SEÁN MacBRIDE

A Life

SEÁN MacBRIDE

A Life

ELIZABETH KEANE

Gill & Macmillan

Gill & Macmillan Ltd
Hume Avenue, Park West, Dublin 12
with associated companies throughout the world
www.gillmacmillan.ie
© Elizabeth Keane 2007
978 07171 3965 1
Index compiled by Helen Litton
Type design by Make Communication
Print origination by O'K Graphic Design, Dublin
Printed and bound in Great Britain by
MPG Books Ltd, Bodmin, Cornwall

The paper used in this book comes from the wood pulp
of managed forests. For every tree felled, at least one
tree is planted, thereby renewing natural resources.

A CIP catalogue record for this book is available
from the British Library.

5 4 3 2 1

To John

CONTENTS

NOMENCLATURE

MacBride was christened Jean Seagan MacBride, presumably given the French variant of his father's name. He is later called Seagan, finally, sometime in the 1920s, settling permanently on Seán, the Irish form of John. For the purposes of clarity, I shall refer to him by his surname or as 'Seán' unless a direct quote commands otherwise.

Throughout the text, I have left intact any irregular spellings that appear in quoted documents, particularly American English spellings, for example 'favor' instead of 'favour'. The Irish acute accent mark, or fada, is included on Irish proper names and words in the Irish language where required, for example 'Seán MacBride' and 'Dáil Éireann', except when the fada is not used in a direct quote. I have employed the term *sic* in brackets for misspellings or odd usage in the original text.

As for the rather murky business of place names: 'the Irish Free State' and 'the Republic' refer to the twenty-six southern Irish counties. 'The Six Counties', 'the North', and 'Northern Ireland' refer to the northern counties currently within the United Kingdom. 'Ireland' may refer either to the Republic or the entire island, depending on context.

PREFACE

'Biography is very like translation — it is not possible and yet it is necessary.'

— FRITZ SENN

A biography of a universally well-liked and admired individual who has never dealt with any type of struggle or adversity is easy to write, but somewhat tedious to read. Fortunately, Seán MacBride's life story presents a different challenge.

MacBride did not elicit lukewarm reactions from those who knew him; people either loved or loathed him. As Charles Lysaght remembered, 'I wrote his obit in the *London Times* but I found it difficult to reach a firm view about him. Different people assessed him so differently.'[1]

Memories of MacBride's accomplishments are also diverse — when I spoke about the subject of this biography, people recalled him as the leader of Clann na Poblachta, a former foreign minister, the co-founder of Amnesty International, or the son of the redoubtable Maud Gonne. Some confused him with his father John MacBride; one academic simply exclaimed, 'that bastard,' calling the MacBride Principles one of the English language's great oxymorons.

MacBride poses a challenge for biographers and researchers not only because he is such an apparently contradictory personality, but more practically because his papers are not available. Like many Irish political figures, he would move from revolutionary terrorist to constitutional politician, but more fascinating is his later role as an international humanitarian. The shift from terrorist to politician is hardly surprising in an Irish context; it is the movement from conservative in government to a seemingly more liberal outlook during the 'elder statesman' phase of his career. There were also many smaller shifts, from a distrust of diplomats and civil servants to expanding the Department of External Affairs and becoming a diplomat himself, from fervent anti-communism while in government to praising the Soviet Union for its position on disarmament during the 1970s and 1980s, from consistently blaming the British for the persistence of partition to enjoying friendly relationships with Clement Attlee, Ernest Bevin, and Lord Rugby.

His career is thought to have had three stages: IRA rebel, constitutional politician and international humanitarian. However, these 'conversions' are not quite as radical as sometimes supposed. MacBride was not really all that conservative before his progression to a humanitarian role and he was not really all that liberal afterward. The usual example of MacBride's earlier conservatism is his behaviour during the infamous Mother and Child controversy, but his reaction can be seen as political expediency rather than true conservative piety. Although he may have espoused humanitarian causes, some of his attitudes toward social issues were not particularly liberal. Like much about MacBride's life, his transformations are not as straightforward as they appear.

MacBride's connection to important individuals and events in twentieth-century Irish history alone would merit a closer study of his life. However, Ireland's participation in European integration and new studies on Irish foreign policy are also compelling reasons for taking a look at his contribution to modern Irish history and politics. As historian J.J. Lee wrote in 1989, Ireland 'has chosen to ignore the study of international relations, including the study of neutrality, to an extent unparalleled in any other small Western European neutral.'[2] Fortunately, this situation has changed and now is an advantageous time to reassess MacBride's influence; particularly in light of recent debates about Ireland's role in Europe and her involvement in human rights issues worldwide, as well as MacBride's own memoir, published posthumously in 2005.

He is most recognised for his international contributions, yet one of the goals in this book is to examine also his role in Irish government and his impact on the nation later in life. Because of their behaviour during the Mother and Child controversy, the inter-party Government's accomplishments have been somewhat eclipsed. F.S.L. Lyons points out that the Government 'did achieve in that direction [the development of modern Ireland] more than posterity has been inclined to give it credit for' and, because of one spectacular failure, has not been recognised for smaller successes.[3]

Despite his having had one of the most extraordinary and varied lives of any Irish figure of the twentieth century, there is only one biography of Seán MacBride, written by Anthony Jordan in 1993. Jordan's work is hampered by a very limited use of primary source material; there are few references to either the private papers of members of the inter-party Government or the Department of Foreign Affairs files located in the Irish National Archives. Jordan does not quite do his subject justice; he calls MacBride a 'kaleidoscopic' man while only tersely demonstrating why.[4]

The most likely explanation as to why there is a dearth of work specifically on MacBride is the lack of access to his private papers. As of now, these papers are not readily available for consultation. He willed his library at Roebuck House to his personal assistant Caitriona Lawlor, who is still in possession of the contents and has not made them publicly accessible; however, she did allow me access to some of MacBride's personal correspondence.

In 2005, Lawlor released a memoir written by MacBride, entitled *That Day's Struggle*. While useful for determining MacBride's version of events, particularly his childhood and feelings about his father's death, in many ways it is incomplete. Firstly, the book spans only from John MacBride's death in 1916 until the end of the inter-party Government in 1951. His early life in Paris and his later political and humanitarian career are not included. The latter is especially surprising considering how important humanitarian concerns became to him. Secondly, there is only the briefest glimpse of a personal life: there are no references to his two children and barely any to his wife. In many ways (and MacBride's memoir is certainly not the only one guilty of this offence), the book serves mainly as a justification, particularly for his treatment of fellow Clann member and cabinet colleague Noël Browne. Stylistically, the book reads as if transcribed. Perhaps he had no time to develop or add to it. Neither MacBride nor Lawlor mentions when the memoir was written, but in a letter to Patrick Lynch, dated 9 March 1981, he alludes to being 'in the throes of completing an autobiography'.[5]

Fortunately, many other sources illuminate both MacBride's earlier political career and his later life. Therefore this study excavates and utilises a variety of primary and secondary source materials, including previously published autobiographies and memoirs, unpublished private papers of MacBride's contemporaries, MacBride's own writings, state papers of Ireland, Britain, the United States, and Canada, as well as documentation from organisations MacBride was involved in. MacBride's daughter, Anna MacBride White, and her husband, Declan White, were kind enough to talk to me about MacBride's life and share their views on his career.

Although this biography provides the most authoritative discussion to date on Seán MacBride's political and personal life, I have no illusion that I am recording the last word. If the papers ever find their way into the public domain, I fully expect future researchers to revise some of my own findings and conclusions. In the meantime, I hope that I have provided an even-handed yet engaging study of a man who, as Dermot Keogh maintains, 'is likely to remain a most controversial figure in the history of the state.'[6]

ACKNOWLEDGEMENTS

This book had its beginnings as a PhD thesis in the Faculty of History at the University of Cambridge. Therefore my first debt is to my supervisor Eugenio Biagini for his cogent insight, frequent help, and seemingly endless patience. Thanks also to Peter Clarke, Joe Lee, Brendan Simms, and Colin Barr for reading earlier drafts of this work. Despite the many comments, suggestions, and criticisms I have received along the way, final responsibility for the historical analysis presented, for good or ill, is mine alone.

In the process of researching and writing this volume, I have greatly benefited from the kind and generous assistance of many people and institutions. Thanks especially to Seamus Helferty and the exceptionally helpful staff of the University College Dublin Archives; the staff of the National Archives, Ireland; Liz Safly and Randy Sowell at the Harry S. Truman Library; Oliver House at the Bodleian Library, Oxford; the staffs of Churchill College Archives, Cambridge, and the Cambridge University Library and Faculty of History; Sunniva O'Flynn at the Irish Film Archive; the staff of the National Library of Ireland; David Sheehy at the Dublin Diocesan Archives; and the staff of the National Archives, Kew. Thanks to Michael MacEvilly for suggesting helpful secondary sources and providing cogent criticism; Caitriona Lawlor for allowing me to see some of Seán MacBride's personal correspondence; Declan Costello for giving me permission to access the papers of John A. Costello; François Danis, Secretary General at the Fondation Paul-Henri Spaak; and Ghislain Malette at the National Archives of Canada for finding and sending relevant documentation. Thanks especially to Declan White and Anna MacBride White for their time and trouble. Our conversations about MacBride were incredibly informative.

Much gratitude to my colleagues past and present for their camaraderie, professional support, and sound advice — in particular, Mgr Tom Bergin, Sr Elizabeth Graham, Nick Vertucci, Kathy O'Riordan, Jane Grant, Justin Nolan, Simon Henderson, Andrew Robinson, Neil Jeffery, David Evans, Gary Savage, Mark Vinall, Robert Shorrock, Peter Southern, Bill Avenell, Mary Ireland,

Sean O'Boyle, Andrew Wines, John Herbert, Julian Roberts, and the members of Christ's Hospital's English and History Departments for being patient with the new kid.

The production of any book is a major undertaking and I am very grateful to Fergal Tobin, Deirdre Rennison Kunz, and the staff of Gill & Macmillan for their expertise and encouragement.

Although the highs of working on this project far outweighed the lows, sincere and heartfelt appreciation to my friends for allowing me to talk about the book or forcing me not to. Thanks to Jane Goundrey, Sonia Osman, Saydan Osman, Stuart Snaddon, Sasha LeGeros, George and Katie Brennan, Roberta Hamilton, James Suter, Charlie Farquharson-Roberts, Adrian Joyce, Christopher Clark, Claire Snellgrove-Hawkins, David Weaver, Roman Roth, and Carrie Roth-Murray. Thanks especially to Fergus McGuire, who hates to be praised but in this case deserves to be.

As always, I am grateful to my late grandparents, E. Richard and Helen Hoffman and Clifton and Bernice Keane, my sisters Nancy Fesko and Catherine Keane (especially for her bravery in reading earlier drafts of this book), and my parents Dennis and Patricia Keane.

Finally, thanks again to John — this time for personal rather than professional reasons.

Elizabeth Keane
Christ's Hospital
July 2007

Chapter 1 ～

MAN OF DESTINY: SEÁN MacBRIDE'S EARLY LIFE

'*What a heavy burden is a name that has become famous too soon.*'

— VOLTAIRE

The only child of 'Ireland's Joan of Arc' and the militant hero of the Boer War was bound to attract attention in certain circles. Seán MacBride's background made a role in Irish politics almost inevitable: his parents were formidable figures in the Irish nationalist movement and a weight of expectation existed even before his birth that the adult MacBride might have sometimes found hard to bear. His mother Maud Gonne once showed Noël Browne's wife Phyllis a photo of him at about age ten with 'Seán, Man of Destiny' written across it.[1]

MacBride's own memoirs say very little about his childhood or his parents' backgrounds. Perhaps he preferred to concentrate on his own achievements, but the lack can more likely be attributed to the bitter end of his parents' marriage and the resulting scandal of their divorce hearings.

Maud Gonne is best known as a fervent Irish nationalist and the muse of poet William Butler Yeats. Her position as the heroine of Yeats's poetry and the details included in her oddly titled autobiography, *A Servant of the Queen*, make it difficult to separate the person from the myth. In her memoir, Maud 'conceals, distorts, alters, and rearranges facts, incidents, and dates for both personal and political reasons.'[2] She was always conscious of her public persona and *A Servant of the Queen* provides an idea of how she wanted to present her life, but the book is not terribly honest or revealing. In her autobiography, she 'continued the fictions she had had to practise throughout her life.'[3]

These fictions were necessary not only to establish and maintain her nationalist credentials but also because Maud had two illegitimate children at a time when this behaviour was seen as morally suspect. Although she referred to the children as adopted relatives, most people seemed to be aware that they were her own. It was never mentioned in the open; at the time in Ireland, 'a certain inconsistency between what one says and what one does seems to be an accepted way of life.'[4] Though Maud was indifferent to many of society's conventions (when told that she would require a chaperone to travel with her, she christened her pet monkey 'Chaperone'), she recognised that others might not be so permissive or understanding. Charles Stewart Parnell's affair with Katharine O'Shea provided a harsh example of what could happen if what was privately acknowledged became public domain. Moreover, *A Servant of the Queen* was written in 1938 when Seán was contemplating a political career and Maud's family did not want her to reveal too much about her private life.[5] It is a shame that *Servant* conceals her allegedly scandalous past or that she never finished a later memoir that might have been more forthcoming.

What is certain is that she was the daughter of Thomas Gonne, a British Army officer, and Edith Cook, and was born on 21 December 1866 near Aldershot and baptised in Tongham, Surrey. Two years after her birth, her father was stationed in Ireland near the Curragh Military Camp in Kildare in the aftermath of the Fenian Rising of 1867. Maud's younger sister Kathleen was born in 1868. The family moved to Donnybrook, a suburb of Dublin, a few months later.

Maud's mother Edith was physically delicate, a trait Maud would inherit, and she died of tuberculosis in 1871, when Maud was five. Edith had been brought up by her paternal aunts and sent to boarding school, both of which she hated. She made her husband promise never to do the same to Maud and Kathleen.

Maud and her father had a very close relationship and, after her mother's death, she helped to run his household. The family lived briefly in England for two years. Maud, Kathleen, and her father moved back to the Curragh in 1876, moving again to Howth the following year. While there, Maud and Kathleen's nurse, Mary Anne 'Bowie' Meredith, took them to visit local families in and around Howth. Despite Maud's claim in *Servant* that her father had expressed an interest in joining the Home Rule movement later in life, the New York *Daily Tribune* reported that 'her father was an officer in the English army . . . and was decidedly English in his sympathies.'[6] In an interview Maud gave in Peoria, Illinois, during an American lecture tour in 1897, she described Thomas Gonne as 'on the English side, a colonel in the British army', making no mention of his support for Home Rule.[7]

The girls were looked after by Bowie and a governess. The family was well off; the Cook family made its money in the linen trade and the Gonnes were wine-importers. In an interview with the St Louis *Globe* on 5 December 1897, Maud described herself as having belonged to the 'Castle set in Dublin', a member of the fading Protestant ascendancy class gradually displaced during the nineteenth and early twentieth centuries. A debutante and hostess for her father, she was presented at court and acknowledged to be a great beauty, attracting the attention of the Prince of Wales. Wary of his daughter's becoming too involved in court intrigue, Thomas sent her to Europe to travel.

Thomas Gonne died on 30 November 1886 of typhoid fever. Maud and Kathleen were sent to London to live with Thomas's stern bachelor brother William. In order to keep Maud reined in, William informed her that she would have very little money coming to her and suggested that she allow her rich great aunt Augusta to adopt her. After Maud threatened to become an actress to earn her own living, William was forced to admit that his nieces did indeed have enough to live on; when she turned twenty-one, Thomas Gonne's will provided a trust fund and a share in the family diamonds and property, giving her a comfortable income.

Shortly after Thomas's death, Maud discovered that she and Kathleen had a half-sister, Eileen, born on 17 July 1886. Maud met Eileen's mother, Margaret Wilson, and made plans for her half-sister's upbringing, sending Eileen to Bowie, now in retirement in Farnborough. Maud arranged for Margaret to work as a governess for a Russian aristocrat, Baron Budberg. Why did Maud separate mother and daughter? According to Paul Durcan, Eileen's grandson, 'it seems she [Maud] felt that it would be a scandal if it became known that her father had a mistress.'[8] However, Thomas's wife had died several years before his relationship with Margaret began and he was no longer alive to suffer the taint of scandal. Perhaps Maud thought that it would be difficult for an unmarried woman with little money to raise a child alone. At the time, Maud believed that she had no real income and probably did not want Eileen raised by her London relatives. Whatever her motives, Maud's life of concealment had begun; in *Servant*, Eileen is referred to as 'Daphne'. Margaret never returned and never saw her daughter again. She died in 1939.

Maud took a trip to Royat in the Auvergne Mountains in central France during the summer of 1887, for a lung condition. There she met Boulangist journalist and politician Lucien Millevoye. At the time he first met Maud, he was hoping for a Franco-Russian alliance and dedicated to regaining Alsace-Lorraine after its loss to Prussia in 1870. Millevoye was married, but separated from his wife. He attracted Maud with his fervent patriotism and his hatred of England. They began a political alliance as well as an affair. She would later call Millevoye 'the only man she ever loved'.[9]

Apparently, she had become politically aware of conflicts in Ireland after witnessing evictions in the west. According to *Servant,* she decided to work on behalf of displaced tenants. She recounts a visit to a hunt ball in the country where her host disparagingly referred to an evicted family lying in a ditch, remarking that the wife was sure to be dead by morning.[10] She was so outraged at his callousness that she left the following morning. This is probably partially correct; her interest in Irish independence was likely ignited by a combination of her infatuation with Millevoye, her childhood in Ireland visiting the families around Howth with Bowie, and the memory of her regimented, stilted life in London. The idea of personal independence held great appeal — it could be that she saw the British oppression and mistreatment of Ireland as parallel to her own experience with her father's relatives in London.

Because of her Anglo-Protestant class lineage, Maud was seen as an outsider in nationalist Ireland; Michael Davitt thought her a spy and the Irish Parliamentary Party saw her as a 'fanatic', using her for electioneering purposes, nothing more.[11] The Fenians, the Land League, and the National League would not have her because of her background and gender, so she '"land-leagued" mostly on my own'.[12] In order to establish her nationalist credentials, in October 1900 she founded Inghínidhe na hÉireann (the Daughters of Ireland), an organisation for women who were not taken seriously by the male-dominated nationalist groups, and edited the nationalist publication *L'Irlande Libre* from 1897 to 1898. She met John O'Leary, Douglas Hyde, Arthur Griffith, and James Connolly, and assisted evicted tenants in Donegal. She was introduced to the Yeats family through O'Leary's sister Ellen.

She had already gained a reputation as a nationalist agitator when she met William Butler Years at his family home in Bedford Park, West London, on 30 January 1889. Yeats 'had never thought to see in a living woman so great beauty'.[13] Likening her to the past Irish legends that intrigued him, he began a long pursuit of her.

He was unaware of her relationship with Millevoye. Maud kept her 'French life' secret, understating the differences between what was tolerated in Parisian society and what would be acceptable in an ostensibly conservative Ireland. She had given birth to Millevoye's child, Georges Silvère Gonne, on 11 January 1890. Georges fell ill with meningitis and died on 31 August 1891. She usually wore black after his death, although most assumed that the mourning gear was for John MacBride after his death in 1916. She travelled to Ireland shortly after, coincidentally on the same boat as the body of Parnell. Yeats met her on 10 October, while she was still in mourning. She told him that a child she had adopted had died, concealing the real situation; 'she was dressed in extravagantly deep mourning, for Parnell, people thought, thinking her very theatrical. We spoke of the child's death . . . speech was a relief to her.'[14]

In her grief, Maud longed for the reincarnation of her son. Two years after Georges's death, she brought Millevoye to the memorial chapel she had built at Samois for Georges, in the hope of conceiving a child. A daughter, Iseult Germaine Lucille Gonne, was born on either 4 or 6 August 1894 at 51 rue de la Tour, Paris.[15] The Gonne family was fond of nicknames and Iseult was known as 'Bellotte' or 'Isolda'. Iseult called Maud 'Moura', an Irish-sounding anagram of 'amour'. Seán would carry the unfortunate moniker 'Bichon', meaning curly-headed puppy, reflecting the family's love of animals.[16]

In 1898, having several times refused to marry him, Maud finally revealed to Yeats the truth about Millevoye and her two children. He was devastated; 'my thoughts have gone round and round, as do miserable thoughts, coming to no solution.'[17] He probably felt foolish; the times when he had hoped that they were growing closer, she was pursuing a secret life apart from and unknown to him. She told Yeats that she could never marry him. The primary reason for her refusal was her intuition that they were not suited to one another. He wanted her to give up politics and live a peaceful life with him and she would have found such a life intolerable. Yeats was devoted to establishing an Irish national theatre and the infighting involved led Maud to insist that it was a waste of his time.[18] Also, she informed him that she had a 'horror and terror of physical love'.[19] It is possible that she was simply not physically attracted to Yeats (she had overcome her supposed aversion with Millevoye and John MacBride) and may have said this to soften the blow. Maud attempted to console him, 'You would not be happy with me . . . you make beautiful poetry out of what you call your unhappiness and you are happy in that.'[20] The two entered a 'mystical marriage' in 1898, where their spiritual selves would be united.

Around August 1900, Maud split from Millevoye. The exact reason for the break-up is unclear. He may have taken a new mistress, a singer from a café-chantant who had similar views on Alsace-Lorraine, which was not a priority of Maud's. It is more likely that the relationship ended because Millevoye's political thinking had changed. He began to support the burgeoning Entente-Cordiale, the co-existence between the French and the British Empires, which gave France influence over Morocco and the west and Britain over Egypt and the east. The Anglo-French accord was signed in London on 8 April 1904 and it virtually ended colonial rivalry between the two nations. As Millevoye no longer considered England the enemy, they had little reason to support each other's political ventures.

Maud did not seem distressed by the end of the relationship. On 7 July 1900, she wrote to Yeats that 'I am not unhappy only supremely indifferent to all that is not my work or my friends.'[21] She was occupied with nationalist causes, running *L'Irlande Libre*, and presiding over Inghínidhe na hÉireann, becoming its president. Her house in Paris became a gathering place for visiting Irish nationalists, including John MacBride.

Yeats biographer R.F. Foster describes John MacBride as 'red-haired, heavy drinking, physically brave, rather inarticulate and utterly unmystical'.[22] In other words, the direct opposite of Yeats — and the incarnation of Irish nationalism that Maud was fighting for.

MacBride, born on 7 May 1865, grew up in Westport, Co. Mayo, the youngest of five sons. His father Patrick owned a merchant ship, trading between his native Antrim and other Irish ports. MacBride was educated at the Christian Brothers school in Westport, then St Malachy's College in Belfast. He became involved with the Irish Republican Brotherhood, taking the Fenian oath at age fifteen. He worked as an apprentice draper in John Fitzpatrick's Drapery Store in Castlerea, Co. Roscommon. He briefly attended medical school, then moved to Dublin, working as a clerk at Hugh Moore & Co., a druggist and grocer, becoming involved in the Dublin IRB.

He was employed as a pharmacist's assistant for seven years. In 1896, MacBride journeyed to the United States for an IRB convention and fund raising. Later that year, he emigrated to South Africa to work in J.B. Robinson's gold mines in Langlaagte, near Johannesburg, persuading fellow nationalist Arthur Griffith to go as well. Griffith joined him in 1898.

In the middle of 1896, MacBride began organising meetings of Irish residents in South Africa. At first, these meetings were generally convened to help the amnesty movement in Ireland and to make plans for the celebration of the centenary of 1798 'to worthily honour the names and memories of Wolfe Tone and his gallant associates in the great movement of the United Irishmen.'[23] These meetings eventually developed into organised opposition to Britain's treatment of the Boers.

In 1881, Prime Minister William Gladstone had granted the Boers internal self-government in the Transvaal following the first Anglo-Boer War.[24] The Boers, under the leadership of Paul Kruger, resented the colonial policy of Joseph Chamberlain and Alfred Milner, which they feared would deprive the Transvaal of its independence. War broke out on 11 October 1899. Having received military equipment from Germany, the Boers met with success on the borders of Cape Colony and Natal. Although they had only about 88,000 soldiers, the Boers were able to besiege the British garrisons at Ladysmith, Mafeking, and Kimberley.

British Army reinforcements arrived in South Africa in 1900 and counter-offensives enabled the British to take control of the Boer capital Pretoria on 5 June. As the conflict escalated, Britain brought in reinforcements from Australia, New Zealand, and Canada, as well as volunteers from other British colonies. For the next two years, groups of Boer commandos raided isolated British units in South Africa. Lord Kitchener, the Chief of Staff, reacted to these raids by destroying Boer farms and moving civilians into concentration camps.

The British activities in South Africa were strongly opposed by many Liberal politicians as an example of the worst excesses of imperialism. The war ended in May 1902 with the signing of the Treaty of Vereeniging. The settlement ended the status of the Transvaal and Orange Free States as Boer republics. However, the British granted the Boers £3 million for restocking and repairing farmlands and promised eventual self-government, which was granted in 1907.

MacBride gained fame as the leader of the Irish Brigade in the Boer War, fighting against the British. He joined because he saw parallels to Britain's domination of Ireland and for a chance to test his physical bravery.

> I read with pain and indignation the news that a body of Irishmen had been organised in Johannesburg to fight with Jameson against the brave burghers of the Transvaal, a circumstance which, of course, was hailed with acclamation by the loyal upholders of the Empire ... I was also very anxious that our countrymen in South Africa should not on the next occasion be found on the side of the would-be grabber and oppressor . . . .[25]

He immediately organised Irishmen in Johannesburg and Pretoria into national organisations which would later develop into the Transvaal Irish Brigade. Five hundred Irish and Irish-American men fought the British in the Boer War, often fighting opposite such regiments as the Dublin Fusiliers and the Inniskillings.[26] MacBride became a naturalised citizen of the Boer Republic, which proved problematic when the Treaty of Vereeniging put the Republic out of existence.

The Boer War became a rallying point for Irish nationalism. It was 'the only place in the English-speaking world where a white nationalist people were effectively standing up to the British Empire.'[27] To capitalise on this surge, Griffith and Maud called a meeting in October 1899, at the Celtic Literary Society, to establish the Irish Transvaal Committee, whose goals were to send an ambulance to the Transvaal, collect funds, find volunteers, and discourage Irishmen from enlisting in the British Army. Griffith, Maud, Yeats, and O'Leary were the founding members. Maud's Inghínidhe na hÉireann also worked to dissuade Irishmen from enlisting. The Irish protest became the most popular and most violent of the European pro-Boer movements.

While in South Africa, John MacBride had a relationship with a Cape Malay woman, which produced a son called Robert John McBride.[28] It is not known whether MacBride ever publicly or privately acknowledged that Robert was his son; yet his photograph ran in the *Sunday Press* of 15 January 1989 and it shows a remarkable resemblance.[29]

At the urging of Griffith and Willie Rooney, founders of the *United Irishman*, MacBride ran for Parliament in South Mayo in the by-elections of 1900. Griffith and Rooney asked the Irish Parliamentary Party (IIP) to withdraw its candidate John O'Donnell on the basis that MacBride would be disqualified because of his Boer War activities and the IIP candidate would most likely get the seat anyway. Suspicious of their motives, the IIP refused. MacBride announced his candidacy from South Africa and urged voters to show their opposition to the war and 'make the attitude of the Irish people to the British Empire plain to everyone'.[30] Both Maud and Yeats cabled support. MacBride lost the election to O'Donnell by the decisive margin of 2,401 votes to 427.[31]

The Boers disbanded the Irish Brigade on 23 September 1900. At a loose end, MacBride travelled to Portuguese East Africa then went to Paris, following the example of O'Leary and other displaced Fenians. Griffith and Maud met him at Gare de Lyon. MacBride and Griffith stayed with Maud at her house at 7 avenue d'Eylau.

Maud's first impression on meeting MacBride was of 'a wiry, soldierly-looking man with red hair and skin, burnt brick red by the South African sun'.[32] She was thrilled to meet someone who had actually been in battle against the English. At this point, she was no longer involved with Millevoye and, as Boer War journalist Henry Nevinson had predicted a year earlier, 'the first man of resolute action whom she meets will have her at his mercy'.[33]

The contrasts between Yeats, Maud's most persistent suitor, and MacBride could not have been more obvious. Yeats was a man of letters whereas MacBride was a man of action, like Maud's beloved father, but perhaps more importantly from a Catholic and nationalist background, unlike her and Yeats. Maud's sister Kathleen also married a military man, Major-General Thomas Pilcher, who fought in France during the First World War.

MacBride embarked on a lecture tour of the United States. As he was a nervous public speaker, he invited Maud to join him, hinting that he would cancel his tour if she refused. Maud had been on two previous American lecture tours in 1897 and 1900. She agreed to join him, meeting him in New

York. The pair went on to Boston, Philadelphia, St Louis, and Chicago, speaking to a variety of Irish societies. Maud prepared his lectures and, during the long train rides between cities, they discussed strategy.

Apparently, MacBride proposed to Maud in St Louis. She delayed answering, responding that she did not intend to marry while there was a war on, but perhaps sensing that she was not the marrying kind in temperament. If such a proposal existed, 'MacBride was no doubt flattered and dragooned into it.'[34] Maud wrote to Yeats on 25 March 1901 from Michigan that the trip tired her but that 'MacBride is going around with me, & is very good & saves me all the worry & fatigue he can.'[35] She did not mention a proposal. Maud left MacBride in Chicago and he followed her to Paris after his tour was over. He had difficulty finding employment, but finally acquired work as a secretary to a correspondent of the American *Sun* and *Laffan's Bureau*, living in an attic room at 140 rue Gay Lussac.

Meanwhile, Maud was busy with her manifold activities in Dublin. She rented 26 Coulson Avenue, Rathgar, in 1902, and that April played the title role in Yeats's *Cathleen Ní Houlihan*, a play inspired by her. However, despite her aversion to marriage, Maud began to relent.

Why this change of heart? Her decision was made partly for her daughter's sake. Maud may not have approved of conventions herself, but she recognised their existence. She was still introducing Iseult as her niece and perhaps she believed that her daughter would benefit from a more traditional home environment, both for her upbringing and for respectability; as she wrote to Kathleen in 1902, 'for Iseult's sake, I make the sacrifice to convention.'[36] Maud also wanted more children — she had never stopped longing for a son after Georges's death.

There may have been another reason to consider the idea: the desire for the harmony of a domestic arrangement, no matter how ill-suited she may have been to it. As she confided to Kathleen, 'Now I see the chance, without injuring my work, of having a little happiness and peace in my personal life and I am taking it . . . with Iseult growing up, I cannot get . . . companionship I need outside marriage.'[37] Despite the suggestive phrasing of the letter, Maud did not marry to begin a sexual relationship; she could take lovers for that. Maud apparently had little interest in sex, but MacBride surely would not be satisfied with a 'spiritual union' similar to the one to which she and Yeats had pledged themselves. She would later tell Yeats that it was anger at Millevoye that influenced her decision.

The idea of marriage may have appealed to Maud, but why wed MacBride? Why not Yeats or other suitors? Both Maud and MacBride shared a consuming interest in the Irish cause, which Yeats, more focused on his poetry, playwriting, and theatre, did not seem as militant about. Yeats had made it clear several times that he thought Maud should marry him and leave politics. She seems to have believed that MacBride would allow her more freedom. She wrote to Yeats, 'Marriage won't change me I think at all. I intend to keep my own name and go on with all my work the same as ever.'[38] There were also political reasons for such a choice: MacBride would be a valuable ally in the fight for Irish freedom. Maud informed Mme Avril that 'I expect that with the husband I have chosen I shall be able more effectively to serve the cause of independence.'[39] MacBride possessed the Catholic nationalist background and the credentials Maud had been seeking. As she later admitted to John O'Leary, in marrying MacBride, she was marrying Ireland.[40]

MacBride's version of events suggests that there was no struggle on Maud's part to accept his proposal. He later wrote that she, not he, initiated the proposal, despite his doubts about a union. According to MacBride, 'I certainly did not want to marry her. I knew we were not suited to one another. For 8 or 9 months before we got married she had been pressing me to marry her until at last I decided on going to America in order to avoid doing so.'[41]

Apparently he relented because he was 'moved by her tears, felt very sad for her, and thinking I was doing a good act for my country and for herself I consented to marry Maud Gonne.'[42] Thus the marriage was a patriotic act on MacBride's part, brought about by her cajoling and pleading. This version reeks of residual bitterness on MacBride's part; he wrote this account during their separation hearings. He is not accurate about going to America to avoid Maud — he asked her to come with him on his lecture tour, which is a strange request if his intention was escape. MacBride maintained that Maud wanted to marry him because her 'tarnished reputation', the rumours about Millevoye and her life in France, threatened to destroy her career in Irish politics. He also refers to Maud's mystical beliefs, claiming that she saw him as the reincarnation of the Irish hero Cúchulainn (a theory she never shared with Yeats, her usual correspondent on mystical matters). She often signed her letters to him with 'Maeve', referring to the legendary queen of Connacht.

Perhaps there is truth in both their accounts of the impetus for their marriage. Maud did want a clean break with the past — however, MacBride hardly seems like the type of man to be forced into a union he did not desire.

Maud converted to Catholicism on 17 February 1903, for personal as well as political reasons. She told Yeats after her marriage that 'I have often longed to denounce the priests and could not because I was Protestant, but now I can.'[43] There was room for Catholic mythology in an already crowded jumble of spiritual beliefs. She wrote to Yeats justifying her conversion on the grounds that she already believed much of it, only in different guises; 'it seems to me of small importance if one calls the great spirit forces the Sidhe, the Gods & the Arch Angels, the great symbols of all religions are the same.'[44] The political aspect of renouncing the Church of England also appealed to her, 'as the head of one's church, I prefer the pope to Edward the 7th.'[45]

Despite her conversion, the contrasts between Maud and MacBride would make their partnership a troubled one. Her liberation got on the more traditional MacBride's nerves. She would later write that he was 'full of queer conventions', noting his shock when she suggested that they take tea in his room rather than going to a café.[46] It is unclear whether she knew about his son Robert; she does not mention it in her memoir or her letters then or later. Robert was never mentioned during the divorce proceedings, so it is likely that Maud was unaware of his existence. She probably would have made some reference to it, as it was something they had in common — especially in view of his response to Iseult's parentage. Maud also had more money, and a female possessing the power of the purse proved difficult for MacBride to handle. He did not earn very much as a journalist and she often gave him money during their marriage.

Others recognised the potential problems the marriage might bring. Kathleen urged Maud to marry Yeats. Maud's response was 'I love him dearly as a friend, but I could not for one moment imagine marrying him. I think I will be happy with John.'[47] Yeats, of course, advised against it. In a highly agitated letter written in late January, he pleaded with her not to convert and not to marry MacBride. MacBride's mother Honoria tried to dissuade her son, as did Arthur Griffith and John's brother Joseph. Maud thought that she heard her father warn her the night before her wedding about the inadvisability of the union: 'I heard Tommy's voice . . . Lambkin, don't do it. You must not get married.'[48] Iseult, at a Carmelite convent in Laval, also expressed unhappiness at the idea and 'cried when I told her I was getting married to MacBride and said she hated MacBride.'[49] However, Canon Dissard of Laval was pleased, especially when Maud told him of her intention to convert to Catholicism.[50]

Despite the warnings of friends and family, the wedding went ahead on 21 February 1903 at the Church of St Honoré d'Eylau, and Fr van Hecke, the Boer War Irish Brigade chaplain, officiated. A civil marriage took place at the English Consulate. The Inghínidhe and Irish Brigade flags served as decorations at the wedding banquet. Maud's final toast was 'to the complete independence of Ireland'.[51] Even their honeymoon had the aura of the political; it took place in Spain, apparently as cover for a plan to assassinate King Edward VII, which allegedly failed because of MacBride's inability to stay sober.[52] The MacBrides returned to Paris and lived in the suburb of Passy in the 16th arrondissement, at 13 rue de Passy, a haven for artists and writers.

Apparently Yeats received a telegram from Maud announcing her marriage as he was about to give a lecture at the Bijou Theatre in London on the future of Irish drama. Biographer Joseph Hone described his reaction: 'Yeats stood aghast, angry as well as very miserable.'[53] To him, Maud's action was not only hurtful, but a betrayal of their spiritual marriage of 1898. He delivered the lecture, which was well received, although he could not remember a word of it later.[54]

Less than two months afterward, Maud admitted to her sister that the marriage was a disaster. Maud had been happy to marry the myth, but found that she disliked living with the man. She realised the extent of his drinking, which had likely increased due to boredom. At a meeting at Kathleen's house in London, she informed Yeats that she had married in a fit of temper because Millevoye had brought his then mistress to see Iseult. After this visit occurred, 'I resolved to get someone to keep him out & make a final breach. I married in a sudden impulse of anger.'[55] Yeats reported this to his patron and friend Lady Gregory and it may have been his assessment rather than Maud's, preferring to believe that she had made an impulsive decision to marry someone else. Her solution seemed to be that she would have to accept the consequences of her decision.

In 1903, Maud discovered that she was pregnant, but the state of the marriage did not improve. As predicted, MacBride resented her independent lifestyle, especially her keeping in contact with other men. He seemed particularly jealous of Millevoye and Yeats, only one of whom was actually a former lover. MacBride commented that he was 'glad weeping William has retired into solitude he so richly deserves and from which he never should have emerged.'[56] Maud later wrote to Yeats that she suspected MacBride had removed all of his poetry books from their house.[57] MacBride complained that 'from the day we were married she wanted to keep up a correspondence with her ex-lovers and bring them into the house for me to entertain. Of course I would not allow such a thing.'[58]

Maud's side of the story is, of course, different. She complained to Yeats that 'my husband is insanely jealous & utterly unscrupulous, he has accused, at some time or other, every man who he has ever heard of being my friend or whose photo he has ever seen at my house of having been my lover.'[59] MacBride took umbrage at Maud's attempt to arrange a meeting between him and Millevoye.[60] Her desire for them to meet is hardly unusual, as Maud's interest in keeping up a friendly relationship with Millevoye was more likely due to the fact that he was the father of her child, not an attempt to cuckold MacBride.

However, MacBride may not have been aware of Iseult's parentage right away, although he claimed to have known about the situation before the marriage; he claimed that Maud had promised him that she would repent and become a Catholic. MacBride stated that 'I knew she had led an evil life before our marriage but did not know it was so bad as I found out afterward.'[61] MacBride's prose is stilted at best and he relies on certain stock phrases that do not clearly explain the situation. He maintained that Maud revealed towards the end of August 1904 that she had been the mistress of three different men. He does not mention who these men were; presumably Millevoye was included in that list.

Aside from Maud's supposed promiscuity, the immorality that MacBride referred to could have been his discovery that Iseult was Maud's illegitimate daughter, that she was not, as Maud sometimes called her, an adopted relative, a fiction Maud kept up all her life. This knowledge could explain MacBride's change of behaviour and his intense dislike of Iseult, whom he called 'a perfect specimen of a decadent having no sense of morality of right or wrong'.[62] Whether this animosity was due to her illegitimacy, her personality, or as the living reminder that Maud had once had another lover is not clear. MacBride continued to find Maud's behaviour crude, complaining that she remained 'incapable of rising to the level of a second-rate French mistress'.[63] He grew more lonely and jealous and began to drink more heavily.

In 1904, Maud bought a house in Colleville, Normandy, with a legacy from her great aunt Augusta; the house was not, as Iseult's husband Francis Stuart later claimed, Millevoye's gift to Iseult. The house, known as 'Les Mouettes', villa of the seagulls, was intended as a legacy for Iseult, but was purchased by Maud, not Millevoye. As it was close to the coast, she hoped that MacBride, brought up near the sea, would like it.

The baby arrived on 26 January 1904. His birth certificate read 'Jean Seagan MacBride', his birthplace listed as Arrondissement 16, Paris. Maud was delighted, as she wrote to Yeats shortly after the birth, 'the baby is a treasure & of course I imagine all sorts of wonderful things for his future.'[64] She had longed for a boy in the hope that he might be a reincarnation of Georges or her beloved father. Moreover, he was her first legitimate child, the first of her children who could be publicly celebrated.

Irish nationalists, who viewed him as the child of heroes, also celebrated Seagan's birth. They, too, had very high hopes for his future. Maud's friend Barry O'Delany sent a telegram to the Pope announcing that 'the King of Ireland had been born.'[65] The baby's mother echoed such sentiment; a scrapbook painted by Maud, adorned with Celtic symbols, bore the inscription 'Seagan Gonne MacBride — belonging to and of Ireland.'[66]

Not surprisingly, Maud insisted that her son be christened in Ireland. John O'Leary was to be the godfather, but was prevented because he was a Fenian and an agnostic. Seagan was baptised at St Joseph's Church, Terenure, on 1 May 1904.[67] Mrs Honoria MacBride acted as sponsor and there was a Special Branch report on the christening which reads 'Chief Commr, DMP informs Inspector General RIC that McBride [sic], accompanied by his mother arrived in Dublin on 30th . . . and returned home on 2nd instant. Most of their time was spent at Mrs McBride's residence, and on 1st they were present at the christening of "Major" McBride's child . . .'[68] Like the wedding, the christening was a political event. The flag of Inghínidhe na hÉireann was prominently placed in the midst of John MacBride's guns and sword from the Boer War.

Despite the birth of their son, the marriage continued to disintegrate. A photograph taken shortly after Seagan's birth shows the stress. Both Maud and John wear tired, tense expressions. Neither looks happy or in love.

MacBride went on another lecture tour of the United States in 1904 and Maud briefly joined him. Maud travelled to Ireland fairly often, staying at her house on Coulson Avenue. MacBride did not join her for fear of arrest.

The Gonne-MacBride marriage was about to end in spectacular fashion. In October 1904, returning to Paris from Dublin, Maud was apparently informed of MacBride's hideous behaviour while she was away.

What happened exactly remains a matter of intense debate. The marriage was certainly not a happy one prior to Maud's filing charges against her husband. However, the seriousness of the charges goes further than mere incompatibility. In her petition for divorce, filed 25 February 1905, Maud accused MacBride of intemperance, cruelty, and worse. A French newspaper reported the accusation: 'That Mr M'Bride even went so far as to compromise a young girl who was under the protection of Mrs M'Bride, and in the absence of the latter at Colleville in the summer of 1903 he had adulterous relations with her.'[69] The charge did not mention the girl's name. The two possibilities were Eileen, Maud's sixteen-year-old half-sister who was living with Maud until her future could be decided, and Iseult, who was nine.

Eileen appears to be the most likely candidate due to her age. Some of Maud's biographers have suggested that she arranged a hasty marriage for Eileen to John's brother Joseph, twenty-six years her senior, in order to quell the scandal, similar to the way she had sent Eileen's mother to Russia. On New Year's Eve 1904, Maud confronted MacBride and asked if he had kissed Eileen. He replied that there was never anything between them and he had kissed her only in Maud's presence. Yet in April 1905, Maud informed Yeats that she had 'complete proof of John's adultery with Eileen'.[70] Yet she did not say what this proof was and the French court did not find MacBride guilty of the charge. Eileen herself denied the allegation in court.

The poet Paul Durcan, the grandson of Eileen Wilson and Joseph MacBride, doubts that the allegation is true, as his grandmother always spoke of John MacBride with warmth and humour.[71] John MacBride's portrait hung over the mantelpiece in the dining room and he was godfather to Joseph and Eileen's daughter Síle. When Nancy Cardozo's biography of Maud was published in 1979, the claim that Eileen had been assaulted and her marriage to MacBride arranged by Maud to save her honour was painful for his mother and sister to read. In Durcan's view, Eileen had been libelled and MacBride 'unquestionably defamed'.

Durcan may have a point. Eileen and Joseph were married on 3 August 1904, long before charges were filed, and it is unlikely that Maud would have kept quiet for so long about an attack on a girl in her care. Eileen was old enough to protest and, given Maud's own feelings toward marriage, forcing Eileen into a union would have been highly hypocritical of her. Marrying Eileen into the family of her attacker would also have been a strange move. Anna MacBride White maintains that Eileen was not forced into marriage and that she always spoke well of John MacBride.[72]

According to Foster, MacBride attacked not only Eileen, but Iseult and the cook as well.[73] In his *Black List Section H*, Francis Stuart mentions that his wife shared 'an anecdote about how her stepfather, John MacBride, had made advances to her as a child.'[74] Maud would not allow Iseult to give evidence in court. This was probably to protect her, as Iseult was terrified of MacBride, and to avoid questions about her exact relationship to Maud.

As for the cook, Marie Bosse, MacBride dismissed this allegation with 'she is 50 years old and extremely unprepossessing.'[75] He added that he was living in Paris and that if he needed that sort of fulfilment, he would hardly need to 'rape a hideously ugly old cook in my wife's house.'[76] As for another allegation that he had tried to seduce Barry O'Delany, he said that she was 'downright ugly' and, as for propositioning her, 'her looks would not tempt any man.'[77] MacBride seemed more offended by the hint that his standards were low rather than the accusations themselves.

MacBride denied the charges vehemently, calling Maud's accusations 'a fairy tale . . . absurd and damnably false.'[78] According to him, he went to Dublin on 25 November just as Maud was returning to Paris. He left her a note, declaring that 'our life was not a happy one owing to her being unable to rise above a certain level . . . she was only the weak imitation of a very weak man.'[79] He advised that, if he were to die, she should marry again as 'she was a woman that could not live without some man or other behind her.'[80]

When he first learned that Maud had filed for separation, he claimed that he believed that she had fallen for someone else or had returned to an ex-lover. When he learned of the charges, he accused her of manufacturing evidence to be sure that she would be successful in obtaining a divorce.[81]

Did Maud fabricate the accusations to ensure that she would obtain a divorce and custody of their son? Did she drag Eileen's name into the mess because MacBride would be unlikely to scandalise his brother's wife? In his *The Yeats-Gonne-MacBride Triangle*, Anthony Jordan makes the case that the charges against MacBride have been universally accepted (and often repeated without real proof) by Yeats scholars. Yet, even without the abuse allegations, she had sufficient grounds for divorce. MacBride had started to drink heavily and Yeats's assessment of MacBride in his 'Easter 1916' as a 'drunken vainglorious lout' is probably accurate.

It appears that Maud did not want a scandal, especially concerning Iseult, and tried to arrive at a peaceful settlement. She travelled to London to see John's brother Anthony in the hope that he could help her to achieve a quiet separation. Negotiations broke down over the custody of Seán. MacBride did seem genuinely fond of his son, writing to Maud that he wanted to see him each day while in London, 'any place and any hour you have will suit me. His happy little face is always with me.'[82] He suggested that the custody arrangements be decided by a tribunal of Irish nationalists, which should include Seán's godfather John O'Leary. MacBride wanted his son brought up in Ireland; otherwise, he dramatically announced, 'I would prefer to see him dead.'[83]

Maud allowed John to see Seán on Mondays. He visited every Monday until April 1905 when he returned to Dublin. Maud filed for divorce on 25 February, on the grounds of cruelty, infidelity, and drunkenness. MacBride denied the charges, responding that he had been intoxicated only once during their marriage and was never unfaithful or cruel, and counter-sued for defamation of character. He claimed that if he did find himself under the influence, his wife's indecent behaviour was the cause. During the proceedings, MacBride did not delve into specifics about his claim that Maud was the mistress of three different men, just stated that she had admitted so before their marriage. He referred to the alleged paramours as C and B, but does not accuse Yeats, mentioning only that there was 'also a distinguished Irish literary man who was in love with Mrs MacBride before her marriage.'[84] As for the custody of Seán, MacBride was 'willing that his wife should have the custody of the child on the condition that the boy spends at least nine months of every year in Ireland, in a Catholic and Nationalist atmosphere.'[85]

Maud was distressed over the break-up, particularly about its implications for the nationalist cause. She wrote to Yeats, 'of a hero I had made, nothing remains & the disillusion has been cruel. I am fighting an uneven battle because I am fighting a man without honor or scruples who is sheltering himself & his vices behind the National cause, knowing that my loyalty to it in part ties my hands.'[86] Many nationalists were afraid that the divorce and the resulting scandal would have an adverse effect on the movement, either by forcing nationalists to choose sides or giving the British fuel to stoke the anti-nationalist fire. As MacBride's lawyer Barry O'Brien cautioned Maud, 'this is no ordinary case of differences between husband and wife . . . this is a case in which Irish national considerations must be taken into account.'[87] John Quinn, an Irish-American lawyer who became a great supporter of Irish politics and art, informed Yeats on 6 May that 'MacBride has had his friends here [New York City] notified and they apparently take his side of the case and those who do not say the scandal is hurtful to the cause generally and that the sooner it is hushed up the better.'[88]

Quinn had helped Maud to obtain affidavits from the United States confirming MacBride's drunken behaviour while on his lecture tours. Annie Horniman, the principal backer of Yeats's Abbey Theatre, travelled to Mayo to gather evidence. She was unsuccessful, largely because she made enquiries regarding Patrick MacBride rather than John. Two Mayo solicitors swore that Patrick MacBride was a 'sober person' of 'solid financial status'.[89] As John had not lived in Mayo for several years, the men were probably speaking about John's father or brother.

Maud mentioned the divorce case in a March/April 1906 letter to Yeats, writing that she found the wait 'wearisome and unsettling'.[90] She was most insulted by the allusion to her father's English background and her lack of true 'Irish' heritage. MacBride drove the knife in further by claiming that her patriotism was insincere, merely an unnatural craving for drama and attention; 'she never went upon the boards until she entered Irish politics, her dramatic talents then, for the first time, found practical vent.'[91]

Testimony ended on 5 September 1906. Five days later, a verdict of judicial separation was granted and Maud was given custody of Seán. MacBride was given visitation rights twice weekly until Seán turned six, then he would visit MacBride every August. Maud appealed this clause and it was eventually amended to only one weekly visit.

The case dragged on until January 1908. As MacBride had proved domicile in Ireland, the court had decided that it could not grant a divorce, as it would not be recognised there. Instead, Maud was given a legal separation and permission to appeal for divorce in three years' time. Immorality was not sufficiently proven, but drunkenness was. More importantly, she was granted full custody of Seán. She accepted the decision and did not appeal further, accepting judicial separation under Irish law administered by French judges, rather than a French divorce. She was content with the decision and 'as long as Major MacBride does not attempt to interfere with me or my child, I don't think I shall take the trouble and go to law again but it is always well to know I can, if I need to.'[92]

Opinion on the separation was polarised in Ireland. Maud's first public appearance in Dublin took place on 20 October 1906 at the Abbey Theatre where she and Yeats saw Lady Gregory's *Gaol Gate*. Writer and actress Mary Colum described waiting in the audience for the play to begin. Yeats arrived late,

> Accompanied by a tall woman dressed in black, one of the tallest women I have ever seen. Instantly a small group in the pit began to hiss loudly and shout, 'Up John MacBride!' The woman stood and faced the hissers, her whole figure showing a lively emotion, and I saw the most beautiful, the most heroic-looking human being I have seen before or since. She was about six feet tall and both of romantic and commanding presence . . . Yeats, standing beside her, looked bewildered as the hissing went on: his face was set in lines of gloom, but she was smiling and unperturbed. Soon a counter hissing set up, the first hisser being drowned by another group and then I realised who she was.[93]

John O'Leary sided with MacBride, which hurt Maud deeply, as she had long considered O'Leary a mentor. Unsurprisingly, the IRB took John's side as well. Maud was expelled from Cumann na nGaedheal, Griffith's nationalist organisation, but she still wrote editorials and gave speeches in Paris promoting the Irish cause.

Maud vowed to concentrate on her son's potential. She wrote to Yeats about 'John whose usefulness is I think over & little Seagan whose work has not yet begun.'[94] She introduced him to the national cause at an early age: when the St Patrick's Society of Paris held its annual celebration, she dressed three-year-old Seán in a white suit, with her Knights of St Patrick membership cross around his neck, and had him distributing shamrocks.[95] He was tutored by the Abbé Combat from Passy Church and later attended St Louis de Gonzague, a Jesuit College a few blocks away from Gonne's house. His potential to take part in the nationalist movement was spotted early on; while lunching at Maud's, outspoken actress and painter Sarah Purser looked at Seán and remarked, 'Aren't you afraid he'll grow up to be a murderer?'[96]

The divorce case took nearly four years. As Seán was only a year old when proceedings began, he may have been too young to understand fully what was happening. Yet he must have later deduced the cause of his mother's antipathy toward his father. The situation is never mentioned in his memoir, but considering his reaction to the potential revelations in Maud's autobiography and his aversion to the airing of family skeletons, his reluctance to mention his view of the circumstances of the divorce is not surprising.

MacBride had returned to Dublin in 1906, where he found a job writing for the *Freeman's Journal* and was seen in the city as 'a fine old soldier who lived very much in the past'.[97] The present must have paled in comparison. His marriage had ended in a storm of negative publicity and he had trouble finding work. Because of MacBride's move, Maud did not feel safe living in Ireland. For the most part, she remained in France, afraid that if she returned to Ireland permanently, MacBride might claim custody of Seán.

Apparently Maud constantly worried about Seán being taken by MacBride and, according to her niece, Thora Forrester, she kept a large sheepdog called Brutus in her apartment and slept with Seán, stowing a revolver under her pillow.[98] She must have communicated these fears to her son. Conor Cruise O'Brien describes a portrait Maud drew of Seán as a young boy, 'an arresting and disturbing portrait. The child's expression is not that of a child but of an ageless being; tense and brooding and apparently confronting dark forces . . . like the picture of a little boy who has been told he is in danger of being kidnapped by his wicked father.'[99] She spoke to him only in French, knowing that if MacBride did try to communicate with him, he would find it difficult, as his grasp of the French language was very poor.

Such stifling security apparently affected his health, which appeared quite precarious. During his parents' separation trial, a Dr Saint Martin testified that Seán suffered from a nervous temperament and had attacks where he briefly lost consciousness.[100] Maud often travelled to Colleville to the sea 'for the sake of my little boy's health'.[101] He had all the major childhood illnesses. In 1912, he contracted acute appendicitis and had an operation, most likely in January. A year later, he caught the chickenpox in Florence. As Maud informed Quinn, 'My boy . . . is never very strong.'[102]

There may have been reasons other than physical delicacy for his illnesses. As Maud was constantly on the move, maladies could have been engineered to keep her in Paris. She was a bit of a nervous mother where his health was concerned, perhaps remembering Georges. Iseult once reported to her cousin Thora that she was certain that Seán could work up a temperature if his mother was going away.[103] It is clear that he wanted his mother near him, either for stability or because he had sensed some of Maud's fear of his being kidnapped. Maud wrote to Yeats on 19 January 1914 that 'I was coming to Ireland next week but the 26th is Seagan's birthday & there was great wailing at the idea of my going away just before it.'[104] Perhaps he was merely sensitive to stress; Maud told Quinn that 'my boy, as usual, when he works hard at school, got ill.'[105]

How founded were Maud's fears regarding an attempt by MacBride to gain custody, especially after 1906 when MacBride was permanently ensconced in Dublin? In the summer of 1910, the family vacationed in Ballycastle, Co. Mayo. Maud, Iseult, and Seán visited John's mother in Westport, probably the first time that she had seen him since his baptism. Although MacBride was not present, he was in Mulrany, not far from Westport. As Quinn inquired about her visit to Mayo, 'I assume from your going there with the children that there is no more trouble in regard to their custody that MacBride feels he can safely try to make.'[106] Maud did not address this question in her reply. She had also brought Seán to Ireland on other occasions and nearly sent him to school in Dublin, prevented only by the outbreak of the First World War.[107] MacBride did not have any real desire to steal his son, nor did he manoeuvre in that direction. His lack of a permanent job or home would have made a custody suit impractical.

Although Maud claimed that it was her fear of MacBride asserting rights over their child, her move away from Irish politics had more to do with the unwelcome publicity of the divorce case. She speculated to Yeats in 1907 that, 'I do not know if my direct work for Ireland is over or not.'[108] Maud had always been a restless person and she kept busy during her exile. She studied painting at Humbert's Academy in the Place Blanche and took classes at the Beaux Arts. She did not appear to dwell on her failed marriage; as Seán's daughter Anna MacBride White explained, 'when it was all over she did not enter into recriminations or explanation.'[109] Yet she seemed disenchanted with her exile, explaining to Quinn that she found Paris dull.[110]

Maud may not have been directly involved in Irish republican matters, but her house was always full of Irish republicans. As Seán later remembered, 'what are now names in history were familiar to me from my boyhood.'[111] He recalled meeting Patrick Pearse in the spring of 1914, as Maud considered sending him to St Enda's, Pearse's bilingual school in Rathfarnham in Dublin. He also met Sir Roger Casement when he came to visit Maud in Paris in 1912 and was 'impressed by this tall, gaunt figure with a beard.'[112] He and Maud spoke, strangely enough considering Casement's role in the Easter Rising, about shipping lines.

She focused on social welfare issues, including a school lunches for children campaign beginning in 1910. An anecdote sees her and Seán feeding ducks in St Stephen's Green when a few small children came and took the crusts meant for the ducks. A little girl explained, 'When we get home from school and mother has no dinner for us I always bring my little brothers to the Green to get bits off the ducks.'[113] The campaign continued through 1911; in February, Maud informed Quinn that she was returning to Ireland for her school meals campaign and 'Iseult and Bichon are rather angry with me for leaving them again.'[114]

Maud's separation from MacBride provided an opportunity for Yeats to re-establish himself in her life. In 1908, they renewed their 'spiritual marriage' and perhaps had a brief sexual relationship at the end of the year in Dublin. Yeats's wife George revealed to Yeats biographer Richard Ellmann that 'W.B. and Maud Gonne were lovers at that time.'[115] However, it did not last. Despite the break from MacBride, Maud had remained a Catholic and she could not marry while her husband was still living. She again alluded to her distaste of sexual love but affirmed her desire to continue a relationship on the astral plane.

Meanwhile, MacBride remained in Dublin, making a living as a journalist. Accounts of the court proceedings were forbidden in France, but were published by the *Irish Independent*. MacBride sued the paper for libel. He did not win, as the court found that although the charges of cruelty and infidelity were libellous, the charge of drunkenness was not. To add insult to injury, he was awarded only £1 in damages. Other than the libel case, he kept a low profile to avoid arrest. In 1910, MacBride was still having trouble finding work. He had applied for various jobs without success. Maud put in a good word for him when he applied for a water bailiff job, where his duties would include inspecting vessels entering the River Liffey and collecting Corporation shipping dues. Although he obtained the position and managed to keep it until his execution, he was 'alleged to have resented her interference in the matter'.[116] MacBride was again active in the nationalist movement, becoming a member of the Supreme Council of the IRB in 1911. However, he was soon forced out in a purge and replaced by Seán MacDermott. MacBride remained on good terms with the new leadership, but they did not trust him enough to confide their rebellion plans five years later.[117]

The couple never spoke to one another again, though it is rumoured that they encountered each other twice but did not acknowledge one another.[118] MacBride never saw his son again; according to Seán's memoir, they communicated mainly through the post.

On 11 March 1911, Seán made his first Holy Communion in France. Later that year, the family travelled to Italy where they attended Pope Pius X's private Mass. The Pope gave Seán a medal with his portrait.[119] Maud continually worried about his health and did not want him to over-exert himself, writing to Yeats that 'my little Jean is making alarming progress in school I do all I can to inculcate idleness & have prevented the master putting him in a higher class than his age warrants.'[120] In June 1912, after their Passy house was pulled down, Maud moved the family about 500 metres down the road to 17 rue de l'Annonciation.

The outbreak of the Great War in August 1914 provided Maud with a focus. When the war broke out, Maud volunteered her services at the auxiliary military hospital housed in the Lycée Janson-de-Sailly at 106 rue de la Pompe, very near her house. She also worked as a Red Cross nurse in Argelis in the Pyrenees. Ten-year-old Seán worked as a page and fed and lit cigarettes for paralysed soldiers.[121] Despite the war enveloping France and her desire to return to Ireland, Maud wanted to keep Seán in France until he was old enough for custody not to be an issue. She had even considered relocating to America, informing Quinn on 4 February 1916 that 'I shall come to America with Iseult and the boy' after the war.[122]

Whether Maud would have made that journey can only be guessed. In less than three months, her plans would change drastically. In March, she was overseeing Seán's recovery from influenza, not realising that events in Dublin were heading toward crisis point.[123]

The Irish Parliamentary Party, split after the Parnell-O'Shea divorce scandal, had managed to reunite in 1900, under the leadership of John Redmond, a Catholic barrister and nationalist. As a result of two general elections in 1910, the Irish MPs held the balance of power at Westminster. In 1912, Prime Minister Herbert Asquith introduced the third Home Rule Bill, and self-government for Ireland seemed certain. Though Ulster unionists opposed it, the bill had the backing of a majority of the population of Ireland and a healthy majority of MPs. Moreover, the powers of the House of Lords had been reduced in 1911; as a result, peers no longer had veto power.

The situation was transformed by the outbreak of the First World War. Both unionist and nationalist leaders agreed to support Britain's war effort and to postpone Home Rule until hostilities ceased. The Home Rule Bill became law on 18 September 1914 but its operation was suspended for one year or the duration of the war, which was expected to be over by 1915. Redmond urged his followers to enlist in the British army, justifying his appeal by arguing that Britain was fighting 'in defence of right, of freedom, and of religion'.[124]

Strategically, there were strong arguments in favour of his response. To support Britain was a way of proving that Ireland could be trusted with self-government, and of disproving the unionist contention that if given Home

Rule, nationalist Ireland would abandon Britain in her hour of danger. In addition, there existed the remote possibility that some unionists might be reconciled to Home Rule once nationalists had provided evidence of their loyalty to the Empire. However, some viewed Redmond's position as a betrayal of Irish nationalism. Others did not trust the British to implement Home Rule legislation after the war.

The Irish Republican Brotherhood, believers in physical force nationalism, sought to act on the old republican dictum, 'England's difficulty is Ireland's opportunity' and had considered an insurrection shortly after the war broke out. This attitude did not have wide support; as Foster points out, the rebels were 'a minority of a minority'.[125] In August 1915, the IRB formed a Military Council. It eventually comprised seven members — Thomas Clarke, Sean MacDermott, Patrick Pearse, Eamonn Ceannt, Joseph Plunkett, James Connolly, and Thomas MacDonagh. They were helped by an Irish-American organisation, Clan na Gael, who shared their aims and provided virtually the only means of contact between the insurgents and Germany, from whom they hoped to receive military backing.

The IRB was too small in number and covert in operation to precipitate a full-scale uprising. For this purpose, they wanted to use the Irish Volunteers, an organisation formed in 1913 in Dublin by moderate nationalists impressed by the impact of the Ulster Volunteer Force and frustrated with Britain's delay in granting Home Rule. The Military Council hoped to employ the Irish Volunteers as a strike force in the planned rebellion. The plan involved infiltration and deceit, as some of the Irish Volunteers leaders, notably Eoin MacNeill, opposed a wartime rising on grounds of principle and wished to proceed only if there was a good chance of success. However, the Irish Volunteers did form an alliance with James Connolly, the revolutionary socialist and commander of the Irish Citizen Army.

During 1915, the rebel leaders' preparations for a rising were gathering momentum. Their plan was centred on an insurrection in Dublin to be reinforced by munitions from Germany, which were to land on the Kerry coast. Germany had agreed to ship 20,000 captured Russian rifles and one million rounds, hoping thereby to divert some British troops from the western front.

Meanwhile, leadership positions in the Irish Volunteers were successfully infiltrated, both in Dublin and elsewhere. By January 1916, the Military Council had set the date for a rising — initially Good Friday, 21 April 1916, later moved to Easter Sunday, 23 April. The Council's intentions were to be masked behind publicly advertised and apparently routine manoeuvres arranged for that day.

On 19 April, Irish Volunteers commanders were given details of the plan of insurrection, despite the risk of this information leaking to members who would oppose it. Disaster threatened on 21 April when MacNeill received word of their true intentions. After initial hesitation, he issued an advertisement in the morning edition of the *Sunday Independent*, cancelling all Volunteer operations planned for Easter Sunday.

To add to the confusion, the scheme to retrieve the expected German arms was a failure. The rebels' emissary, Sir Roger Casement, was arrested on 21 April, hours after landing on the Kerry coast via a German submarine. The Royal Navy captured the arms ship, the *Aud*, on the same day. Because of inept planning by the rebel leadership, local volunteers had not been expecting the *Aud* to arrive when it did. News reached Dublin that the ship had been captured. The Military Council met in an emergency session on Sunday morning to consider its options. It was decided to proceed on the following day with whatever forces could be mustered.

The Easter Rising is generally seen as having been doomed from the outset, and to have been understood as such by its leaders; historians have seen in it elements of a 'blood sacrifice' in line with some of Pearse's writings. However, Joe Lee convincingly demonstrates that blood sacrifice was not the original intention 'however profusely blood sacrifice sentiments spatter the later writings of Pearse and MacDonagh . . . it seems unhistorical to interpret these sentiments as the basis of the actual planning of the Rising' but because of the hopelessness of the venture it was placed in those terms.[126] There was hope that the mission might succeed; citizens of Dublin might rise to join them. A Britain preoccupied with fighting a world war might take the rebellion as a sign that Ireland could not be controlled and choose to grant it freedom. The rebellion itself might not go well but the act might make enough of a nationalist stand to ensure a place at the eventual peace conference following the Great War.[127]

For the rebellion to have the slightest hope of success, the insurgents would need ample weapons and clever planning. They had neither. The Rising was virtually confined to Dublin. The capture of the German arms greatly reduced its scale outside the capital. Moreover, the flood of conflicting orders and the postponement of the rebellion led to fewer numbers.

At about 11 a.m. on Easter Monday, the Irish Volunteers, along with the Irish Citizen Army, assembled at various prearranged meeting points in Dublin and set out to occupy a number of buildings in the centre of the city. These had been chosen to command the main routes into the capital and because of their strategic position in relation to certain military barracks. Given the advantage of surprise, the properties were taken virtually without resistance and the rebels set about making them defensible.

During the Rising, the Second Battalion under MacDonagh occupied Jacob's Biscuit Factory. John MacBride was second in command. Again, there are a few contradictory tales about how MacBride came to be at the factory. One anecdote puts him at Thomas Clarke's tobacco shop, where he heard of the plan and volunteered directly to MacDonagh. Another sees him passing the factory, observing what was happening and joining in. At his court-martial on 5 May, MacBride claimed that he set out that Monday morning with the

> intention of going to meet my brother who was coming to get married . . . I went up as far as Stephen's Green and there saw a band of Irish Volunteers . . . I considered it my duty to join them. I knew there was no chance of success and I never advised nor influenced any other person to join. I did not even know the positions they were about to take up — I marched with them to Jacob's Factory. After being a few hours there I was appointed second-in-command.[128]

It is certain that MacBride had no prior knowledge of the insurrection; witnesses confirmed that he was not dressed in military garb, and his landlady, Frederick Allan's wife, testified at his court-martial that she remembered him 'leaving my house last Easter Monday morning dressed in civilian clothes'.[129] She explained that MacBride's brother 'was coming up from Castle Bar and [asked] the accused to meet him in the Wicklow Hotel Dublin' as he was 'to be married the following Wednesday and . . . the accused was to be best man.' MacBride was not part of the IRB Military Council nor was his name on the 1916 Proclamation.

The General Post Office on O'Connell Street was the nerve centre of the rebellion. It served as the rebels' headquarters and the location where Pearse issued his 'Proclamation on Behalf of the Provisional Government of the Irish Republic'.

The British did not take action right away. When the Rising began, the authorities had just 400 troops to confront roughly 1,500 insurgents. Their immediate priorities were to amass reinforcements, gather information on volunteer strength and location, and protect strategic positions, including the seat of government, Dublin Castle, which had been initially undefended.

As the week progressed, the fighting in some areas became intense, characterised by prolonged, fiercely contested street battles. In some instances, lapses in military discipline occurred. Soldiers were alleged to have killed fifteen unarmed men in North King Street near the Four Courts during intense gun battles on 28 and 29 April.[130] The pacifist Francis Sheehy-Skeffington, the best-known civilian victim of the rebellion, was arrested on 25 April, taken to Portobello Barracks and shot by firing squad the next morning, without trial.

Reinforcements were sent into the capital and, by 28 April, the rebels were facing about 19,000 soldiers. The GPO had been cut off from other rebel garrisons from 27 April. On 29 April, the rebel leaders evacuated the GPO and accepted the only terms on offer — unconditional surrender. The decision was made known to all the battalions still fighting and was accepted, sometimes reluctantly. MacBride learned of the surrender on Sunday, and, though he might have been able to escape capture, he thought that doing so would be dishonourable.[131]

In total, the Easter Rising left 450 dead, 2,614 wounded, and devastated much of central Dublin.

The British response was swift and brutal. Martial law was imposed, and all suspected 'Sinn Féiners' were arrested. Ironically the small Sinn Féin party was not involved in the uprising but was blamed by the British Government and the Irish media for being behind it — a charge that stuck. Those who signed the Proclamation and all battalion commanders were to be executed.

On 4 May, MacBride was brought to Richmond Barracks for his court martial. He pleaded not guilty. He was taken to Kilmainham Gaol and executed on Friday, 5 May. His part in the rebellion was relatively small and he had had no part in planning the uprising. He was earmarked for execution largely because of his role against the British in the Boer War. Apparently MacBride refused a blindfold on the morning of his execution, declaring, 'Fire away. I've been looking down the barrels of rifles all my life.' According to poet and economist Tom Kettle, that was a magnificent lie: 'he had been looking down the necks of porter bottles all his life.'[132] Still, his execution raised his status in Dublin, and Quinn called his death 'a fine one . . . the best end possible for MacBride, a better end than a small place-holder and going on living in the past and drinking and talking out his life.'[133]

The rebels apparently had little public support, though Lee points out that it is difficult to reconstruct the exact public response because little concrete objective information was available to the public at the time.[134] Yet the shooting of Sheehy-Skeffington, the secret courts martial, and the executions of the leaders mobilised public opinion behind the failed rebellion. The speed and severity of the actions against those fifteen did for the Irish independence movement what years of public appeals could not.

Maud was only vaguely aware of what was happening in Dublin, reading in the French press small, heavily censored accounts of 'Dublin Riots'. She pleaded with Yeats from Colleville, where the family was staying for the Easter holidays, 'I am fearfully anxious for my friends & for news of what is really taking place . . . PLEASE send me papers quickly.'[135]

Maud read in the newspapers of her husband's execution. According to Yeats, Seán was informed of his father's death by his mother, who took him aside in Colleville while he was making a boat, and told him, 'Your father has died for his country — he did not behave well to us — but now we can think of him with honour.'[136] Maud probably did say words to that effect several times after MacBride's death, but in an RTÉ interview and in his memoir, Seán claimed that he learned of his father's death from the priests at Gonzague College in Paris; at school, the rector announced his father's death among the war dead by stating that John MacBride was 'executed by the British for fighting for the freedom of his country.'[137] He appreciated the gesture, especially considering that France was fighting alongside Britain only miles away.

Maud's feelings about MacBride had altered completely. His death was redemption for his behaviour and, more importantly, provided Seán with the legacy of an honourable father. He had died for the cause, earning her forgiveness and perhaps a re-estimation of his potential for heroism. As she informed Quinn shortly after his death, 'My husband is among those executed . . . he has died for Ireland . . . I remember nothing else.'[138] And more significantly from Maud's point of view, 'his son will bear an honoured name.'

Maud became known as Maud Gonne MacBride even though she had shied away from using that surname during their short marriage. The addition of 'MacBride' was seen by some as hypocritical and opportunistic, but she did this more to establish Seán's legitimacy; she had always been mindful of his political future. Now that John had proved himself worthy, his name was without stain: 'Major MacBride by his Death has left a name for Seagan to be proud of. Those who die for Ireland are sacred. Those who enter Eternity by the great door of Sacrifice atone of all.'[139] No matter what his behaviour in his other life, to Maud, MacBride had atoned for all by that grand gesture of facing a British firing squad. Again, like the rebels themselves, John MacBride did in death what was impossible for him to do in life.

She wore black more often in public, which was also viewed as hypocrisy, but she had been wearing mourning clothes since the death of Georges. She did not become a staunch defender or commemorator of MacBride's memory but she disliked Yeats's tribute to the Rising, 'Easter 1916', where he famously described her former husband as a 'drunken, vainglorious lout . . . ' who had 'done most bitter wrong/To some who are near my heart', calling it 'not worthy of Willie's genius and still less of the subject.'[140]

She would correct the errors of others if she felt it was necessary. She complained to Quinn that 'It is characteristic of the English to insult a fallen adversary — the *Daily Mail* Paris Edition, announcing his execution had an article full of lies, which I had to contradict in the French press.'[141]

How did Seán feel about his father's execution? The death of a parent, even one to whom he was not close and did not know well, must have affected him. He contracted enteritis after Easter, perhaps as a result of the emotional trauma of recent events. He had not seen John MacBride for years, and prior to his execution, MacBride had been reviled by his mother and, 'whatever vague information he had been given about his father, he cannot have been unaware of the fear surrounding him.'[142] Yet his mother's image of MacBride was suddenly transformed after 1916. Such an about-face must have been difficult for a boy of twelve to process, but Maud had brought him up as a fervent nationalist, so perhaps he could accept such a change. Conor Cruise O'Brien, who later worked with Seán in the Department of External Affairs, theorised that

> the father whom he had never known, and towards whom he must have entertained feelings of aversion and apprehension (at best) was now metamorphosed into a sacred being in the eyes of his mother, who had loathed his father, for as long as Sean's memories could go back. Yet he must have instantly recognised the legitimacy of the totally unexpected metamorphosis for he had been brought up, by his mother, on a peculiarly intense mystical-nationalist form of the cult of those who died for Ireland.[143]

Cruise O'Brien wrote about the power of the ghosts of a nation and that 'Sean MacBride was brought up under that power and it had been strengthened by the addition of his formerly alienated father to the number of the ghosts in question.'[144] To paraphrase Yeats, all were transformed utterly.

Years later, people would remark about Seán's lack of warmth or humour. If his personality is sometimes described as cold, it is easy to deduce where this aloof manner originated. His experiences during the First World War, the lack of a real relationship with and the execution of his father, and his career both as an IRA man and a lawyer surely toughened him and placed him in situations where signs of emotion were not welcomed.

Maud was anxious to return to Ireland; custody was no longer an issue and, in October 1916, she decided to travel to Dublin with Iseult and Seán, as 'Paris doesn't suit him & I have always wanted him brought up in Ireland.'[145]

After MacBride's death, Yeats again proposed to Maud, again on the condition that she abandon politics, and was again refused. He then proposed to Iseult in the summer of 1917. She eventually turned him down. As both Lady Gregory and his astrological chart suggested that he should wed at once, Yeats married George Hyde-Lees on 20 October 1917. George was probably a more suitable choice for the poet, as he wrote to Lady Gregory, 'she has made my life serene and full of order.'[146]

Living in Ireland would place Seán in the thick of events in the fight for freedom, similar to an Irish Candide. The weight of expectation for Maud's 'man of destiny' would become much heavier. Many of MacBride's later concerns would be formed and solidified during his first years in Ireland.

Chapter 2 ∿

A SORT OF HOMECOMING: SEÁN RETURNS TO IRELAND

'To understand a man, you have to know what was happening in the world when he was twenty.'

— ATTRIBUTED TO NAPOLEON BONAPARTE

Seán's own memoir, *That Day's Struggle*, begins roughly after his father's execution. The book provides information about his activities after his permanent return to Ireland, but Seán's recollections are selective and his grasp of names and dates slightly suspect.

John MacBride's death removed any of Maud Gonne's fears of living in Ireland. After her virtual exile, the possibility of returning must have seemed exciting. She could once again be involved in nationalist politics having been absent for so long.

However, returning was not quite so simple. The First World War had wiped out a considerable portion of her trust and economising became necessary. Far more important to Maud's immediate plans to return was the mood in Ireland following the Easter Rising. In June, John Dillon had told David Lloyd George, 'the temper of the country is extremely bad and the temper of this city [Dublin] ferocious',[1] and the political climate meant that British authorities did not want any more fervent nationalists stirring up trouble. When Maud pointed out that 1916 rebel Constance Markiewicz was allowed a visa, the response was that the British did not want two such mad women running around Dublin.

But Maud was determined to return to Ireland, both to encourage agitation and to allow Seán to live in a nationalist environment and to attend school in Ireland. Maud wrote to the British Home Office on 30 June 1917, pointing out that as all Sinn Féin prisoners had been allowed to return, there should be no difficulty for her to obtain permission.[2] Maud was told that, under the Defence of the Realm Act, the British would allow her only into England and, although Maud wrote that 'no reason was assigned',[3] Home Office paperwork explained that she posed a danger; not only was she the widow of John MacBride, but she had once taken an active part in anti-British movements, and, while in Paris, she had associated with Indian seditionists. Warnings were sent to all ports and directives issued to stop her leaving Britain. Maud was later told that she could embark for Ireland if she agreed to sign a document promising to take no part in politics. She refused and asked her friend John Quinn for help. He was unable to do anything.

Maud was certain that she could find some way to return. According to MacBride's memoir, the family arrived in London at the end of 1916 or the beginning of 1917 and lived at a house on King's Road, Chelsea, over a shop between Chelsea Town Hall and a cinema.[4] Their arrival date was most likely 17 September 1917; according to Home Office records, Maud, Iseult, Seán, and their cook Josephine Pillon arrived at Southampton accompanied by Yeats. They were informed that they would be unable to proceed to Ireland. By 24 October, the family had changed quarters, ensconced in Yeats's rooms in Woburn Buildings.

London must have had a temporary, waiting-room feel for Seán, as he was aware that his mother had not stopped wishing to travel to Ireland. He was maturing quickly, perhaps becoming the man in charge now that his father would never assume that role. As Iseult reported to Yeats in July 1917, 'You will not know Bichon when you meet him again, he is nearly as tall as we are, speaks with a man's voice and has at last acquired some smoothness and grace of manner.'[5] Maud had not enrolled him in school. Instead Seán was tutored by Ezra Pound, a young American poet and the driving force behind several modernist movements in twentieth-century poetry; he had recently befriended Yeats.

The lessons did not last long. Pound claimed that Seán 'has never forgiven me for trying to jam some Ovid into his very allergic head',[6] but it is more likely that Pound's affair with Iseult offended Seán. Pound was married to Dorothy Shakespear, the daughter of one of Yeats's former lovers, and depended on her income, making it impossible for him to marry Iseult, who had no real income of her own. Pound initially found Seán to be very intelligent, but later told Quinn that 'the months in Ireland have ruined his mind and left him, as might be expected at his age, doomed to political futilities.'[7]

Fearing that she would get restless, Scotland Yard arranged for Maud to be shadowed by detectives after her arrival in London. Seán proved useful in outwitting two of the men following Maud. While at Woburn Buildings, he noticed that the detectives normally went to the pub while Maud went for her daily Turkish bath. He formulated a melodramatic plan to help Maud get to Ireland. In January or February 1918, she ducked into the bathhouse and waited for the detectives to depart. She then emerged shortly after, disguised as an old woman, a disguise which helped to hide her height of 5 foot 11 inches.[8] Having sneaked off to the railway station, she managed to get to Ireland safely. Seán did not accompany her, but was very pleased that his efforts had borne fruit, 'Naturally I enjoyed doing this a great deal; it was a very thrilling game.'[9]

Seán followed her a few days later. The British knew that she was in Ireland; a Home Office Report, dated 13 January 1918, revealed that Maud had been seen around Dublin with Seán, but she was not arrested for fear of creating a sensation.[10] As the War Office had made clear to the Home Office before Maud's departure, 'we wish to prevent her from embarking for Ireland but have agreed that it is a pity to make a martyr out of her by arrest or prosecution.'[11] Her escape a success, Maud rented 'cold, bleak, and miserable' rooms in North Great George's Street while she searched for a house.[12] She purchased 73 St Stephen's Green in March 1918.

Maud was encouraged by the activities in Ireland. The threat of conscription and identification of Sinn Féin with the now-martyred Rising men gave a new cohesion to the nationalist effort. But the British Government was equally determined to keep this resurgence in check. On 19 May 1918, Maud was returning from dinner at the home of George Russell (Æ), with Seán and Joseph King, an English MP. She was arrested, along with nearly the entire leadership of Sinn Féin and the Irish Volunteers, under suspicion of engaging in a conspiracy with Germany. Seán ran after the Black Maria that was carting his mother away. The authorities provided no evidence as to this 'German Plot'. Maud was sent to the Bridewell, then Holloway Prison.

Constance Markiewicz was also incarcerated in Holloway. Prisoners were allowed free association and could send out for food, but they were not allowed visitors because they refused to submit to the prison rule that politics not be discussed during visits. Maud worried about Seán, particularly his plans for school. He had not been receiving any formal education since they had left Paris and it would be important, as 'he will have to make an income someday for his Mother has no longer enough for herself & him & Iseult. She will be able to give him something but not a livelihood.'[13] Markiewicz wrote to her sister that 'my companions [Kathleen Clarke], I think of as "Niobe" and "Rachel" as they are the most complete and perfect — though now, alas! mournful — mothers that I have ever met!!'[14]

Yeats took Seán to Ballinamantane in Gort in July 1918 where he and George were living until his newly refurbished tower, Thoor Ballylee, was habitable. The village schoolmaster tutored him, teaching him Irish, Latin, arithmetic, and algebra.

He was content with the Yeatses but insisted on returning to London to campaign for his mother's release, travelling to London on 5 September. Either Iseult or Seán would go nearly every day to try to visit with her.

Here he would get his first glimpse of the injustices of the prison system. His conversations with his mother were monitored. During a visit of 8 July 1918, they spoke about Seán's education and provisions for the Dublin house, but their discussion was interrupted when Maud tried to talk about her treatment in prison.[15] Prison officials believed that Maud might use a cipher to send messages to the nationalist community via Seán; 'a woman like Mrs McBride [sic] might have taught her son a sort of code . . . which would not attract the attention of the ordinary English official but might sound suspicious to anyone acquainted with Irish matters.'[16] Who she might be trying to speak to and what information she could possibly acquire while in Holloway was not apparent in the directive.

His mother's imprisonment and treatment affected Seán deeply. In a letter to Yeats written after Maud's temporary release, Iseult worried about 'Bichon's present state of agitation and drastic plans' regarding Maud's imprisonment.[17] Whether he had overstated his mother's health problems to ensure her release or whether he had formulated an actual escape plan is unclear.

The situation became so dire that Seán reported in a letter to the Home Office on 11 September 1918 that his mother threatened to go on hunger strike unless her conditions were improved.[18] John Quinn helped to secure Maud's release from prison; both Quinn and Seán wrote often to the authorities regarding the state of Maud's health — she was tubercular and losing weight. Having been seen by a doctor, she was taken from Holloway Prison on 29 October to a nursing home on a one-week temporary release. Seán requested that she be allowed to go to her regular doctor in Dublin but before he could receive an answer to his request, she had moved to Woburn Buildings, apparently without permission from prison authorities.[19] Again Seán pleaded for her release for health reasons and was told that Maud must remain at 18 Woburn unless the Home Office gave her permission to move.[20]

Maud heeded this warning like she heeded all the others. In November, in disguise again (this time as a nurse), she slipped past the detectives and boarded a train at Euston. Upon arrival in Dublin, she went to her Stephen's Green house, which was then occupied by Yeats and his wife George who was pregnant with their first child. Yeats turned Maud away — because of the nursing staff there was no room and he did not want his wife subjected to a possible military raid. Maud was very upset; she had recently been in prison, she was worried about her children, and she now felt betrayed by someone who had always helped her through her troubles and who had promised to leave her house when she returned.[21] Iseult relayed the quarrel to Pound, taking neither side, telling him that 'they have both behaved as badly as they could.'[22] However, the quarrel was soon mended and the family lodged with friends until George could safely travel.

The family was close, perhaps too close; Iseult wrote to Yeats referring to her 'scrubbing Bichon in his bath'.[23] Bichon was fourteen at the time. The two siblings were of very different temperaments: Iseult could be dreamy and vague but also full of furious temper at times, while Seán was more cerebral. Yeats commented on his logical and just mind: 'he is the most remarkable boy I have met — self-possessed and very just, seeing all around a question and full of tact.'[24] Yeats praised Maud's children to John Quinn, reporting that Seán and Iseult were the 'most able courteous people & do Madame Gonne's ideas of education, that seemed wild, great credit. The boy like the girl has great sense of justice & both have strong gentle minds.'[25] However, three months later, he complained to Lady Gregory that 'Seagan has not fixed habits or discipline.'[26]

Although he lacked a clear routine, Seán's health seemed to have improved. While with Yeats at Gort, 'all his illnesses, aches, and pains were long forgotten.'[27] The key psychological reasons for his childhood illnesses had been removed. He no longer had to fear his father and, as he was older, he needed less attention from his mother. Securing his mother's release from prison gave him a practical goal and he began to demonstrate a desire to reform the injustices of the legal system.

The issue of his schooling was also resolved. He began at Mount St Benedict in Gorey, Co. Wexford, in 1919. Maud had thought of sending him there earlier, but Victor Collins, a friend of John MacBride's, taught at the school. He had been Maud's godfather at her baptism in 1903 but had taken MacBride's side during the divorce case.[28] Collins also held Maud responsible for the death of his nine-year-old son who had drowned while staying at Colleville during the summer of 1903. Maud thought Collins a bad influence and did not want Seán under his wing. After MacBride's death, Collins's connection with Mount St Benedict was no longer important. The abbot at Mount St Benedict, Fr John Sweetman, was a strong nationalist and involved with Sinn Féin. James Dillon and Cecil Lavery, future members of the inter-party Government, were schoolmates of Seán's. In his memoir, Seán recounts a story of how boys were given one tree for fires in their bedrooms and they had to plant six trees to make up for the one they burnt.[29] Such activity may have been the spark of his interest in afforestation.

After leaving Mount St Benedict, he took lessons in Latin, Irish, and English literature from George Erwin, the Protestant captain of the IRA company in Mount Pleasant Square. Erwin suggested that he join the Fianna, a training ground for the IRA and 'recognised as such though denied officially'.[30] Founded by Markiewicz, the Boy Scout-type group aimed to turn young Irish boys into 'good and patriotic men and will help to soon win the glorious future fate has in store for our land'.[31] His mother approved the move, probably seeing it as an opportunity for Seán to meet other like-minded nationalists of his own age.

Aside from his schoolmates, he did not seem to have many friends when he was young. This may be because he did not grow up in Ireland or because he was protective of his family situation — his half-sister's illegitimacy and his parents' separation. It is more likely that his analytical personality did not make camaraderie easy for him. Upon meeting him in 1918, Arthur Symonds commented that he seemed like a nihilist revolutionary student, always conspiring.[32]

He would develop into an unusual Irish nationalist. Like Éamon de Valera, he was born outside Ireland and had little contact with his father. Unlike de Valera, he had spent much of his early childhood outside Ireland and did not have the same background in Gaelic sport or language as his compatriots did. As C.S. (Todd) Andrews commented, Seán's 'sympathy with Gaelic Ireland was minimal'.[33] In his *Over the Bar: A Personal Relationship with the GAA*, Breandán Ó hEithir related a very telling story about him. At an August 1936 meeting to discuss how to establish a republic, Seán noticed that delegates, especially those from Kerry and Mayo, who had been engaged in passionate debate, now seemed silent and restless. He asked Máirtín Ó Cadhain what the problem was. Ó Cadhain replied that Kerry were playing Mayo in the All-Ireland football semi-final later that afternoon and that most of the delegates wanted to get to Roscommon in time to see it. 'I see,' said Seán. 'So a game of football is more important than the future of the Irish Republic?' Ó Cadhain wrote, 'I knew then that he would never do any good in politics because he did not understand Ireland.'[34]

The Commander of the Dublin Brigade of the Fianna was Barry Mellows and their meeting place was called Skippers Alley near Fleet Street. He and Markiewicz would give speeches, lead military drills, and go camping. Though underage, Seán secretly managed to transfer into the IRA 'B' Company, Third Battalion, operating from North Brunswick Street.

Membership consisted of more drills, revolver lessons, and parades.

Seán became active in politics, canvassing for Markiewicz in the 1918 general election. Iseult believed that this activity was beneficial for him, writing to Pound that Seán seemed 'to show some sense and perhaps this complete immersion in political life may be his salvation.'[35] Sinn Féin won 73 of Ireland's 106 seats, making Markiewicz the first woman elected to the House of Commons. However, following Sinn Féin policy, she refused to take her seat.

After the elections, Sinn Féin MPS gathered in Dublin's Mansion House and set up an alternative parliament, which they called Dáil Éireann, 'Assembly of Ireland'. The Dáil pledged to work for the creation of the Irish Republic by any means possible. In conjunction, the military wing of the IRA burst into action. The War of Independence had begun.

Despite his active involvement in the War of Independence, Seán decided to read for a degree at University College Dublin. His choice of subject, law, was probably influenced by his mother's experiences with the legal system in Britain and Ireland. His other subject, agriculture, was slightly odd as Seán had no farming background. He explained that he had visions of a quieter future for himself: 'I started off with a strange idea of being a farmer and a lawyer, of having a small farm in the country, living from the farm, and doing an occasional law case, for interest or to be able to vindicate justice from time to time.'[36] He abandoned agriculture after a year.

Seán sporadically attended the 1920–1 session at UCD, apparently arrested on his second day of attending lectures. He managed to combine law lectures with creating chaos in and around Dublin: 'when we'd see a patrol or a lorry coming along we'd fire on it, or lob a bomb and fire on them when they'd jump out. Then we'd run like hares, dump the revolvers and I'd get back to college. The professors weren't too keen on what we were doing, but it didn't matter. So long as I got back quickly to Earlsfort Terrace I could pretend I was attending classes when the ambush took place.'[37]

Law student was not Seán's only disguise. 'I used to wear a yellow waistcoat, not that I especially liked fine clothes, but I was usually a dapper on these occasions. I felt that I would get away more easily with the police and in that way I was able to walk into police stations pretending to be a newspaperman.'[38] Like his law-student disguise, it was based in fact — he would later work as a journalist.

He appeared to be managing his double life well, even with his arrest on 26 September 1920 for driving without a military driving permit while chauffeuring Constance Markiewicz, a member of the illegal Dáil. The car's 'engines, horns and lamps all [were] out of order.'[39] The police noticed a broken light and then realised who the female passenger was. He was released in a few days but his incarceration meant that he missed an exam. He was taken to Mountjoy, where Maud was afraid 'they will punish him for being his father's & his mother's son.'[40] She also worried about his time away from college, but he managed to pass his exams in March of 1921.

Maud discovered Seán's IRA membership when he accidentally let off a shot while cleaning a rifle in the attic of their house. The bullet went through floorboards to the room where a priest, recovering from nervous breakdown, was trying to relax.[41] Having heard Seán's explanation, she feared for his safety, but could hardly stop him. She had brought him up on the notion of bravery, of 'dying for Ireland', and dying for Ireland had made a hero out of his previously reviled father.

The idea of dying for Ireland may have been romantic but the reality of it actually happening proved frightening.

> I remember one evening myself and another volunteer were pinned down on the railway line by Tans firing at us. I could see sparks from the bullets striking the tracks. I noticed blood coming from my friend's head and suddenly I realised he was dead. I had to see his parents and go to the wake and that sort of thing. It was my first experience of death. I was about sixteen at the time.[42]

During his first important military action on Pearse Street, Seán and seven others were in charge of guarding the Catholic Working Men's Club where an IRA council meeting was taking place. A convoy of five or six Black and Tan vehicles stopped at the building. Seán opened fire. The Tans fired back and his partner Leo Fitzgerald was killed.

These events obviously terrified Seán. Having considered what was at stake, 'I faced death quite calmly and coolly and decided well if death is to come, there it is and I'm going to do what I believe to be right, and that is to continue.'[43]

The realisation that he could easily die in combat was not the only upheaval taking place at this time. His sister Iseult had attempted to elope with Francis Stuart, a writer eight years her junior and another of Yeats's protégés. After their return from London, Maud insisted that they marry properly. Francis duly converted to Catholicism, with Seán as his godfather, and married Iseult on 6 April 1920 at UCD's Newman House Church. Seán does not mention his sister's marriage in his memoir, most likely because it was a stormy union and Seán felt that Stuart was unkind to Iseult. Geoffrey Elborn contacted him about his biography of Stuart. Although Elborn told him that he could speak freely, Seán replied, 'Francis Stuart treated Iseult disgracefully, and I will have nothing to do with you or your book.'[44]

In July 1921, Iseult's first child Delores died. To help her recover, Maud took Francis, Seán and Iseult to Munich. Seán used the holiday to buy guns which he hid in a recess cut into books and posted to a safe address in Ireland. In August 1921, he was sent to Hamburg to assist in the transport of weapons. He found the ship under guard and somehow managed to have the arms transferred to another ship.

In addition to his gun-running activities, he worked to prepare defences for prisoners, gathering evidence, preparing statements, and finding witnesses. In one case, Seán knew that the prisoner was innocent, but when tried by court martial, the man was found guilty and sentenced to death.[45] Seán became convinced of the unreliability of judicial systems believing of capital punishment, 'certainly death sentences should never be carried out . . . perhaps I was more sensitive because I was a law student and had a lot of sympathy with the people who were charged and tried.'[46] Certainly his viewpoint must have been influenced by his own father's execution.

His guerrilla work in the Mount Street area near the South Dock brought him to the attention of Michael Collins, Minister of Finance and Director of Intelligence for the IRA. Collins gave him special assignments, such as buying guns on the Continent, leading attacks on the Royal Irish Constabulary (RIC) barracks in Wicklow, Wexford, and Carlow, and running a training camp outside Dublin.

During an attack on the RIC barracks in Wicklow, his men took refuge at the Glendalough Hotel. It was there that he learned of the Truce in July 1921. His immediate reaction to the truce was one of 'considerable annoyance'.[47] He felt that it came too soon and that if the Irish had waited, they might have got a better deal. The IRA's popularity was growing because of its own success and the draconian behaviour of the Black and Tans sent to squelch the uprisings.

However, the odds of the IRA being able to continue the conflict at strength were weak. During the previous May, IRA units occupied and burned the Custom House in Dublin. The occupation was intended to show that British rule in Ireland was untenable. However, from a military point of view, it was a fiasco, which revealed that the IRA was not trained or equipped well enough to take on British forces in a conventional manner. By July 1921, most IRA units were chronically short of both weapons and ammunition. Seán did allow that the weapons they had were 'antiquated and terrible'.[48] By the time of the Truce, many republican leaders, including Michael Collins, were convinced that if the war went on for much longer, there was a chance that the IRA campaign as it was then organised could be brought to a standstill.

Despite the Truce, the IRA continued to build up its forces and conducted more training. Seán was assigned to a camp in Glenasmole. While he was there, Collins informed him that he would be going to London as Collins's aide-de-camp. Seán was pleased to have been chosen, but said that he was already on assignment. Collins instructed him to see Chief-of-Staff Richard Mulcahy who told Seán that it was more important to carry on with the training. Collins replied, 'Tell him [Mulcahy] to go to hell. I want you to come and you're coming. Go back and tell him you're coming, whether he likes it or not.'[49] Faced with Collins's demand, Mulcahy agreed to let him go.

In October 1921, representatives of the Dáil went to London to negotiate with the British. Seán's job in London was to make arrangements for a quick getaway if things didn't work out and to carry dispatches between Dublin and London. Seán claimed that he never read the letters.[50] There were two separate groups within the delegation; the military men stayed at Cadogan Square while the politicians lodged at Hans Place. There was little contact between the two houses.

Seán stayed with Collins at 15 Cadogan Gardens but often played chess or bridge at Hans Place. Such behaviour did not go unnoticed by the military men, who mocked his pretentiousness in associating with the politicians. Seán's incongruities showed in other ways. He was amazed by the amount of drinking Collins did, as he thought that such behaviour was a bad influence on the delegation. Such opinions did not stop Seán from joining in: 'I was rather revolted by it, though I did drink a good deal with them.'[51]

The negotiations lasted for three months. During that time, Seán went to Hamburg to postpone a gun-running mission as Collins feared that it would damage the negotiations. Collins instructed him not to abort the mission entirely, but to complete the deal after the Treaty was signed.[52] The arms would then be used to train for Northern activities. If Seán's recollection is correct, this deal demonstrates that Collins had little faith in the Boundary Commission drawing borders in favour of the South. The guns did arrive: a few shipments came into Waterford followed by a considerable amount of collaborating between Collins and Liam Lynch. According to Seán, 'We were aware that arms were being transferred between the Four Courts and Beggars Bush . . . This was done to impede the new Six County Government and also as an aid to the Catholic minority.'[53]

During the negotiations, Seán began to change his mind about Collins. The image of Collins going in guns blazing against the British had been replaced by a Collins who had been swayed to compromise. As Seán recalls, 'he had been impressed by the possibility and even the desirability of remaining in the Commonwealth, provided Ireland was given an equal share in the responsibility of the Commonwealth.'[54] In Uinseann MacEoin's *Survivors*, Seán remembers Collins returning from the day's negotiations and telling the group that Lloyd George had brought him over to a map showing the British Empire in red, put his arm around him and joked, 'Come on, Mike, why don't you come in and help us run the world?'[55] Collins seemed amused, but Seán was convinced that it had made an impact.

On 6 December, a treaty was signed which ended the War of Independence. It gave Ireland dominion status within the British Empire and provided an option for Northern Ireland to opt out, which it did. The Treaty stated that if Northern Ireland chose to withdraw, a Boundary Commission would be established to draw the boundary between the Irish Free State and Northern Ireland.

Perhaps even more controversially, the Treaty required that the Irish Free State's head of state would be the British monarch, who would be represented by a Governor-General, and members of the new Irish parliament would be required to take an Oath of Allegiance to 'be faithful to His Majesty King George v, his heirs and successors by law, in virtue of the common citizenship'. This oath stung more than the partitioning of the North, which had already taken place under the Government of Ireland Act in 1920. As F.S.L. Lyons observed, of the 338 pages of debate printed in the Dáil report of the Treaty debates, only nine pages were devoted to partition.[56]

Most historians and political scientists seem to agree that the division of the island was an inevitable consequence of Irish demands for independence and the fervent unionist desire to preserve the connection to Britain. Partition was not the major contention with the Treaty; the Oath of Allegiance to the King and dominion rather than republic status were the divisive issues. The debaters in the Dáil left the question of partition aside and focused on questions of sovereignty and alliance instead of what later generations might regard as the more fundamental problem of a divided country. During the 1920s, the belief that economic and other factors would eventually lead to reunification meant that William Cosgrave's Cumann na nGaedheal Government did not make an issue of it. Establishing the Free State in the aftermath of civil war and curbing periodic IRA activity meant that dealing with partition was not a priority. The feeling in the Free State was that partition was fleeting and Ireland would soon be reunited.

As the delegates were envoys plenipotentiary of the Irish Republic, negotiators empowered to sign a treaty without reference back to their superiors, de Valera did not have to be consulted. Misunderstandings about the Treaty might have been minimised if the delegation had had more contact with home, but as Joe Lee argues, it is unlikely that the outcome would have been different.[57] Collins would maintain that he had got the most he could from the British and that the Treaty provided a 'stepping stone' from which an Irish Republic could be achieved.

Seán later laid blame at de Valera's door for not taking part in treaty negotiations or exercising more control over the delegation. The loss of contact and loss of touch with the cabinet at home allowed the delegation to fail in its attempt to secure the Republic. As Minister of External Affairs,

> I certainly would not have allowed any delegation of officials to go negotiate even a minor trade or other agreement, with the British or any other country, without being in daily contact with them, finding out exactly what was happening from day to day and giving them very clear cut instructions as to what they could or could not do, what they should or should not do, what they could or could not agree to.[58]

The Treaty would split the country and lead to more armed conflict, with the irony of Winston Churchill offering Michael Collins arms to enforce its terms. Although he was friendly with Collins during the negotiations, Seán was completely opposed to the Treaty. As he wrote later, 'I felt we could have gotten much more if we had waited. Secondly, I felt that the imposition of allegiance to the crown would never be acceptable and should never be accepted. Thirdly, the treaty would probably involve the partition of the country which again should never have been accepted.'[59]

This viewpoint is very likely influenced by what came later; the worry at the time seemed to be the oath rather than partition. During the Dáil debates concerning the Treaty, most speakers focused on the issue of sovereignty and the oath, not partition. In his memoir, MacBride claims that the lack of focus on partition surprised him. It is not clear whether he means that it surprised him at the time he was writing or at the time the Treaty provisions were being debated. Although partition was not the prominent concern with the Treaty, all parties in the South would speak vehemently about bringing it to an end. Seán would campaign against partition throughout his political career.

However, partition was a firm fact before the Treaty. The Government of Ireland Act in 1920 had already partitioned Ireland and created a six-county Northern Ireland. Although Sinn Féin protested the Act and continued to fight for a united Irish republic, partition was already in place before the Treaty. As Roy Foster indicates, the Treaty of 1921 did not enable partition to take place; partition actually cleared the way for the Treaty.[60] Most of the negotiators, including Collins, believed that the Boundary Commission would transfer many large nationalist areas to the Free State, reducing

Northern Ireland's size so as to make it too small to be a viable political entity.

Apparently there was hope that better terms could be won and that the truce was Collins's ploy to regroup. As Seán wrote, 'Many thought that this was a device, that soon Collins would again take leadership, put an end to the truce and resume fighting for the republic.'[61] He also claimed that Collins handed over substantial quantities of arms to the IRA so that the struggle could continue in the North. Apparently there was contact and there were transfers of arms between Collins and Rory O'Connor right up until the Four Courts raid in April 1922.[62] However, the IRA did not have many weapons to begin with, which made Collins argue that the truce was incredibly timely.

Despite the Oath of Allegiance and the prospect of permanent partition, many of Seán's compatriots accepted the Treaty. His mother was in favour of it which he understood, as 'most of her lifetime, the struggle had largely been for Home Rule, for some measure of independence and control of our own affairs. To Mother, this looked like a tremendous step forward.'[63] Apparently, the issue did not cause enmity between the two, 'when I say fell out, we weren't bitter, but we agreed to disagree. We ceased to exchange views very much — political views.'[64] For two people with such strong opinions whose lives were so devoted to politics, such silence must have been difficult. Seán and his family lived with her until her death in 1953, so perhaps silence was necessary to keep the peace.

The Treaty was accepted by 64 votes to 57. De Valera resigned as President of the Dáil and was replaced by Arthur Griffith, founder of Sinn Féin and one of the Treaty negotiators. Seán officially joined the anti-Treaty forces. He offered his services to de Valera and helped him to open an office on Suffolk Street.

One of Seán's first tasks was to finalise plans for an Irish Race Congress. The Congress aimed to bring people of Irish descent together — mainly for cultural purposes but there was a political element as well. The Congress was held in Paris in January 1922. Among the speakers was William Butler Yeats. To get to France, de Valera disguised himself as a priest, as he had no passport.

While working for de Valera, Seán became involved in reconstruction of the IRA along anti-Treaty lines. He was appointed Assistant Director of Organisation, reporting to Ernie O'Malley. His task was to analyse the strengths of different units in the army. He received instructions from Collins for at least one arms deal. Seán was certain that Collins's involvement was post-Treaty; he recalled meeting Collins in the Gresham Hotel.[65] The meeting made Seán believe that the Treaty was mere 'breathing space' and that Collins would resume the fight against the British. Despite the Civil War, Seán claimed that he and Collins remained on friendly terms. It was the last he saw of Collins, who was killed in an ambush on 22 August.

Because of his involvement in the struggle and the inconvenience and distraction of being on the run, Seán abandoned his law studies in 1922. He had been promoted to the rank of staff commandant at the Four Courts, the anti-Treaty military headquarters. As he had worked closely with Collins and Liam Tobin in procuring weapons during the War of Independence, he was well connected to do so for the anti-Treaty side. He was on an arms mission to Berlin and returned to the Four Courts six days before it was shelled on 22 June.

The Proclamation at the Four Courts was couched in language similar to that of Easter 1916. The pronouncement addressed the 'sacred spirits of the Illustrious Dead' and asked them to support the struggle.[66] At 4 p.m. Ernie O'Malley surrendered the Four Courts to Brigadier General Paddy Daly. All were taken prisoner, including Seán.

He was in prison for sixteen months, spending most of the Civil War in jail. He heard about Arthur Griffith's and Michael Collins's deaths while in Mountjoy, where he shared a cell with Rory O'Connor, a staunch anti-Treatyite who had led the charge on the Four Courts in April. On 7 December, both O'Connor and Seán were ordered to get up, get dressed, and pack their things. The command was not a surprise; both men had heard rumours of a transfer to the Seychelles or St Helena where their escape would be less of a worry. Seán was told to stay behind while Rory was shot at around 6 or 7 a.m. The circumstances of O'Connor's death are often used as an example of the deeply personal divisions in the Civil War — O'Connor had been best man at Cumann na nGaedheal Minister for Justice Kevin O'Higgins's wedding, yet O'Higgins must have approved his execution. O'Higgins affirmed that the executions were necessary for 'the welfare and safety of the Irish people', but broke down in tears when referring to O'Connor.[67]

The execution affected Seán deeply. He later recalled how O'Connor had two golden guineas on him, given to him by O'Higgins six months before at the wedding. Seán had suggested that he sew them into his trouser pockets in case they could be used to bribe warders in foreign prisons.[68] The shock of losing a friend was coupled with the idea that he could just have easily been shot along with him. Afterward,

> I carefully folded Rory's blankets neatly in a corner . . . I used to do this every day. I kept them there that way for some days. I also put away the set of chess which Rory had made during the time we were in jail. He had carved them out of pieces of wood with a penknife. And I put those away feeling that I must keep these as a kind of memento. We had developed a certain order in the cell. We had each folded up our blankets and put them

into corners, using them to lean against as a kind of an armchair during
the day. Several days passed by and by then I decided I might as well use
some of Rory's blankets. It was cold at night. I remember having a funny
kind of feeling that in a way I shouldn't use them, they are his blankets,
but then arguing with myself, well, he's gone after all, and I'm sure he
would like me to use them.[69]

In early 1923, both Maud and Iseult had been interned and Francis was also in
jail. It is easy to see why Seán's interest in prisoners' rights was so constant and
well developed, but he never mentions his family's experience in this context.
Seán's father, mother, and wife had been imprisoned, yet he wrote nothing
about Maud's imprisonment or conditions and only briefly mentions that his
wife had been in jail.

Seán's time in prison was eventful. He attempted to escape several times,
once by sawing his handcuffs off, another time by hiding in a bread truck.
When these attempts proved unsuccessful, he tried to build a tunnel out of
the prison, which was ultimately discovered. His chance finally came in
October 1923 when he jumped from a lorry during a transfer to Kilmainham.
The lorry driver lost his way and Seán slid away in his pyjamas and dashed
across the road. He and Michael Price managed to cross the canal to Maureen
Buckley's house in Glasnevin. En route they ran into two soldiers. One said,
'Knock me down, for goodness sake, knock me down quickly.' The soldier
threw himself to the ground and was later court-martialled for cowardice in
not capturing Seán.[70]

Maureen's parents took them in for three days, having ascertained that he
was Seán MacBride by making him speak French. He stayed in various safe
houses then hid in Galway and Mayo. Disguising himself was difficult because
of his accent, so he attempted to cultivate a British one to make his
masquerade more effective.

Some clergy refused to give absolution unless prisoners signed a paper
saying that they were sorry for having opposed the Free State Government.
Seán viewed this as a 'complete abuse of power . . . they had no business to use
their religious functions in order to try to force the acceptance of political
status.'[71] Such a position may have outraged Seán, but it should not have
surprised him. The Catholic Church had excommunicated Fenians and
members of the IRA and denounced Parnell from the pulpit after his affair
became public knowledge.

Seán had more cause to be outraged about the execution of men without
trial or charge. He expressed surprise that O'Higgins, who he believed was
'honestly and sincerely devoted to trying to establish some rule of law in the

country', had consented to these executions.[72] The IRA had been badly defeated and the executions left a tremendous amount of bitterness in the country.

While Seán was in prison, Maud bought Roebuck House, a large Georgian mansion with gardens and outhouses, with Charlotte Despard, in August 1922, after 73 St Stephen's Green had been maliciously raided by Free State forces. The two women started a home-made jam business in 1924 to aid republicans who had trouble finding jobs. Seán's daughter, Anna MacBride White, remembers Maud holding meetings every Sunday throughout the 1920s and 1930s at Roebuck for political prisoners.[73]

Two months after the lorry escape, William Cosgrave granted a Christmas Amnesty. Seán no longer had to worry about being apprehended. He remained an active officer on the headquarters staff of the IRA, and occupied some of his time in 1924–5 attempting to trace sums of money lodged in German banks before the Civil War. But his main activity was spearheading the last great IRA naval mission, the *St George*.[74]

Naval activities had been carried out intermittently by the IRA from 1921 to 1924, concerned mainly with arms smuggling. In November 1924, Chief-of-Staff Frank Aiken proposed a rescue attempt to transport prisoners from an internment camp in Larne. The plan involved prisoners digging a tunnel and marching to the shore, where a rescue boat would be waiting. Seán had 'always been interested in boats, sailing and indeed ships of all kinds', and kept a boat called the *Lady Di* on the Shannon in the early 1930s.[75] He immediately agreed and went about finding a boat and crew. His crew consisted of Tom Heavey, Tony Woods, and Frank Barry. Seán used the alias 'Lt. John Swift' and invented a back-story about being the nephew of a retired Royal Navy admiral — proof that he could fake a British accent.

He found a suitable boat in a Belfast shipyard, paid £200 for it, and gave it a British sounding name, the *St George*. The boat needed an overhaul, which was completed in Belfast. There was a curfew at the time; men had passes for going in and out of the dock area, but the harbour police never seemed to suspect them.[76]

The boat was ready before the tunnel had been completed so the crew had to remain in the dockyard, claiming that the boat needed further modifications. On or about 13 December 1924, Seán received word that the tunnel had been discovered. The plan might have been abandoned, but rumour was that some of the prisoners had managed to escape. Despite the possibility that the Royal Navy had been alerted, the *St George* left the dockyard the following day.

No prisoners had actually escaped. Seán planned to sail to Kingstown (now Dún Laoghaire) for fuel and instructions. A storm meant that they had to leave the boat on a sandbank. The crew eventually salvaged what they could for auction. There was no real suspicion of 'Lt. Swift' and his crew; 1924 was a winter of frequent storms and sea rescues were common. During their stay in Newcastle, the crew received the co-operation of the RUC and the Coastguard, and 'Lt. Swift' was entertained over New Year in an officers' mess in Ballykinlar army camp.[77]

Seán was disappointed at the loss of the boat, as GHQ saw its possibilities as a useful rescue boat for future military exercises. He was also frustrated as he considered himself a very able sailor. Authorities eventually figured out who the crew members were, but 'Lt. Swift' managed to escape detection. Neither Seán nor Michael MacEvilly mention if he managed to disguise his exotic accent, but his cover was so effective that in early 1925 he attended an enquiry into the wrecking of the boat and, in March or April of 1925, a case of salvage rights brought by a Newcastle man. 'Lt. Swift' won his suit.[78]

Seán became de Valera's secretary in 1925. He went with him to Rome to meet Archbishop Daniel Mannix of Melbourne, a Cork-born former philosophy professor at Maynooth. The Archbishop had been very supportive of the republican cause, but de Valera was not certain that Mannix would see him. He asked Seán to arrange an interview with the Archbishop, who was coming to Rome. Seán managed to get de Valera a false passport and they travelled to Florence where de Valera would await Mannix's answer.

Mannix replied that he would be delighted to meet with de Valera. His opinion was that it was necessary for him to accept the establishment of the Free State and seek election to government so that he could participate in the political development of the country. De Valera appeared to see the wisdom of Mannix's advice. Seán argued with him, believing that 'if it was once accepted that Ireland was part of the British Commonwealth, and that the Irish Free State was the lawful and legal government, it was reneging completely on the republican position.'[79]

It is likely that de Valera had already made up his mind and Mannix merely gave him the advice he wanted to hear. Fr John Hagan, Rector of the Irish College in Rome, also gave de Valera advice about forming a new party and the morality of entering a Dáil that de Valera had claimed was illegitimate. According to Dermot Keogh, Hagan 'exerted whatever influence he could from the ending of the civil war to try to persuade de Valera to give up his policy of abstentionism from the Dail.'[80] Hagan favoured the idea of a new political party, even if it meant a split. If John O'Leary's judgment that in Ireland one must have either the Church or the Fenians on his side was accurate, de Valera was ensuring that at least the Church was on board.

The Free State Government was consolidating its power. If de Valera didn't forge a path into government, he would find himself exiled into the political wilderness. Once he and his new party got into the Dáil, he could make changes. The first step was to discover a 'principled' way that would gain him the necessary support. Sinn Féin's March 1926 ard-fheis met to consider de Valera's plan to abandon abstentionism and allow members to take their seats in the Dáil. This divisive announcement was ultimately rejected. The following day, de Valera resigned and began to organise a new political party. Fianna Fáil officially came into being on 16 May 1926. Having fought two elections in 1927, Fianna Fáil TDs entered the Dáil on 12 August. De Valera denied that he or any member of his party had taken the oath: they had merely signed their names in the book.

Seán was approached by Frank Aiken, the Chief-of-Staff of the IRA, about playing a part in Fianna Fáil. Aiken suggested that Seán might gain a post as Adjutant General of the army. Seán did not warm to the offer, believing that he was not a military man: 'I had done this [soldiering] with a considerable amount of dislike partly because I considered it my duty to try and help the country at that time.'[81] He wrote in his memoir that he did not believe in wars as a method of solving problems, but would allow them 'only as a last result'.

Seán found himself having to choose sides once again. He thought that de Valera's willingness to join the Dáil was a sell-out and remained firmly on the anti-Treaty Sinn Féin side. The 'synopsis of political history of Sean MacBride s.c.' found in Seán MacEntee's papers, notes that after the general release of prisoners MacBride worked in the GHQ staff of the IRA and from 1926 to 1929 his 'position is somewhat obscure'.[82]

The vagueness of Seán's role during those years can be ascribed to his marriage in January 1926 to Catalina Bulfin. Catalina, though born in Argentina in 1900, was of solid Irish republican stock. Her parents, William Bulfin and Annie O'Rourke, had emigrated to Argentina. They met while working on the Dowling Estate in the Pampas. While there, William wrote *Rambles in Erin* and *Tales of the Pampas*, edited the Buenos Aires based *Southern Cross* newspaper and introduced hurling to Argentina. Catalina was the youngest of five, hence her nickname, 'Kid'. Even Seán called her Kid, although she was four years older than her husband.

The Bulfins returned to Ireland in 1902, living in William's childhood home in Birr, Co. Offaly. William divided his time between Ireland and Argentina until his permanent return in 1909. Catalina's only brother Eamonn attended Patrick Pearse's school, St Enda's, and fought with him at the GPO during the Easter Rising. Kid went to boarding school in Banagher then followed her elder siblings to Dublin.

Kid intended to do a short-hand typing course, but was quickly roped into working for the republican movement. She worked with Austin Stack in the Department of Home Affairs office until the Civil War and continued in his employ after the Treaty split. She carried dispatches for republicans. Like her husband, she was imprisoned after the Four Courts raid, first at Kilmainham then in North Dublin Union. She met Seán as a result of her republican activities.

Kid merits only a brief mention in *That Day's Struggle*, which said that she was involved in the cause and had been imprisoned. Seán never mentions what she was like or why he chose to marry that particular woman at that particular time. The wartime atmosphere of Dublin in the early 1920s may have contributed to the desire to marry as may have Seán's family background — he may have been anxious to start his own family to mitigate a past that embarrassed him.

It helped that his mother liked her; Kid's devotion to both Seán and the republican cause endeared her to Maud. She wrote to Ethel Mannin that 'Sean was the lucky boy when he got her to marry him.'[83] Like Maud, Kid was tall, thin, and striking, and had taken an active part in the movement. C.S. (Todd) Andrews remembered her as well read, 'a typical woman of the Twenties, elegant, smoking cigarettes through a very long holder, short skirted and not sparing décolletage.'[84]

The affection Maud felt for Kid was returned. By all accounts, Kid was a spirited woman and anyone able to manage a household that included the redoubtable Maud and the menagerie of animals, political prisoners, and republican exiles that came with her must have had patience as well as strength of character. When *The Irish Times* printed an unflattering article about Maud after her death in 1953, Kid immediately wrote a letter praising her mother-in-law, writing that 'All over the country there are people who bless her name . . . Nothing ever really stopped Madame once set on a course, as various Governments and people have found out from time to time. She was an outstanding personality while as yet in her teens, and remained so until the hour she drew her last breath. She was also a great, kindly, lovable human being.'[85]

Seán may have thought the same about his wife, but his memoir keeps her in the background and she remains somewhat of a mysterious figure who quickly disappears after the couple's marriage. In *Against the Tide*, Noël Browne mentions that early in his association with MacBride, Kid, dangerously ill, had been taken to Jervis Street Hospital in urgent need of a blood transfusion.[86] The story is nowhere in Seán's memoir.

The announcement of Seán's engagement came as a surprise to his contemporaries in the movement. Marrying at that age was unusual at that time, as most were not financially secure enough to contemplate such a step. A party at 21 Dawson Street, a flat famous as a young republican hangout, the evening before the wedding was a great success. Seán asked Tony Woods, who ran his father's garage, to pick him up in a car to take him to the church. Woods thought that this request was a joke and did not show up. Seán was forced to hitch a ride, arriving forty-five minutes late. Apparently Kid was 'completely unperturbed'.[87]

The marriage took place on 26 January 1926 on Seán's twenty-second birthday. According to Seán, the wedding was supposed to be 'a great hush, hush secret. But there were, nevertheless, about two or three hundred people at the church, at six o'clock in the morning.'[88] Seán was still on the run, hence the secrecy and the early hour of the ceremony. His best man was Tom Daly, an IRA man from Kerry.

The couple moved to Paris, renting a small flat in rue d'Annonciation in Passy where Seán had spent most of his childhood. He found work as a journalist with the Havas Agency and with the *Morning Post* in London, writing under the pseudonym Maguire. Whenever the couple had some money, they would dine out in Paris.

Shortly after arriving in Paris, he was informed that Ireland wanted him to be extradited. At one point, he caught the British Secret Service in his flat going through documents. The culprit was arrested by the French police and warned not to do it again. Seán laid a trap just in case and caught him in the act a second time.[89]

Seán may have being lying low in Paris, but IRA intrigues would soon catch up with him. Colonel Lacassi, a colonel in the French army, called on Seán to warn him that Ernie O'Malley was involved with Colonel Francesc Macià, founder of the Catalan nationalist party, Estat Català, and leader of a separatist group planning an invasion of Spain. A restless and slightly disoriented Ernie had been staying with the MacBrides since August, but would disappear frequently. Lacassi asked Seán to dissuade them from invading. Seán, with great difficulty, persuaded Macià to postpone the invasion. About three weeks later, plans were afoot once again. Lacassi again requested that Seán intervene. Seán went to see Macià again and he agreed to postpone again.

However, the third time Macià refused to put it off and Lacassi decided to arrest them in France, halting the rebels' commandeered train before it reached the border. He allowed Macià to stay in Paris and run a Catalan government in exile. Although the invasion was aborted, Macià gained popularity for his cause. Home Rule was eventually granted to Catalonia and

Macià later became President of the Catalan Republic.

Kid returned to Ireland in December 1926, followed by Seán. He claims in his memoir that the reason for their return was that, as many republican prisoners had been released, they had been assured by both Kid's uncle Frank Bulfin and Seán's uncle Joseph MacBride that it was safe to come back. The more compelling reason was that Kid was pregnant with the couple's first child, born on 24 November, and if it had been a boy born in France, he would have been required to serve in the French military.

Seán never mentions the birth of his first child, Anna, or her younger brother Tiernan anywhere in his memoir. Anna surmised that it might be because 'he didn't like children' and never really bonded with her or her brother. He was particularly perturbed at his daughter's intention to publish Maud's letters, which she did after his death, as well as his son's suggestion than he deposit his papers.[90] He seemed to be the type of father who expected unquestioned obedience from his children.

After her marriage, Kid supported her husband, but did not have any direct role in the IRA or other national movements. She gamely took over the running of Roebuck House, including the jam and shell factories. Seán convinced UCD to allow him to return to his law studies, while still remaining involved in republican activity. Anna remembers her father as being 'always ready to go'.[91]

His association with such activity would lead to his arrest in connection with one of the most notorious IRA murders of the twentieth century. On 10 July 1927, Cumann na nGaedheal Minister for Justice Kevin O'Higgins was assassinated by three gunmen on his way to Booterstown Catholic Church.

Seán heard about the murder while he was in Brussels getting fruit and equipment for the jam factory. He remembers being surprised at the action: 'I was not aware of any particular antagonism to Kevin O'Higgins on the republican side at that period.'[92]

Luckily for Seán, while on the boat trip to Belgium, he had run into a Cumann na nGaedheal MP for Sligo, Major Bryan Cooper, who would thus have known that Seán could not have had anything to do with the crime. Nonetheless, on 24 August, Seán was arrested in the middle of the night, taken to the Bridewell and charged with the murder. He was then put in a line-up and mistakenly identified as one of the gunmen.

Yeats, by now a Free State Senator, tried unsuccessfully to have him released. Major Cooper confirmed that Seán had been travelling at the time of the assassination, but, although the evidence the Government had was slim, the Public Safety Act allowed the Government to hold him indefinitely. He was unable to receive letters, but could see visitors; IRA Chief-of-Staff

Moss Twomey wrote to Kid during Seán's imprisonment asking her to write a coded message to see if he would be able to read correspondence.[93]

He spent most of his internment in Mountjoy, at this point probably more familiar to him than Roebuck House. He was held there until October when he was suddenly released in the middle of the night with no explanation.

Although many suspects were questioned, no one was brought to justice for the O'Higgins murder. Terence De Vere White's biography reveals that O'Higgins lived for five hours and was able to speak, but never named his assassins. However, in 1985, with the publication of Belfast republican Harry White's biography, their identities were revealed. White named Archie Doyle, Bill Gannon, and Timothy Couglan.[94] After the shooting, the assassins escaped capture by driving to Wexford and playing in a pre-arranged football match.[95] The O'Higgins murder was not officially sanctioned by the IRA; it was an impetuous act by a splinter group that thought that the IRA was not being active enough against the Cosgrave Government.[96]

In his memoir, most likely written in the early 1980s before White's biography was published, Seán maintained that he

> never found out who assassinated Kevin O'Higgins. I have heard the reports of different republicans alleging that they carried it out. But these reports are so numerous and conflicting, that in the end I began to disregard them all. There is a strange tendency — I don't know whether it is only confined to Ireland — that when something of that kind happens, somebody has to claim credit when they think they render themselves popular for doing it.[97]

He may have suspected who the true culprits were. Peadar O'Donnell revealed that the names of the assassins had been given to the IRA Army Council 'pretty promptly' after the attack.[98] White wrote that the identities of O'Higgins's killers were not common knowledge in IRA circles, and Seán's apparent lack of information might demonstrate that he was not completely trusted within the IRA. However, as is often the way in Irish politics, Seán later worked with both Gannon and White. Gannon was later involved in Saor Éire in the 1930s, so must have had contact with Seán. Seán also defended White on the charge of murder during the 1940s, and the inter-party Government was responsible for pardoning him in 1948.

If Seán did know who had carried out the assassination, he never publicly revealed it. When *The Irish Times* asked him to comment on White's revelations, he responded that the names came as a surprise: 'I think I know one of them — Archie Doyle who was in the fourth battalion, a wild person

... I had heard names mentioned, but not these names.'[99]

Seán was again subject to frequent arrests after returning from Paris, usually charged with unlawful assembly or belonging to an illegal organisation. Roebuck House was also repeatedly raided. Seán put it down to the Government's mangling of security issues and subsequent support for the IRA: 'the Free State Government realizes this national resurgence exists and is preparing new coercion and public safety bills and a new reign of terror has been launched to frighten and terrorize us.'[100]

In 1929, Maud and Seán joined Comhairle na Poblachta (the Republican Council), a loose group of republicans who ultimately could not agree on a firm programme, at least not one that could effectively compete with Fianna Fáil. Comhairle's members had too many conflicting views for it to last.

Despite the failure of Comhairle to ignite, Seán was slowly becoming more politicised. As a representative of the IRA, he attended an anti-imperialist conference organised by his childhood friend, Indian nationalist Chato Padaya. The Congress of the League Against Imperialism was held in Frankfurt in 1929, the first major public anti-colonisation meeting. While there, Seán met Pandit Nehru and Ho Chi Minh. Peadar O'Donnell also attended and the two had a discussion about the future of the IRA. The group was losing political significance; reduced in size, it was fighting a sporadic terrorist campaign with little success. The IRA of the early 1930s, as Seán Cronin points out, was a talented bunch, but with no real plan of campaign, 'a revolutionary army in search of a revolution'.[101] The lack of focus would become evident in the division regarding aims and methods.

The IRA realised that it would need a political arm to attract republicans tempted by Fianna Fáil. Seán felt that 'nationalism was very important and that we should keep nationalism to the forefront while at the same time working towards world socialism, without necessarily accepting socialism as it was being practised in the Soviet Union or elsewhere in the world.'[102]

The combination of republicanism and socialism is not as surprising as it may seem — though a fervent anti-communist while in government, Seán's feelings about the Soviet system had more to do with its atheism than its politics. In its early stages, Clann na Poblachta's programme had shades of socialism. The trick was not to appear too communist as that would alienate public and clerical support.

What is far more surprising is Seán's willingness to directly engage in politics at all. At an IRA Convention in 1934, he declared that 'I have very little faith in the mass of the constitutionalist republicans nor in the opinion of the mass of the people.'[103] Later during Clann na Poblachta's peak, he would insist that he disliked politics and the accompanying ballyhoo. Seán's lack of trust in 'the people' surely makes him an unlikely campaigner and candidate for political office. Perhaps such distrust shows the elitism in revolutionary movements: the sense that 'people' don't always know what's good for them — they have to be told. Seán most likely saw politics, like warfare, as a necessary evil. If Fianna Fáil refused to work with the IRA and discounted its aims, then the IRA must remain pledged to the complete independence of Ireland and establishment of a republic.

Saor Éire, Seán's first attempt to found a political party, began on this basis. Saor Éire's main men were Moss Twomey, Michael Fitzpatrick, Donal O'Donoghue, and Con Lehane — some of whom would later appear in Clann na Poblachta. The official launch took place on 26 September 1931 at Iona Hall, North Great George's Street, Dublin, and the party platform called for 'an independent revolutionary leadership for the working class and working farmers towards the overthrow . . . of British Imperialism and its ally Irish capitalism.' Its dangerously Marxist goals were to organise and consolidate the future Republic on the basis of possession and administration by the workers and working farmers of the land, instruments production, distribution and exchange, and to restore and foster the Irish language, culture, and games.[104] Some of these policies would later reappear in more polished form in the Clann na Poblachta platform and in the inter-party Government manifesto.

There was not supposed to be any formal relationship between Saor Éire and the IRA. Despite this severance, Saor Éire was declared illegal in the Free State. The Government warned bishops that it was dangerous and communist, reports that Seán called 'completely unreliable and grossly exaggerated.'[105] Like all decent republican groups, it was denounced by the Catholic Church, which feared that Saor Éire would 'mobilise the workers and the working farmers of Ireland behind a revolutionary movement to set up a Communistic State.'[106] Its members faced excommunication. For the Fenians and the Civil War Sinn Féin, such ecclesiastical criticism did not prohibit an increase in membership and status. Saor Éire, perhaps because of its communist taint or perhaps because Fianna Fáil was already feeding the republican demand, did not benefit from being denounced from the pulpit, and the party soon dissolved.

In March 1932, Fianna Fáil secured seventy seats at the general election and de Valera was able to form a government with the support of the Labour Party. This was a crucial event, first because it was a peaceful transfer of power where Cosgrave handed over office to men who, a mere decade earlier, had challenged the Free State's very existence, and second because it began sixteen years of Fianna Fáil domination.

When de Valera became head of the Irish Free State, many in the IRA hoped that he would break ties with England and renew the fight for a republic. However, de Valera had decided that Ireland could advance through peaceful means and his Government seemed to look no more kindly on IRA extremism than did Cosgrave's administration.

More realistic was the belief that the new Government would free political prisoners and end various emergency powers legislations and the harassment of republicans. The first act of the new Government was to release the prisoners in Arbour Hill. Seán drew up a list of prisoners who should be released, and Fianna Fáil complied, but if the IRA believed that de Valera would be more in line with their cause, they were in for a surprise.

As Roebuck Jam had been sold to Donnelly's in 1932 and membership in fledgling political parties did not provide a very stable income, Seán returned to journalism and became a sub-editor of the pro-Fianna Fáil *Irish Press* and *Evening Telegraph*. When the newsboys' union went on strike, Seán wanted the Union of Journalists to strike in sympathy. They opposed the idea. He joined the newsboys and left the *Irish Press*. Son-in-law Declan White maintains that the newsboy strike was the event that led to the falling out between Seán and de Valera, though the abortive negotiations between the IRA and the newly empowered Fianna Fáil surely threw fuel on the fire.[107]

Kid began to help run Irish Sweepstakes as the income from the Gonne trust was dwindling. The money had been reinvested in Irish government bonds, which was patriotic, but not fiscally beneficial. Maud had sold her house in Normandy, using the proceeds to enable Iseult and Francis to buy a house in Glendalough. As previously discussed, Stuart claimed that the Colleville house was a gift to Iseult from Millevoye whereas in fact Maud had purchased it using a legacy left by her aunt Augusta. Millevoye had left Iseult no inheritance after his death in 1918.

Meanwhile, the inhabitants of Roebuck were increasing. Seán and Kid's second child, Tiernan, was born on 19 March 1932. Iseult's two children, Ion, born in 1926, and Katherine, who arrived in 1931, would often visit.

Spurred on by the early success at getting republican prisoners released, in early 1933 Seán attempted to negotiate with de Valera over the role of the IRA in the new Government. The talks ended in stalemate. In a letter to Joseph McGarrity, the leader of Clan na Gael, dated 31 January 1934, de Valera explained his reasons: 'since 1921 the main purpose in everything I have done has been to secure a basis for national unity . . . But is this need and desire for unity to be used as a means of trying to blackmail us into adopting a policy which we know could only lead our people to disaster?'[108] At the final meeting, Seán suggested an informal connection between Fianna Fáil and the IRA, but de Valera wouldn't hear of it. To add insult to alienation, on 26 March

1935, the Government tried to arrest Seán, but he was not at home and managed to avoid incarceration.

Relations between Fianna Fáil and the IRA would deteriorate throughout the 1930s. In addition, Eoin O'Duffy, the dismissed Commissioner of the Garda Síochána and head of the right-wing organisation known as the Blueshirts, was increasingly hostile to the new Government. Fearing the prospects of a takeover, de Valera, with Minister for Justice Patrick Ruttledge and O'Duffy's successor Eamonn Broy, decided to create a new auxiliary police force. Its official name was S[pecial] Branch but it was more commonly known as the Broy Harriers, a pun on the well-known Bray Harriers hunt. The Government met the Blueshirt threat head on and neutralised it.

Having moved against the Blueshirts, the Government then decided to move against the IRA, which had increased its attacks on the state apparatus and on members of the police force. The IRA was suffering from internal tensions and public backlash against its activities. This allowed de Valera to ban the organisation in 1936. Common republican roots counted for little when Government felt under threat from fringe republicanism, and sentimental attachments were jettisoned with unseemly haste. De Valera demonstrated throughout his time in power that he was a constitutional leader to the core.

At the time of its suppression, the IRA was depleted, as some had joined the Broy Harriers or Fianna Fáil's Army Volunteer Reserve. Despite Tom Barry's forbidding Volunteers to volunteer, others had left to fight on the republican side in the Spanish Civil War. A number of IRA men were among the Irish fighters, later known as the Connolly Column, who fought for the Spanish Republic. Frank Ryan was perhaps the most prominent IRA participant.[109]

Still attempting to find a political outlet, Seán joined another party, the abstentionist Cumann Poblachta na hÉireann, officially launched on 7 March 1936. The party participated in the June elections, but none of its candidates was elected, not even Maud Gonne. The party held only one ard-fheis, in November 1936.

However, Seán claimed in 1980 that 'I was not involved in Cumann na Poblachta, the IRA political party set up in March 1936. I stayed out of it.'[110] This is not strictly true, though. Seán had helped to draft a detailed constitution of a 'Confederation of a Republic' that later metamorphosed into Cumann na Poblachta and he attended its inaugural meeting. He also ran his mother's unsuccessful campaign. In his study of the IRA, J. Bowyer Bell mentions that Seán's work with Cumann na Poblachta made him suspect in the eyes of the IRA's military activists.[111] He himself did not stand as a candidate, but he hardly stayed out of it.

A new opportunity to develop a political movement within the IRA would soon present itself, as Seán ascended to the position of Chief-of-Staff. Though it now seems that the IRA's track toward rogue militancy was inevitable, in 1936 it may have been possible to drive the movement towards a more constitutional solution.

Chapter 3 ∼

FROM CHIEF-OF-STAFF TO CHIEF COUNSEL: SEÁN MacBRIDE IN TRANSITION

'Would you tell me, please, which way I ought to go from here?'
'That depends a good deal on where you want to get to,' said the Cat.

— LEWIS CARROLL, *Alice's Adventures in Wonderland*

Moss Twomey's arrest on 1 May 1936 led to Seán's being named Chief-of-Staff of the IRA. Even if the position was only a temporary one, it was an impressive title and it gave him an opportunity to make a mark on the movement.

However, Seán did not hold the top job for very long. Two reasons contributed to his decline: divisions within the IRA, and personality characteristics that did not meld well with running a paramilitary organisation.

MacBride inherited the mantle at a difficult time. The IRA lacked direction and was divided about how to proceed. Some elements in the movement, notably Seán Russell, advocated physical action and wanted to build up an armed-force wing in the republican movement. Others, including MacBride, favoured a political solution.

He attempted to patch up these differences of opinion, but he felt that launching a war against Britain was unrealistic and irrational. He wanted the new abstentionist republican party, Cumann na Poblachta (League of the Republic), to provide a political outlet. For Russell and his supporters, the connection with England could be broken only by force and the IRA's task was to supply that force. Politics would only distract from obtaining and storing arms and training and preparation for combat.

One of his first acts as leader drew the battle lines. MacBride, precise and exacting, called Russell to task for failing to account properly for funds. He called a court-martial and proved his complaints about Russell, forcing him out of the centre of activity.

His victory would be short-lived. Russell has been described by J. Bowyer Bell as 'a simple and overwhelmingly honest man'.[1] Despite Russell's carelessness, everyone knew that he was not an embezzler, merely disorganised. Many of those in the movement who disliked MacBride rallied around Russell and began a quiet campaign in favour of his plan to attack Britain from Ireland.

MacBride may have been pushed out not because of his policies but because of his personality. More than his desire to find a political solution to the conflict, it was his 'differentness' which apparently grated, 'making him unpopular for a variety of often contradictory reasons.'[2] He had always been granted a certain deference due to his lineage and republican connections. Seán's contemporary, Todd Andrews, described his upbringing: 'he was brought up in situations where he only met the important people in the Independence movement. He behaved from boyhood as if he were one of them. He was accepted as such by everyone he met.'[3] Despite his 1916 name, the average Volunteer felt that Seán was a strange Irishman: he had a peculiar accent, too much education, and was very, very clever. As David Norris recalled, 'His early education in France left him with a pronounced French accent which he cultivated to the end of his long life and which caused some derision among his opponents, who suspected that a less vain man might have acquired an accent more in keeping with his passionate identification with Mother Ireland.'[4]

Some felt he was too rigid, IRA member Bob Bradshaw remarking that 'MacBride was a very punctilious person in the respect of timing and efficiency but I respected him.'[5] Others were put off by his cleverness. He revelled in starting arguments and winning them; he was seen as too much of an intellectual to be truly trusted within the movement. Andrews also mentions Seán's obvious interest in the pursuit of power, a trait that may not have endeared him to his comrades.[6]

According to Andrews, Seán 'was treated by everyone with a diffidence dissociated from his personal qualities, the principal one of which was charm.'[7] Yet such charm was not sufficient: MacBride was clearly not a wily enough politician to hold on to power and quell division within the IRA. Seán Russell knew that reasoned argument needed to be augmented: he realised the necessity of and had the talent for getting votes and pitching to an audience — a talent that allowed him to outmanoeuvre MacBride.

MacBride agreed to step down in November 1936. He had become Chief-of-Staff by accident following Twomey's arrest, and the Army Council had approved him in June 1936 only in a 'caretaker capacity'.[8] Still, it must have stung to be removed from power. The new chief, Tom Barry, appointed him Intelligence Officer and, in an effort to placate both sides, called for action against the British not in England but in the North.

MacBride left the IRA shortly afterwards. He insisted that the 1937 Constitution paved the way for effective legitimate government. However, the new constitution is probably not the only motivation for his departure.

In 1937, de Valera had introduced a new constitution to divest Ireland of the elements he found abhorrent in the Treaty. The 1922 Constitution was seen as a product of the bargain with Britain, a typical liberal-democratic document suiting a country with any religious complexion. The 1937 Constitution was much more marked by Catholic thought. Fianna Fáil tried to build up the image of being a more Catholic party than Cumann na nGaedheal, the party that had passed the 1922 Constitution based on the Treaty's conditions.

Bunreacht na hÉireann asserted in Article 1 that Ireland 'hereby affirms its inalienable, indefeasible, and sovereign right to choose its own form of Government, to determine its relations with other nations, and to develop its life, political, economic and cultural, in accordance with its own genius and traditions.' More controversially, Article 2 stated that 'the national territory consists of the whole island of Ireland, its islands and the territorial seas. It is the entitlement and birthright of every person born in the island of Ireland, which includes its islands and seas, to be part of the Irish nation.' This was the first time the claim to the Six Counties had been given legal form and permanence.[9] However, Article 3 allowed temporary recognition of partition by stating that the document applied only to the twenty-six counties until Ireland was once again united.

Articles 2 and 3 claimed political and territorial control over the entire island while Article 44 claimed religious control or at least partiality: 'The State recognises the special position of the Holy Catholic Apostolic and Roman Church as the guardian of the Faith professed by the great majority of the citizens.' The Catholic Church was singled out and Protestants and other religious denominations were grouped afterwards. It can be argued that de Valera added this proviso out of political necessity as well as deference to the Church. De Valera operated within somewhat narrow electoral limitations and 'his proposals had to be acceptable to the largest and potentially most influential pressure group in the country, the Catholic Church.'[10] Yet he did not make the Catholic Church the official or established Church, giving it 'symbolic primacy but no additional authority'.[11]

Despite de Valera's clever political manoeuvring, the clause indicated to unionists further proof of 'Rome Rule'. In addition, Article 41, which prohibited divorce and encouraged women to remain in the home while raising their families, demonstrated a pervasive Catholic influence that could be used to justify unionist claims that the Free State was a papal state. Article 41, though a social rather than political constraint, demonstrated the close church–state relationship and provided fuel to unionist fire that, if Ireland were united, unionists would be forced to live under Catholic ideology.

De Valera's Constitution made the Irish state appear wholly committed to the maintenance of Catholic values, especially because it led to the repeal of rights enjoyed under previous British law. Unionists could not help but view these Articles as a tyranny of a religious majority that would oblige Protestants to accept constraints that their own religion did not require. Fianna Fáil was returned to office in the 1937 general election with a minority but the Constitution referendum, held on the same day, passed with a majority vote, 685,000 to 527,000.

De Valera had previously removed from the Constitution the Oath of Allegiance to the British monarch. He had also omitted the British monarch from the previous Constitution after the abdication in 1936 of King Edward VIII, making the king's successor the nominal head of External Relations. Britain accepted this External Relations Act as a sufficient link to retain Commonwealth membership.

For Seán, the new Constitution meant an end to most of the elements he had found objectionable in the 1921 Treaty. The oath of allegiance was long gone and, although partition was still around, the 1937 Constitution seemed certain of its eventual end.

Seán may have felt that the new Constitution altered the situation and he could now support the Government: 'It was a rational decision. Yes, if you like . . . I changed my mind. Once de Valera removed the Oath it was possible to pursue Ireland's aspirations by constitutional means.'[12] Similar to Michael Collins's idea of the stepping stone, the Constitution was not perfect, but it could lead to perfection. Apparently he 'decided that I would terminate my connection with the IRA as from then.'[13] Both his daughter Anna and his personal assistant Caitriona Lawlor confirm that Seán decided to leave the IRA on the adopting of the 1937 Constitution.[14]

His explanation may very well be true, but the power struggles within a marginalised organisation cannot be discounted — nor can any ill-feeling over his dismissal from the leadership and the rise of Seán Russell, who became Chief-of-Staff in 1938 and set about preparations for a bombing campaign against Britain. MacBride opposed the indiscriminate and terrorist bombings. The campaign aroused no sympathy for the movement or its goals and probably confirmed in MacBride's mind that he had made the right decision to leave.

Bob Bradshaw claims that Seán retired a year after being appointed Chief-of-Staff because he 'may have come to see the movement as a spent force.'[15] Not only was the organisation losing ground but his place in it had diminished. He realised that his influence had waned in the IRA and perhaps searched for another way to gain position.

It has been rumoured that MacBride advised the IRA long after his formal connections had been severed. During the 1948 general election campaign, Seán MacEntee referred to MacBride's IRA past, questioning his claim that he had left in 1937. MacEntee offered proof that he had not been truthful about this, citing a letter dated 1 October 1942 where the IRA wrote that 'Sean MacBride will be only too pleased to do it for us.' MacEntee allowed that the quote might not demonstrate direct links, but said that it showed 'confidence in his willingness to co-operate with them in carrying out their plans.' MacEntee also mentioned MacBride's legal career where he defended the IRA and questioned who paid him.[16]

MacEntee was correct in that last regard. MacBride did not completely break the connection, as he defended IRA prisoners free of charge, becoming the leading legal defender of the IRA. He had long been unimpressed with the way the Irish Government, both the Cumann na nGaedheal and Fianna Fáil administrations, handled the treatment of prisoners, and felt that much of their legislation was reactionary and unconstitutional. Relieved of his IRA responsibilities, Seán persuaded UCD to let him continue his legal studies. He was called to the Bar in 1937. Ironically, de Valera's son Vivion was also working toward the Bar at the same time. Seán would later act as a defence lawyer for those arrested by his father's Government.

The year 1939 was a significant one for Seán. Having suffered from a variety of illnesses for a number of years, William Butler Yeats died in Cap Martin, France, on 28 January 1939, aged seventy-three. Yeats had been a surrogate father to Iseult and Seán, though he merits only a brief reference in Seán's memoir. Although Yeats and his mother were not as close in later years, his death affected Maud deeply. Seán does not mention that one of his first acts as Minister for External Affairs was to arrange for the re-interment of Yeats's remains in Drumcliffe Churchyard in Sligo, in accordance with the poet's wishes. Yeats's coffin was removed from Roquebrune on 6 September

1948, driven with a military guard of honour, and placed on the Irish navy corvette *Macha*. The boat was met in Galway by Yeats's wife George, their children Anne and Michael, and his brother Jack. Maud did not attend the ceremony due to arthritis, but Seán was closely involved. In gratitude, George gave him three of Yeats's manuscript books as a memento.

The year 1939 also saw the start of the Second World War. De Valera immediately reiterated Ireland's neutrality in the conflict. One of the reasons for this position was partition; de Valera believed that civil strife would occur if Ireland allied with Britain. Declaring neutrality was also an opportunity for Ireland to demonstrate her independence: 'the right to pursue a policy of neutrality in wartime has generally come to be considered in the twentieth century as the ultimate yardstick of national sovereignty.'[17] The Emergency, as it became known in Ireland, provided the first opportunity to assert independence and strike a small blow for the freedom of small nations to opt out of big power conflicts.

Despite the declaration of neutrality and de Valera's offer of formal condolences upon Hitler's death and his refusal to close Axis legations or hand over Axis personnel or property, Irish neutrality was hardly strict, rather, as Attlee wrote, it was a 'benevolent neutrality' that favoured the Allies. Ireland was also heavily dependent on Britain economically and this relationship continued during the war. Ireland cooperated with Britain by supplying volunteers[18] and agreeing to support Britain in the event of a German invasion.[19] However, it made sense to take an official neutral stance; Ireland was militarily weak and in no real danger as long as Britain held out.[20] The policy enjoyed popularity; Ireland united behind it, and sustaining the policy in spite of pressure from the old enemy provided a sense of satisfaction. As Mansergh writes in *Problems of War-time Cooperation and Postwar Change*, neutrality was 'the final vindication of independence'.[21]

Martin S. Quigley, who was sent by America's Office of Strategic Services to find out how sincere Irish neutrality really was, concluded that German activities outside Dublin were unfounded. Most of the stories making the rounds were ludicrous.[22] The Irish Government gave secret help to Allies, but none to Germany and, although there were a number of pro-Germans, there were probably never more than a thousand and this group dwindled as the character of Nazism became more clear.[23]

Despite the power of de Valera's stance, it is doubtful that Ireland could have remained neutral if Northern Ireland were not in the hands of the British. Northern Ireland's connection to the United Kingdom actually made it possible for the Irish to implement a neutrality policy. Even more than the strategic benefit the North provided, Britain now felt she owed something to

Northern Ireland for participating in the war. As Churchill said in 1943, 'the bonds of affection between Great Britain and the people of Northern Ireland have been tempered by fire and are now, I firmly believe, unbreakable.' In a later victory speech in 1945, he also stated that 'a strong loyal Ulster will always be vital to the security and well-being of our whole empire and common-wealth.' Neutrality, though it provided Ireland with its first independent foreign policy opportunity, made Ireland a 'moral debtor' while strengthening the relationship between Northern Ireland and Great Britain.

Ireland may have possessed a benevolent neutrality, but some in the IRA saw the conflict as an opportunity. The movement's attitude toward fascism, particularly towards Hitler's Germany, is difficult to gauge. Not surprisingly, no individual or movement will readily acknowledge support of a genocidal regime and such connections or sympathies to the Nazi regime would be denied or played down in later years. However, the brief Blueshirt upsurge (although most modern historians do not generally perceive it as a serious fascist movement, though de Valera feared it might become so) coupled with the 'England's difficulty is Ireland's opportunity' mindset makes it no surprise that the IRA might look for German aid.

Was there a 'coven of German activity' in Ireland during the Second World War? The IRA did send a delegation to Berlin in 1940 to enquire about German aid for Ireland. Seán Russell was a delegate. The Germans wanted the IRA to attack Northern Ireland to help weaken Britain. Negotiations proved difficult and were apparently fruitless. On the way back to Ireland via German submarine, Russell suffered from perforated ulcers and, as there was no doctor on board, died on 14 August. He was buried at sea with full naval honours, wrapped in a German flag. MacBride was later asked in the Dáil about Russell's fate; in reply to Michael Fitzpatrick he said, 'it appears reasonably certain that the late Seán Russell died as a result of illness while a passenger on a German submarine in 1940.'[24]

There have been suggestions that Germany planned to use Ireland as a jumping-off ground for an invasion of Britain. If this plan were seriously considered, would the Nazis actually have needed IRA help to achieve it? Invading and occupying neutral countries to improve their strategic positions had not previously been difficult for Nazi Germany. As Joe Lee points out, however indifferent or sympathetic Irish observers might have been to Nazism, they were sure to notice the fate of other small neutral states before considering cooperation with Berlin.[25] In his tome on the IRA, Tim Pat Coogan calls allegations of an IRA-Nazi tie-up groundless, throughout the war.[26]

The idea of help from Germany was another divisive issue within the IRA. Both Russell's trip to Germany and the fact that parachute-jumping spy Hermann Goertz had been given the name of an IRA connection in Ireland demonstrate that some contact had been made. However, not everyone in the movement favoured help from Germany. For some, Fascism might prove just as oppressive as Britain, and 'whether Churchill would be supplanted by Mosley', Ireland would still have to fight for freedom and 'no section of our people should attempt to induce either the British or the Germans to invade Southern Ireland.'[27]

The Dominions Office wrote to Maffey in 1940 that there was 'little doubt that German funds do reach the I.R.A. and quite possibly via the United States, though there is no definite evidence to that effect.'[28] The FBI reported in September 1943 that Clan na Gael leader Joe McGarrity had gone to Germany before war broke out but that he had decided that there was no merit in forcing Britain out only to bring Germany in. This appeared to be the sentiment of most of the IRA. It is possible that the Germans used the IRA for propaganda purposes rather than to foment an actual attack on Northern Ireland or Britain.

It has been suggested that Seán had made contact with Nazi Germany in the hopes of obtaining help for the cause. Eunan O'Halpin believes that he courted German aid, writing in his *Defending Ireland* that 'ironically in view of his eventual metamorphosis into a patron saint of Irish radicalism and of the international struggle for human rights, he then reportedly made the "first contact" with the agents of Hitler's Germany.'[29] O'Halpin does not mention when this contact took place, but Seán's claim that 1937 was the year of his departure from the IRA absolved him from having to defend his position about the war.

Seán's own connections to Germany were numerous. He had been on many previous gunrunning missions to the country. According to Francis Stuart, both Iseult and Maud were pro-German during the war.[30] Such support might not have been considered completely appalling; Ireland was neutral, the newspapers were censored and the news of concentration camps did not reach Ireland until the end of the war. Seán had been introduced to the German Minister to Ireland, Edouard Hempel, by Helmut Clissman, the head of the German Academic Exchange Service. Clissman had helped Germany to make contact with the IRA and was suspected of espionage. Hempel and his wife Eva regularly visited Roebuck. Seán gave him advice, warning him not to be on the wrong side of the law at any time.[31] Prior to Hempel's ministerial appointment, the Department of External Affairs had specified that it did not want a Nazi party member as ambassador. At the time he took up the appointment, he was not a member of the party, but he joined the following year.

Even more interesting than his connection to Hempel was Seán's connection to a Germany spy who came to Ireland in 1940. A German Intelligence Officer, Captain Hermann Goertz, landed in Meath on 5 May 1940 and marched seventy miles to Laragh, Co. Wicklow, to Iseult Stuart's home.

Goertz's version of events was published as a series of articles in *The Irish Times*. According to Goertz, he wanted to make contact with the IRA to communicate that Germany was 'interested in a unified independent Irish State.'[32] He claimed that his position was independent, that of a free agent. His orders were not to cause any friction between Germany and the neutral Government of the Republic. Goertz knew of Iseult through Francis, who according to Goertz 'had no contact with or knowledge of, the I.R.A.' Although technically not true, Goertz seems to have believed that Stuart had no IRA connection.

Germany was considering an invasion of the Six Counties. In order to help foment the invasion, Goertz had planned his parachute jump to end in Tyrone. Instead, he landed in Meath and proceeded to try to find Iseult in Wicklow. He was 'not expected' but 'treated with the greatest hospitality'.[33] Iseult bought clothes for him in Dublin, as he had nothing to wear. Goertz stayed for about three days then contacted the IRA. A 'gentleman' arrived and took him away to Dublin where he went to see Stephen Carroll Held. Goertz never mentioned Iseult by name in the interview. In November 1941 he was arrested by the Irish police.

According to Anna MacBride White's narrative in the published collection of Iseult's letters, a visitor was expected and Seán disapproved unequivocally.[34] Iseult was arrested on suspicion of assisting a foreign agent. The situation was awkward, as Hempel often went to Iseult and Francis's home in Laragh for weekend visits. Iseult was questioned, charged, tried, and given three months in jail. She refused to give away Goertz's name and claimed that she did not help him out of loyalty to Germany or the IRA, but because Francis asked her to. She was acquitted on 2 July 1940. Goertz was mentally unbalanced towards the end of his life and poisoned himself in May 1947 as he was about to be deported to Germany.

Both the Goertz incident and Seán's own position during the Second World War are nowhere in his memoir. His apparent silence regarding his sympathies caused him problems. During the 1948 general election campaign, Seán MacEntee would repeatedly attack MacBride about his alleged pro-German sentiment, commenting on the 'frigid restraint which has characterised all his utterances in this controversy' as well as MacBride's apparent disappearance when Ireland needed defending during the Emergency.[35] The IRA raid on the Magazine Fort on 23 December 1939 deprived the Irish Army of munitions and MacEntee wondered why MacBride had not stopped the raid, claiming that MacBride's silence indicated approval of IRA activities during the war.[36] In a speech at Swords, MacEntee charged that he 'has kept his attitude in regard to neutrality as a closely guarded secret . . . perhaps he is merely "pro-MacBride".'[37]

MacBride called MacEntee's hint of German sympathies 'a lie . . . I had no sympathy with authoritarian dictatorships of any kind, whether German or Russian. I was not associated throughout the course of the war with a political movement of any kind.'[38] He threatened MacEntee (through his solicitors) with legal action for spreading 'false and misleading statements and innuendoes'.[39] MacEntee did continue to malign MacBride; and as for the threat to sue, MacEntee protested in the *Irish Press* of 25 October 1947 that a suit wouldn't come to trial until after the elections and questioned whether MacBride could prove that any of the allegations were false. This may have been merely the typical mudslinging of a political campaign and no lawsuit was ever filed.

MacBride apparently supported the Government's policy of neutrality. He wrote a letter to the newspapers urging the avoidance of violence and other acts that might jeopardise neutrality, but he maintained that it was suppressed by the Government.[40] A year before the war's end, Seán wrote to de Valera offering help, 'if in the course of the present crisis, my services can be of any value to the Government, I shall be at your disposal. If I may be permitted, I should like also to express confidence in the manner in which you have handled the situation.'[41] Such an obsequious note appears odd, as for most of the Emergency he had been criticising de Valera's Government on its treatment of prisoners. Though outwardly cordial, MacBride and de Valera's relationship had deteriorated since MacBride's tenure as his secretary. MacBride had not approved of the founding of Fianna Fáil and its Government's subsequent treatment of prisoners, and de Valera would never forgive MacBride for accusing him of betraying the Republic.

Seán's main activities during this period seemed to be constitutional politics and legal cases rather than active espionage. He was still attempting to make his mark politically. The successor to the short-lived Cumann na Poblachta was Córas na Poblachta (Company of the Republic), founded at the Mansion House, Dublin. Córas na Poblachta was launched within weeks of the execution in England of the alleged Coventry bombers, Peter Barnes and James McCormack, in February 1940, just as Clann na Poblachta had had its genesis soon after the death of Seán McCaughey in 1946. Córas's nucleus consisted of old IRA men angered by de Valera's policies.

Not satisfied with the Constitution's territorial claim, Córas sought the formal declaration of a republic. Though its members must have realised that such a declaration would run only in the twenty-six counties, they would claim that its authority pertained to the North. As Coogan points out, 'Nobody bothered too much about how this writ would be enforced, either on a wartime England or a wartime North of Ireland. In fact this declaration of a Republic was made eight years later by the coalition which ousted Fianna Fáil.'[42]

Five candidates ran in the 1943 general election and all lost their deposits. Most of its members would later become involved in Clann na Poblachta but in 1940 its leaders were not capable of making an impact nor were the times right for a change. Nor did it have much popular support; 'people tended to discuss the party rather than join it.'[43]

With the latest republican party failing to ignite, Seán focused on his legal career. While he had opposed the IRA's British bombing campaign and he knew that people did not agree with IRA methods, he said, 'they have a good deal of sympathy with the ideals for which the IRA has stood. You cannot treat young men who are actuated by idealistic motives of patriotism on the basis that they are criminals without evoking sympathy, and continuing forever a state of latent civil war.'[44]

He first came to prominence as a lawyer on the *habeas corpus* case of Seamus Burke in December 1939 where he successfully challenged the constitutional validity of internment without trial under the Offences Against the State Act. Justice George Gavan Duffy ordered Burke released. On 1 December, fifty-three men were released as were other IRA men as they completed their sentences. The case led to the Second Amendment to the Constitution in 1941, which included restrictions on the right to *habeas corpus* as well as an extension of the right of the Government to declare a state of emergency.

Certain members of the IRA, keen to capitalise on Britain's difficulty, stepped up their bombing campaign in Britain. In order to contain the IRA and keep Britain content with Irish neutrality, Fianna Fáil set up military tribunals and arrested known IRA members. The IRA was not the Government's only problem, but it had the potential to do great damage and 'the time for tolerance had long passed.'[45]

Patrick McGrath was arrested on 9 September 1939. He began a hunger strike, demanding unconditional release. McGrath's strike put the Government in an awkward position. Allowing him to die would engender the wrath of a people all too familiar with heroes sacrificing themselves for their beliefs, and it would confer martyrdom upon McGrath. Releasing him too quickly would be a sign of weakness and the first step toward the collapse of public security. Public outcry forced the Government's hand. On 9 December, McGrath was in the twenty-third day of his strike and was told that he would be released and moved to a hospital. With the IRA threat declining, the Government could afford to be magnanimous.[46] McGrath actually escaped from custody and would figure again in Seán's legal career.

Internment and hunger strikes continued through the Emergency. Minister for Justice Gerald Boland was determined not to show weakness. Boland wanted a no-nonsense, firm approach, with no political status for prisoners. This position led to several going on hunger strike. Count Plunkett's son Jack Plunkett, Thomas MacCurtain, Jack McNeela, and Tony D'Arcy went on strike on 25 February 1940, demanding the right to walk around the prison freely without being confined to cells at four o'clock each afternoon. They also wanted two prisoners on penal servitude to be transferred into military custody. Boland warned that the Government would remain firm: 'my duty is to see that the law is obeyed and that those who defy the law are suitably dealt with.'[47]

On 16 April, D'Arcy died and McNeela followed three days later. Boland insisted on appearing as a witness for the state at McNeela's inquest. Seán appeared for the family. He had the opportunity to cross-examine Boland, asking him, 'Do you realise that the whole country was against the Government for letting these men die?'[48]

On 16 August 1940, Detectives Patrick McKeown and Richard Hyland were murdered in Dublin. Thomas Green (alias Thomas Harte) and Patrick McGrath were arrested for the crime and were tried before a military court. The prisoners refused to plead and offered no defence. They were found guilty and sentenced to death by shooting. Seán made a last-minute attempt to save their lives by obtaining an order of *habeas corpus* to bring them before the High Court, as he argued that the military court that had tried them was unconstitutional. The case went to the Supreme Court. After a three-day hearing, the appeal was rejected. McGrath, whom Seán had saved once before, was executed in August, and Harte followed a month later.

Six teenage IRA men were found guilty of murdering Patrick Murphy, an RUC man, in Belfast. All were given death sentences. Seán organised a reprieve committee in Dublin. Acting as secretary, he collected 200,000 signatures and held meetings to prevent the upcoming execution of the six men, all of whom were under nineteen years old. Five of the six were ultimately reprieved; only Thomas Williams (aged nineteen) was hanged, on 2 September 1942.[49]

By 1943, Seán had become a Senior Counsel of the Irish Bar. He had accomplished this in only seven years, the shortest period in Irish legal history.

He became known for his scaring cross-examinations. The Bernard Casey inquest provides a notable example. Casey, an unconvicted internee, had died at the Curragh; the inquest report revealed that he had died of shock and haemorrhage from a gunshot wound that had entered through his back. At the inquest, Seán repeatedly asked, 'Why was Casey shot in the back?'

The Seán McCaughey inquest would become a turning point in both Irish politics and MacBride's career. McCaughey was a Tyrone man who had been charged in connection with the kidnapping and holding of Stephen Hayes, acting Chief-of-Staff of the IRA, on suspicion of being a spy. After a savage beating and torture, conducted by McCaughey and others, Hayes had 'confessed'. Before he could be shot, he had escaped and reported his ordeal to the Garda Síochána, who had arrested McCaughey. McCaughey's crime was normally punishable by fine or imprisonment for up to two years. However, in September 1941, he was sentenced to death. The sentence was commuted to penal servitude for life. While in Portlaoise prison, McCaughey refused to wear a prison uniform, donning the blanket instead. As a result, he was not allowed outside, was not able to have visitors for four and a half years, was held in solitary confinement until the end of 1944, and was not permitted to use the lavatory. He died on 11 May 1946, after twenty-two days on hunger strike.

De Valera's secretary, Maurice Moynihan, informed MacBride of McCaughey's death. He asked MacBride to let McCaughey's friends and family know. McCaughey's family asked MacBride to appear at the inquest, which was held in Portlaoise.

The deputy coroner refused to allow Seán MacBride, counsel for the next of kin, to cross-examine the Governor but during his cross-examination of the prison doctor, T.J. Duane, he described the conditions McCaughey had lived under at Portlaoise. He then asked the doctor if he had a dog. When Dr Duane responded in the affirmative, Seán followed up the question with, 'Would you allow your dog to be treated in this fashion?' After a pause, the doctor responded that he would not allow his dog to be treated in this way.[50] The prison argued that McCaughey's condition was mainly his own doing, but Seán maintained that 'my remarks were intended to show the inhuman treatment that led this boy to go on hunger-strike.'[51]

The jury's verdict was 'that the conditions existing in the prison were not all that could be desired according to the evidence provided' but there was no reflection on the Governor, Medical Officer, or staff.

The verdict was mild, but was critical enough of the Government's treatment of prisoners to please Seán. The inquest had exposed the conditions McCaughey had endured before his death and the report received considerable publicity. Conditions at Portlaoise became public only during the inquest on McCaughey and subsequent questions in the Dáil; 'there was no appreciation that there were so many political prisoners, and that they were being so badly treated.'[52]

Informal discussions between republicans grew into meetings about beginning a new political party. Kid would bake scones for visitors to Roebuck on Sunday afternoons. Anna remembers that McCaughey's inquest was the genesis of Clann na Poblachta.[53]

Perhaps Seán came to believe that more could be accomplished by constitutional methods than through violence. He had tried to start political parties before. He states in his memoir that 'I find it very hard to place the exact point in time at which I seriously began to think about the formation of a party *that would have as its purpose the bringing about of a change in government.*'[54] Perhaps the move was selfishly pragmatic; he had no future in the IRA and the movement was diminishing in influence and public support. Seán's trajectory repeats a pattern in Irish politics, echoing de Valera's move from militant to constitutional nationalism twenty years earlier.

Whatever Seán's motivation, his new party had to be more than a republican party offering mere platitudes about the necessity for complete independence. The opportunity to take the Government to task had finally arrived.

Chapter 4 ~

FIGHTING YOUR BATTLES: SEÁN MacBRIDE AND CLANN NA POBLACHTA

'Remember I never liked politics. I just hated politics from beginning to end. I hate the ballyhoo of politics.'

— SEÁN MacBRIDE

The political climate of the 1940s provided a promising atmosphere for the founding of a new party. Since coming to power in 1932, Fianna Fáil had gradually moved to the centre, losing much of its original radicalism, leading to disenchantment among some former supporters. While in power, Fianna Fáil adjusted its interpretation and application of republican ideology as well as its social welfare policies.[1] Taoiseach Éamon de Valera's, and consequently Fianna Fáil's vision of the Irish state, was summarised in his St Patrick's Day speech in 1943. He famously described the ideal Ireland as:

the home of a people who valued material wealth only as the basis for right living, of a people who were satisfied with frugal comfort and devoted their leisure to the things of the spirit — a land whose countryside would be bright with cosy homesteads, whose fields and villages would be joyous with sounds of industry, with the romping of sturdy children, the contests of athletic youths and the laughter of comely maidens, whose firesides would be forums for the wisdom of serene old age.[2]

Yet the Ireland that de Valera governed did not correspond with this vision. At a time when, in Noël Browne's words, 'they [the Fianna Fáil Government] had offered nothing but unemployment, much human distress, and mass emigration',[3] de Valera at best seemed to be rolling backward; at worst he appeared to have completely lost touch with reality.

However, in the general election that followed that speech, de Valera was returned to office and was again victorious in yet another election the following year largely because there did not seem to be any other promising alternative. As a result of the long period of Fianna Fáil dominance and a lack of able party organisation and dynamic leadership, Fine Gael (the former Cumann na nGaedheal) seemed poised for a slow descent into obscurity. In several important by-elections in 1945, the party could not find candidates. The Irish Labour Party, never a real threat to the two major parties when united, split in the 1940s. Even without the division, Labour proved too afraid of being labelled socialist or communist to develop a strong left-wing programme that could benefit from Fianna Fáil's lack of direction in the realm of social welfare policy. Clann na Talmhan, a farmer's party founded in 1938, seemed too small and specialised to pose a threat to Fianna Fáil. Thus, Fianna Fáil seemed invulnerable.

In addition to the apparent stagnancy in the party system, Ireland's neutrality policy during the Second World War also affected the political climate. F.S.L. Lyons famously compared post-war Ireland to the inhabitants of Plato's Cave, who, after spending a long time seeing only shadows of the world beyond, are suddenly thrust into sunlight.[4] As *The Irish Times* editorialised in July of 1948, Ireland resembled 'a sleeping beauty who has slept through a long winter and is now stirring her limbs to life.'[5] Neutrality possessed a positive side; the policy commanded overwhelming popular support; it saved the country from war, emphasised the consciousness of sovereignty, gave the Irish a sense of confidence and common dedication to a national purpose — which went far in mollifying Civil War divisions — and it marked the beginning of an independent foreign policy.[6] However, the debit side proved to be harsh; neutrality weakened an already inactive economy while engineering a sense of apathy in politics and society. Most of all, it marked Ireland's isolation and insularity from a quickly changing world. Post-war modernisation came later to Ireland than other Western European nations partly because Ireland did not directly suffer from the war and was not in need of rapid rebuilding.

Food and fuel rationing continued after the war and a sluggish economy, poor housing conditions, poverty and illnesses associated with it like tuberculosis, a depressed agricultural sector, high prices, low incomes, an increasing rate of emigration, growing industrial unrest, and a series of strikes and proposed strikes undermined confidence in the Government and began to drain support from Fianna Fáil. The Government's hard-line response to a teachers' strike in 1946 left a legacy of bitterness. Teachers were an enormous base of Fianna Fáil support, their participation in the party positive proof of Fianna Fáil's commitment to the Irish language and culture. Their defection proved to be quite beneficial for Clann na Poblachta, as teachers would become the organisational foundation of the new party.

As well as harnessing teacher support, the harsh treatment of political prisoners under the Fianna Fáil Government, notably Seán McCaughey, served as a catalyst for the creation of a new alternative to Fianna Fáil. According to Seán's memoir, the party developed as a result of chats with Con Lehane, Noel Hartnett, and Peadar Cowan, in the Law Library.[7] Most of the party's Provisional Executive, like Seán, were lawyers.

Clann na Poblachta officially came into existence on 6 July 1946 in Barry's Hotel in Dublin; the first mention of the Clann in the press appeared on the front page of *The Irish Times* on 8 July 1946. By the end of August an office in Bachelor's Walk was secured and branches were being set up all over the country. The party's first ard-fheis was held in the Balalaika Ballroom in November 1947.

Seán was to lead the new party. Apparently Cowan and Hartnett encouraged him, saying that they would help; 'Finally, after resisting for some time, I eventually agreed.'[8] Seán's account may be true; his first two attempts at cultivating a party had been unsuccessful and he might have been reluctant to try again. Despite his claim that he detested the 'the ballyhoo of politics', he had been supporting republican political movements within the IRA while he was a member. Perhaps he craved the recognition that being the leader of a successful party would bring. He may have been conditioned by his mother's belief that he was destined for greatness and encouraged by reminders of his father's contribution to Irish republicanism. Perhaps the most likely reason is that Seán was guided by the pattern within Irish politics of the movement from violent action to constitutional methods typified by the movements of Daniel O'Connell, Charles Stewart Parnell, and more recently, de Valera himself. His political career was progressing in a relatively predictable path from IRA militant to constitutional politician. Seán found himself frustrated with the IRA and was willing to endure the ballyhoo in order to accomplish objectives that he thought would improve the Irish nation. Seán echoes journalist Brian Inglis, who felt that becoming politically conscious was essential to the Irish character; 'I must find a way to embrace Irishness; and the obvious one was to join a political party.'[9]

The Clann has sometimes been referred to as a 'flash party', but in 1948 it seemed to be the party of the future — the most serious challenge to complacent Fianna Fáil power in the 1940s, taking Fianna Fáil to task for its failure to tackle severe social and economic problems and resolve the problem of partition while also claiming to be the more sincere republicans. The party possessed an instant nucleus of support from those, like Seán, who had been republican activists in the 1930s and 1940s.

Capitalising on post-war frustration and winning over discontented supporters from all parties, the trick for Clann na Poblachta was 'to sound more nationalist (or "national") than de Valera but less nationalist than the IRA.'[10] They succeeded in mobilising almost all of the remaining extra constitutional republicans, former IRA members and those disenchanted with Fianna Fáil's move toward the centre. Clann na Poblachta contained people of diverse ideological backgrounds who managed to remain intact due to the prospect of electoral success, the idea of defeating Fianna Fáil, and the excitement of campaigning. The party attracted republicans disheartened by the widespread imprisonments of the 1930s. Noel Hartnett, Seán's junior counsel in many defences of IRA prisoners, became disillusioned by Fianna Fáil's move away from republicanism, especially in regard to the Government's treatment of political prisoners. Clann na Poblachta also attracted those concerned with social welfare like Noël Browne, who according to his wife Phyllis was unfamiliar with Seán's political background, joining the party because of his desire to eliminate tuberculosis.[11] Peadar Cowan, Clann na Poblachta's director of finance, was an executive member of the Labour Party. Inglis calls the Clann 'vaguely progressive', maintaining that it was merely a disparate group linked only by dissatisfaction with Fianna Fáil and thus did not promise to be stable.[12] An accurate assessment, but in 1946 such dissatisfaction was enough to gel such a varied collection of people.

There is little comment from the press after the Clann's initial meeting. No editorials or letters followed and they did not publicly issue any new or more detailed policy statements. For the moment, de Valera and Fianna Fáil possessed a comfortable majority in the Dáil and the latest splinter parties, National Labour and Clann na Talmhan, had posed no real threat. Fianna Fáil had introduced an Electoral Amendment Bill in the Dáil on 2 July, four days before the Clann was officially founded, so this extra cushion would give them even less to fear from the new party. In 1946, Clann na Poblachta had not formulated any specific policies or programmes and a general election would not be necessary until May 1949. As Eithne MacDermott indicates, nothing about the Clann appeared in Fine Gael leader Richard Mulcahy's correspondence until the general election of 1948.[13] It seems that although Clann na Poblachta made an impression on individual discontented party members, it did not initially have a significant impact on their rival parties.

Clann na Poblachta can translate to 'family of the republic,' though 'clann' can also mean 'children', 'people', or simply 'clan'. It was the only Irish political party to refer to a republic in its name; both Fine Gael ('Tribe of the Gaels') and Fianna Fáil ('Soldiers of Destiny') used past mythology choosing their names whereas Clann na Poblachta looked toward the future with its choice.[14] As the republic did not formally exist yet, its name made it obvious where the Clann stood. Despite the republican emphasis, the party aimed to be broadly based, and to concentrate on social and economic problems. Seán wanted to win a wide measure of popular support for his party by promising a fresh, objective approach to politics. As MacDermott points out, very little about the party was totally innovative: 'it looked new, and radical, and challenging, and different, without really being many of these things.'[15] Clann na Poblachta cannot be termed truly extreme in any sense; the claim to radicalism must be judged in the context of Irish political and social traditions. In a country with a strong Catholic and democratic culture, it was radical in a 'thoroughly safe, unthreatening manner, sculpting its proposals around the traditional framework of Catholic social teaching.'[16]

The party was influenced more by Catholic social principles and the new trend of Christian Democracy in Europe than by any staunch socialist philosophy. While deciding on the Clann na Poblachta programme, Seán may have been influenced by the trends in European politics at that time, as he says in his memoir, 'I had been in touch with the European movement and followed a number of developments in the post-war period in Europe.'[17] Christian Democracy, as Kees van Kersbergen posits, was not merely a political party, but a political movement.[18] Seán never publicly compared Clann na Poblachta to Christian Democrats, but his desire to cultivate a European perspective and the similarities in his party's programme, for example the belief that economic policies must go hand in hand with social policies assuring that members of society had equal opportunities for self-development, demonstrate that he was somewhat influenced by Christian Democracy.

Clann na Poblachta was similar to European Christian Democracy in that its members were vigilant about the defence of Catholic doctrine and institutions and believed in an integrated Europe. Seán was a strong supporter of the embryonic European economic, political, and military integration and he wanted Ireland to participate. However, there were notable differences between Clann na Poblachta and the continental Christian Democrats. On the Continent, cooperation with other Christian denominations was seen as the way forward. Yet, in Ireland, which possessed a homogenous religious environment where the 'special position' of the Roman Catholic Church was enshrined in the Irish Constitution, 'all sorts of forces were at work to make Ireland a more totally Catholic state than it had yet become.'[19] John Charles McQuaid, the Archbishop of Dublin, wielded immense religious, political, and social power, to such an extent that he is sometimes viewed as the co-author with de Valera of the 1937 Constitution.[20] According to biographer John Cooney, this power was used to build up an intensely conservative Catholic-dominated state in which dissent of any sort was not welcome.

Catholics in other parts of Europe began leaning toward the socialist tradition; Austria's Catholic Party entered a coalition with socialists as did Christian Democrats in the Netherlands and France, whereas Clann na Poblachta was careful not to be equated with politics that were too left wing, fearing any suspicion that its members might sympathise with communism, despite the lack of any socialist or communist movement in Ireland. In July 1947, the Standing Committee decreed that members of the Communist Party were not eligible to join the Clann.

Experiences of world war had made Ireland's development in relation to Christian Democracy different from that of the rest of Europe.[21] The Continent had been bombed, fought over, and occupied by enemies, which led to barriers and established patterns being broken down. Resistance movements brought diverse people together and encouraged cooperation. In neutral countries that did not have these experiences, including Portugal, Spain, and Switzerland as well as Ireland, the post-war passion for cooperation that influenced Catholics in other parts of Europe seems to have been missing or subdued.

Regarding the early steps toward European integration, Seán and the Clann's position could be construed as 'radical' within Ireland simply because such ideas were not in keeping with de Valera's concept of neutrality or Fine Gael's desire to remain tied to the British Commonwealth. Seán himself had gained a reputation as a radical, or at least a liberal, which probably originated from his concern with civil rights evolving from his legal practice. However, such a reputation is very hard to sustain in light of his deference to the Church at the start of the inter-party Government, the decision to go into government with Fine Gael, and the disastrous outcome of the Mother and Child controversy.

Radical or not, the genesis of Clann na Poblachta was notable because it was the first broadly based political party in Ireland not to come out of Treaty politics, taking the republicans to task for preventing political development. The initial statement of the founding members demonstrates this attitude:

Various causes combined to prevent political development. Not least of these was the low standard of political morality set by those who in the name of republicanism secured office. The continual inroads on elementary personal rights (quite apart from Emergency legislation) also rendered it difficult to instil in republicans confidence in political action . . . The Nation is being weakened by the forced emigration of its youth. A small section has been enabled to accumulate enormous wealth while unemployment and low wages, coupled with an increased cost of living, are the lot of the workers . . . It has been apparent that if these evils, and the system responsible for them, are to be ended there must arise a strong political party that will set up an ideal before the nation and a new standard of political morality in public life.[22]

The reference to a 'new standard of political morality in public life' alluded to recent Fianna Fáil scandals, notably the suspect sale of Locke's Distillery which received considerable press attention during the 1947 by-elections. The distillery was sold to foreign investors, some of whom were alleged to have had criminal pasts, and the Government was accused — falsely — of having facilitated the sale in order to help its own political supporters. Seán's thoughts were that 'political life in this country had got into a rut and Clann na Poblachta had been founded to stem the decadence and set a clean ideal for the nation.'[23] An early election manifesto for MacBride declared

Seán MacBride is fighting your battles for a right to live in reasonable comfort in your own country; for a lower cost of living; for food subsidies and price controls; for increased old age pensions; for free secondary education for your children; for decent housing; for proper social services; for municipally owned transport; for a Christian state in reality, not merely in name.[24]

The Clann also represented the first major attempt since 1932 to create something more republican and more concerned with social welfare than anything offered by Fianna Fáil at that time; here was a challenge to Fianna Fáil on its own territory. The similarities between early Fianna Fáil and Clann na Poblachta are ironically demonstrated by Fianna Fáil Minister for Local Government Seán MacEntee's labelling of Clann na Poblachta as communists, which is exactly the response Fianna Fáil had once elicited from its opponents in the 1920s and 1930s.

An obvious divergence existed within the party, with one side favouring nationalist-political issues and the other emphasising socio-economic goals

— the republican aspect competing with the social programme for prominence within the party. In a 1946 handbill, the Clann's first pledge was 'to reintegrate the whole of Ireland as a Republic' but it went on to state that, though this was the ultimate objective, it was also the intention that Clann 'should take an active and independent part in the political life of the Nation.' The most urgent problem was 'political decadence' and it was also necessary to address social security, emigration via a scheme of national planning, improving rural life, cultural aims including preserving the language, and then ending partition. Everyday struggles were of more consequence; a vague concept of 'republic' might not be the first priority of someone with relatives in an underfunded tuberculosis sanatorium. In a speech at the Mansion House, Seán declared that 'if we get a Republic in name, it would mean nothing unless it ensured economic and social freedom for all the people of the country.'[25] Clann na Poblachta also promised to remove taxes on beer, tobacco, cinema seats, and greyhound racing, which was sure to be popular with most of the electorate.

Were such statements merely populist rhetoric designed to win votes? How committed was Seán to social welfare issues in general? Peadar O'Donnell commented that he was clever, 'but on political matters he was almost an amateur and had no real contact with life or living problems.'[26] Clearly if the party hoped to succeed, the day-to-day concerns of the voting public had to be addressed: in a letter to *The Irish Times* on 27 January, Seán wrote that although the republic was the ultimate aim, 'problems in the economic and social spheres . . . are of paramount importance and . . . require immediate attention.' He knew that he could not make a 'politics, not personality' plea without addressing socio-economic issues. He also recognised the localist character of Irish politics. Though as Phyllis Browne observed, 'Seán was really more of a diplomat than a politician'; he knew that it would be necessary to please his constituency and work within the broker/client relationship of Irish politics if only to ensure re-election.[27]

For a party so linked to republicanism, Clann na Poblachta did show a genuine and vigorous concern for domestic issues. Seán's own speeches focused to a large degree on the general economic situation and his final speech before the by-election concerned moving Ireland away from British sterling. Most early speeches concentrated on domestic reform, particularly halting emigration and improving the situation of Irish workers. As he said, 'The Christian State must be based on the family unit; but to-day the family is being broken up by forced emigration.'[28] He believed that Ireland's problem was a fall of production caused by the enforced exile of Irish workers to England because of higher wage rates in that country. The plan to limit emigration was to provide jobs by developing Ireland's natural resources, particularly afforestation and hydro-electricity, as well as housing and 'other constructional works of national or social importance', faintly echoing the American New Deal. Seán would later ask Archbishop McQuaid's opinion regarding a government ban on the emigration of women under the age of twenty-one, a plan which severely limited civil liberties and would have proved unworkable in practice.[29]

The Clann supported the Bishop of Clonfert's scheme for a national health insurance closely following Catholic teaching, a proposal that Seán MacEntee had rejected as too costly. MacBride cited the examples of New Zealand and Sweden as models for successful social insurance schemes. He believed that the state should take responsibility for the employment of those who were unemployed and hoped to eliminate 'the wasteful and harmful system, whereby those who are unable to secure employment have to exist on doles and public charity, while essential work remains undone.'

This essential work would help to provide the funds necessary to implement his party's proposed programme. MacBride pledged to make Ireland self-supporting; to electrify rail transport, create a deep-sea fishing fleet, provide state forests, and adequate housing with a kitchen and bathroom in each dwelling. As well as developing the country's resources, national planning would provide the funding for the proposed economic policies. MacBride suggested the establishment of a National Monetary Authority to 'equate currency and credit to the economic needs of full employment and full production' and to provide 'credits free of interest for full employment and national development of industry and agriculture'. 'Our Party will support a policy of economic development of our natural resources and full employment to return to full production.'[30] He wanted to use the money invested in British banks and securities to develop forestry and education.[31] Forestry was worthwhile because land was available, it would provide employment, and the product could be used for timber, fuel, paper, and alcohol. As MacBride pointed out at a meeting in Tuam, Ireland possessed two million acres of wasteland that could be utilised.[32] He claimed that Ireland had the best tree-growing climate in Europe, yet planted fewer trees than any other European country, preferring to use the land for agriculture, which provided a more immediate return on the investment.[33]

Culturally, the Clann wanted to get rid of 'alien, artificial and unchristian concepts of life', to establish a national theatre and film industry, to extend the Irish-speaking Gaeltacht, and to create a council to help spread knowledge of music and the arts. Another council would be set up to coordinate all branches of education, to build additional schools and modernise the existing ones. Such decentralisation, 'instead of concentrating vast armies of civil servants in Dublin', would secure the development of civic responsibility as well as reduce inefficiency and bureaucracy. Admission to universities would be regulated not only by aptitude, but also by the needs of the country in different professions — though this part of the programme would be successful only if emigration rates among graduates declined considerably, and would be nearly impossible to implement in a free society. An *Irish Independent* editorial of 2 February 1948 praised the Council of Education idea and agreed with raising the school-leaving age, but nothing was mentioned regarding university admission, and surprisingly educators from the National University or Trinity College Dublin did not respond to the proposal.

Clann na Poblachta also claimed to be dedicated to the special concerns of women, a claim which amounted to keeping prices of consumer goods and food down and limiting the emigration of women to Britain. One of the Clann's initial pamphlets 'You and the Future' focused on social insurance, price controls, and improving the economy. Problems like inadequate medical care and a high cost of living probably had more immediate resonance with voters. As Browne noted, 'There were many of my age with a general radical outlook who were weary of the gross incompetence of a succession of civil war generation politicians.'[34]

The division within the Irish Labour Party helped Clann na Poblachta. Labour had suffered a bitter split between leader Jim Larkin and General Secretary of the Transport Union, William O'Brien. O'Brien, claiming that the Labour Party had been infiltrated by communists, formed the National Labour Party. J.J. Lee's assessment that the division had more to do with personality conflicts between Larkin and O'Brien than politics, that O'Brien was 'the type of man, only too common in Ireland, who prefers to wreck a movement rather than lose control of it'[35] was more likely than any alleged communist influence. Labour Party members who did not want to involve themselves in such political minefields but desired, like Noël Browne, to ally themselves with a party concerned with social welfare, found an outlet in Clann na Poblachta.

The Clann's policies sounded good on paper and on the platform, but the price tag seemed very steep. If the plan was to lower taxes, how could all of these social welfare programmes be funded? Minister for Finance Frank Aiken commented that the proposed social insurance scheme, modelled on Sweden and New Zealand, would have likely required an income tax increase, as taxation per head in Sweden was £22 and New Zealand £54 compared to

Ireland's £20.[36] Aiken criticised the Clann's unemployment insurance scheme, wryly observing that 'the weekly stamp necessary to pay benefits on this scale would be so heavy on the men at work that there would be a definite and positive inducement for them to get into the ranks of the unemployed.'[37] However, if income taxes were reduced, money could come from several alternative sources: an Excess Profits Tax and a proposed tourist tax collected either on arrival into the country or added to hotel bills. Yet these revenues would not cover all that Clann had planned. As the 11 November editorial in the *Irish Independent* posited, 'We seem in many directions to allow our ideas to outstrip our needs, and to propose plans more suited to an imperial standard than to the strictly-limited resources of the people.'

Through generally praising the party, an *Irish Times* editorial of 1 November 1947 stated that Clann na Poblachta's 'economic programme scarcely deserves to be taken seriously,' and *The Economist* predicted after the by-elections that 'a Coalition Government of the Republican Party and Labour now becomes a real possibility. Such a combination would be less likely to follow a rational trade and economic policy than Fianna Fáil.'[38] Perhaps Seán, not an economist, was naïve about how a free market economy functioned and saw the evils of communism only in terms of religion, not economics. It is very likely that he did not have the time to work out his policies properly or the foresight to see their consequences and may have realised this later on. In an RTÉ radio interview with John Bowman in 1980, Seán posited that 'we lost in the last ten days of the election campaign . . . Our economic policies frightened the people . . . I could feel the people being scared that last ten days.'[39]

Lyons sums up the party philosophy as an 'apparent combination of republican orthodoxy with social radicalism.'[40] The orthodoxy was not always comfortably compatible with the radicalism. Though Seán's and Clann na Poblachta's commitment to social welfare issues was sincere, an IRA culture dominated the party. The basis of the party, after all, was the committees formed to help republican prisoners, and the party organisation retained similarities to the IRA structure. Over time, Seán fell out with nearly every senior member of Clann na Poblachta — Noel Hartnett, Noël Browne, Jack McQuillan, and Peadar Cowan — whose immediate ancestry did not lie with the IRA.[41] Perhaps this is because Seán was used to taking command of a revolutionary organisation, not constitutional politics. Cruise O'Brien recalls that Seán was pleasant to work for 'except that he expected you to be available at all hours, whenever required, like a member of a revolutionary organisation . . . There were always distant semi-revolutionary overtones when he was around: a rather somnambulistic obeisance to the Pearsean call.'[42] There appeared to be five 'tendencies' within the party: the parliamentary, the extra-parliamentary, the Catholic intellectual, the reformers, and the Fenians. But the overriding imperative, according to McQuillan, was unswerving loyalty to the leader.[43]

Seán's attitude may have been akin to that of the leader of a revolutionary movement, yet he did not want the Clann to be seen as another IRA party rather than one for social change, a 'party of protest' rather than a 'party of government'.[44] Was he taking care to emphasise social welfare to distract from the Clann's IRA background? The choice of Noël Browne as cabinet minister seems to bear this theory out; Browne was thirty-two, a young age for a government minister, had no IRA connections or controversial political past, and was obviously committed to social welfare, particularly the eradication of tuberculosis. Seán proved astute in this case, choosing someone whose presence would 'eradicate a lot of the criticism, suspicions that there had been, that the Clann was only a group of old IRA men parading under a new façade.'[45]

Yet social issues were tied to the Clann's foreign policy concerns. Seán pointed out that 'one of the realities that has to be faced is that until we set up social services and an economic system that are at least as good as those offered to the people of the Six Counties by the British Labour Government, no serious advance can be made towards the ending of partition.'[46] MacBride was trying to persuade extreme republicans that a focus on improving social welfare would be useful in achieving the ultimate goal of a united Ireland. Clann na Poblachta's policies in social and economic areas could make unification more likely.

Despite Seán's stance that economic and social problems required immediate attention, solving the problem of partition and proclaiming Ireland's independence from Britain superseded issues of social welfare for many party members. Such a dichotomy could eventually prove harmful to Clann na Poblachta, but in 1947 the prospect of defeating Fianna Fáil provided the necessary cohesiveness between the two groups.

Three vacant Dáil seats, in Dublin, Tipperary, and Waterford, became available in October 1947, giving Clann na Poblachta its first campaigning opportunity. In that same month, the cabinet approved an Electoral Amendment Bill that increased the number of three-member constituencies from fifteen to twenty-two, as the *Irish Independent* wrote, loading 'the electoral dice in favour of the big party. Moreover, there seems to be no good reason, in geography, population, or convenience, for some of the groupings now proposed.'[47] Under proportional systems with the single transferable vote, large constituencies tend to favour smaller parties; yet in three-member constituencies, the largest party typically wins two of the three seats, leaving the third to be fought over by the smaller parties. Thus Fianna Fáil's solution was to break up the number of large constituencies to ensure a Dáil majority. The Dáil grew from 138 to 147 members despite a fall in population. Here was a sign that Fianna Fáil was worried about the increasing popularity of Clann na Poblachta.

The MacBride family got involved in the Clann's first election. Kid, Anna, and Tiernan helped to campaign for the Clann in Dublin and Maud contributed to Clann literature and wrote letters to Irish newspapers highlighting the deficiencies of the Government of the time, especially in regard to its treatment of political prisoners.

Clann na Poblachta fought both the 1947 by-elections and the 1948 general election on the basis of social welfare proposals first and a militant republican stance second, roughly adopting as its own the programme of early Fianna Fáil. But unlike Fianna Fáil in the 1930s, the Clann desired to dispense with the political and social divisions defined by Treaty politics, end any residual bitterness of the Civil War and the 1930s, and begin a new type of political discourse. Thus policy differences rather than personality debates played an enormous role in the 1947 and 1948 elections; '"Home front" policies have provided the main issues for the political orators during the past few weeks. The cost of living has loomed largely with agriculture and housing supplying equal good material for political discussion and argument.'[48] Seán tried to keep to the issues, limiting broad nationalist rhetoric. As he later told MacDermott, 'I had campaigned very strongly on the basis that people should be appointed in government irrespective of their past political affiliations, and that had a progressive political viewpoint, and were capable of trying to change conditions in the country.'[49] In a speech at Roscrea on 26 October 1947, he suggested 'that they [government ministers] were subject to the influence of their political and personal friends in the granting of licences involving vast sums of money to trading concerns.'[50] Roddy Connolly, the son of James Connolly, wrote in The Irish Times that Clann na Poblachta 'is looked upon by the people as a battering ram to break the power and privilege of the present Government and that combined with Labour and Clann na Talmhan would contribute largely to the overthrow of Fianna Fáil.'[51]

During the by-election campaigns, the Clann went on the offensive, baiting the Government, and attempting to grab public attention and get public support. Seán's letters most often appeared on the pages of The Irish Times, a paper supportive of his campaign or at least antagonistic to Fianna Fáil.[52] The Irish Press was an unapologetically pro-Fianna Fáil paper while the

Irish Independent was partially, but not overtly, favourable to Fine Gael. MacBride and Seán MacEntee engaged in a letter-writing duel; as the radio was government-controlled[53] and television was not widespread, letters to newspapers were the main method by which political arguments could take place and spread to a wider audience.[54] MacEntee referred to MacBride half-heartedly supporting the Germans during the Second World War, 'sitting on the fence waiting to see what side would triumph in the end', and credited MacBride with 'a singular lack of judgment, foresight and political sagacity . . . He has always been among those who have chosen to exploit the difficulties which confronted the nation in order to advance their own political views,' and later stated that 'I am doing my utmost to secure the defeat of Mr MacBride and his fellow-candidates.'[55] In his reply, MacBride facetiously began, 'Mr MacEntee is a Minister of State. He therefore has plenty of leisure at his disposal,' and is 'afraid to face the actual issues involved in the present by-elections,' instead resorting to 'invectives and personal abuse . . . Mr MacEntee's accusations and innuendoes in so far as they conflict with my views as stated in this letter, are as inconsistent with each other as they are untrue.'[56] The 'Letters to the Editor' served as a venue for political debate; replies to letters usually appeared a day or two after the original. In his letters, MacBride tried to dispense with 'flag-waving "national records" and personalities', writing that 'what is needed is a policy based on realities. Instead of recriminations and self-glorification based on past events, the need is vision and planning for the future.'[57]

The by-elections took place on 29 October. Two of the three candidates were successful, including MacBride, who ran against Fianna Fáil candidate Thomas Mullen in Dublin. Both Tipperary and Waterford were considered Fianna Fáil strongholds. Fianna Fáil did manage to hold on to Waterford, which was expected. Before the Tipperary election, the *Irish Independent* commented that the 'general impression throughout the country is that [Clann candidate Patrick Kinnane] will upset the ordinary gauge of the Tipperary election by taking votes from each of the other four parties.'[58] MacBride and Kinnane's main support came from those affected by economic depression rather than those with a strong republican agenda; Kinnane's election 'showed very clearly the trend of feeling in the country. It showed that the people of Tipperary only wanted a lead to show their desire to get back to the old track again.'[59] *The Irish Times* noted that 'this totally illogical development is a sign of the times.'[60] An *Irish Independent* editorial of 1 November theorised, we venture to think that a high proportion of those who voted for Clann na Poblachta were former supporters of Fianna Fáil who have been disillusioned. Whatever may be the people's views of the policy of the new party, it has certainly aroused the interest of many young citizens in public affairs at a time when apathy was a disturbing feature of political affairs.

After the election results were announced, MacBride declared that he was pleased to be the 'first spokesman of a new movement in Ireland.'[61] The success in the by-elections led to an atmosphere of optimism and more prominent people willing to join, for example Kathleen Clarke, wife of 1916 martyr Thomas Clarke; Joseph Brennan, a key civil servant in the early years of the state; and ex-IRA activist Dr Patrick McCartan. The general reaction to the by-elections in London was chiefly concern as to how it would affect the ongoing Anglo-Irish trade talks.[62]

Seán MacBride entered the Dáil on 5 November 1947. The first issues he addressed were the desirability of an inquiry regarding the proposed sale of Locke's Distillery[63] and the necessity to reduce the cost of living, thus preventing emigration by making it more cost-effective to live in Ireland:

In other words, in Britain at all times the increase in wages and salaries was twice the increase in the cost of living. That is the fundamental cause of emigration. The fundamental cause of emigration here is that we allowed a position to develop whereby the wage earners, the small farmers, the agricultural labourers, were unable to earn an economic living in this country, whereas they were able to go across to England to earn an economic living there which enabled them to send money home. Therefore, if we really want to stop emigration, we must reduce the cost of living to at least the level which prevails in the neighbouring island.[64]

In the Dáil, Seán proved to be well prepared and spoke more about domestic issues than foreign policy; from 5 November 1947 until 11 December when the Dáil was dissolved, he did not speak about partition or the republic at all. The topics he addressed varied from fishing rights, sanatoriums, and amnesty for political prisoners to taxation, emigration, and decreasing the cost of living.

Though an election was not necessary until May 1949, de Valera had promised to call an early general election if Fianna Fáil candidates were not successful in the by-elections, a move that the 29 October *Irish Times* editorial called 'petulant'. He kept his promise and called a general election for February 1948 in the hope of securing power and curbing the Clann's development by embroiling that party in a nationwide contest before it was ready. In Seán's opinion, 'De Valera felt the shorter time I was given to organise, the better, because he had an exaggerated opinion of me as a good organiser.'[65] The ploy was clever; Clann na Poblachta had no breathing space and did not have the time to build up and strengthen its organisation or fine-tune its policies. At the time of the election, the party had no established structure and skeletal organisational systems in many parts of the country.

As Seán admitted during the by-election campaign, he would not be in a position to alter government policy or bring about a change of government if elected. But the general election now offered the chance of government removal and formation. Campaigning began in late November and one advantage the party did have was excellent public relations and advertising, largely due to the efforts of Noel Hartnett. The Clann was the first Irish political party to employ 'spin doctors' and effectively used available media to publicise its platform.

All competing parties ran small advertisements in the newspapers. Fine Gael highlighted specific candidates like Liam Cosgrave and Richard Mulcahy. Fianna Fáil's 'information series' was packed with small print expounding on election issues and using the tagline 'These are Facts'. Fianna Fáil was also the only party not to ask for funds. Clann na Poblachta's ads were succinct: focusing on its platform, its diverse membership and, notably, answering its critics:

> We serve no duce, no marshal, no fuehrer, no dictator, no taoiseach . . . but Ireland. If Clann na Poblachta has converted Blueshirts — is it to be called Fascist? If it has converted Leftists, is it to be called Communist? If it has converted De Valerites, is it to be called Fianna Fáil? That would be the last straw.[66]

Clann na Poblachta produced an eight-minute film, *Our Country*, addressing rural depopulation, poverty, urban deprivation, emigration, shortages, and unemployment. As cameraman Brendan Stafford remembered, the footage was genuine; 'If we showed bare-footed newsboys, there were bare-footed newsboys — we didn't ask them to take their shoes off.'[67] However, MacDermott spoke to one of the actors, Liam Ó Laoghaire, who pointed out that very few people went barefoot in Dublin in December and that a young man was given sixpence to remove his shoes. However, Ó Laoghaire also said that the shortages and depictions of the slums were indeed accurate.[68] Browne was interviewed regarding tuberculosis. MacBride was also interviewed, declaring, 'it's your country', and only the voters themselves could change the situation, presumably by changing the Government. Noel Hartnett acted as narrator, commenting, 'Communism will not solve these problems. State control will not solve these problems. Only you, the people, can solve them.' The film never mentioned 'Clann na Poblachta' at all, but the point had been made. Browne found it 'an enlightened effort in the political education of an electorate whose politics were of the crudest emotive civil war tribal variety.'[69]

Our Country was offered to cinemas without charge and, as no political party or affiliation was mentioned, Liam Ó Laoghaire claimed that the broadcast was free of narrow party bias.[70] However, most major cinema organisations banned it, deciding that it was indeed too political. Undeterred, the party showed the film on sides of buildings.

Ian McCabe's assessment that there was a lack of serious ideological debate during the 1948 election is not entirely true. MacBride attempted to concentrate on politics, asking voters in Clare (de Valera's constituency) to 'vote for a policy rather than a personality'. According to Inglis, Seán 'spoke . . . of matters which were hardly calculated to grip the audience; the repatriation of Ireland's external assets was one theme, reforestation another.'[71] MacBride was attempting to break the 'cult of personality' and so tried to keep his focus on prosaic concerns; 'little has been heard of their [republican] policy on the hustings.'[72] He was not a dynamic speaker; he disliked shows of spontaneous enthusiasm and preferred to speak seriously about relevant issues. A major memory of the campaign for Liam and Colm Ó Laoghaire was Seán solemnly lecturing some dishevelled slum youngsters about 'the incompatibility of sterling' with Irish economic independence.[73] At the final speech on the eve of the general election, there was excitement, but no wild cheering; yet *The Irish Times* concluded that 'the crowds were thinking, instead of bursting into enthusiasm for a single individual.'[74] Such a lack of showmanship may have been Seán attempting to focus on issues.

This strategy may have proven difficult because the party platforms were not very diverse. There was no tangible difference between Fine Gael and Fianna Fáil; the parties agreed on the methods for solving domestic issues such as improving agriculture, industry, education, housing, and healthcare, increasing the standard of living, and lowering taxes. Labour and Clann na Poblachta had similar social welfare programmes; the difference lay in Labour's emphasis on the workers and trade unions and Clann's more republican stance. During the election, Labour seemed to accept that it would not gain a majority and looked to support or coalesce with a suitable party. In such a political climate, not only does personality become incredibly important, but candidates must also find some way to make themselves or their party stand out. With a lack of real distinction between the competing parties, the focus shifts to symbolic rather than substantive issues. Thus, the questions of Ireland's connection with Britain and which party comprised the true republicans were dealt with. However, repeal of the External Relations Act was not a major theme in the election campaign. MacBride and Clann na Poblachta continued avoiding relying on past glory, pointing out the dangers of doing so: 'Political issues have for the last quarter of a century been judged on the basis of past affiliations rather than on their merits. Likewise, public life has largely been the monopoly of persons whose only qualifications were derived from their associations with events that occurred 20 or 30 years ago.'[75] In a speech during the 1948 election, Browne stated that 'we are sick and tired of hearing about 1916 and 1922 and of the futile wrangling about the past. There are present social and economic evils which need resolution.'[76] Browne's sentiment certainly could be interpreted as radical; it was nearly impossible in the environment of Irish politics to escape from the rhetoric of 1916/1922, especially while a party was called the 'family of the republic'. Yet, the heckling cry of 'Where were you in 1916 and 1921?' was replaced by 'Where will you be tomorrow?' Of course, such sentiments were easier for Seán to articulate, as his republican lineage was firmly established.

The election focused on the shortcomings of Fianna Fáil, and the Clann had the advantage of being able to chide Fianna Fáil for not carrying out its policies.[77] As MacBride stated in a speech in Tralee,

> the Fianna Fáil party have been 15 years in office. They claim that they have done everything that could be done. They claim there is no remedy for emigration, poverty, squalor. They are satisfied with existing conditions. As that is their attitude then let them stand out of the way and let the people with faith in the future take over.[78]

Government corruption, stagnancy, and failure to achieve proposed goals in both the domestic and foreign spheres provided Clann na Poblachta with election material. As the British Representative to Ireland, John Maffey, later Lord Rugby, reported, support for Clann na Poblachta originated from 'a strong gesture of disgust with the de Valera Government for the usual economic grievances of failing to satisfy popular demand to keep prices down.'[79] Moreover, Fianna Fáil did not take the opportunity to rebut seriously the Clann's economic policies, nor did the other parties.

Public perceptions of Seán himself varied. *The Observer* cynically commented before the election, 'MacBride has caught hold of the popular imagination . . . His following is composed of extreme chauvinists or incorrigible Celts, disgruntled IRA, a few ex-communists, and some political adventurers.'[80] Brian Inglis kept a diary of Clann na Poblachta progress during the election for *The Irish Times*. To Inglis, Seán MacBride seemed refined and modest, yet 'not impressive on the platform. His face, skull-like in its contours, split rather than relaxed by his rare smile, was a little intimidating, and the foreign inflection was not as attractive on the hustings as it could be in conversation . . . Seán did not have the personality needed to create a revolution in voting habits.'[81]

However, most observers felt differently: 'Unfortunately for his party, it has not been organised sufficiently long to enable it to select or attract many candidates who have either Mr MacBride's popular personality or background.'[82] Seán's speeches and rallies were well attended, including the largest public meeting in Ballina for years, on 11 January, complete with torchlight processions and bonfires.[83] At the high point of the campaigning, Seán was speaking at up to four meetings a day in inclement weather which strained his voice. Both *The Irish Times* and the *Irish Independent* refer to 'huge gatherings' where MacBride received an 'attentive hearing'. The *Irish Independent* estimated that Seán had attended 100 meetings over 3,000 miles and 'the appearance of his party created an interest not apparent since 1932.'[84] At one rally in Cork,

> a tumultuous welcome awaited Mr MacBride when he arrived at Cork from Cobh. He was met at the entrance to the city by a cheering crowd of several thousand people who mobbed his car. He was later driven to the scene of the meeting — said to be the biggest election meeting ever seen in the city.[85]

John A. Murphy writes that the exotic element of Seán's personality provided 'an additional attraction in an Irish political chief'[86] and Ronan Fanning credits MacBride with personifying 'the impulse for change in Irish politics and he had the advantage, more unusual in politics than is commonly realised, of knowing what he *wanted* to do.'[87]

The Irish papers continued to receive 'Letters to the Editor' from both MacBride and MacEntee. MacBride felt that these missives went beyond mere campaign mudslinging. In a speech at Kilrush on 15 January, he claimed that MacEntee was engaged in 'a campaign of lying and personal vilification'. MacEntee, in a letter to *The Irish Times* on 16 January, once again labelled Clann na Poblachta as communist, citing MacBride's organisation of Saor Éire in 1931. An *Irish Times* editorial of 17 January called MacEntee a 'political Don Quixote, tilting gaily at Communist windmills and smelling Bolsheviks behind every bush', and further stated that 'many voters who are sick of the ancient feuds between the older parties will be tempted to give the "new man" [MacBride] a chance.'

Clann na Poblachta nominated ninety-three candidates, which vastly overstretched the party's time and resources. Though MacBride's speeches were cautious and restrained, some of his followers boasted of repeating the 1918 Sinn Féin landslide. MacBride himself mused that the party could gain an overall majority: 'at one stage of the campaign, I thought it was going to be a landslide victory . . . We were not only going to gain a majority, but a large majority.'[88]

Ultimately, Clann na Poblachta won ten seats; 13.2 per cent of the national vote. This number did not meet expectations but a young political party winning ten seats in its first general election in a conservative Irish political climate could be seen as very promising.[89] If not for the previously mentioned Electoral Amendment Act, Clann na Poblachta would have won nineteen seats based on the proportion of votes the party acquired. Over-ambition made the 1948 election feel like a failure, yet 13.2 per cent was, after all, the highest ever won by a minor party in its first general election, and in the long term, Clann na Poblachta was able to cause a break in the conventional pattern of the Treaty-based pattern of voting. Its numbers provided enough presence to help form the Dáil's first inter-party government, dominated by Fine Gael and united mainly to keep Fianna Fáil from returning to power.

As a result of the election, Fianna Fáil lost its overall majority but remained the largest single party in the Dáil. De Valera would not enter a coalition as a rule, but he believed that he would have the support of National Labour and Dáil Independents. Instead, at the impetus of Fine Gael leader Richard Mulcahy, the opposition parties agreed to form a coalition government. In an *Irish Times* interview with Michael McInerney in 1979, MacBride recalled, 'I think I was the first to enunciate policy. I was aware at the time that this was awaited anxiously by Fine Gael and others.'[90] The four points Seán put forth were more public investment in Irish resources, increased forestry planning, release of Hospital Trust Funds to build hospitals and sanatoriums, and increases in social welfare benefits. 'There was a sigh of relief because I had not mentioned the External Relations Act or the political prisoners, although I had campaigned on those issues in the election. Everybody around the table agreed to the points I had proposed.' MacBride did not raise those issues because 'while I had campaigned on those issues the others had not, and I felt it would be putting an impossible strain on them to ask them to agree to things for which they had not campaigned.'

The 1948 general election was one of the most unusual elections since

1932–1933 not only because it ushered in the first inter-party Government, but because it also led to the electoral trend of Fianna Fáil versus the rest. Clann na Poblachta had campaigned with the slogan 'Put Them Out' and now it had its chance, even if it meant joining a Fine Gael-led government, proving Ronan Fanning's assertion that coalition governments in Ireland 'have more to do with taste, temperament, and environment than with party labels.'[91]

The question of whether to enter a coalition proved to be divisive and may have been the beginning of the end for the party, as many within Clann na Poblachta could not stomach the party serving in a pro-Treaty, pro-Commonwealth Fine Gael government. There were some accusations of opportunism and some resignations from the party. Seán defended his decision: the Clann had campaigned to 'Put Them Out'; it couldn't very well vote to put them back in again.[92] The reasons for entering the inter-party Government may have been more pragmatic than just the desire to oust Fianna Fáil; the Clann was largely financed through loans and may have been unable to fight another election if de Valera had returned to power and called another election right away.

MacBride could not agree to Mulcahy's becoming Taoiseach, as Mulcahy had been commander of the Free State forces during the Civil War and had once signed an internment order for MacBride.[93] Mulcahy offered to stand down, a gesture that Seán admitted was 'magnanimous', and John A. Costello, who had not been involved in the Civil War, was chosen to be Taoiseach. The Clann agreed to the choice because its members regarded Costello as 'innocuous and malleable'.[94]

That Mulcahy and MacBride could serve in the same Government having been on opposite sides in a bloody, contentious, and recent civil war showed that tensions had abated and that the desire to stop Fianna Fáil from forming another government was quite fervent. The lack of strong ideological differences among the parties also made it easier to form a coalition.

As the first inter-party Taoiseach, Costello found himself in a bind. He was not the party leader, his party did not have a Dáil majority, and because of the compromise situation of coalition, he was able to make only one senior governmental appointment. MacBride managed to secure two ministries for Clann na Poblachta, External Affairs for himself and Health for Noël Browne. Because of the wide range of interests Seán had demonstrated as TD, it is not implausible that he could have been given Finance or Lands. Yet he was content with External Affairs because the Ministry would provide him with a way to further Clann na Poblachta's aims and would keep the party (and himself) in the public eye. The cabinet also consisted of Labour leader William Norton as Tánaiste, Clann na Talmhan leader Joseph Blowick as

Minister for Lands, Independent James Dillon as Minister for Agriculture, and Mulcahy as Minister for Education, completing what Dermot Keogh called a 'cabinet of talent, temperament and torpor'.[95] Despite being from different parties, the cabinet members all had close ties: MacBride and Costello moved in the same legal circles, MacBride and Dillon had gone to school together. An example of such camaraderie took place a few days after Seán entered the Dáil. Frank Aiken sniped that 'I was delighted to see Deputy Dillon welcoming with open arms and almost kissing the Kingstown republican [MacBride] who came in here the other day.' Dillon replied that 'Deputy MacBride and I were at school together under Father Sweetman.'[96]

In his first radio speech as Taoiseach, Costello stated that his Government believed that the main challenges were of a socio-economic nature rather than a political-constitutional one, but did claim 'as a priority' the reunification of the island. As party leader, Seán continued to pontificate in the Dáil on social welfare issues, yet it would be in foreign policy that his influence would be most clearly seen.

Four important relationships would define MacBride's time in cabinet. Two of those relationships, those with Britain and the United States, were already in place. Seán would attempt to strengthen those ties, while cultivating successfully closer connections with Europe, and not so successfully those with the Catholic Church hierarchy.

Chapter 5 ∿

THE HARP WITHOUT THE CROWN: IRELAND AND BRITAIN

'*The more precisely the position is determined, the less precisely the momentum is known.*'

— WERNER HEISENBERG, *The Uncertainty Paper*

As Minister for External Affairs, Seán established strong relationships with both the inter-party cabinet and diplomats working in Dublin. He would share a weekly lunch of boiled egg on toast with John Maffey, later Lord Rugby, as well as the American Ambassador George Garrett and the French Ambassador Count Stanislaus Ostrorog. In his memoir, Noël Browne described Seán and British Prime Minister Clement Attlee arriving unannounced at Browne's home near Louisburgh where his wife Phyllis cooked omelettes over the fire.

Despite the risk to his cholesterol level, MacBride was quickly gaining a reputation as a charming diplomat and hard worker, often forgetting to come home for supper. Despite his diplomatic position, he was the leader of a party which attracted republicans disenchanted by the lack of movement on partition. He would have to demonstrate that his Government was trying to solve the problem.

Ireland's relationship with Britain continued to be defined by partition. As with every politician and party since 1922, Seán MacBride and Clann na Poblachta campaigned vigorously for its end. While in power, the inter-party Government continued to produce anti-partition rhetoric, and as its members blamed Britain for partition's existence, put the onus on Britain to reunite the island.

There were two facets to the anti-partition policy; attempts to bring about cooperation and propaganda at home and abroad. The latter quickly eclipsed the former. Seán's method consisted of raising the issue in the international arena at every possible opportunity in the hope that publicising the 'unnaturalness' of division and appealing to people's sense of a nation's right to self-determination would provide the necessary pressure for Britain to rejoin the country. Clann na Poblachta had proposed equalling the benefits of the British welfare state in Ireland, establishing concentrated contact with both Northern nationalists and Catholics, and allaying unionist fears about 'Rome Rule'. Yet Seán abandoned these ideas to undertake a propaganda campaign that showed no sign of working. He and the inter-party Government made the mistake, common in Irish nationalist politics, of underestimating unionist tenacity and expending too much energy on publicising partition in the international arena rather than focusing on reconciliation at the national level, discarding opportunities to improve the relationship or at least assuage the unionist siege mentality.

While campaigning and while in office, Seán unceasingly affirmed that the removal of 'unnatural' partition was inevitable; he believed that a basic bond of love of Ireland united the peoples of the North and South. The difficulty was that they loved different concepts of 'Ireland'. Seán unwittingly provided an example of this: 'An English friend of mine recently complained bitterly to me because we [Ireland] were celebrating the 150th anniversary of the United Irishmen and of the 1798 Insurrection. He saw in this an overt act of unfriendliness. We, on the other hand, thought it the most natural thing in the world.'[1] Ulstermen may have had more sympathy for 1798 commemorations, but in a country where history and commemoration are so vital, notable historical events like the Siege of Derry, the Battle of the Boyne, and the 1916 Easter Rising have very different meanings across the border. How would 'national' events be commemorated if partition ended? It was likely that the unionist tradition would be subsumed and it is also likely that unionists realised this. As Clare O'Halloran argues, 'the rhetoric was primarily that of "one nation", [but] there was an implicit exclusion of northern unionists from a nationalism which was wholly gaelic [sic] and Catholic in ethos.'[2]

The concept of nationalism that MacBride and the Government were trying to invoke put them on uncertain ground. As he stated in the Dáil,

Our sole claim is that the Irish people should be allowed to determine their own affairs democratically and of their own free will, without interference by Britain. The fact that Britain succeeded, over 25 years ago, in retaining a corner of our island and that she has since occupied it, in no way entitled her to divide the historic Irish nation and to pretend that our island now consists of two separate nations.[3]

However, nationhood does not always follow geography and some see partition as an institutional recognition of pre-existing and genuine divisions within Ireland. Despite having been employed by the Department of External Affairs to write anti-partition tracts, Conor Cruise O'Brien feels that the alleged occupation of Northern Ireland was sustained by the will and votes of the majority living there and that this essential fact was ignored in anti-partition propaganda.[4] Scholars and politicians have argued over whether Ireland is or is not two nations, but it cannot be denied that there exist two traditions, two aspirations, and two philosophies of life.[5]

The inter-party Government gave little attention to such arguments and began almost immediately to increase anti-partition rhetoric. Propaganda attempts to end partition targeted Britain as the Government believed that the ultimate responsibility for ending partition lay with the British. The Government parties were also confident that Britain could solve the problem with no consequences, such as civil war, and that doing so was in Britain's best interest, 'that a united and free Ireland is as essential to Britain's welfare as it is to Ireland's.'[6]

The Conservatives, normally staunch unionists, were no longer in power and the new Labour Government, which had seemed more amenable to movement on the issue, provided hope that Britain would soften its position on partition. Seán believed that Prime Minister Clement Attlee was sympathetic to the problem; during his holiday in Ireland in 1948, Attlee 'was very friendly' and would remark on 'how anxious he was to end partition'.[7]

However, the positions of the British political parties were not so set in stone; Winston Churchill stated in casual conversation in 1948 that 'I still hope for a united Ireland. You must get those fellows from the North in, though you can't do it by force',[8] and the Labour Government proved just as determined as the Conservatives to maintain the status quo. On 14 August 1948, Attlee, Seán MacBride, Secretary for Commonwealth Relations Philip Noel-Baker, and Minister for Health Noël Browne met informally in Mayo where both Attlee and Noel-Baker ruled out any movement on partition. Even when it became obvious that a British initiative was not forthcoming, MacBride told United States Secretary of State Dean Acheson that the British Government was 'over-cautious about partition for fear of eliminating middle-class support.'[9] Seán held out hope that Attlee's personal feelings would result in a change of government policy.

Placing responsibility with Britain was convenient in some sense; 'by insisting that Britain alone was to blame, Nationalists absolved themselves of any possible guilt for partition and therefore of any obligation to find a solution.'[10] At a lecture to the Royal Institute of International Affairs, MacBride disputed the view that the problem should be settled by the Irish. He pointed out that partition had been affected by an Act of the British Parliament, passed in 1920. British Customs operated the border, British troops occupied the territory, and British finances were inextricably mixed with those of the Belfast Government. Therefore it was Britain's responsibility to take some action. Seán again alluded to the right of national self-determination, clearly defined boundaries, and a national history. Despite the amenable relationship that Ireland and Britain possessed, 'No matter how much one may like one's neighbour, one does not like him to squat in a corner of one's garden. We merely want our garden. It is not really so unreasonable.'[11] Seán protested Britain's attempt to 'reinforce the unjust partition of our country and to encourage the Belfast Government to persevere in their intransigence.'[12]

Seán had misjudged the chain of command; the Belfast Government was reinforcing partition and the British Government was merely responding to its wishes. Regarding his Royal Institute of International Affairs lecture, H. Duncan Hall observed that 'the audience, while uncertain about his logic, thought he should argue his case with Belfast rather than London.'[13] Public statements by both Churchill and Attlee should have made Seán and the Government realise that the British were not going to change their stance on partition. Northern Ireland Prime Minister Sir Basil Brooke was confident that 'their basic ideas were the same,'[14] highlighted by their past experience of the Second World War and the future security of the United Kingdom. Instead of badgering Britain, it would have been a better plan to work with Belfast.

As well as the underestimation of Northern unionism, the 1937 Constitution proved to be another barrier to Irish unity. The document not only claimed political and territorial control over the entire island but also claimed religious control or at least partiality. Whatever the political manoeuvring behind it, de Valera's Constitution made the Irish state appear wholly committed to the maintenance of Catholic values, especially because it led to the repeal of rights enjoyed under previous British law.

While in government, Seán exhibited a willingness to alter the Constitution to guarantee civil rights, but did not seem to see much difficulty with the existing document:

Under our Constitution, full and adequate safeguards are rigidly imposed to protect the religious and political minorities that may exist, but in so far as it might be suggested that these are inadequate to safeguard the views of any of our fellow-countrymen in the Six Counties, I think I can say, not merely on my own behalf but on behalf of any Irish Government, that we would be prepared to give them any other additional rights and guarantees that were reasonably required.[15]

Yet the inter-party Government did not make any attempt to change the Constitution, possibly choosing to wait for overtures from Britain or the North. The contentious articles were amended, but not until much later.[16] If such amendments had been carried out earlier, it might have led to a more cordial relationship between North and South because it would have demonstrated willingness on the part of the Irish Government to compromise and to mollify unionists by assuring them that their civil rights would not be threatened in a united Ireland.

Ireland's neutrality policy during the Second World War also helped to sustain partition. Although neutrality isolated Ireland from the damaging effects of war and provided a successful test of self-determination and an independent foreign policy, Irish neutrality was a principal factor in influencing the decision of Britain not to lean on Northern Ireland to unite with the Irish Free State. A united Ireland would in all likelihood remain technically neutral, which would be detrimental to both Britain and America with regard to the Cold War. As the American State Department's Director for European Affairs, John Hickerson, observed:

With the United Kingdom in control of Northern Ireland we have, according to the past record, every reason to count on the use of bases in that area in the event of need. I am sure that you will agree that this is a powerful argument for this Government's favoring the continued control of Northern Ireland by the United Kingdom.[17]

The partition issue was forced into the background during the war, but as both Inglis and Davis observe, the change of government in February 1948 rekindled it as a live issue in Irish politics.[18] Partition was not a divisive subject in the twenty-six counties; all parties agreed that it should be removed as quickly as possible and that no physical force should be used. From 1922 on, it was a domestic ritual to refer to partition in almost every political speech. Not surprisingly, during the 1948 general election, MacBride and Clann na Poblachta campaigned for the end of partition and had the newcomer's advantage of being able to chide Fianna Fáil for not solving the problem.

Seán suggested two noteworthy ideas: improving conditions within Ireland to rival the benefits that the North was receiving under the British Welfare State, and the proposal 'to give the right of audience in the Dáil to the elected representatives of the Six Counties' as well as nominations to the Seanad, an idea similar to the power-sharing Government instituted fifty years later; as Seán said during the campaign, 'In the Constitution, it is claimed that the Dáil is the Parliament of the whole country. Yet Mr de Valera's Government refused to allow elected representatives of Northern Ireland to sit in Leinster House.'[19] Both ideas were far-sighted; at best an improved relationship between North and South could provide an incentive to end partition, at worst a better relationship between the North and South could develop.

The idea of having Northern Ireland in the Dáil met with some approval in the North. Eddie McAteer, a Derry MP elected to Stormont in 1949, expressed enthusiasm, but admitted that it would merely be a 'token attendance'.[20] Other nationalist MPs agreed. Seán's plan was well-intentioned, but Attorney General Cecil Lavery later pointed out some major difficulties: representation would occur without taxation or similar constituent responsibilities which might appear unfair, the difficulties of determining election rules and citizenship requirements could prove arduous, and the proportional representation election system might make the prospect difficult. When asked in the Dáil whether these deputies would take their seats, Costello responded,

> Having regard to the constitutional, legal and other difficulties involved, the Government do not intend to make any proposals for the admission to Dáil Éireann of the representatives referred to in the Deputy's question. The Government, however, have been considering whether Seanad Éireann should not be consulted with a view to making provision for giving them a right of audience in the Seanad.[21]

The proposal was put on the agenda for the cabinet meeting of 23 May, then postponed until 4 July, then withdrawn completely.

As a result of the 1948 elections, Fianna Fáil also became more vocal about the issue. As Maffey observed, 'the platform which won most applause was the one which put out the most violent anti-British ranting.'[22] De Valera embarked on an anti-partition speaking tour of the United States, Canada, and Australia. However, de Valera's tour did not lead to an increase in the anti-partition movement; his audience was largely composed of the converted and his speeches were 'tribal rallies, not political meetings'.[23] John Bowman believes that de Valera completed the tour mainly to secure his and Fianna Fáil's ideological territory at home, and his speeches were really aimed at the Irish to ensure them of his commitment. This belief is given some credence by the fact that anti-partition activity in the United States received little active support from the Government when de Valera was in power. As Fine Gael candidate Seán MacEoin declared to the *Westmeath Examiner*, 'They [Fianna Fáil] had been 16 years in office, and had done more talk about partition in the few months they had been in opposition that they did during that 16 years.'[24] The tour caused more problems for the inter-party Government than for Belfast, as the Government lost an opportunity to differentiate itself from de Valera and Fianna Fáil by not relying on propaganda. The inter-party Government had to take some action to neutralise Fianna Fáil, and repeal of the External Relations Act provided an opportunity to do that.

The repeal of the External Relations Act and the establishment of an Irish Republic have been lauded as the most important achievement of Ireland's first inter-party Government. Both initiatives demonstrate Seán MacBride's influence within that Government, although repeal ultimately benefited Costello and Fine Gael at the expense of MacBride and Clann na Poblachta and cemented the partition of Ireland, which Clann na Poblachta had vowed to end. Despite those circumstances, Ireland did gain from repeal by being able to ensure continued Commonwealth benefits while also making an important psychological claim to true independence.

There is a tendency to view Ireland's departure from the Commonwealth, as Anthony Jordan does in his biography of Seán MacBride, as the single most important act of the coalition Government.[25] Though a patriotically potent sentiment, it actually does a disservice to the Government, which did accomplish more, though not on such a grand or public scale. However, the available evidence, although some is contradictory or circumstantial, points to a different interpretation, bringing about a need for a more critical approach to the events concerned and their impact.

Ireland's move away from the Commonwealth was a gradual one. In 1931, the Statute of Westminster gave Commonwealth members the legal right to revoke treaties and to withdraw from the Commonwealth if they so wished. Upon becoming President of the Executive Council a year later, de Valera took advantage of the Statute and proceeded to remove from the Constitution the oath of allegiance to the British monarch. The link with the Commonwealth was further weakened after the abdication of King Edward VIII in 1936. De Valera's Government recognised the abdication and took the further step of omitting the King and the Governor-General from the Irish Constitution. He then decided to reappoint the King's successor by making him nominal head of External Relations. Britain accepted this External Relations Act as a sufficient link to retain Commonwealth membership. De Valera's Constitution omitted the previous Constitution's passage stating that 'the Irish Free State is a co-equal member of the community of Nations forming the British Commonwealth of Nations.' De Valera informed the British that this omission did not mean that Ireland would no longer be a member; it was there because he had assured his followers that when the new constitution came into existence, it would be written so as not to require an amendment if it was later decided to leave the Commonwealth.[26] Again, there was no protest from the British Government.

For de Valera and Fianna Fáil in 1932, the goal was to win power, then remove the restrictive features of the 1921 Treaty they had fought against. The main problems that de Valera had with the Treaty were that it did not provide the Irish Republic (merely a 'Free State') and it necessitated an Oath of Allegiance to the British monarch. He removed the Oath after the Statute of Westminster, but hesitated in declaring Ireland a Republic, largely because he believed that such a declaration would strengthen partition, and if he declared the Republic, he would do so for thirty-two counties, not twenty-six. However, it can be argued that he held back more out of a sense of political timing and a wish to avoid direct challenge to Britain than his professed concern for the ending of partition.[27]

When asked in the Dáil whether he intended officially to proclaim Ireland a Republic, he replied:

> we are a democracy with the ultimate sovereign power resting with the people — a representative democracy with the various organs of State functioning under a written Constitution, with the executive authority controlled by Parliament, with an independent judiciary functioning under the Constitution and the law, and with a Head of State directly elected by the people for a definite term of office.[28]

De Valera thus maintained that Ireland already functioned as a republic and proceeded to read out dictionary and encyclopaedia definitions of the word 'republic' to prove the point.

De Valera's reluctance provided the impetus for Seán's newly formed Clann na Poblachta to make the claim that it was the true republican party. De Valera and Fianna Fáil had had sixteen years in office to declare Ireland a republic; the fact that they had not, bolstered the Clann's claim that tedium had set in. In a letter to *The Irish Times*, Seán criticised the notion of a 'dictionary republic' which 'in no way satisfies the traditional aspiration of the republican section of our own people' and stressed his party's desire for a *de jure* rather than *de facto* republic.[29]

Clann na Poblachta had pledged to establish an Irish republic during the 1948 general election. Having secured only ten seats in the Dáil, Seán admitted that his party could not

> claim that in this election we secured a mandate from the people that would enable us to repeal, or seek to repeal the External Relations Act and such other measures as are inconsistent with our status as an independent republic. These, therefore, have to remain in abeyance for the time being.[30]

Fine Gael, the party with the majority of seats in the new Government, had campaigned on retaining the Commonwealth connection. After the first Dáil session, *The Irish Times* editorialised 'we may assume, therefore, that so long as the new Government remains in office there will be no interference with the existing condition of affairs.'[31]

Despite the Government's assertion that declaring Ireland a republic would have to wait, Costello announced after a mere seven months in power that the Government would be declaring a republic. The eventual repeal of the External Relations Act itself was expected, but the time and place of the announcement led to conflicting rumours and interpretations.

It was becoming obvious within the Government that Ireland planned to leave the Commonwealth at some stage. As Seán stated in July, 'The Crown and outward forms that belong to British constitutional history are merely reminders of an unhappy past that we want to bury, that have no realities for us and only serve as irritants.'[32] A letter from Assistant Secretary of External Affairs Frederick Boland to the High Commissioner in Canada, John Hearne, dated 21 August 1948, reads 'it is generally accepted here now that the days of the External Relations Act are numbered . . . you will probably have deduced as much from the Minister's statement when introducing the External Affairs Estimate in the Dáil.'[33] While Taoiseach, de Valera had prepared draft bills for repeal in November 1947 and in January 1948, and Fine Gael Deputy James Dillon stated in the Dáil that 'I observe that Deputy MacBride contemplates a long postponement of some objectives near his heart [achievement of the republic], but I am more optimistic than he.'[34]

It may have been apparent that Ireland's days in the Commonwealth were coming to an end, but it was not clear as to whether a formal cabinet decision had been reached to depart officially. There was no record of any decision made in cabinet meetings prior to Costello's trip to Canada, where the official announcement was delivered. According to an interview Nicholas Mansergh had with Boland, the inter-party Government had unclear views on repeal until the summer of 1948 when the issue of attendance at the October meeting of the Commonwealth prime ministers' conference led to discussion on Ireland's role within the Commonwealth.[35] F.S.L. Lyons believes that there had been a prior cabinet decision to repeal the act but uncertainty remains about when such a decision was reached.[36] The discussion could have taken place at a cabinet subcommittee meeting, as there were no minutes taken at such meetings. Both Costello and MacBride maintained that a decision was reached that summer. It can be surmised that an 'unofficial' decision had been made and there is evidence that Ireland's connection to the Commonwealth was on the Government's mind. Issues of citizenship legislation were under discussion between London and Dublin and the accreditation of the new Argentinean Minister directly to the President of Ireland rather than the King appeared to be another small but important severance in the Commonwealth connection. Seán felt that the Minister's accreditation signalled 'what I would regard as the first step towards the repeal of the External Relations Act and towards Ireland's departure from the Commonwealth.'[37]

On 21 July, Independent (former Clann na Poblachta) Deputy Peadar Cowan stated in the Dáil that 'we in this House should make it perfectly clear that we do intend to take the steps that will establish this country as an independent Republic, whatever those steps may be, and whatever sacrifices may be necessary in the process.'[38] On 6 August, Tánaiste William Norton put the question to de Valera, now leader of the Opposition:

> AN TÁNAISTE: I said it then and I repeat it again now . . . I think it would do our national self respect good both at home and abroad if we were to proceed without delay to abolish the External Relations Act.
>
> MR DE VALERA: Go ahead . . . You will get no opposition from us.[39]

It is reasonable to say that by August the scene had been set. On 10 August 1948, at a cabinet meeting, Seán recommended that Ireland should not attend the October Commonwealth conference.[40] Yet there was no sign of preparation for an upcoming declaration, repeal of the External Relations Act was not on Seán's proposed agenda for the October cabinet meeting, and there is no record of him seeking any type of preliminary forum to discuss with either Britain or any Commonwealth countries Ireland's departure from the Commonwealth. Thus the cabinet had informally decided on repeal, but had made no substantial plans.

Not only was there controversy regarding any official cabinet decision, but the choice of venue for the public announcement has been the subject of some debate, as vastly conflicting versions exist of what, why, when, and how the announcement happened. As Costello said later,

> the most extraordinary, fantastic and completely unfounded statements were issued from various sources, generally to the effect either that I had without any consultation or authority from my colleagues in the Government 'declared the Republic in Canada' or else in a fit of pique at something that is supposed to have happened at a function.[41]

The Taoiseach was invited by the President of the Canadian Bar Association to attend a gathering in Montreal from 31 August to 4 September. The Canadian Government then invited Costello to be its 'official guest' for the duration of his visit, and several receptions were held in Costello's honour. Yet the trip was not an 'official' or state visit; he was there in his capacity as a barrister who happened to be Taoiseach of Ireland.[42] It was Costello's first trip abroad in an unclear capacity; he was not yet fully confident of his role, and he was there without MacBride or any departmental 'minders'. According to Costello, when drafting his speech for the Bar Association dinner, entitled 'Ireland and International Affairs', he was aware that a government decision had already been taken to repeal the External Relations Act, and the process was supposed to begin when the Dáil resumed in October.

Costello delivered the speech on 1 September. He criticised the 'lack of a precise and formal definition of legal and constitutional relationships' between Britain and Ireland, declaring that 'the harp without the Crown symbolised the ideal of Irish independence and nationhood . . . the whole purpose of our national struggle was to free ourselves from those British institutions which, as the inevitable consequence of our history, had become associated in our minds with the idea of national subjection.'[43] The talk was well-received and Costello prepared to attend several dinners in his honour.

Problems began due to issues of diplomacy. Costello was asked in Montreal by Louis St Laurent, the Canadian Minister for External Affairs, if a toast to the King would cover him as well. Costello attempted to explain: 'I had to argue, that it did not, because we were not real members of the Commonwealth',[44] but he was not positive that the distinction was clear. A dinner with the Governor-General, Lord Alexander, had been planned to take place in Ottawa on 4 September, and the Irish Embassy had previously 'indicated to the Department that the Taoiseach would not attend the dinner unless the toast of the President was honoured. The Governor-General's Private Secretary confirmed by 'phone that the procedure regarding toasts would be observed as agreed with the Department of External Affairs.'[45] However, the Governor-General did not toast the President of Ireland, a serious breach of protocol. The King was honoured and Costello complied, but he was disconcerted by the slight. He was not enraged, however, and seemed to believe that the toast situation was a confirmation of the confusing status of Ireland within the Commonwealth.

According to Noël Browne, Costello felt that there was 'a certain coolness' at the reception. The Governor-General had seemed stand-offish in his few exchanges with the Taoiseach, including snubbing him at a garden party at McGill University in Montreal.[46] Costello was unhappy with the seating arrangement at the banquet table, and the replica placed in front of him of 'Roaring Meg', a cannon used by Protestants against Catholics in the Siege of Derry in 1689 bearing the legend 'The walls of Derry and no surrender'. A Canadian External Affairs briefing reported that the replica 'is constantly used by the Governor General as a centerpiece on the dining room table at formal functions.'[47] However, Alexander was a member of a prominent unionist family from Tyrone and would have realised the significance of the replica. Costello was annoyed, but according to his assistant, Patrick Lynch, he was restrained and polite to his hosts.[48] He made no comment during dinner but later asked John Hearne what should be done, as, at the time, he believed that the Governor-General's actions were intentional: 'I was of the opinion for some considerable time that the failure to honour the Toast of the President was a deliberate action on the part of the Governor General. I am now convinced that for some reason, whether through negligence or otherwise, the Governor General was never informed.'[49] As for Roaring Meg, Costello merely remarked that the replica was in 'very bad taste', but not a calculated insult.[50] Hearne reported later that

> I have got no explanation on why the Governor General did not give the toast of the Uachtarán. As I told you I had mentioned the matter of toasts to the Chef de Protocol . . . I have not asked why the Governor General did not give it; nor whether he was asked why he had a particular replica as a centre-piece on his table when you were his guest of honour. But I shall not leave Canada without letting Pearson know how we felt about it.[51]

In his autobiography, Browne wrote that Costello simply lost his temper and, in a burst of anger, declared that Ireland was leaving the Commonwealth;

Boland confirms this explanation.[52] Mansergh calls Costello an 'impulsive and somewhat inexperienced' politician who took umbrage at his treatment in Canada.[53] He further states that ill-temper is the only way to explain the odd timing of the announcement.

However, these assessments seem inaccurate, as Costello did not make the announcement until three days after the dinner, which would have given him time to consider such a move. In those three days, he could have calmed down, communicated with the cabinet, and carefully considered his position. British Prime Minister Clement Attlee believed that the announcement was spontaneous and once Costello declared that Ireland was leaving, he could not retreat from what he had said,[54] similar to Cortes burning his ships upon reaching the New World. Yet it seems unlikely that he delivered an impromptu speech, later realised its consequences, and then felt that he could not back down. Lyons's personal impression of Costello was that he was an admirable chairman equipped with tact and patience who made the coalition harmonious — hardly someone who would commit to a rash course of action without considering the outcome.[55] He was a skilled lawyer who had experience on the international stage and was not easily tempted into indiscretion. The American Minister to Ireland, George Garrett, agreed: 'Mr Costello is inclined to be a prudent, conservative lawyer not given to irresponsible statements.'[56] In any case, it is not clear that Costello took the Ottawa slight seriously. Indeed, David Johnson of Canada's Department of External Affairs, wrote that 'on the numerous times that I have seen Mr Costello . . . he has never made any reference to these slights or given the impression that he was upset by any incident that happened in Canada.'[57]

There is another very plausible explanation to account for the strange timing of the announcement. Costello was pushed into an awkward situation; on 5 September, the *Sunday Independent* reported that the Government intended to repeal the External Relations Act. When Canadian journalists inquired about the article, he responded with 'no comment'. But a press conference had been arranged two days later in Canada's House of Commons, where the question was sure to come up again.

Costello suspected that someone with insider information had leaked the story (which assumes that there was a story to leak), but the author of the article, Hector Legge, assured him that he had no inside source, that he had just drawn astute conclusions based on what had been said in the Dáil and on MacBride's recent press release quoting parts of Costello's speech. The *Sunday Independent* was known as a Fine Gael paper. Its editor was friendly with members of the party; therefore suspicion would fall not only on Seán, the staunch republican, but also on other, equally likely, sources, such as James Dillon. However, Louie O'Brien, Seán's secretary, would later reveal that he was the source, though she claims that she herself did not know it at the time.[58] In a conversation with Mansergh in 1952, Costello revealed that he believed that Seán was indeed the source.[59]

Had he grown impatient with the progress being made towards repeal of the External Relations Act, even though he recognised that the inter-party Government did not have a mandate for such a decision? Did he use the opportunity presented by Costello's Canadian tour to hurry legislation along? Legge has consistently denied that a leak occurred, and after the article appeared, Seán telegraphed Costello immediately, instructing him to say 'no comment'. Advising Costello not to say anything is a strange response if Seán had been the leak. It is more than likely that he would have encouraged Costello to confirm it and comment on the Government's plans. Maffey assessed Seán MacBride by writing, 'in office he so far shows restraint and a strong sense of responsibility.'[60] If Maffey's opinion is correct, surreptitiously leaking the information appears out of character. Seán had no ostensible reason for wanting a republic declared so quickly; it would be wiser to wait and ensure that he and his party could claim credit.

Costello gave consideration to how he should respond. According to Lynch, Costello had discussed the repeal of the Act with Hearne and himself on 6 September, the day before the press conference, and had also spoken to Seán. Costello decided not to comment, but before going to bed, he changed his mind, 'as he feared that if he equivocated Mr de Valera would take the initiative.'[61] Ultimately the newspaper article forced the decision much more than the diplomatic slights.

Costello did not follow MacBride's directive. He believed that issuing a 'no comment', though 'well intentioned, was one that I felt would not be permitted by my questioners to adopt.'[62] At the press conference on 7 September, he confirmed the accuracy of the report and revealed that the cabinet 'unanimously agreed' to repeal the External Relations Act on resumption of the Dáil.[63] In an *Irish Times* interview in 1967, Costello said that the announcement had nothing to do with the diplomatic slights in Canada, but had been brought about from questions arising from the newspaper article. As he wrote to Norton, 'It was really the article in the *Sunday Independent* that decided me, although I had intended to tell Mr Mackenzie King [the Canadian Prime Minister] . . . of our intentions in that regard.'[64] He had been bludgeoned with examples of the ambiguities in both the External Relations Act and in the relationship between Ireland and the Commonwealth during his trip and since he was sure that a cabinet decision, however unofficial, had been made, there was little reason not to verify the story.

Most commentators then and now agree that repeal itself was not an unexpected development. Despite its inevitability, the announcement was badly timed, leading to the thought that 'a crucially important constitutional decision had been made in an arbitrary fashion several thousand miles away.'[65] Costello obviously felt that he had to address the *Independent* article, but as Lyons wrote, the Irish people deserved to have the proclamation made on their soil.[66] The announcement made international news and Costello was the guest of honour at official dinners as the Canadian Government tried to ascertain what was happening.

Apparently, Costello's decision to announce impending repeal came as a surprise to some cabinet members like Browne, Dillon, and perhaps MacBride, who was informed while at dinner at the Russell Hotel with Maffey. He stated that Seán appeared surprised at the news: 'I certainly got the strong impression that he was a little surprised — indeed perturbed — by this sudden unconventional development.'[67] Seán appeared to express shock, but later in two separate interviews with *The Irish Times* said that he was not surprised, that 'this was no surprise to me or to any other Minister.'[68] This is incorrect, as many of the ministers were indeed surprised. He stated that

> Lord Rugby may have been quite right when he says that I looked surprised when, on the night of September 7th, 1948, I received copies of news agency reports indicating that our intention to repeal the External Relations Act was being treated as an unexpected sensation. I *was* astonished that anyone should be surprised, particularly in view of the speeches made for some months and the banner headlines which had appeared in one of our leading newspapers only four days before.[69]

Certainly Seán would not want to admit that he was not aware of what was happening in Canada, as this not only implied a lack of control over his department but also represented Costello usurping an issue that the Clann had made its own. He may have been puzzled that Costello had not followed his advice not to comment on the situation.

According to Browne, after he returned from Canada, Costello told ministers that he had decided on repeal while attending a government dinner in his honour. Apparently, he later realised that he had no authority to make the statement and was distressed. He called a cabinet meeting to explain and apologise and offered to resign. As MacBride was not present, Browne spoke for Clann na Poblachta and told Costello not to resign, as the Clann was glad to see the act go.

Whether this meeting ever took place provoked yet another controversy. When Browne told this story in a radio interview in 1976, Dillon, Daniel Morrissey, Seán MacBride, and Patrick McGilligan claimed that no such meeting had ever happened. But in 1983, Browne reviewed Ronan Fanning's *Independent Ireland* and again stated that Costello had held a cabinet meeting after the Canadian trip and had offered to resign, as well as reassuring Fanning that 'no Cabinet decision or papers could exist since no formal Cabinet decisions had taken place.'[70] Within days, Seán once again countered Browne's claim about the aftermath of Costello's Canadian trip: 'there was no such Cabinet meeting and Mr Costello did not offer his resignation.'[71] When Seán, in the process of writing his memoirs, asked Lynch what his recollection was, Lynch replied,

> On Tuesday 7 Sept. at 10.30 a.m. Taoiseach gave press conference. He announced Government's intention to repeal the External Relations Act and said 'yes' to a question relating to Ireland's leaving the Commonwealth . . . I have no recollection of any meeting of Ministers in Mr Costello's own house during the week after his return from Canada as alleged by Dr Browne.[72]

Browne's account may have some basis in fact; minute-taking at meetings was notoriously careless, Boland agreed with his account, and Browne did stand in for MacBride when he was away. A vulnerable cabinet had to present a united front at the time and may have continued to do so long afterwards. An unrecorded cabinet meeting may have taken place on 7 October.[73]

Yet Browne's attendance at cabinet meetings was admittedly erratic; he missed the 19 August 1948 meeting where the cabinet discussed attendance at the Commonwealth Conference. Seán had complained many times about Browne's frequent absences. Meetings themselves departed from the normal administrative convention. In large part because of Seán's suspicion of civil servants, Chief Whip Liam Cosgrave took notes and, as Lynch recalls,

> Often there were ad hoc meetings of Ministers: these could be tantamount to government meetings because they frequently took decisions. Not all Ministers need be present at any government meetings . . . and if Mr Cosgrave were not present the procedure for recording a decision for transmission to the Secretary to the Government could easily be overlooked.[74]

Not all decisions were fully and accurately recorded which led to the suggestion that repeal and republic were Costello's personal decisions. Seán would always maintain that the decision was a cabinet one with the implication that the impetus came from Clann na Poblachta.[75]

The cabinet did meet on 9 September immediately after Costello's press conference. Six members did not attend, including Cosgrave, so there is a question of who took the minutes. Because of the slipshod nature of recording and the persistence of conflicting memory, with everyone equally definite that their version is correct, the exact sequence of events will remain unclear. Seán quickly drafted a bill transferring the functions of the King to the President of Ireland. A month passed before a meeting attended by all government ministers formally and retroactively approved the action taken by Costello in Canada, thus averting any constitutional crisis, and another month elapsed before the Government finally considered its repeal legislation in detail.[76]

Attlee commented that one of the ironies of Ireland's declaring the Republic was that de Valera, thought to be the extremist republican, did not sever ties, but Costello of Fine Gael, still seen as the 'pro-Commonwealth' party, did.[77] After the announcement, those who had voted for Fine Gael felt betrayed. As Garret FitzGerald recalled,

Joan and I had canvassed for Fine Gael from door to door in Mr Costello's constituency of Dublin Townships (now Dublin South-East). My understanding . . . was that Fine Gael supported Commonwealth membership, and Joan and I canvassed accordingly, we particularly remember reassuring the inhabitants of Waterloo Road on that point.[78]

Senator J.W. Bigger remarked during the Seanad debates on the Republic of Ireland bill,

I and thousands of others in this country voted at the last election for Fine Gael, confident that the Leaders of that Party were honest men, upon whose good faith we could rely. It was believed that their policy might be taken on its face value and not subject to legal quibbles. The statements upon which I chiefly relied were those of General Mulcahy and of Mr Costello. When General Mulcahy was elected President of Fine Gael he said: — 'We stand unequivocally for membership of the British Commonwealth.' That plank in the Fine Gael Party programme, as far as I am aware, has never been withdrawn.[79]

Bigger was correct; during the campaign there had been no mention by any Fine Gael cabinet members of repeal. MacBride was also correct about the lack of a mandate for leaving the Commonwealth. Maffey observed, 'They [Fine Gael] are all somewhat bewildered by their own sudden illogical iconoclasm and must now find high sounding phrases to justify it.'[80] The press focused considerably on the accountability of Fine Gael: 'many thousands of Fine Gael's electoral supporters are thoroughly disgusted at the whole business' whereas MacBride and Clann na Poblachta 'have at least been consistent.'[81]

Why did Fine Gael, who, only a few years earlier had extolled the benefits of belonging to the Commonwealth, decide to take Ireland out of it? Frustrated with the imprecise definition of status, Costello himself found the External Relations Act 'untidy and inadequate.' He knew that it had been a divisive issue since the Civil War and solving it would justify breaking with Fine Gael tradition. As Nicholas Mansergh wrote, dominion status 'evoked only misgiving in Irish minds. They craved, whether wisely or not is beside the point, for precise, logical definitions.'[82] The nature of the link between Britain and Ireland remained vague, despite de Valera's attempts to define it through 'external association', sovereignty in internal affairs but associated with the Commonwealth for the purposes of external concerns.

In addition, the balance of parties in coalition made the Dáil highly susceptible to initiative from what Costello called 'some person not well disposed to the government' — for example, someone like Peadar Cowan introducing his own bill in the Dáil — and an absence of any agreed government policy could mean the end of the coalition. All that the parties had in common was a desire to oust Fianna Fáil and to end partition. They had already replaced Fianna Fáil and since ending partition was not immediately possible, repeal may have 'appealed as something to which all might subscribe without the straining of some few tender consciences.'[83] The inter-party Government was especially vulnerable on the republican flank, especially in light of de Valera's recent anti-partition tour through the United States. Repeal could help the Government to prove its worth on the all-important national question. Some may have felt betrayed by the change in Fine Gael policy, by (as Seán MacEntee called them) 'Republican wolves masquerading as Commonwealth sheep',[84] but the party did strengthen its position in the 1951 general election, gaining nine seats in the Dáil, so perhaps the disappointment had worn off in time for the next election.

The Republic accomplished a great deal for Fine Gael: it gave the party the opportunity to best Fianna Fáil; it helped to reinvigorate Fine Gael's image as a serious party whose patriotism was just as fervent as that of its competition.

As his son-in-law Alexis Fitzgerald wrote to Costello, 'by one stroke of genius, politically, you have placed Fine Gael back in the centre of the national tradition right where Mick Collins had it.'[85] Fine Gael would no longer be seen as pro-British or anti-national; it was 'in government doing things rather than an ageing party of sterile opposition living on its memories.'[86]

Repeal signalled both the first steps toward Fine Gael's political ascendancy and Seán MacBride's inability to safeguard his ideological territory.[87] Not only did it benefit Fine Gael, it helped Costello to assert his authority as Taoiseach and showed him to be a clever political tactician. He gained the upper hand, both by declaring the Republic in Canada, away from his cabinet and without Seán's approval, and by introducing the Republic of Ireland Bill in the Dáil. Though declaring the Republic was largely accidental and forced by circumstance, Costello managed to take control and make the issue his own. He 'took the gunman out of Irish politics' by pacifying the IRA, whose members were probably pleased that de Valera could not take credit for establishing the Republic. The Republic of Ireland Act showed Seán's clout, therefore it would be supported by the IRA, where it was rumoured that he and the Clann still had ties.

MacBride possessed the highest public profile of any cabinet member. Because of his lineage and prior career, his republican credentials were incontestable. His appointment as Minister for External Affairs guaranteed that the issue of repeal would come up; the Clann had put repeal of the External Relations Act and declaration of the Republic at the forefront of its programme during the election campaign.

Did MacBride directly influence Costello to declare the Republic? The Secretary of Commonwealth Relations, Philip Noel-Baker, believed so, as he said to High Commissioner of Ireland John Dulanty on 7 September: 'My own guess is that Sean put him up to it.'[88] Yet Costello denies that he made the statement because of pressure from Seán who was allegedly under pressure from the IRA. Repeal was not a price paid by Costello for Seán and his party's support in government; the confusing situation of a republic at home and a monarchy abroad had provided the impetus for Costello's decision, a decision made without formal cabinet consultation and apparently without consulting his own party. Costello later stated, 'Seán MacBride did not influence me in the slightest . . . I must give him full credit that while it was an issue of his party's policy, he never at any stage tried to influence me in that direction.'[89] But Costello, without MacBride, may not have pushed the issue of repeal as far as it would go. The *Clann na Poblachta Bulletin* of 1950 encapsulates this opinion:

Sean MacBride generously gave the Government . . . whole credit for this
republican step. But does anyone seriously imagine that the Act would
have been repealed if Clann na Poblachta had never existed? Fine Gael was
a Commonwealth party. Fianna Fáil had passed the External Relations
Act, thereby helping to drive genuine republicans to extreme measures.[90]

Whether Seán 'generously' gave credit to the Government is debateable; it
seems that he merely made the best of Costello's appropriation. However,
Costello's repeated denials that repeal was the 'pound of flesh' owed to Seán
for his party's continued participation in government paradoxically
demonstrates that he did influence the situation even if he did not directly use
repeal as a bargaining device.

Because of the coalition situation, Seán was in a position to exert more
influence than his portfolio would normally allow and he proved to be a
highly active minister in terms of both expanding his department and
adopting policy initiatives.[91] Although Costello eventually overshadowed
him, MacBride's name will always be closely linked with the decision to repeal
the External Relations Act. As Cruise O'Brien wrote in his *Leader* piece on
Seán, 'His main achievement — apart from giving the Fianna Fáil
Government a short holiday — was to get the Commonwealth party to take
Ireland out of the Commonwealth.'[92]

Costello announced on 13 November that he, not MacBride, would
introduce the Republic of Ireland Bill to the Oireachtas, stating that he
wanted 'to place the question of Irish sovereignty and status beyond dispute
or suspicion or guesswork.'[93] Normally, Seán, as Minister for External Affairs,
would have introduced the bill. Costello may have decided to proceed in this
way because of his impatience with the ambiguities of the External Relations
Act and his determination not to have any uncertainties with the bill, or to
show his resolve 'to assert his position as the principle source of foreign policy
in the government.'[94] MacDermott posits that Costello wanted to assert
authority over MacBride, who he suspected of backing him into a corner.[95] It
may have been done to placate pro-Commonwealth Fine Gael supporters: as
Fitzgerald advised him, 'people [must] be taken behind the scenes of your
own mind before you made the decision and that your justification when the
Act is introduced by you (as you must *insist* it should be) should have regard
to your own Fine Gael origins.'[96] Costello's introduction of the bill in the Dáil
made a statement. He was the one in charge. He asserted his position at the
expense of MacBride, and even Browne, hardly a fan of MacBride, thought
the usurpation ungracious.[97]

The bill was passed by the Seanad on 15 December 1948 and signed six days later by President Seán T. O'Kelly in a ceremony attended by Costello and MacBride. Seán stated publicly that the Bill 'will enable Ireland to be regarded internationally as a republic, and will thus enable her to play her part in international affairs.'[98] The Republic would be inaugurated on Easter Monday 1949, thirty-three years after the Easter Rising. Goodwill messages were received from all world leaders, except those from communist countries.

According to Browne, Seán protested his diminished role by not appearing at the Easter Monday celebrations. Actually, he did not attend because he was in the United States at a State Department Conference.[99] As Maud Gonne MacBride attended, it does not seem likely that Seán was exceedingly irritated. In Samuel Levenson's biography of Maud, he mentions a photo in *Life* magazine detailing the Easter Monday celebrations describing 'important figures leaving the Pro-Cathedral after Mass on that day; among them was Maud Gonne MacBride, leaning on the arm of her son.' This was actually Seán's son Tiernan.[100]

No matter what his reasons for not attending, Seán failed to capitalise on this symbolic turning point which, at a later stage, would be remembered as an act of great statesmanship. De Valera and Fianna Fáil boycotted the festivities, stating that celebrating was out of place as long as partition still existed. Instead, he spent the day at Arbour Hill, praying for the men of 1916.

Despite the later packaging of repeal as a high point of the inter-party Government, there are signs that the Irish public was slightly cynical about the move. A barman commented, 'Sure, it's all politics. Costello and his crowd have wiped Dev's eye and now Dev is trying to get his own back on them.'[101] As *The Times* reported a day after the celebrations, 'the truth is that the people are not greatly enamoured of Mr Costello's republic. They regard the introduction of the repeal of the External Relations Act as a piece of rather cute politics on the part of Mr Costello . . . They believe that the declaration of the republic will make little constitutional change and that it is intended largely as window dressing and as an attempt to embarrass Mr De Valera.'[102] Brian Inglis wrote in 'An Irishman's Diary', 'There were loud cheers, but they were the cheers of people tired of just standing there waiting for something to happen.' The Irish Grand National at Fairyhouse Racecourse competed with the celebrations, which may explain not only the absence of huge crowds but also the priorities of the Irish people.

There was a noted lack of genuine warmth in Easter festivities; Inglis quotes a spectator:

Who did you expect to do the cheering? Not Costello supporters after the way he went back on them after the Commonwealth link. Not de Valera after the way he has taken it himself, and not the Clann; they won't start cheering until we get back the six other counties. I don't know who you thought was going to cheer.[103]

If members of the Irish cabinet were surprised by the announcement, the British Government had even less warning. The Government may have believed that repeal would happen in the future, but was not aware of any firm immediate plans. In a report dated 17 August, Noel-Baker stated that Anglo-Irish relations were friendly and that he did not expect any action before the Dáil resumed at the end of the summer recess.[104] Foreign Secretary Ernest Bevin wrote to John Hearne that he 'regretted the declaration of the Republic and that it was a great surprise to him when Costello went that far.'[105]

Yet there were hints that the British were not terribly enthusiastic about the idea of external association. Ireland's role within the Commonwealth was ambiguous, as Maffey wrote to Sir Eric Machtig before the general election:

> Personally I should not be sorry to see this strange device removed. The Irish have handled it in such a way as to discredit it. Furthermore, it is now clear that it will not provide the bridge to closer association, as was once hoped. Indeed, it may well be that its removal will make closer association easier.[106]

In Bevin's own papers, there is a notable absence of material relating to Ireland's repeal of the External Relations Act. But then Bevin did not believe that the Foreign Office should take responsibility for Irish business.[107] The Commonwealth Office was responsible but Secretary Noel-Baker left in his papers no personal letters or correspondence regarding Ireland, just a few newspaper clippings. Attlee's own memoirs include only a brief treatment on Ireland leaving the Commonwealth.

There are several explanations for the absence of extensive material relating to Ireland. Many other matters were preoccupying the British at the time. The need to convert from a wartime to a peacetime economy, an almost continuous succession of currency and trading crises, and the division of global politics into hostile, competing Cold War camps kept Attlee's Government busy during the late 1940s.

In the area of colonial policy, Labour did not yet have a coherent political philosophy linking attitudes of colonial issues with socialist policy. Imperial/colonial policies were not an obvious or impressive aspect of Labour policies before the Second World War and its 1945 election manifesto, *Let Us*

John MacBride, 'a wiry, soldierly-looking man with red hair and skin'. (*Topfoto*)

Maud Gonne, c. 1890, 'with beauty like a tightened bow... Being high and solitary and most stern.' (*Hulton Archive/Getty*)

William Butler Yeats and his wife George in 1923. (*Hulton Archive/Getty*)

Dubliners celebrate the release of IRA men imprisoned at Arbour Hill Prison after Éamon de Valera's new Fianna Fáil government authorised their release in 1932. (*Hulton Archive/Getty*)

'Extreme chauvinists or incorrigible Celts, disgruntled IRA, a few ex-communists, and some political adventurers…' An early Clann political rally. (*Time Life Pictures/Getty*)

'The ballyhoo of politics': Seán speaking at a political rally in Dublin during the 1948 election campaign. (*Time Life Pictures/Getty*)

'It's your country.' Speeches during the 1948 general election. (*Hulton Archive/Getty*)

Seán speaking in Arklow, Co. Wicklow, in February 1948. (*Time Life Pictures/Getty*)

Seán at Clann na Poblachta headquarters shortly before the 1948 general election. (*Time Life Pictures/Getty*)

Maud Gonne MacBride, with Seán, casting her ballot in the 1948 election. (*Bettmann/Corbis*)

The Irish Times announces the election results. (*Time Life Pictures/Getty*)

The MacBride family, 1948. *(Left to right)*: Anna, Maud, Seán, and Kid, with one of the many family pets. (*Time Life Pictures/Getty*)

John A. Costello and Seán being interviewed in 1948. (*Hulton-Deutsch Collection/Corbis*)

The inter-party Government: 'a cabinet of talent, temperament and torpor'. Front row (*left to right*): Noël Browne, Seán MacBride, William Norton, John A. Costello, Richard Mulcahy, Thomas O'Higgins, Timothy Murphy. Back row (*left to right*): Dan Morrissey, James Everett, Patrick McGilligan, Joseph Blowick, Seán MacEoin, James Dillon. (*Topfoto*)

Seán and US Secretary of State Dean Acheson during Seán's visit to America in April 1949. (*Topfoto*)

Iseult Stuart, Seán's half-sister, at Laragh Castle. (*Time Life Pictures/Getty*)

Roebuck House, Clonskeagh. It was purchased in 1922 by Maud Gonne MacBride and Charlotte Despard, and Seán lived there until his death in 1988. (*Time Life Pictures/Getty*)

Seán MacBride, second from left, waits to speak at an anti-partition meeting in Trafalgar Square on 16 September 1951. (*Topfoto*)

The launch of Amnesty International's campaign for the abolition of torture, on 11 December 1972. (*From left to right*): Lord Gardiner, Seán, and Secretary General of Amnesty Martin Ennals. (*Hulton Archive/Getty*)

Seán giving a telephone interview after learning of his Nobel Peace Prize, October 1974. (*Bettmann/Corbis*)

Seán pictured with his Nobel Peace Prize, received in Oslo in December 1974. (*Topfoto*)

The first meeting of the UNESCO International Commission for the Study of Communication Problems, on 14 December 1977. Seán is on the right. (*Topfoto*)

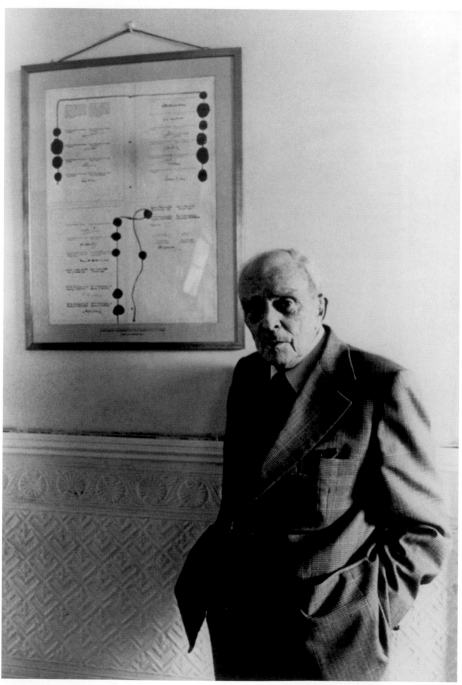

Seán stands beside a copy of the European Convention of Human Rights in 1983, 'a positive achievement of the first importance'. (*Topfoto*)

Face the Future, contained little detail on colonial proposals, showing dominion policy to be a peripheral concern. However, Britain still retained control of an enormous amount of territory including large blocks of Africa and the Middle East, as well as scattered territory, from the Fiji Islands to Hong Kong to the Falklands. So, in addition to solving Britain's post-war crises and establishing the welfare state, Attlee had to deal with the changing structure of colonial relations and help Labour to formulate and nurture a consistent colonial policy.

Furthermore, keeping Ireland within the Commonwealth was not all that vital. The negotiations following Costello's announcement seem similar to an amicable divorce with some squabbling over property. If Britain could continue a beneficial economic relationship, still retain territory in the North for defence purposes and could guarantee the constitutional status of the North, Ireland's presence within the Commonwealth was not crucial. In any case, domestic problems came first at the time. Indeed, even the much more momentous independence of India in 1947 had elicited little public concern, and the resolution of India's role in the Commonwealth took on far more importance than Ireland's imminent departure. One of the ironies of the situation was that as Ireland left, efforts were being made to ensure that India could remain within the Commonwealth even though the new Government was determined to establish a republic.

The Dáil recommended that Ireland should attend the October Commonwealth conference, but the invitation had been withdrawn and the Government then had to 'angle' for an invitation and persuade Commonwealth leaders to ensure that Ireland received it. MacBride and the Minister for Finance Patrick McGilligan attended the Commonwealth conference on 17 October at Chequers, as 'observers'. The challenge for the Irish Government was to preserve the advantages that had been Ireland's, while severing the symbolic ties that bound the two countries.

Britain's overseas dominions had a significant influence in Britain's not taking a hard line about repeal. Commonwealth nations affirmed that they would continue close relations with Ireland after it seceded. With the possible exception of Canadian Prime Minister Mackenzie King, Commonwealth ministers had no advance information, and the secession of Ireland was decided apart from the Commonwealth, but members, especially those with large Irish populations, like Canada, New Zealand, and Australia, respected Ireland's decision. The Canadian Government seemed to feel that 'the repealed External Relations Act would only formalize what for some time had been the de facto situation.'[108] A communiqué from T.J. Kiernan, the Irish Minister in Australia, to External Affairs, dated 11 February 1949, reported, 'it seems clear that the attitude, all around, to Ireland is unchanged by the legislation . . . they have no difficulty understanding the different historical background in Ireland and the objectivity and absence of rancour in our declaring the Republic.'[109] New Zealand passed the Republic of Ireland Act, stating that New Zealand law would operate toward Ireland 'as it would have if the Republic of Ireland had remained part of His Majesty's dominions.'[110]

The Chequers meeting was arranged on the initiative of Canada, Australia and New Zealand's representatives and would not have gone so well for Ireland without Commonwealth support. Lord Chancellor Jowitt stated in the House of Commons, 'If we had taken a different line from the one we decided to take, we should have acted in the teeth of the advice of the representatives of Canada, Australia, and New Zealand.'[111] Attlee, Noel-Baker, Lord Jowitt, and Secretary to the Cabinet Sir Norman Brook met with MacBride and McGilligan at Chequers to discuss informally the practical aspects of Ireland's secession. Attlee's cabinet thought that 'if they insisted on treating Eire as a foreign state . . . the practical difficulties would be greater for the United Kingdom than for Eire; and, furthermore, that they would thereby forfeit the sympathy and support of Canada, Australia, and New Zealand.'[112]

MacBride informed Attlee that repeal was not a hostile action — it was intended as 'a necessary preliminary to the restoration of friendly relations between Eire and the United Kingdom' because Ireland's difficulty of feeling subordinate to the crown prevented the development of friendly relations with Britain and the Commonwealth. McCabe calls the negotiations 'tortuous', but that did not seem to be the general perception; both *The Times* and *The Irish Times* noted that negotiations were cordial.[113] After further negotiations in Paris, the basic arrangement of trade, citizenship and immigration policies remained favourable to Ireland. There was no inconsistency in the British position; as Fanning argues, the abolition of the oath of allegiance, the External Relations Act, the 1937 Constitution, and the Republic of Ireland Act show a consistent pattern of the British Government choosing to ignore Irish policy, rather than to resist.[114]

It also helped that Attlee and MacBride had a good personal relationship; in August 1948, Attlee and his wife went on holiday in the west of Ireland, staying with Sir Anthony Bevir, one of his Downing Street advisors. Seán acted as tour guide, playing golf, and going sailing with the Prime Minister and Mrs Attlee. When the Republic of Ireland Bill passed in the Dáil, MacBride said,

I should like to pay a special tribute to the assistance which we received from the British Government in this matter. They met us with understanding and goodwill. Mr Attlee, the British Prime Minister, gave the matter a considerable amount of his personal time and I think I would express the views of my colleague the Minister for Finance, who was present during the discussions we had with him when I say that he impressed us by his high degree of integrity and his understanding approach to our problems.[115]

On 25 November, when the Republic of Ireland Bill was announced, Attlee informed Parliament that Irish citizens were not to be regarded as foreigners; the British Nationality Act of 1948 would continue to govern the position of Irish citizens in the United Kingdom, despite the Republic no longer being part of his Majesty's dominions, and the status of Irish residents in the United Kingdom would not be adversely affected.

In May 1949, Parliament's Ireland Act recognised Ireland's departure from the Commonwealth and was particularly beneficial to Ireland regarding citizenship and trading rights. These measures did not pass without argument — Lord Simon and Serjeant Sullivan inquired as to why Ireland was permitted to keep Commonwealth privileges if it was technically a foreign country. Conservatives were worried that the favourable treatment Ireland was receiving might upset relations with other Commonwealth nations. Despite these protests, the Bill became law and Attlee declared in the House of Commons, 'It is to be hoped that the Bill will be accepted both in the United Kingdom and in Eire as a common sense solution and a further step towards eliminating friction and bitterness.'[116]

But this was not to be, because of the Act's reaffirmation of Northern Ireland's status, declaring 'that Northern Ireland remains part of his Majesty's dominions and of the United Kingdom and affirms that in no event will Northern Ireland or any part thereof cease to be part of his Majesty's dominions and of the United Kingdom without the consent of the Parliament of Northern Ireland.' The Act denoted the official end of the 1922 Boundary Commission, which Michael Collins and other Treaty negotiators had hoped would redraw the border in the Free State's favour. Ultimately, the new Republic meant that the Irish question was no longer an issue for the British political elite; the position of Northern Ireland was secure and the rest of Ireland claimed republic status.[117] For the British, then, the Irish question had been answered.

Attlee believed that Britain must be firm about maintaining the position in Northern Ireland. Such action would please Conservatives, particularly after clashes over India. It was also necessary to reassure Northern Ireland, where the reaction was one of fright. Ireland's Constitution claimed jurisdiction over the entire island which, to unionists, meant that the declaration of the Republic was merely a prelude to a violent campaign to absorb the North. Unionists were afraid that Britain might waver in its commitment to Northern Ireland and did not see why Ireland was permitted to keep most Commonwealth benefits.

Attlee recognised the paradox involved, stating that it was 'obvious that the action of the Government of Eire in deciding to leave the Commonwealth would increase the difficulty of arriving at any agreement on partition.'[118] He concluded that the Irish 'considered that cutting the last tie which united Eire to the British Commonwealth a more important objective of policy than the ending of partition.'[119] Churchill believed that by declaring Ireland a republic 'Mr Costello and his colleagues have constituted themselves the authors of permanent partition.'[120]

How did the inter-party Government reconcile repeal and the ongoing demand for the removal of partition? Lyons points out that Clann na Poblachta saw no incompatibility between the two, which may indicate that they misjudged the strength and tenacity of both Northern unionism and the British willingness to protect the connection. Seán MacBride believed that unionists would eventually concede, writing to *The Irish Times* that 'their attachment to the Crown is more apparent than real' and that the feeling that a thirty-two-county Republic would not respect civil liberties was a 'prejudice' which, he said, 'I believe, will die with the generation that is now passing out.'[121] Even with the benefit of hindsight, his view of the situation seems remarkably naïve and confirms that MacBride did not recognise the finality in unionist rhetoric, preferring to see Ulster unionism through green-coloured glasses.

He believed that the development of an integrated Europe or the United Nations would provide a forum that a newly independent Republic could use to raise the issue of partition without having to appease the unionists. Costello argued that neither waiting to declare the Republic nor remaining in the Commonwealth had evoked the slightest response from the North, therefore it was pointless to continue to hope for a reconciliation that would not come.[122] As Costello said in the Dáil, 'Friendly overtures by this Government or any Government in this part of the country to the Northern Ireland Government would still be opposed by the same cascade of scorn and derision as had been directed by the northern ruling classes towards every constructive suggestion from Irish leaders for the ending of Partition.'[123] As Lee argues, if Northern Ireland Protestants were not convinced to consider unification to persuade Dublin to enter the Second World War, which in 1940 may have been an option, they would hardly be likely to unite because Dublin chose to remain in the Commonwealth.[124]

There may still have been opportunities for unity; the plan seemed to be to declare the Republic first, then solve the partition problem, much like a bear chewing off its leg to get out of a hunter's trap. Costello seemed to believe that repeal would help solve the partition problem; 'every section of this community in Ireland, every section of the Irish people, can unite with all their energies directed and not distracted towards a solution of this last political problem . . . We will have removed one of the two remaining causes of friction between this country and Great Britain,'[125] once again leaving Ulster unionists out of the equation. As in 1921, when the objective was to gain freedom from Britain and then solve unionist issues, de Valera and other nationalists may have failed to notice which difficulty was more intractable. It seemed that the inter-party Government was in a similar situation with repeal.

Aside from Commonwealth membership not providing a path to reunification, Ireland was uncomfortable with dominion status because it came too late and it came as a result of violence. As Costello argued in his Ottawa speech, 'by reason of their seven centuries of struggle with England and because of the fact that the political situations which grew up naturally in Britain and her Dominions . . . were imposed on Ireland, those could never really be acceptable to Irishmen.' Seán said in an interview with the *Manchester Guardian* on 21 September 1948 that there was no parallel between the history of Ireland and the other Commonwealth countries because

> descendants of the British pioneers who built the Commonwealth naturally take pride in their common British origin; they feel an affection for their home country and for the crown . . . Accordingly, the British Crown served as a traditional rallying point for them. But there is no similarity between our history and the history of the Commonwealth countries.

He made a similar point in his lecture to the Royal Institute of International Affairs, stating that Ireland had no real attachment to the monarchy based on national sentiment; rather the relationship involved protracted struggle where the crown was a symbol of oppression.[126] Such a symbol served as a psychological disadvantage and a rallying point for more extreme forms of nationalism. It would have been difficult to raise the issue of partition if Ireland were still a member of the Commonwealth; partition would remain a domestic issue, whereas leaving the Commonwealth could turn it into an international one. As Lyons eloquently wrote, Ireland remained deaf to the lure of the Commonwealth and 'in the end heard only the ghosts of Roger Casement and all those other dead men knocking on the door.'[127]

The Ireland Act was the first time the Parliament of Northern Ireland was given a veto over the political unification of the country, a high point of Ulster unionism.[128] Two days after the introduction of the Ireland Act, MacBride met with Attlee, then with Bevin and Noel-Baker, and Bevin explained to Seán that many in the Government were sympathetic to a united Ireland, but that

> we could not ignore the history of the last forty years. Northern Ireland had stood in with us against Hitler when the South was neutral. Without the help of the North, Hitler would unquestionably have won the submarine war and the United Kingdom would have been defeated . . . as a reward for this loyalty and until the majority in the North decided otherwise the British people would oblige us to give them guarantees that they would not be coerced.[129]

In a report to External Affairs, MacBride's reply to Bevin 'pointed out what should be obvious to a layman, that Partition was already legally in existence on the British statute book and it was unprecedented to re-enact a law that was already valid.'[130] Also the Irish had consulted with the British and Commonwealth governments regarding the Republic of Ireland Act, yet 'until the day before the "Ireland" Bill was introduced in the House of Commons no intimation, direct or indirect, was given to the Irish Government that it would contain these provisions.'

In response, Bevin exposed the irony of the situation, 'you are complaining of our having given no indication to you of this Government of Ireland Bill, why couldn't you have given us even a hint about the Republic of Ireland Act?'[131] The provision safeguarding the North was the only issue that the inter-party Government could argue with and they protested vehemently, leading to more anti-partition campaigning. R.F. Foster believes that the naïve reaction of Dublin to the Ireland Act showed both Costello's lack of skill and the insularity of post-war Ireland — the official line of Dublin continued to place on London all the blame for sustaining partition.[132] Placing responsibility there was unfair, as Attlee had informed MacBride that there would be no change in the status of Northern Ireland and the unionists would obviously protest the declaration of the Republic and want reassurance of Britain's commitment to maintaining the connection,

The inter-party Government officially protested in the Dáil, with Costello [placing] on record its indignant protest against the introduction in the British Parliament of legislation purporting to endorse and continue the existing partition of Ireland, and [calling] upon the British Government and people to end the present occupation of our six north-eastern counties, and thereby enable the unity of Ireland to be restored and the age-long differences between the two nations brought to an end.[133]

On 13 May, demonstrations were held on O'Connell Street in Dublin, featuring speeches by Costello, de Valera, MacBride, and Norton. Costello later stated that he thought the Ireland Act's reference to the North was an effort to please opposition leader Winston Churchill and the Conservative Party (once again paying little attention to the influence of Ulster unionists), but that Ireland was successful in securing its main demands, retaining all benefits without losses.[134]

It did not solve ambiguity issues on Britain's part; Ireland had once been 'excluded inside the Commonwealth', now it was 'included outside the Commonwealth'.[135] But Britain allowed Ireland to keep the Commonwealth perks because it benefited Britain as well. Other Commonwealth countries defended Ireland's position, and the Statute of Westminster provided Ireland with the legal right to secede and, as Attlee echoed de Valera, 'Eire was already a Republic in fact.'[136] Because of its close geographic location and tragic history, Ireland occupied a different position from other Commonwealth countries and 'few things in the relationship between the two countries have been logical.'[137]

In April 1949, the British Government announced the London Declaration, mainly as a means to keep India within the Commonwealth. The Declaration stated that Commonwealth countries could become republics, but the British monarch must be recognised as Head of the Commonwealth. Attlee felt that if Ireland had been patient, this might have been a possible solution to combine independence with improved constitutional relations with the UK.[138] This scenario is not likely; the promise of independence was essential to the Irish psyche, and following India's example may have created even further confusion in the relationship with Britain. Yet, within thirty years, Ireland would not have been out of place, as by then there were a majority of republics within the Commonwealth.

Ireland's departure did not fundamentally affect the Commonwealth. Mansergh predicted an obvious disadvantage to secession: Ireland being deprived of an opportunity for a voice in world affairs and Commonwealth countries not being able to exercise great influence on Ireland.[139] Lee takes an opposing view and speculates that Irish diplomats might have made worthy contributions, but it seems doubtful if an Irish absence made much difference to Ireland or to the Commonwealth.[140] The Council of Europe, the United Nations, and the OEEC could provide other avenues of partnership and cooperation, and the idea of wanting to pursue these avenues as an independent nation may have been tempting. The emphasis and direction of Irish foreign policy was changing from de Valera's method of working within the Commonwealth to MacBride's strategy of looking towards Western Europe.

Twenty years afterward, Costello claimed that the declaration of the Republic was one of the major achievements of the inter-party Government.[141] Seán MacEoin agreed and praised both Costello and MacBride: 'we now looked forward to a new dawn in Ireland's history, thanks to the statesmanship of John Costello and Seán MacBride and the unanimous support of the Dáil and Seanad.'[142] This is not an undisputed conclusion; Lee feels that the 'whole performance of the government . . . seems to have been a shambles from start to finish, perhaps the most inept diplomatic exhibition in the history of the state.'[143] Coogan contends that leaving the Commonwealth had harmful consequences which are still being felt, particularly in the relationship with Northern Ireland, 'as a result of Dublin's severance of its link with the Crown, a far stronger one was forged between Belfast and London.'[144] If the establishment of priorities is a fundamental feature of a productive foreign policy, then the events surrounding repeal show a lack of clear design and forethought in Anglo-Irish relations. The inter-party Government was indeed 'overwhelmed by the momentum of circumstance'[145] and repeal remains a dubious legacy. Essentially, fortunate timing and the intervention of other Commonwealth countries ensured that Ireland did not suffer negative consequences of leaving the Commonwealth.

However, MacBride should be recognised for his contribution to repeal because in the short run his negotiations helped to disguise the reactive rather than active posture of the inter-party Government, bolting the barn door after Costello had allowed the horse to escape. In the long term, his tactics helped Ireland to become involved in an integrated Europe, demonstrating his 'obsession with Ireland's international position'.[146] He showed an interest in politics of European cooperation and integration, which is not surprising considering his French background, and more generally, Irish nationalists' past habit of looking to France and Germany for help in 1798 and 1916 respectively.

Despite MacBride's Marshall Plan negotiations, OEEC, and Council of Europe dealings, these did not count as 'real' matters of foreign affairs — the action was in the nature of Ireland's relationship with Britain. Britain was, for a long time, the way Ireland defined herself, and Seán was attempting in those other examples, to move away from this, to define Ireland without Britain. Seán's personal assistant Caitriona Lawlor lists repeal among MacBride's prized accomplishments, 'MacBride was happy enough about the achievements of Clann na Poblachta in government — the repeal of the External Relations Act, the fact there were no political prisoners, and the significant increase in the afforestation figures.'[147]

Additionally, repeal was important from a psychological perspective. When asked by *The Irish Times* if repeal would improve relations with Britain, George Bernard Shaw answered, 'It will improve relations with everybody. This is not politics, but psychology.'[148] It removed much of the ambiguity and tension of the relationship between Britain and Ireland and gave the Irish a sense of self-determination and would help Ireland to establish an international identity separate from Britain. MacEoin believed that the External Relations Act 'lowered our own dignity as a nation.'[149] MacBride echoed this sentiment, stating that the Act 'was as repugnant to our national sentiment as it was unreal. As a constitutional fiction, it pleased no one.'[150] Furthermore, the move was politically astute for both Fine Gael and Clann na Poblachta.

Otherwise, repeal was not truly a radical move — it did not change much of the day-to-day relationship between Britain and Ireland, 'the country at large . . . will lose little sleep over this decision', and other formalities were discarded with little effect.[151] Leaving the Commonwealth had no discernible effect in practice; as Cruise O'Brien points out, de Valera's success in maintaining Ireland's neutrality during the Second World War had established the independence of the Irish state more convincingly than the declaration of the Republic.[152] The boundaries remained the same, as did Ireland's economic relationship to Britain. Repeal was successful because of the benevolent indifference of both Great Britain and the Commonwealth countries. There was little disapproval and no severe retaliatory action; the consensus was that Ireland's withdrawal should not affect friendly relations between Ireland and Commonwealth nations. Leaving the Commonwealth did not provide an answer to the deeper problem of partition; as MacBride commented, 'all obstacles to the creation of a better relationship, with the exception of partition, have now been removed.'[153] Of course, that particular obstacle was immense. Attlee later wrote, 'Much of the old bitterness between the English and Irish had passed away . . . but the division between the North and South was still a rankling sore.'[154]

What it did provide was a sense of autonomy and independence,

fundamental to how Ireland wanted to be perceived both by herself and by
other nations. Achievement of sovereignty took precedence over aspiration to
unity and sovereignty was incomplete as long as a formal link existed. In a
speech delivered on 8 April 1949, MacEoin declared that 'thirty-three years
after Padraig Pearse's historic declaration, we will be able to say, and have it
accepted all over the world, that in this part of the country we are an
absolutely sovereign Republic.'[155] Other countries were made aware of Irish
independence, providing a chance to find forums where Ireland was not seen
as a British appendage, which would please MacBride and perhaps provide a
way to publicise, if not solve, the problem of partition.

With Ireland a republic, ending partition became the last unachieved
nationalist goal. Partition would become the first great test of the inter-party
Government's foreign policy and ability to think in the long term rather than
bow to rhetoric. Irish diplomacy, for better or worse, would centre around the
issue and foreign policy would be seen mainly in the light of partition.

The inter-party Government's basic formula for ending partition involved
turning it into an international issue in order to put pressure on the British
Government to concede. According to Costello:

> We have faith in our capacity to persuade other nations of the justice of
> our cause as well as the harmful effects of Partition in preventing a united
> Ireland from playing that part in international affairs which our strategic
> position warrants. In our efforts to rouse world opinion on Partition we
> are securing the whole-hearted supported and influence of millions of
> Irishmen and the friends of Ireland throughout the American continent,
> the British Commonwealth and the world generally.[156]

It is easy to understand why the inter-party Government thought this 'sore
thumb' strategy might be successful. Attlee himself appeared amenable even
if his Government did not. Though still not a member of the United Nations,
Ireland was becoming more involved in European cooperative bodies, which
would allow them to raise the partition question within those bodies. A large
emigrant population in America and the British Commonwealth gave Ireland
the ability to 'punch above her weight'. As Costello declared in the Dáil,
'Though we are a small nation, we wield an influence in the world far in excess
of what our mere physical size and the smallness of our population might
warrant.'[157] As the inter-party Government believed that partition was unjust
and unnatural, surely all they would need to do was expose the injustice to
gain sympathy.

However, there were several flaws. The inter-party Government may have overestimated Ireland's strategic position, counting too much on the United States, who wanted to maintain a close relationship with Britain during the Cold War and who still held negative memories of Irish neutrality during the Second World War, and placing too much blame on Britain for sustaining partition. Constant reference to the issue left the impression within the international community that Ireland had no interest in wider concerns. Perhaps the greatest flaw was that the plan depended too greatly on altering world opinion and not enough on cooperation between the Republic and the North.

In order to coordinate and strengthen the propaganda campaign in Britain and Ireland, the Irish Anti-Partition League was founded in November 1945 in Tyrone by Northern nationalists. In the beginning, the League did emphasise grievances and adversities endured by the nationalist community in Northern Ireland. During Clann na Poblachta's 1948 campaign, Seán promised cooperation with the Anti-Partition League, especially on publicity and propaganda. The goal was to persuade foreign governments and the public of the moral case for uniting Ireland. Irish exiles in Britain, Australia, and the United States were targeted. The anti-partition campaign received support from Irish-America in its early years. In November 1947 the American League for an Undivided Ireland was formed to coordinate a campaign, collecting 200,000 signatures on a petition asking Truman to try to end partition.[158] The US Government's response was that the problem was for the British and Irish Governments to resolve. The League did have some success in raising the cause in Congress; in March 1950, Congress voted to withhold Marshall Plan funds from Britain as long as partition continued.

The inter-party Government's all-party Mansion House Conference began in January 1949 and also emphasised inequities faced by Northern nationalists, especially political aspects like gerrymandering constituencies, limits of the franchise, and inadequate representation.[159] The *Irish Independent* commented on the 'splendid beginning' and display of party unity and purpose.[160] Yet the activities of the Mansion House Conference soon turned to propaganda; in their opening statement, the parties declared,

we assert once more the right of the Irish people to the ownership and control of all the national territory and we repudiate the right of Britain to carve up the Irish nation or to occupy any portion of it, even though a local majority against unity can be procured in the area which was deliberately selected for that purpose by the British Parliament.[161]

One of the first initiatives taken by the group was to begin a campaign fund for nationalist candidates in Northern Ireland for the election of February 1949. Collections were taken on the steps of Catholic churches after Mass and money was provided from the Department of External Affairs. There were comparatively few attempts to collect outside Protestant churches, which gave the collections, and consequently the initiative, a sectarian`air. A few days after the church-gate collections, Brooke observed that the inter-party Government 'appear to be holding out to us the hand of friendship and . . . have . . . the effrontery to complain that we do not respond.'[162]

Involvement in Northern Ireland elections proved to be counter-productive; the unionist share of the vote rose from 50 per cent in 1945 to 63 per cent, with a gain of four seats. The interference in the elections of what was a foreign country divided Irish public opinion, some believing that intervention was justified because the elections were an 'unequal fight which the Nationalists of the Six Counties have to wage against the odds set against them. At least they can be given added courage from the assurance that their countrymen south of the Border are with them'[163] while others thought that 'interference with the internal affairs of what is legally — even if not in accordance with the sentiment of a great majority of Irishmen — a separate State can have one consequence . . . to anger the Northern majority, and reinforce its determination to stand aloof from the South.'[164] The attempt to influence the elections appeared to be pointless political window-dressing and only allowed unionists to continue their siege mentality rhetoric, Brooke stating that 'the whole constitutional structure of Northern Ireland was being assailed from every angle and it was an elementary duty of the Government to answer any attacks which may be made upon its structure.'[165] Irish propaganda in this case failed in its objective and strengthened the resolve of the Northern majority.

Seán MacBride was anxious to develop a programme of publicising the partition issue. On 13 July 1949, he introduced a bill in the Dáil requesting to begin an Irish News Agency to ensure that the case for a reunited Ireland received more attention abroad, an idea that Fianna Fáil had vetoed in 1947. Seán summarised his reasons for developing such a venture:

> First of all . . . we have a national objective to achieve. We still have to gain full control of our own country. We still have to assert the rights of the Irish people to determine their own form of Government and their own affairs without outside interference. In the second place, for one reason or another we have to counteract a good deal of hostile propaganda . . . that is published constantly in the Press of the world. From the third point of

view, we need news channels of our own in order to encourage the development of our industrial life, of our foreign trade, of our tourist traffic, to make known our cultural developments and also to make known our viewpoints in the field of international affairs as the need arises.[166]

At the time, all Irish newspapers were members of the London-based Press Association, a holdover from when Ireland was part of the United Kingdom. This link was oddly overlooked after Ireland became a Free State. The Irish media received a great portion of their information from Britain, and Seán believed that 'undoubtedly, the viewpoint of a country must become distorted if it is presented through a channel other than a national channel.' Therefore major news and features about Ireland should originate from Ireland to avoid any bias. The proposed Irish News Agency was 'not intended to be a propaganda machine'; it would break through the 'paper wall' of English-owned newspapers and news agencies and 'place Ireland on the map and to that extent then it will be serving a propaganda service by making Ireland known throughout the world in different spheres.'[167] MacBride requested appointments of additional staff for the Irish News Agency as well as additions to External Affairs based in the United States in cities with substantial Irish populations like Boston, Chicago, and New York.

The Dáil passed the final bill to fund the Agency on 24 November 1949. Seán's first choice for head of the Agency was Clann na Poblachta member Noel Hartnett, whom Cruise O'Brien called a 'dedicated republican propagandist'.[168]

Hartnett was Clann na Poblachta's Campaign Director and deserved much of the credit for Clann's early success. Having lost the Dáil seat he was vying for in the 1948 election, he hoped to receive one of the two Clann-nominated Seanad seats. Seán did not choose him and he was hurt by the slight. Cruise O'Brien described Hartnett as 'able but angry and bitter' and believed that their falling out culminated in Hartnett being abruptly relieved of his speechwriting duties on Seán's American tour.[169] MacBride then asked Cruise O'Brien to run the Irish News Agency. Cruise O'Brien refused the appointment at first but realised that fighting with Seán would have a detrimental effect on his career in External Affairs.[170] He also hoped that the public assurances would be true and ignored what he suspected MacBride's intentions really were. Cruise O'Brien wanted to develop a bona fide news agency and chairman Roger Greene agreed to this. Hartnett also agreed not to indulge in propaganda; Cruise O'Brien thinks that if Hartnett had been on good terms with Seán, he would have run it as a propaganda unit, but as they were quarrelling, Hartnett was 'devoting himself heart and soul to thwarting and tormenting Seán MacBride.'[171] He made no effort to change the direction of the Agency; both internal party conflicts and duties as Minister were diverting his attentions and he did not make any attempt to influence Agency decisions.

The goal of the Agency was to counter-balance 'incorrect' interpretations of the partition issue, and was organised into news, photo, and features departments. Talented people became involved, O'Dowd Gallagher, a well-travelled Fleet Street foreign correspondent was in charge of the news division, as well as Peadar O'Curry, Noel Hartnett (who ended up taking a position on the board), former Irish ambassador to the United States Robert Brennan, and journalist and historian Brian Inglis, and many went on to become major figures within Irish journalism. Yet Cruise O'Brien's biographer Donald Akenson calls the Agency an 'all star cast putting on a pantomime'.[172] It was difficult to maintain the public belief that the Agency was not a propaganda machine. In addition, the Agency did not possess all the technology necessary, as one staff member commented, 'we were just marginally faster than Reuter's original pigeon post, one hundred years before.'[173]

The Agency did not formally begin operations until the summer of 1950 and did not get off to a promising start. Agency representatives were sent to cover the first major meeting of the Council of Europe Assembly in Strasbourg. It was Ireland's turn to provide the chairman of the Council of Ministers and MacBride was sent. Held up by trying to install a teleprinter, the Agency representatives decided not to meet the Irish delegation. Instead, the Associated Press, the chief rival of the Agency, arrived to meet the delegates. Thus, the Agency was scooped. On the other hand, the reporting regarding the debate on European defence went well, at least in Inglis's opinion.[174] *The Irish Times* published the Agency's report in full on its front page. The story was a straightforward account of the debate, but it made Irish intervention seem unpopular and unwise, as the Irish delegates had raised the issue of partition and this seemed to make the other delegates impatient. MacBride and de Valera were present and de Valera's plea for an end to partition met with silence, not because the other delegates were necessarily unsympathetic, but because the overwhelming desire of those present, including Churchill, Ernest Bevin, Robert Schuman, Georges Bidault, and Paul-Henri Spaak, was to set up a structure for bringing about improved European cooperation. The prevalent feeling was that the Irish issue was not relevant. The Irish delegates were not happy with the Agency's report; in their view, bringing up partition may have been unpopular but they attracted attention by inflicting the issue on both elder and up-and-coming statesmen, who might have been irritated at the time but surely would begin to take notice of the problem. Therefore, the debate should have been reported as a strategic advance.[175] The Agency argued back that it was not its duty to slant stories and the news must be presented as it appeared — if word got out that the Agency was a propaganda outfit, it would become impossible to sell stories. The delegates, especially MacBride, did not agree.

Despite the talent involved and the potential for such a venture, the Irish News Agency did not meet expectations. Seán failed to sell the idea to even the Irish press, who did not oppose it, but did not actively promote it either.[176] Despite assertions to the contrary, the Agency gained a reputation abroad as a propaganda machine, and foreign newspapers, with the exception of Irish-American ones, were reluctant to purchase articles. In Britain, the National Union of Journalists was against the Agency because it could prove to be a rival. Moreover, there were financial problems; the Agency was set up with £5,000 from the Government and never broke even. Eventually under the direction of Brendan Malin, the Agency broadened its scope beyond events relating to Northern Ireland and began covering European developments and Irish life through its news and features divisions. The Agency began a deal with United Press International, but the controversy of the Mother and Child scheme and the fall of the inter-party Government led to Agency business being placed on the back burner.

De Valera allowed it to carry on, hoping that it would eventually pay its way, but since it was government-funded, it could not issue the kind of story which would lead to angry questions being asked in the Dáil. Features putting Ireland in a favourable light were sent to editors and a great majority came back with rejection slips. The Agency's weakness was that it could only report what happened in a straightforward manner, while others could be more salacious and more critical. In June 1959, a Fianna Fáil Government under Seán Lemass took over and decided to close it. The Irish News Agency was associated with the anti-partition policy of MacBride and the politics of the inter-party Government, which were no longer popular.[177] Ten or twelve years later it would have been of value not just to Ireland, but also to the world press when Northern Ireland became major news. As Douglas Gageby laments, 'it died, not without honour, but with so much unfulfilled.'[178] Another opportunity to prove that Ireland was not obsessed with the partition issue appeared to be lost.

Seán may have been more successful in gaining publicity for his cause, as the Anti-Partition League did at the start, by concentrating more on the denial of rights to the Catholic minority in the North. There were legitimate human rights complaints: dubious electoral practices, discrimination in public and private employment and public housing, regional policy and policing as well as local electoral boundaries being blatantly manipulated to ensure unionist power. If partition could be seen as a human rights issue rather than one of self-determination and geo-political unnaturalness, the Government might have had more luck with its propaganda campaign. The international post-war climate might have been more favourable toward correcting problems such as religious intolerance. On 19 August 1949, at a speech in Strasbourg on human rights, Seán tried to link partition with human rights abuses, stating that partition was a problem 'which is so pertinent to the establishment of peace and concord in Western Europe.' This point is hard to argue; the relationship between Britain and Ireland was good despite Ireland's departure from the Commonwealth and more significant issues such as Soviet violation of human rights and threats of military infringement into Western Europe appeared more menacing than the Irish dispute.

In the first month of the inter-party Government, MacBride stated that

> we should have closer contact with our brothers and sisters in the North, whether Protestant or Catholic, Unionist or Nationalists. There should be as much economic and cultural relations as possible. This would be helpful and make them appreciate that we are all human beings; that we are prepared to recognise their rights, and expect that they will be prepared to recognise ours.[179]

Seán suggested beginning with a customs or economic union and declared in the Dáil that he would be

> glad to take steps that would in any way bring about a closer relationship between our people and those of the partitioned counties. Rather than the exchange of representatives, I feel that a much more useful purpose would be served by the establishment of direct contact on matters of mutual concern between the two Governments. Accordingly, I should be willing, at any time, to meet representatives of the Belfast Government for the purpose of discussing matters of economic co-operation which might be of benefit to Ireland as a whole.[180]

There were many opportunities for such cooperation in late 1940s Ireland. MacBride said that 'in so far as cooperation on economic matters may be of assistance in minimising the effects of Partition and in bringing about a better understanding between those in defacto control of the Six Counties and ourselves, I should welcome it.'[181] Though not the best turn of phrase, it did demonstrate willingness to begin cooperating with the North, which had not been attempted since the Boundary Commission. Brooke was willing to collaborate on issues of security and trade. The Great Northern Railway (GNR), Erne hydroelectric scheme, and River Foyle fishing rights were non-political in nature and showed that cooperation was possible.

The Great Northern Railway (GNR) linked the North and the Republic and operated an extensive rail network on both sides of the border. Based in the Republic, the GNR was a privately owned company in an era of state-owned transportation. In 1946, the Ulster Transportation Authority (UTA), set up by Stormont, took over Great Northern Railway's road services in Northern Ireland. GNR chairman Lord Glenavy warned the Northern Ireland Minister for Commerce Brian Maginess of probable company losses that year, saying that something must be done if services were to be maintained. GNR also approached the Government in Dublin. Maginess became worried that Dublin would use the crisis for political purposes, believing that Dublin could afford to buy out the company.[182] The Córas Iompair Éireann-UTA joint report was presented to Dublin and Belfast in April 1950; rather than have two commerce ministers discuss the situation, the permanent secretaries of the departments met in Dublin. Yet, by mid-August, Brooke had changed his mind and William McCleery, the new Minister for Commerce, met Dublin's Minister for Industry and Commerce, Daniel Morrissey, in Dublin. The meeting went well and McCleery reported back that 'the Republican government are just as unwilling to have to buy out the railway . . . no likelihood of Dublin trying any "quick ones" and that none of the unpleasant possibilities which were recently under consideration is likely to arise.'[183] A later meeting between Parliamentary Secretary (Junior Minister) to the Minister for Industry and Commerce Liam Cosgrave and McCleery ended in disagreement; Cosgrave suggested subsidies or establishing an all-Ireland Transport Board while McCleery advocated purchasing GNR. A purchase was finally agreed upon at £3.9 million, but it was not finalised because Dublin wanted to run it as a joint venture and Belfast wanted the UTA to take over in the North, allowing only the cross-border services to be jointly run, feeling that a joint venture was 'wholly undesirable from a political point of view.'[184] The disagreement was left for the next Fianna Fáil Government to settle.

At the same time, a major agreement to drain the lands around and develop Lough Erne began. A proposal was brought forth by the Republic's Electricity Supply Board (ESB) to establish a hydroelectric scheme that would also allow Stormont to control flooding on Lough Erne. Brooke was enthusiastic, primarily because it would make his constituents in Fermanagh happy. The Erne Drainage and Development Bill, published on 8 May 1950, came before the Dáil and Stormont the following day, stating that 'any works necessary in Fermanagh shall be carried out by the Northern Ministry, but to the satisfaction of the Electricity Supply Board.'[185] It was technically an agreement between the Northern Ireland Ministry of Finance and the ESB rather than between the two governments, but it laid the foundations for further partnerships. An *Irish Times* editorial praised the scheme, asking, 'Is there any good reason why the example of the Erne should not be followed in other directions?'[186]

Fishing rights to the River Foyle, located in Donegal, Derry and Tyrone, were held by the London-based Honourable Irish Society, who had once held the charter for Derry city, though the area they claimed the right to was located entirely in Donegal. This was challenged in Dublin High Court by eighty Donegal fishermen, who won their case, the judge deciding that the fishery was public, not private property. The Society appealed the decision to the Supreme Court. In 1949, Northern Attorney-General Major Lance Curran wrote to Cecil Lavery suggesting a 'get together with a view to the adequate regulation of the fishing in the River Foyle', with the caveat, 'I hope that you and those concerned in your Government will regard this in its true light, namely as an attempt to arrive at a practical solution of the problem in a friendly spirit. You will appreciate that my approach to you is informal.'[187] The two governments agreed to buy the fishing rights and set up a joint authority to manage them. This was the first such initiative between Dublin and Belfast. At the February 1951 Fine Gael ard-fheis, Costello stated that the North 'have given some grounds for the belief that friendly relations can do much to achieve eventual unity more certainly than threats of bloody warfare.'[188] Liam Cosgrave commented in the Dáil:

> For some time, I believe, the whole approach to Partition has been based too much on showmanship and not enough on statesmanship, and that a great deal of reckless talk on both sides of the Border has prevented practical steps or, on some occasions, has hindered certain practical steps, that might be taken towards achieving a united Ireland ... I think that the proper approach to this problem lies along the lines that have been adopted in relation to the Erne hydro-electric scheme and the Foyle fisheries agreement, and, although there may be some temporary divergence of view, the discussions that took place in connection with the Great Northern Railway.[189]

All of these were practical circumstances, not political concerns, which forced collaboration. North–South cooperation was acceptable to Belfast as long as it did not encourage Dublin to hope for unity.[190] Seán Lemass would later institute North–South relations and practical cooperation, after becoming Taoiseach in 1959, and developments might occur as a result of greater unity with the European Union; in a few years' time 'one can expect the border between the North and South to mean less in practical terms than it does now.'[191] MacBride, Costello and Cosgrave recognised the benefits of cross-border cooperation, yet this indirect but pragmatic approach might not have solved the problem quickly enough for the Government and they might have felt that indulging in too many cross-border initiatives would be equal to recognising the North and the permanency of partition. If cooperation had continued without strident propaganda, then behaviour and policies might gradually have become more compatible. Like the Good Friday Agreement of 1998, it was not a resolution of difference, but a structure within which difference might possibly be managed.

Seán contended 'that Ireland is one nation is beyond the realm of argument.'[192] He made the mistake of underestimating the strength and tenacity of unionism and did not make allowances for unionists' viewpoint. As Basil Chubb proposes, 'because the nationalist frame of reference included a woefully inadequate concept of Ulster Unionism, people simply did not take realistic account of the views of the million and more Northern Protestants, let alone accord them value.'[193] Partition was not merely a rock in the road; it was, as Brooke said, a 'barrier of race, history, and outlook' and the Irish Government needed more inventive plans for linking the two sides.[194]

The inter-party Government's error was not to consider developing and strengthening links to Northern Catholics and not to try real grass-roots initiatives to court unionists. The Republic should have put more effort into publicising unfair discriminatory treatment instead of focusing on ideals like self-determination and geography, and should have developed practical rather than elevated concepts. Instead, politicians put propaganda in place of real policy initiatives and looked like they were merely posturing. Was the Government trying to prove its commitment to the issue without actually doing anything about it? The concept of unity seemed to be of minor importance in practical politics, but fundamental in terms of ideology.

In his address to the Anti-Partition League in Manchester, Costello, in keeping with government policy, referred to the North as an 'artificially created political structure' and urged the audience to inform, educate, and condition public opinion about partition and the need for settlement. He did show some insight as he spoke about cultivating an appreciation of the

Northern Irish point of view, but such insight was hard to sustain in light of the Mother and Child controversy, which was brilliantly exploited by unionists as further proof of a theocracy where individual liberties are sacrificed to religion.

Though the inter-party Government's anti-partition strategy did lead to an expansion of the Foreign Service, a united Irish people within the Republic, and the end of diplomatic isolation, the strategy also demonstrated the reactive nature of the Government as its members did not seem fully to examine alternative methods to solve the problem. The strategies that the Government adopted at first, such as creating an Irish News Agency, establishing friendly relations with the North, and revamping the Council of Ireland, dwindled in favour of more anti-unionist rhetoric and anti-partition propaganda, which alienated Cruise O'Brien and Boland, who, according to MacBride, was 'horrified' by repeal and the anti-partition campaign.[195] Equalling the benefits of the British Welfare State in Ireland may not have been economically possible, but concentrated contact with both Northern nationalists and Catholics, and allaying unionist fears about 'Rome Rule' were feasible and would have been the best course of action for ending partition, or at least improving the relationship between the North and the Republic. Yet such actions may have proven too slow to suit, and the inter-party Government demonstrated an unwillingness to think long-term toward a better relationship with Belfast. In its relationship with the United Kingdom, the Government seemed overwhelmed by momentum of circumstance, responding to events rather than directing them.

Chapter 6 ～

RATTLING THE SABRE: IRELAND AND THE UNITED STATES

'All politics is local.'
— THOMAS P. O'NEILL

Ireland and the United States have historically had a significant relationship. In his time in office, Seán MacBride was involved in negotiations with President Harry Truman's Government regarding Marshall Plan aid and proposed entry into the North Atlantic Treaty Organisation. The combination of Irish neutrality during the Second World War, the escalating Cold War, and Seán's fixation on the partition issue would greatly affect the relationship between Ireland and the United States. His attempts to make Irish Marshall Plan cooperation as well as Irish NATO membership conditional to the ending of partition were unsuccessful. MacBride made a tactical error in believing that the United States would be willing to mediate in respect to partition. Did this mistake show an incomplete understanding of both the Irish-American relationship in the recent past and power politics at the time? Was he really unable to recognise that the American political climate was the most important issue, that the Cold War was not the best time to try such an approach, or were other factors at work? It seems likely that the inter-party Government knew that enlisting American help would not work; instead, it was done to please home constituents rather than solve the problem.

Seán may have misread American willingness to help on the partition issue but there were some benefits deriving from this policy. For example, his virtual dominance in Marshall Aid negotiations, despite such negotiations being within the domain of the Department of Finance, gave the Department of External Relations a more prominent profile.

The Irish Government thought that America would be sympathetic to ending partition. This belief is not surprising considering the amount of political clout that the Irish-American community possesses. The claim that Ireland has a special relationship with the United States is an enduring feature of Irish foreign relations. In a 1922 memorandum that explained why Ireland would be well suited to begin a career on the international stage, Irish Minister for Foreign Affairs George Gavan Duffy stated that 'we are supposed to have great influence upon American politics and policy.'[1] However, that supposition is not as straightforward as it at first appears and the relationship between Ireland and the United States is more complex than it seems. Furthermore, Irish-American politicians did not use their clout to the advantage of Ireland itself. As Deputy Donal O'Callaghan admitted in 1921, 'it was all a myth talking about 20 millions of [the Irish] in America. There never was more than half a million in the Irish movement in America.'[2]

There was a mass exodus of Irish to America after the Famine in the late 1840s. It is estimated that from 1846 to 1891, three million Irish went to the United States.[3] Many also emigrated after smaller crop failures in 1863–66 and 1880–83. The newly arrived ethnic and urban-centred Irish clashed with nativist society, and American suspicion of Catholicism reinforced the Irish immigrants' cohesiveness.[4] The Irish in America tended to remain in self-contained communities and tended to marry 'within the tribe'.

The White Anglo-Saxon Protestant establishment in the United States seemed to parallel British domination of Ireland. Irish emigrants and the succeeding generations took an interest in events in Ireland mainly because 'many of the American Irish continued to feel that they lacked the respect that other Americans enjoyed, and they came to pin their hopes for greater prestige and acceptance among their fellow citizens on events in Ireland itself.'[5] 'The Irish nationalist effort in the United States was very much a part of the impulse to improve the standing of immigrants from Ireland, for a conquered homeland offered living proof of the inferiority of her people.'[6] The Fenians were founded in the United States in 1858 and Clan na Gael in 1867. It would appear that the combination of Irish nationalism and the Irish-American talent for gaining political power might work in Ireland's favour.

Yet, after assimilation, the descendants of emigrants had other concerns. The idea that the Irish were 'America's political class' is quite true, but they used political power for local concerns, not wider Irish ones. Gradually 'the story of the Irish in America had become the story of Americans of Irish descent.'[7] An example of this mindset was that a majority of Irish-Americans voted for Woodrow Wilson in 1916, despite his attack on Irish-American 'hyphenism'.[8] Such activity shows American interests prevailing over Irish ones.

Irish-Americans of this era were less interested in politics in Ireland than those of a generation earlier. Rather, their interests lay in American perceptions; the ethnic solidarity of Irish-American communities, a result of nativist Protestant discrimination, helped form and fuel political machines in New York, Boston, Chicago and Philadelphia. Gradually the descendants of Irish immigrants became less conscious of Ireland and more interested in local concerns. American isolationism after the First World War encouraged this outlook.

However, the United States was the most important target for Sinn Féin propaganda in 1919 and the party did a lot of fund raising in Irish-American communities. The Irish nationalists put faith in American support. After the end of the First World War, Seán T. O'Kelly was dispatched in 1919 to the Paris Peace Conference to try to win international recognition for Ireland, in the hopes of taking advantage of President Wilson's desire for 'self-determination' for small nations. However, Wilson himself was an Anglophile of Ulster Protestant descent and had no sympathy with the Irish case for self-government.[9] The Irish delegation was unsuccessful.

Ireland, then, would not benefit from the Irish-American talent for politics; 'by 1916 Irish nationalism in America had little to do with Ireland.'[10] Even before then, Irish-American organisations did not focus on Ireland; 'essentially they were pressure groups designed to defend and advance the American interests of the immigrant.'[11] Even when a descendant of Irish-Catholic immigrants became President in 1960, John F. Kennedy's administration concentrated on Cold War politics rather than policy regarding Ireland and had a cordial relationship with Britain's Macmillan Government.

Some argue that the Irish gift for politics is misunderstood. Lawrence McCaffrey points out that the Irish have had no trouble gaining political power, but 'once in office Irish politicians have either abused power or failed to direct it constructively.'[12] Daniel Patrick Moynihan, a well-respected Irish-American Senator, concluded that the Irish are skilled at acquiring political power, yet inadequate at its application; 'in a sense the Irish did not know what to do with power once they got it.'[13]

Moreover, the British could also claim a special relationship with the United States; legal and linguistic likenesses existed and at least one-third of Americans could claim British descent.[14] England and America had been drawing closer together and American administrations consistently favoured

Britain whenever Anglo-Irish issues came up. American foreign policy, motivated by self-interest, required cooperation with Britain.

The Second World War would further the divisions between Irish-America and Ireland. Ireland's declaration of neutrality affected Ireland's rapport with the United States, as the US did not respond well to the decision. The Irish position during the war 'placed a strain on traditional Irish-American friendship.'[15] As John Hickerson, the head of the State Department's Division of European Affairs, wrote to the American Representative in Dublin, David Gray, in January 1945, 'the people of the United States, I believe, will not soon forget that the one time in history when Ireland had an opportunity to do something to assist this country the Irish Government turned a deaf ear.'[16] A communiqué from the British Embassy in Washington in March 1949 explained that 'whilst there has, of course always been a measure of sympathy in this country for Ireland, it has been markedly strained by Eire's strict neutrality during the war ... [including] her refusal of United States' requests for naval and/or air facilities in the anti-submarine campaign.'[17]

To add to the tension, Gray, an Anglophile and uncle by marriage to Eleanor Roosevelt, did not get along with de Valera and did much to malign him and Irish policy to the US Government. According to T. Ryle Dwyer, Gray's machinations to discredit de Valera and the Irish neutrality policy led to a freezing of relations between the two nations.[18] His campaign to discredit the Irish Government during and after the war worked and 'Irish-American relations at the end of the conflict were altogether poisoned and the strain between the two nations seemed set to continue for some time to come.'[19]

The point has been made that Irish neutrality was not 'strict' at all, rather a 'benevolent neutrality' that favoured the Allies. As Nathan Becker of the State Department remembered, 'of course, the Irish were very good as neutrals, they let us do most anything that was reasonable.'[20] This included supplying volunteers, allowing the Office of Strategic Services to establish an official liaison in Ireland, and agreeing to support Britain in the event of a German invasion.

Despite this, many in the US Government continued to see Irish neutrality as traitorous. Hickerson vented to Gray's replacement George Garrett, 'The British were our allies in the last war when Ireland's neutrality operated to the advantage of Germany.'[21] Myron C. Taylor, the Representative of the President to the Holy See, informed President Truman that he had once suggested to Truman's predecessor Franklin Roosevelt in 1941, 'that he ignore De Valera, grant him no favors, and treat him with contempt ... De Valera's vanity had grown out of all proportion to the importance of his area of Ireland and its relatively small population.'[22]

Taylor also informed Roosevelt that 'there can be little doubt that the i.r.a. is being financed and in part directed by German agencies in Eire.'[23] The Irish refused to hand over the Treaty ports to the British during the war and would not close the Axis legations. These were proper actions for a neutral nation but were not appreciated by the United States, who thought that the ports were vital to the British war effort and the legations 'centers of espionage'.[24] After denial of the ports, 'Ireland was off America's conscience for good, if indeed she'd ever been on it.'[25]

On 2 May 1945, de Valera paid a visit to the German legation to offer condolences upon Adolf Hitler's death. While this was proper diplomatic protocol for a non-belligerent state, de Valera's visit was widely criticised. The *New York Times* commented that 'considering the character and record of the man for whose death he was expressing grief, there is obviously something wrong with the protocol, the neutrality, or Mr de Valera.'[26] Why did de Valera behave in such a manner, in what Maffey called a 'conspicuous act of neutrality'?[27] De Valera's behaviour at Roosevelt's death a few weeks earlier had been far more effusive; he adjourned the Dáil as a mark of respect, stating that 'personally I regard his death as a loss to the world.'[28] He made no favourable comments and did not dismiss the Dáil after Hitler's death. Perhaps he was irritated with Gray and wanted to stress Irish sovereignty. De Valera was 'tweaking the tail of the British Lion; but a more correct analogy would probably have been that he was ruffling the feathers of the American Eagle.'[29] De Valera also respected Dr Edouard Hempel, the German Minister in Dublin, 'for whom he had a much higher regard than he had for Gray.'[30]

Neutrality had not only coloured how the us Government viewed Ireland; it had also dulled Irish minds to the nature of the Irish-American relationship as well as the improved Anglo-American relationship and how the war had altered both. As Lewis Douglas wrote to British Foreign Secretary Ernest Bevin in 1948, referring to the Anglo-American relationship cemented by the war, 'Unity among our two peoples can and will, I believe, lead us through the troubled times of the present to a long period of tranquillity. Division between us can only mean a catastrophe for us both.'[31] America was unlikely to risk alienating Britain, then their most important single ally, for the sake of a country that had remained neutral throughout the Second World War; 'Americans were less ready to offend the British than to offend the Irish.'[32]

In addition, for many Americans, the Second World War altered the way they perceived their nation's place in world affairs. The isolationism of the inter-war years was firmly in the past. This change can be seen in the enthusiasm for membership in the United Nations, which contrasts to the American attitude in joining the League of Nations. The burgeoning Cold

War meant that the United States needed to be a strong presence in world affairs. This outlook also strengthened the relationship with Britain, who vigorously supported the containment of communism.

In 1945, the position of the US Government toward the partition of Ireland was very clear; it was a problem for the United Kingdom and Ireland to solve and 'the partition question is one in which the United States cannot become involved.'[33] In the years between 1945 and the formation of the inter-party Government in 1948, there were no signs that this position would change. Yet the Government continued to try to use the Americans to bring about an end to the problem. In a letter to Seán Nunan, the Irish representative in Washington, MacBride supposed that 'the attitude of the State Department has always been opposed to giving any assistance to the solution of the Irish question. But I feel now that an opportunity really offers to do it.'[34]

He had some reason for believing this. One of the issues during the 1948 general election campaign was the lack of movement on partition. Here was an opportunity to best Fianna Fáil. Seán believed that the British Labour Government would be more sympathetic than the normally unionist Conservatives. George Garrett succeeded Gray as United States Minister to Ireland in summer 1947 and he had a much more cordial relationship with the Irish Government and appeared prepared to examine the partition question on its merits.[35] Perhaps the new Government thought that more propaganda would reawaken the commitment of Irish-Americans.

The large numbers of Irish-Americans and their apparent political clout probably influenced MacBride's thinking. One of the goals of the inter-party Government's anti-partition propaganda campaign was to marshal the support of Irish-Americans to petition their Government to intervene. As has already been mentioned, MacBride had created the Irish News Agency to provide a favourable impression to American newspapers. Putting Ireland in a positive light could influence more Americans to support the cause. That said, it seems clear that MacBride was in denial about partition and the formidable barriers in Northern Ireland to its removal. Looking to the United States rather than to the root causes of the problem was a means of deflecting an unpalatable reality into a more benign sphere.

In a later interview, Seán recalled that 'As far as policy-making, I was conscious I was dealing with a very hostile State Department and my only leverage was the Irish-American members of Congress.'[36] He may have overestimated how much help Congress could provide. From 1948 to 1951, sixteen anti-partition resolutions were proposed in Congress: three in the Senate, thirteen in the House of Representatives. Only one resolution came out of committee and the vote on whether the House should consider it was defeated 206 to 139. In 1949, four Congressmen, John Fogarty (Rhode Island), Thomas Lane (Massachusetts), Enda Kelly (New York), and Mike Mansfield (Montana) and one Senator, Everett Dirksen (Illinois), moved unsuccessful resolutions against partition and, on 29 March 1950, Fogarty announced an amendment to a Foreign Aid bill, suspending Marshall Aid to Britain until partition ended. His amendment did not mention Britain by name, stating that the United States would withhold

> any assistance under this act, where it appears that any participating country is impairing in whole or in part its economic recovery by reason of the expenditure of any portion of its funds, commodities or services in the maintenance or subsidization of any dependant country, which naturally is or should be, an integral part of some other participating country, until such time as such participating country shall sever its control of, and refrain further from maintaining or subsidizing such dependant country.[37]

However, he followed that statement up with 'in plain English it means that all funds that shall be appropriated through the authorization of this bill will be withheld from the United Kingdom as long as partition exists in Ireland.' The bill passed 99 to 66.[38]

At first glance, this would appear to be a victory for the Irish-American lobby in Congress. However, there were few members in the House of Representatives at the time and many who were there were well-known supporters of the previous resolutions. Perhaps Fogarty, a representative with a large Irish-American constituency, was looking for a symbolic victory. Mid-term elections were coming up in November so the amendment could be viewed as a bid for Irish-American support. Also, as the relationship between President Truman and Congress was tense at the time, the Republicans in the House were willing to support the bill because it provided an opportunity to embarrass Truman.[39] Under the House rules, changes in bills were tentative and depended on a formal role call vote at the end of the debate. Thus prior arguments could be reversed. The *New York Times* headline of 30 March 1950 read, 'House cuts off aid until Britain ends Ireland partition', with the subhead, 'Action likely to be reversed.'[40] The article pointed out that the vote followed assurances by the sponsors that 'there would be ample opportunity to reconsider the action.' The *Washington Post* hinted that the Representatives were 'in a playful mood' and 'nobody seemed to take the vote very seriously.'[41]

The Irish Government's assessment was quite different; Costello called the amendment 'a justification for putting the question of partition on the international plane.'[42] MacBride remained silent about Congress's action, merely stating that Britain was 'violating the fundamental principles of democracy by keeping Ireland divided.'[43] There does not appear to be any direct connection between Seán's lobbying and the bill; there is no correspondence in the Department of Foreign Affairs files between Seán and any of the Congressmen who spoke in support of the amendment, though the Irish Embassy did send Senators and Congressmen copies of Seán's anti-partition speeches.[44] The Irish Government did not provide the impetus for the amendment. Bill Peer, a Brooklyn Irish-American who had recently been made a director of publicity for the American League for an Undivided Ireland, apparently suggested the idea to Fogarty while on a trip to Washington.[45]

The leading American press considered the action irresponsible on the part of the House. A *New York Times* editorial surmised that the amendment was 'intended merely as a demonstration' and further felt that the 'European Recovery Program is being made a football of domestic politics.'[46] The *Washington Post* called the vote an 'outrageous and schoolboyish exhibition.'[47] Even *The Irish Times* remarked that 'we could wish that the Congressional friends of our sundered country had chosen a more tactful, and less perilous, means to make their sentiments felt.'[48] Moreover, the amendment ignored both the practical side of denying Britain Marshall Plan aid and that denial's potential economic effect on Ireland.

The amendment was rejected in committee on 31 March and the Foreign Aid Bill passed 266 to 60. Further evidence that the Amendment was a symbolic stance was that all the Congressmen who had spoken in favour of the Amendment voted for the final version of the bill.[49]

Seán MacBride was probably correct about the State Department: a likely reason why most of the resolutions died in committee was that Congress often asked the Department for advice in matters of foreign relations. The State Department's memo to Tom Connally, Chair of the Senate Foreign Relations Committee, affirmed that partition was 'not a matter in which the United States could properly or usefully intervene.'[50] There is no doubt that sympathy for the cause of Irish unity existed; several state legislatures and Congress passed resolutions opposing partition, but this had little practical effect other than to sustain the hopes of the Northern nationalists.[51]

This does not mean that the US Government ignored anti-partition activity. The American League for an Undivided Ireland had gathered 300,000 signatures for a petition, which they had sent to Secretary of State George Marshall on 12 May 1948 with the demand that 'European Recovery funds should be withheld from Great Britain in order that the growing source of irritation be eliminated in Ireland.'[52] The petition gained attention, but not the kind that the League was looking for. Threats to Marshall Plan aid irritated the State Department; on 28 May 1948, Hickerson wrote to Matthew Connelly, President Truman's Secretary, that

> this Department has been receiving a number of communications from Irish societies and individuals expressing the view that economic aid should not be given to Britain as long as the northern counties remain separated from Eire . . . this Department would prefer that publicity regarding this petition [from American League for Undivided Ireland] be kept at a minimum.[53]

The insistence that this was a serious issue to world peace was similar to crying wolf; 'this last named policy [American non-involvement] is imminently sound and the u.s. can do nothing but lose by meddling into a matter which is not nearly as serious as the [Irish-American] extremists would have us believe.'[54]

Yet it was necessary to appear strong on partition to satisfy the electorate in Ireland. After his defeat, de Valera embarked upon an anti-partition tour of the United States, Australia, New Zealand and Britain. Thus the new Government could not be outdone in expressing its nationalist zeal; de Valera was manoeuvring in a field where it was almost impossible to attack him, so 'MacBride duly banged the anti-partition drum.'[55] He and Taoiseach John A. Costello also made trips to the United States. From 8 April to 2 May 1949, Seán travelled to Chicago, San Francisco, Boston, New York, and Washington, DC, where he gave speeches, all of which were well-covered in Irish newspapers, about avoiding world conflict, the benefits of European integration, the Irish position on NATO, and the injustice of partition, missing the official Irish Republic celebrations in Dublin on 18 April, as discussed in the previous chapter. The US Government recognised the dilemma of Irish political parties in respect to partition, the CIA explaining that 'if political parties keep the issue before the people, it is because they cannot do otherwise and continue to exist.'[56]

The British were not very concerned about the anti-partition rhetoric. Lord Rugby reported to the Dominions Office that Irish-Americans were 'slightly less frenzied' than they had been about the problem.[57]

It was unwise to add the United States to the 'sore thumb' strategy if ending partition was the Irish Government's aim. It got to the point where whenever MacBride visited government officials, prior warnings would be issued. One such brief for President Truman read:

It is anticipated that Mr MacBride's appointment will be in the nature of
a courtesy call. In the course of the conversation, however, Mr MacBride
may refer to the Irish partition issue, Irish defense requirements, ECA aid
to Ireland, and the civil aviation issue. It might prove highly embarrassing
to our relations with the United Kingdom if announcement were made
that the Partition Issue had been discussed. Therefore it is suggested that
this subject be avoided if possible.

If MacBride did introduce the subject, the response should be that the United
States 'cannot intervene in this issue between two friendly Governments.'[58]

The meeting between MacBride and Truman took place on 23 March 1951.
Seán did mention partition in an oblique fashion, referring to the 'political
difficulties' involved if Ireland were to join NATO.[59] Truman kept to his brief
and replied that he hoped that Ireland would join but that the matter was
between two friendly nations, and the United States could not intervene. Seán
then mentioned the possibility of military assistance to Ireland, but not a
specific bilateral defence pact. Truman said that the 'strain now being placed
upon the United States to provide arms for both itself and for the most urgent
need of allies who are more exposed than was Ireland' might prohibit this
request, but promised to consider the possibility.

The US Government had little sympathy with Irish-American posturing
despite the fact that there were vocal efforts in the United States to address the
partition question. Many Ancient Order of Hibernians chapters requested to
Truman several times that partition be ended and sent copies of the pamphlet
'Ireland's Right to Unity' from the Dublin Mansion House Conference. Irish-
America managed to keep the partition issue alive, but did not influence the
Government to change it.

The United States also maintained a cordial relationship with Northern
Ireland. Truman wrote to Sir Basil Brooke that 'the interests and attachments
binding us to our friends in Northern Ireland are deep seated and esteemed.
To you and the people in Northern Ireland may I express the good wishes and
hope for continued happiness and well-being.'[60] Brooke replied on 9 August
1949 that 'we in Northern Ireland are proud to know that so many Presidents
of the United States have been men of Ulster descent and that large numbers
of Ulster men and women are playing an important part in the life of your
country today.'[61] He reminded Truman of Northern Ireland's role during the
war: 'this bond of kinship and friendship between the United States and
ourselves was immeasurably strengthened during the world war when 300,000
members of the United States Forces came to Ulster for the completion of their
training and found an abiding place in the hearts of our people.'

If it had chosen to involve itself, could the United States have succeeded in making the British end partition? And did an 'unsympathetic' attitude ensure its permanence? Would the British even have responded if the US Government had put pressure on them? Britain had already made its stance on partition clear; the Ireland Act of 1949 stated that partition would remain unless a majority in the Northern Ireland Parliament agreed to its removal. The British Government would not have allowed mediation without Northern Ireland's consent and it is highly unlikely that unionists would have willingly participated. Seán Cronin argues that the United States, by allowing Britain to influence unduly its policy toward Ireland, was 'taking sides against a united Ireland'.[62] While Cronin's point that the United States and Britain had a close post-war relationship is correct, Davis convincingly counter-argues that there is nothing to suggest that the United States would have opposed any solution to partition agreed on by Britain and Ireland.[63] The US decision not to involve itself in the partition issue did not mean that it took any positive action against Irish unification.

The motives of Irish-American politicians taking a vocal anti-partition stance seemed to mirror those of Irish politicians — such a stance was necessary to impress their constituents. Gaining votes was the goal rather than achieving unity. The use of partition as a political weapon rather than a genuine problem to be solved continued.

After the general election in May 1951, the American anti-partition campaign ebbed upon de Valera's return to power, and his Fianna Fáil Government maintained a policy of 'silence and discretion' regarding unity.[64] When asked in the Dáil what he thought about the partition movement, de Valera answered, 'If I am asked: "Have you a solution for it?" in the sense: "Is there a line of policy which you propose to pursue, which you think can, within a reasonable time, be effective?" I have to say that I have not and neither has anybody else.'[65]

One of the major hallmarks of the Irish-American relationship at this time was Ireland's participation in the Marshall Plan. The basis of the plan lay in Secretary of State George Marshall's Harvard University commencement speech of 5 June 1947, where he pledged US help to restore 'the confidence of the European people in the economic future of their own countries and of Europe as a whole . . . to assist in the return of normal economic health in the world, without which there can be no political stability and no assured peace.'[66]

The Marshall Plan, also known as the European Recovery Programme (ERP), was open to allies, former allies, enemies, former enemies, and neutrals during the war. Thus Ireland was permitted to participate. American motivation could be viewed as 'an attempt by the United States to create a bloc of states centred around itself. In addition, each European state was considered valuable in terms of promoting key United States foreign policy interests,'[67] the paramount one being anti-communism.[68] Like participation in the Council of Europe, this may have signalled a violation of neutrality. In his introduction to *Ireland, Europe and the Marshall Plan*, Till Geiger points out that involvement could be viewed as a threat to Irish sovereignty and the desire to conduct affairs free of outside interference.[69] However, the financial benefit made it worth participating and Ireland had already expressed its views on communism. In addition, Whelan argues that Ireland was drawn into the Marshall Plan because of demands of British and United States economic, political, strategic and diplomatic policies — Ireland had 'little or no control over its own destiny on this matter.'[70]

The case for Ireland to be offered aid was very strong. Neutrality may have put a strain on Ireland's rapport with the United States, but its geographical location made a good relationship important to both British and United States security.[71] Marshall Aid would also provide some relief to Britain's strained dollar reserves and improve Irish agriculture to help alleviate the post-war food shortage. The Irish economy was suffering from stagnating production, inflation, and balance of payments in deficit with every country except Britain. Raymond J. Raymond correctly argues that the United States extended the offer in order to reduce Ireland's drawing on the dollar pool of the sterling area so that the United Kingdom would be financially viable.[72] Spain, in a similar post-war position to Ireland, did not receive Marshall Plan help.[73]

The lack of a potent communist threat may have prejudiced any aid. The CIA had determined that 'Communism has little appeal to the Irish, whose views on political, social, and economic matters are conditioned by religious beliefs' and the ideology was an 'almost insignificant force, and internally at least offers no conceivable threat to the State.'[74] The Irish Government did not hesitate to declare its aversion to communism. MacBride had declared in the Dáil that 'I am not aware that there can be the slightest doubt as to where Ireland stands in regard to the general world conflict.'[75] Despite a lack of a threatening communist presence, Ireland's immediate economic difficulties were similar to those of most Western European countries and there were political, diplomatic, and security arguments for inclusion.[76] There was no real public opposition in Ireland itself and the state of the Irish economy meant that Ireland did not have much choice but to investigate.

On 4 July 1947, Ireland received an invitation to attend a meeting in Paris on 12 July to 'take part in the drawing up of a programme covering both the resources and needs of Europe for the following four years.'[77] Representatives of sixteen Western European Countries met in Paris to frame a joint response to the American offer. On 16 April 1948, the Committee of European Economic Cooperation (CEEC) met in Paris and adopted a convention, which established a permanent organisation of sixteen participating countries, thus officially forming the Organisation of European Economic Cooperation (OEEC). An *Irish Independent* editorial supported the idea, stating that there was 'good ground for hoping that the agreement signed yesterday in Paris will endure and be of lasting value to the world.'[78]

After the general election of 1948, organising Irish participation in the ERP and meeting the steps to qualify for aid fell to MacBride and his department, as did how the money should be spent. Seán would distinguish himself in the OEEC but he was not quite as successful in dealing with America itself.[79]

The first controversy involved loan versus grant status. In May 1948, Ireland was offered a $10 million loan to be dispersed during the period of June through October from Marshall Aid funds. It was decided to give Ireland loans rather than grants because there were 'no over-riding political considerations which would warrant preferential treatment for the Irish . . . the decision [loan or grant] should be made on an economic basis in comparison with the other CEEC countries.'[80] The aim of the ERP was to restore the Western European economy as a whole, thus making the area less vulnerable to communism, and Ireland was peripheral to this aim. The country 'didn't have a relatively high rate of priority on our program at that time.'[81] Moreover, Ireland was of comparatively minor economic importance and not badly damaged by the war, not suffering to the same extent as other countries. Raymond argues that political reasons, specifically lingering American annoyance at Irish neutrality, were also factors.[82]

On 18 May, MacBride led a delegation to Washington to argue for a grant. At a meeting on 20 May, he met with Hickerson. His main argument was that 'we have, as a nation, a fundamental objection to undertaking obligations we see no prospect of meeting.'[83] Seán tried to emphasise the need for a grant, stating that, as an agricultural nation, Ireland had suffered war damage due to a lack of fertilisers and feeding stuffs and Irish agriculture had suffered 'as effectively as if it had been ravaged by war.'[84] He also pointed out that Northern Ireland benefited from the Marshall Plan, through London, largely in grant form.[85] Despite Raymond's conclusion that Seán made a good case, it was unwise to use these arguments, as Britain was far more war damaged than Ireland and it only emphasised Northern Ireland's more active participation in the war effort.

Hickerson replied that increasing Irish aid was an unnecessary burden to

American taxpayers. The favourable terms of the loans ensured that the Irish would find repayment fairly easy; there were four separate loan agreements and the repayment of the $128 million total was not to commence until 30 June 1956 with twenty-seven years to remunerate at an interest rate of 2.5 per cent, beginning 31 December 1952.[86] The economic recovery that would result from the loans would make repayment possible, as J.J. Lee recapped, 'Ireland would have no difficulty meeting the repayments out of the increased output which the delegation confidently predicted would result from Marshall Aid!'[87]

In May of 1948, the Executive still needed full Congressional approval for allocation of Marshall Aid funds. The State Department wanted to ensure that nothing would go wrong.[88] Any attempt by Seán to enlist the Irish lobby could weaken support for the entire aid package. The House of Representatives Appropriations Committee questioned why Ireland was receiving aid while other wartime neutrals such as Sweden, Switzerland and Portugal were not in line to receive any. The response was that Ireland needed ERP funding because of its close relationship with the sterling area. Congress had also insisted that some proportion of aid be given as loans; thus the United States had to make choices. Ireland was seen as able to handle loans. Paul Hoffman, the Administrator of the Economic Cooperation Administration (ECA), was clearly irritated by Ireland's behaviour; if Ireland rejected a loan, that might be the end of ERP offers to Ireland. Moreover, if the Irish could contemplate rejecting the loan, perhaps they did not really need it.

The discussion brought out the second issue, tying ERP aid to partition. This was alluded to when MacBride brought up the funding that the North would be receiving, hinting that the United States was encouraging partition by 'increasing the disparity between the economies on both sides of the border.'[89] Seán mused to Hickerson that it was difficult to comprehend why the United States would not want to help cure a 'sore spot' in Europe. Hickerson replied,

> I then explained that, frankly, as they knew, during the last war bases in Northern Ireland had been of great assistance in the anti-submarine campaign and had undoubtedly saved many American and Allied lives. At present we and the British [sic] were working together on the closest possible terms . . . If Ireland had taken over the Six Northern Counties, where would this leave us if Ireland remained neutral the way she had in the last war? I finished by expressing the hope that Ireland would one day be a member of the Brussels group [the forerunner of NATO].[90]

Seán returned to Dublin and asked the cabinet what to do. The Secretary of the Department of Finance, J.J. McElligott, believed that the loan would be advantageous; $10 million for June–October would benefit the sterling pool, and the British Treasury was also in favour. Yet, at a cabinet meeting on 11 June, the Irish Government voted to reject Marshall Aid for the time being.

However, the situation would soon change. The British dollar reserve was so depleted that Sir Stafford Cripps, the Chancellor of the Exchequer, announced in June that Ireland would not be able to withdraw dollars from the sterling pool after 30 June. The Irish could have restricted access if Ireland agreed to participate in the ERP. Geiger has posited that this was not entirely the Exchequer's decision; that 'indirect American pressure on the British Government forced the Irish Government to accept ERP loans after Irish ministers had decided to refuse any assistance except in the form of grants.'[91] Daniel Davies further noted that America asked the British to remove Ireland from the sterling pool.[92] Whatever the impetus, on 25 June, the cabinet agreed to accept the initial offer of a loan and, on 1 July, the Dáil voted to accept Marshall Aid.

MacBride may have misjudged American willingness to intervene, but he did manage to boost his authority within the inter-party Government. His early pre-eminence in the cabinet enabled him to ensure that ERP concerns, OEEC business, applications for Marshall Aid, and plans for spending the money were handled by the Department of External Affairs rather than Finance. MacBride was put in charge rather than the Minister of Finance because the European Economic Cooperation Agreement stated that the Administrator of the ECA would negotiate directly with the OEEC and the OEEC must approve each country's national programme. Seán was Vice-President of the Council of Ministers of the OEEC and was given the task of negotiating with the ECA on behalf of the sixteen countries involved.

His friendships with Garrett and European Ambassador at Large for the ECA, W. Averill Harriman, certainly helped to increase his influence. He was well thought of in United States Government circles; a CIA assessment of MacBride called him

> the outstanding personality of the present Government . . . MacBride has an impeccable revolutionary pedigree . . . Like Costello, a brilliant and successful barrister, he is noted for his forceful advocacy and remarkable talent for cross-examination. He is probably the best debater in the Dáil. He is definitely of Prime Ministerial caliber. He is charming, affable, and intelligent, an excellent diplomat.[93]

The CIA believed that MacBride was 'likely to remain a powerful force in Irish politics'.[94] Despite his near-constant harping on about partition every time they met, Secretary of State Dean Acheson seemed to enjoy Seán's company. When Nunan's replacement, John Hearne, realised that he had scheduled Acheson to be at two separate dinners for MacBride and provided him with a potential excuse for missing one, Acheson replied that 'I saw no reason why I should not dine twice with Mr MacBride.'[95] The OEEC also provided another European forum for Ireland. With the ERP, Seán managed to extend his influence beyond diplomacy into foreign and domestic economic policy.

Despite the popular support and Seán's enthusiasm, the response of the Department of Finance to the Marshall Plan was sceptical. McElligott believed that 'we cannot expect any measure of salvation from the so-called Marshall Plan', as he stated in a review submitted on 1 August 1948.[96] The Department of Finance did not see the benefits of long-term economic planning. As T.K. Whitaker later remarked, 'no one who took part in preparing the recovery programme (and that includes myself) ever looked on it as a development programme, but rather as an exercise that had to be undertaken to persuade the Americans to give us Marshall Aid.'[97] In addition, Marshall Aid proposals could threaten the Department's close relationship with the British Treasury; after 1922, the Department had been modelled on the British Treasury, and collaborated closely with it; the Irish and British economies were linked and close personal ties and friendships existed between Finance and Treasury officials — many Finance officers were on a first-name basis with their Treasury counterparts but not with their colleagues in Irish departments. Finance was afraid that Ireland would be unable to pay back any loans. The Department also thought more conservatively; increased heavy borrowing might provide 'a standing temptation to governments to incur expenditure without regard to the economic consequences.'[98] Cabinet hegemony was at stake; as External Affairs had assumed the leading role in negotiations and planning, that department could be strengthened at Finance's expense. If it did accept a loan, Finance would also have preferred to use the money to repay the national debt.[99]

In the end, MacBride won out. The cabinet approved his plans in December 1948. Most of the Marshall Aid loan went toward long-term projects such as public investment to stimulate industrial development, land rehabilitation, rural electrification, telephones, and improvements in fishery and harbour facilities, and afforestation — projects with little immediate return, though viable in the long run, and strikingly similar to Clann na Poblachta's economic policy presented during the 1948 general election.

As a condition for participating, an economic programme had to be submitted to the OEEC. The *Long-Term Recovery Programme*, published as a white paper in January 1949, was the responsibility of MacBride and Frederick Boland, Secretary of the Department of External Affairs. This nascent attempt may have demonstrated a lack of imagination toward development possibilities; but it proved useful for future economic planning. As John A. Murphy accurately states, the beginnings of economic planning were found in the first inter-party Government rather than Whitaker's better-known memo in November of 1958.[100] Despite the improvised nature of the document and the dependence on projects with little immediate return, the white paper was the first attempt at an overall economic plan since the establishment of the state. As Seán remarked in a speech to the National Press Club on 14 March 1951, the ECA was 'constructive and helpful' and the 'direct financial aid which we received was valuable but far more important in my view was the economic planning which we had to undertake in conjunction with the E.C.A.'[101]

In subsequent years, Ireland did not qualify for as large a share of aid; the United States believed that the Irish economy had shown signs of recovery. In late 1951, the US Government announced that economic assistance was to be considered solely in terms of strengthening NATO and promoting European political unity. Ireland did not want to participate in a mutual assistance pact and, in January 1952, its involvement ended.

As Whelan has contended, Marshall Aid had no dramatic economic impact and Ireland did not share in the Western European recovery of the 1950s. Economic growth and prosperity did not result and the balance-of-payments situation worsened and led to a period of economic depression. Yet Marshall Plan participation did have some tangible benefits: it accounted for 50 per cent of the total inter-party Government's investment, it improved Ireland's standard of living, and it gave the Government economic planning experience and a modernised planning system. Involvement also offered Ireland a chance to re-enter the mainstream of European diplomatic life, to consider its position on European cooperation, to rehabilitate the national image, and to establish a harmonious working relationship with both the United States and the United Kingdom.[102] As Fanning indicates, the Marshall Plan was the 'first great milestone in the path leading tortuously but inexorably to increased Irish involvement in European affairs.'[103]

MacBride's Department also benefited from Marshall Plan involvement. As Michael Kennedy maintains, the ERP helped the Department of External Affairs to expand from a small operation not always taken seriously by its peers in Irish administration to an influential department ranking alongside Finance as one of the senior departments in the Irish civil service.[104]

Participation not only provided the motivation for a restructuring of the Department; it allowed External Affairs to expand its brief into foreign economic policy and multilateral diplomacy; the ERP section developed into the Economic Section, which would handle relations with the EEC.

In the case of the Marshall Plan, the Irish Government could not afford to put principle above practical concerns. By the end of Ireland's participation in the plan, it had received $128 million in loans, $18 million in grant aid, and $1.25 million in technical assistance. Most agree that the Irish Government did not demonstrate good political judgment, either in the way it responded to getting a loan rather than a grant and by attempting to raise the issue of partition. The meeting between MacBride and Hickerson about the Irish receiving loans rather than grants should have made the American position on partition clear to the Irish Government. However, Seán chose either to ignore or to downplay the US position.

MacBride's approach to the Marshall Plan overestimated Ireland's bargaining position with the US administration of the time. The Irish response to the invitation to join the North Atlantic Treaty Organisation also demonstrates an incorrect appraisal of contemporary power politics, but this time with more dire consequences.

On 7 January 1949, the United States informally approached the Irish Government through its embassy in Washington about issuing to Ireland an official invitation to consider becoming a NATO founding nation. The United States was still miffed about Irish wartime neutrality, but, as with the Marshall Plan, Ireland's strategic location and close connections to Britain meant that it could not be completely ignored. A CIA situation report determined that Irish participation would be useful

> because of its strategic location athwart the chief seaways and airways to and from Western Europe. Its terrain and topography lend themselves to rapid construction of airfields which would be invaluable as bases for strategic bomber attacks as far east as the Ural Mountains . . . because hostile forces in Ireland would outflank the main defences of Great Britain, and because it could be used as a base for bombing North America, the denial of Ireland to an enemy is an unavoidable principle of United States security.[105]

The Government responded to the American invitation in an *aide-mémoire* handed in on 8 February 1949 stating that the Irish Government agreed 'with the general aim of the proposed treaty'; however, any military alliance with, or commitment involving military action jointly with, the state that is responsible for the unnatural division of Ireland, which occupies a portion of our country with its armed forces, and which supports undemocratic institutions in the north-eastern corner of Ireland, would be entirely repugnant and unacceptable to the Irish people.[106]

The *aide-mémoire* suggested finding a solution to partition for the reason that 'any detached or impartial survey of the strategic and political position must lead to the conclusion that a friendly and united Ireland on Britain's western approaches is not merely in the interest of Britain but in the interest of all countries concerned with the security of the Atlantic area.'

When asked in the Dáil later that month to summarise the Government's policy on NATO, MacBride responded:

Ireland, as an essentially democratic and freedom-loving country, is anxious to play her full part in protecting and preserving Christian civilisation and the democratic way of life. With the general aim of the proposed Atlantic Pact in this regard, therefore, we are in agreement. In the matter of military measures, however, we are faced with an insuperable difficulty, from the strategic and political points of view, by reason of the fact that six of our north-eastern counties are occupied by British forces against the will of the overwhelming majority of the Irish people. Partition is naturally and bitterly resented by the people of this country as a violation of Ireland's territorial integrity and as a denial in her case of the elementary democratic right of national self determination. As long as Partition lasts, any military alliance or commitment involving joint military action with the State responsible for Partition must be quite out of the question so far as Ireland is concerned. Any such commitment, if undertaken, would involve the prospect of civil conflict in this country in the event of a crisis.[107]

MacBride surmised that Ireland was of vital geographic and strategic importance, so the United States would at least acknowledge the grievance, if not aid in its removal, in order to secure Ireland's presence in NATO. He was not aware that the invitation to join was actually at the suggestion of the British Foreign Office. A note from Ernest Bevin to the State Department the day before Ireland received the official invitation warned that, 'if the Irish raised partition as a barrier to joining the pact', the response should be that the issue was 'beyond their competence' to discuss.[108] The State Department was not as anxious to secure Ireland's membership as Seán thought, and the us Government's response to the *aide-mémoire* was that the partition issue was 'entirely the concern of the governments of Ireland and the UK' and the situation was not relevant to membership of NATO.[109]

MacBride then made 'tentative overtures' about abandoning neutrality and joining NATO in exchange for American support for ending partition.[110] In his view, neutrality would not prevent Ireland from participating in NATO; Ireland joined the OEEC and the Council of Europe and only the Soviet veto kept Ireland out of the United Nations. A CIA report stated that MacBride 'considers it politically impossible for Ireland to join a military alliance while Partition continues',[111] but that political impossibility referred to partition, not Irish neutrality. MacBride was much more preoccupied with partition than with neutrality. Noël Browne confirms this, writing that Seán wanted to abandon neutrality and join NATO, which went against Clann na Poblachta party policy; Browne cites the example of MacBride's 'strange nomination' of Denis Ireland, a NATO supporter, to the Seanad.[112] The Catholic Church was also keen to join; according to Garrett, Archbishop John Charles McQuaid 'assured me that the Roman Catholic Church was in favor of Ireland's accepting the invitation to join the North Atlantic group.'[113] Seán himself stated that 'my overall attitude was if a choice came of ending partition by joining NATO, I would say let's join NATO . . . anything destabilizing partition was worth doing.'[114]

On 4 April 1949, the North Atlantic Treaty (NAT) was signed in Washington. Seven days later, MacBride met with Acheson. They discussed the then state of Europe and partition and NATO membership. Once again, Acheson reiterated the American unwillingness to become involved.[115]

MacBride suggested that Ireland would be happy to join if partition did not exist. He expressed the hope that North Atlantic Treaty signatories could try to create a situation where the problem could be discussed. Seán may have been hoping that Article 4 of the North Atlantic Treaty, which stated that 'the Parties will consult together whenever, in the opinion of any of them, the territorial integrity, political independence or security of any of the Parties is threatened' could be utilised in this regard. Of course, MacBride would have to make sure that this tactic, similar to the 'sore thumb' strategy being employed by the Irish in intra-European groups like the OEEC and the Council of Europe, would be feasible before committing Ireland to the Atlantic Pact.

This approach was also unsuccessful. On 3 June 1949, the State Department informed Nunan that the North Atlantic Treaty has been concluded by the participating nations for their collective defense against aggression and for the preservation of their common Christian and democratic heritage. It was not intended to settle long standing territorial disputes or similar matters which might be at issue between the parties or between a party and any other state.[116]

A year later, the Irish Government was still peddling this idea. The National Security Council (NSC) reported:

the United States replied to the Irish Government to the effect that NAT was not a suitable framework within which to discuss a problem solely the concern of the United Kingdom and Ireland, and that we failed to see any connection between partition and NAT, which was not intended to provide a new forum for the settlement or discussion of long-standing territorial disputes. All other signatories took similar positions.[117]

MacBride's overtures were refused by the United States for four reasons. First, Seán misjudged Ireland's necessity to the pact. An NSC note indicated that 'in the early development of NATO, the United States Government made a study of [Irish ports and airbases] and concluded that although Ireland's military potential was by no means an element essential to the success of NAT, Ireland should be given an opportunity to join the organization.'[118] Irish participation was not necessary for NATO's success and the ultimate conclusion was that there was no military reason to pursue Ireland. As Britain was a member, Northern Ireland's bases and ports would be available for NATO's use. Irish military facilities would be merely complementary to those already available to North Atlantic forces in this area through the adherence to the North Atlantic Treaty of Great Britain and Northern Ireland.[119] It was *Northern* Ireland that was important to North Atlantic defence — if Britain were a member, Northern Ireland would be as well. Therefore partition was not a problem in the context of Western European defence.

In addition, despite official neutrality, Ireland was ideologically aligned with the West and the 'power of the pulpit' ensured that Ireland would remain so. An example was Irish intervention in the Italian election of 1948, where it seemed that the Italian Communist Party might win a majority. If there were conflict, it was easy to see where Ireland's loyalties would lie. An NSC report surmised that

despite strong anti-communist sentiments, the Irish Government for domestic political considerations still adheres strongly to its traditional policy of neutrality which was militarily embarrassing to the Allies in World War II. In a war against communism, a policy of Irish neutrality undoubtedly would be more benevolent to the Western Allies than in World War II and less useful to the Soviet Union, which has no diplomatic representatives in Ireland, than Irish neutrality was to the Axis.[120]

If war broke out, pressure from the Church hierarchy, the Dominions, and the United States would ensure Dublin's participation. Indeed, as MacBride stated in the Dáil, 'we in Ireland are not much troubled by conflicting ideologies. We are firm believers in democracy in its true sense and are firmly attached to the principles of Christianity. Our sympathies, therefore, lie clearly with the nations of Western Europe.'[121]

Moreover, MacBride misjudged the friendship between Britain and the United States. After the Second World War and in a Cold War context, they were close allies. The United Kingdom was the most responsible for getting the US involved in Europe and was an original signatory of the Brussels Pact. The British were undisturbed about Ireland's absence; they were not surprised by the Irish response to the offer and they were certain that Ireland would be an ally in any war with the Soviets. Furthermore, the Ireland Act of 1949 had guaranteed that Britain would not abandon partition unless a majority in the Northern Ireland Parliament consented. Acheson, Cronin argues, was an 'Anglophile', the son of an Anglican bishop with 'little sympathy or patience with Irish nationalism or its advocates'.[122] This is not a fair assessment of Acheson; he proved willing to listen to Irish concerns and he should not be singled out as the only Anglophile in the State Department.

Irish-American NATO negotiations appear to reflect Lyons's well-known summation of Irish neutrality creating an atmosphere similar to Plato's Cave, where what the prisoners see and hear are shadows and echoes cast by objects that they do not see, mistaking appearance for reality and knowing nothing of the real causes of the shadows.[123] Perhaps neutrality had dulled Irish minds to the nature of the Irish-American relationship as well as the improved Anglo-American relationship and how the war had altered both. The United States was unlikely to risk alienating Britain, then its most important single ally, for the sake of a country that had remained neutral throughout the Second World War. As an NSC note indicated, 'Irish participation was by no means essential for NATO's success. Irish military facilities would be merely "complementary" to those already available to North Atlantic forces in this area through the adherence to the North Atlantic treaty of Great Britain and Northern Ireland.'[124] When Dublin argued that partition meant that Ireland could not join NATO, Washington concluded that it meant that Ireland need not join NATO.

Finally, MacBride was blind to the realities of Cold War power politics. He did not put the issue in a global framework; rather he placed partition in terms of an Anglo-Irish framework. A Foreign Office report correctly pointed out that 'Anglo Irish politics influence Eire's approach to every problem.'[125] Of course, the United States had other concerns. The nation was moving from a period of non-involvement in European affairs to becoming more involved in a tense atmosphere. Despite James Dillon's comment that sustaining partition was in 'the prime interests of Communism in the world to-day' by fomenting division between the United States and the British Commonwealth, the United States did not take that idea seriously.[126] As NATO's basic purpose was to 'keep the Soviets out, get the Americans in, and hold the Germans down', a comparatively minor political squabble between two friendly nations was not a major concern.[127]

Domestic political concerns provide some explanation of the Government's behaviour. MacBride thought that joining NATO might lead to Northern nationalists accusing the Government of selling them out, which could bring about the fall of his Government. In a speech to the National Press Club on 14 March 1951, Seán declared that 'Partition is the cause of such feeling in Ireland that no Irish Government could attempt, without immediately being driven from office, to enter into a military alliance with the power which is responsible for it.'[128] Of course, this was based on the assumption that Northern Ireland would join the Republic if permitted, an assumption that was a miscalculation. If the inter-party Government had proved willing to join, it would have left itself open to criticism from de Valera and Fianna Fáil for selling out the Northern minority and accepting partition. MacBride told Garrett that 'anti-partitionists would feel that Eire was giving something to Western Europe and America without getting anything in return and it would be considered foolish to have thrown away such a promising opportunity to bargain.'[129] Once again, the undesirability of appearing soft on partition prevented the Government from imagining the bigger picture.

De Valera and Fianna Fáil backed the policy, which is not surprising as they had upheld neutrality in the last world war. MacBride revealed later that

> there was no one in the Government who wanted to join NATO. I didn't have to fight for it in the Cabinet. Each member had his own set of reasons, I'm sure. Some objected because of partition, others because it was a military alliance. We had emerged from a war in which we had been successfully neutral and this was a bipartisan policy.[130]

This was not entirely accurate; some in government were pro-NATO, like Minister for Finance Patrick McGilligan and Dillon, who had advocated abandoning neutrality to aid the Allies during the Second World War. Yet, they did not protest too much because they did not want to appear soft on partition. *The Irish Times* criticised the Government, pointing out that partition 'will not be ended by a childish refusal to help the British, Canadians, Americans, and the rest to insure themselves against the dire hazards of a possible war.'[131] The paper called not joining 'a serious mistake' and stated that the Irish Government's position did not reflect the true attitude of the people.[132] No popular vote was ever held to gauge the Irish electorate's reaction to the prospect of joining NATO.[133] De Valera's anti-partition tour and removal from the Commonwealth were taking place at the same time, which may account for the Government's desire to 'cleave fast to neutrality if only for domestic political considerations.'[134]

The American Ambassador to Ireland, George Garrett, reported that Church intervention might be able to convince Ireland to join; Archbishop McQuaid assured him 'that the Roman Catholic Church was in favour of Ireland's accepting the invitation to join the North Atlantic group.'[135] But Garrett pointed out that 'the Church's opinion on the issue would cut very little ice, as whenever in recent Irish history politics and the Church have clashed, politics have always come out on top.'[136] This, of course, is true only in the context of civil war and partition; in domestic politics, the Church had much more say.

From 1949 to 1950, MacBride tried to negotiate a bilateral defence treaty between the United States and Ireland, maintaining that, in the event of an invasion, Ireland would be defenceless. Garrett thought that a defence treaty was a good idea:

> It is unfortunate all around that political considerations make it impossible for any Irish Government to accept membership in the North Atlantic Council until the question of Partition has been resolved. Military aid, I feel convinced, would furnish the impetus that could lead to a bilateral treaty, which, although in the nature of a side-door entrance, would, nevertheless, bring Ireland into the defense picture against any aggression on the part of the U.S.S.R.[137]

The final decision on that matter was that 'United States–Irish bilateral arrangements would create friction and resentment among the NAT signatories who have assumed collective mutual assistance obligations.'[138] A bilateral treaty would probably be unnecessary; the Truman administration's containment policy, shown in response to increasing communist influence in Greece and Turkey, demonstrated a US willingness to protect countries under communist threat.

As late as 13 March 1951, with the inter-party Government's days dwindling, MacBride paid a courtesy call on Acheson. They spoke about the struggle against communism and Seán once again brought up ending partition. Acheson noted that

> he [MacBride] thought there was an increase in the realization of this point of view even in London but that he did not think that, by itself, the United Kingdom would do anything about it. He expressed the view that if the United States were to encourage the United Kingdom to do something result would flow from such a step.

Acheson replied that, 'I had always regarded the problem as one which should be decided by his Government, the United Kingdom and the people of the northern counties.'[139] Neither side had altered its perspective.

The unwavering position of the United States is encapsulated in an NSC Statement of Policy written on 17 October 1950: 'the United States should . . . Continue its present policy of maintaining an attitude of readiness to welcome Ireland as a member of the North Atlantic Treaty Organization, at this time leaving the initiative to Ireland . . . Avoid discussion of bilateral arrangements for a military assistance program outside NATO.'[140]

The Government would later try to package not participating in NATO as a foreign policy success, one that protected neutrality and kept the Irish people from revolting. Cronin agrees with that evaluation, arguing that in 1949, Ireland successfully avoided being drawn into a military alliance that would have limited its sovereignty at home and independence in foreign affairs.[141] Yet, that 'success' was not intentional; it was not the goal of the policy. As Boland wrote to Ambassador to the Holy See Joseph Walshe, 'the major objective of our present efforts is to get the United States or Canada, or both to act.'[142] Cronin further argues that 'if partition was a good enough reason to stay out of the second world war, then it was sufficient reason to stay out of the cold war.'[143] Yet, although partition was a decisive factor, it was not the only reason Ireland stayed out of the Second World War. De Valera claimed that the principal reason was that a small country would only be damaged in a conflict involving major states.[144] When offered the opportunity to end partition in exchange for Irish participation in the war, de Valera refused.

Ultimately, if the Government was serious about not joining NATO because of neutrality, it should not have shown itself willing to bargain. If it sincerely wanted to solve the partition problem, it should have joined. As Dermot Keogh observed, MacBride and the Government's 'posturing on NATO was as gauche as it was naive. It introduced a note of crude horse-trading into high diplomacy.'[145] The argument that 'the Alliance itself would be an ideal means by which Ireland could emerge from isolation, play an active part in international affairs, and contribute to the containment of communism' is correct; it would also have erased some of the stigma of Second World War neutrality.[146]

Joining NATO would have been beneficial to Ireland in the long term and would have been possible to justify to public opinion. Taking part would have provided another opportunity for functional cooperation between the North and South. It might also have influenced Britain: 'the United Kingdom are in no way opposed to North and South coming together when they can agree to do so and . . . co-operation on Western European affairs would seem to point in this direction.'[147] As McCabe correctly surmised, 'Eire's acceptance of participation in NATO would have presented Britain with the major difficulty of justifying her continued support for the Unionists' position on the partition of Ireland.'[148] Taking part would have demonstrated that Ireland was willing to cooperate and might have made the United States more amenable to mediation. As a CIA report of April 1949 explained, 'the end of partition is conceivable only in connection with Ireland's adhering to an alliance such as the suggested North Atlantic Pact, in which case bases would presumably be available under the terms of the alliance.'[149]

In addition, NATO was a good ideological fit: the Irish were hostile toward atheistic communism; The Irish Times editorialised that non-participation was 'a direct contradiction of the Irish people's natural instincts'.[150] NATO was led by the United States, not Britain. The treaty was strictly defensive, which would have suited a neutral nation, where it is permissible to respond when threatened. On the other hand, the Soviet Union was not specifically hostile to Ireland, which meant that defence considerations were minor.[151]

Also, participating would have helped to increase Ireland's influence in European politics, where the Irish were trying to make an impact. Choosing not to join the North Atlantic Treaty Organisation seemed to be an exception to the partition strategy rule of entering international organisations to publicise the problem. Bevin and Paul-Henri Spaak were the chief European proponents of the Atlantic Pact. Bevin and Anthony Eden were disappointed that Ireland did not join.[152] Apparently 'Spaak was indignant over the Irish position', the United States Ambassador in Brussels reported and 'thought their contingent proposition was absurd and typical.'[153]

Regarding defence, Ireland kept to a neutrality policy, but as an expression of anti-partitionism rather than national sovereignty, and remained a non-aligned country in a Europe split by NATO and the Warsaw Pact. Ireland never became a member and MacBride's own attitude toward the organisation altered as he became more involved in human rights causes and less obsessed with partition. In 1983, he was

> much more hostile. He grew totally opposed to membership, even by a united Ireland, citing three main reasons: NATO's commitment to nuclear weapons; its support of undemocratic and colonialist regimes, notably in South Africa; and his belief that the division of the world into power blocs accelerates the arms race and increases the likelihood of a world war.[154]

The United States would later become much more involved in negotiations between Ireland and Britain, playing a major part in the Good Friday Agreement. However, involvement came only when violence had intensified in the North and after the Cold War had ended, at a time when the British, Irish, and Northern Irish were willing to talk together. The United States was also more comfortable with a peacemaker role, as Richard Bourke observed, 'since the end of 1980s, conflict resolution has been a minor growth industry.'[155]

MacBride may have appeared over-optimistic and naïve, especially if he expected the United States to respond to the partition issue and, like the larger campaign to end partition, he and the inter-party Government persisted in a policy that was not working. However, they did this largely for the benefit of domestic political concerns so that the Government would not appear weak on partition. Irish-American politician and former Speaker of the House of Representatives Thomas P. 'Tip' O'Neill's assertion that 'all politics is local' was true in two senses: the Irish at home determined foreign policy in respect of partition, and the Irish abroad were more focused on America than on Ireland. Both Irish and Irish-American politicians were perhaps also more concerned with their constituents' response than with practical solutions to the partition situation. Hickerson wrote to Garrett in May 1948 that 'as a result of Mr De Valera's use of the American public as a sounding board to demonstrate his firm position against partition, the Costello Government has been required to demonstrate to the Irish electorate that it is equally zealous.'[156]

The policy toward the United States cannot be considered a triumph in terms of ending partition, yet it might be seen as successful if the goal was to appear firm on the partition issue. It can be argued that the Irish Government was fully aware that the US would be unwilling to help solve the problem, that it would be impossible to 'press a great power into the services of a small nation'.[157] Thus the Irish saw no harm in beating a dead horse, even though it might jeopardise a good relationship with the United States.

Chapter 7 ∿

COMING OUT OF THE CAVE: IRELAND IN THE WIDER WORLD

'No man is an island entire of itself; every man is a piece of the continent, a part of the main.'

— JOHN DONNE

One of Seán MacBride's most important contributions during his time in ministerial office is involvement in the Council of Europe and other multilateral organisations. As Minister for External Affairs, he was directly responsible for Ireland's growing role in European politics. By expanding Ireland's international presence, he was attempting to forge an independent identity for the country. Institutions like the Council of Europe allowed MacBride an international forum to seek support for ending partition, and his apparent obsession with the topic sometimes led to the impression that partition was all that Ireland was concerned with. Yet, despite the shadow of partition, Ireland made many positive contributions to European integration, and events taking place during his tenure led to the expansion of the Department of External Affairs and long-term economic planning. MacBride's attempt to internationalise Irish politics would also play an influential part in shaping his later career.

After the repeal of the External Relations Act and the departure from the Commonwealth, Ireland played a more significant role in international relations than is sometimes credited. Scholars of modern Irish history have tended to focus more on Ireland's relationship with Britain and the situation in the North than on other foreign policy issues.[1] As well as comparatively little being written on Ireland and Europe during this period, there are a few misconceptions about Irish foreign policy. Such errors include overestimating the Irish obsession with partition and describing the period as stagnant. This situation is unfortunate because the burgeoning Irish presence in international relations may be the one notable area where MacBride and the inter-party Government demonstrated an active, rather than reactive policy.

His contribution has also been overshadowed somewhat by later politicians and advocates of European cooperation such as Frank Aiken and Seán Lemass. As Patrick Keatinge, from a political science perspective, correctly concludes, MacBride 'can be said to have grasped firmly the few opportunities open to Ireland in those years for pursuing an active foreign policy.'[2]

Opportunities for an active foreign policy were relatively new to the Irish. As Ireland was part of the United Kingdom until 1921, Britain insulated the island and prevented it from developing a distinct foreign policy.[3] The important exception was the 'England's difficulty is Ireland's opportunity' mindset. Hence, Ireland did not involve itself in Europe, except to ask for help in battling the British, establishing ties to the French in 1798 and the Germans in 1916, for, as Seán T. Ó Ceallaigh colourfully put it, 'whipping John Bull'. There were no feelings of attachment or antagonism toward any other European country; Ireland's main gripe was with Britain, which coloured its relationship with other countries. Furthermore, the tradition of emigration was limited mainly to Britain and its dominions and to the United States. Ireland shared no borders with another foreign power, so it had no close contact with neighbouring countries and its only property dispute was with Britain.

With the important exception of the Six Counties, Ireland was a Free State within the British Commonwealth after 1921. Not surprisingly, the Irish were more concerned with the formation of statehood than with foreign policy issues; 'new states, in their formative years, need first to establish their sense of national and international identity before entering into international organisations where they may have to dilute their sovereignty for the greater good.'[4] However, the country was not completely insular: Ireland was a member of the League of Nations and Michael Kennedy concluded that the League provided Ireland with 'an international identity, purpose and sense of place' in the crucial years of consolidation.[5]

Ireland adopted an official neutrality policy during the Second World War and managed somewhat successfully to keep to this policy. However, many argue that the country was not truly neutral, what Norman MacQueen calls a 'peculiar neutrality'.[6] If Ireland was not truly neutral during the war, it was even less so afterward: 'neutrality had been a wartime expedient but was not necessarily a peacetime preference.'[7] De Valera's primary concern was sovereignty, not neutrality. Despite the successful show of independence, for geographic, economic, and historical reasons, Ireland maintained a close relationship with Britain and the increasing post-war bipolarisation of Europe also put Ireland and Britain on the same side. By 1949, even MacBride admitted that, in the future, Irish security 'would be bound up with Britain's security.'[8]

The Cold War also affected Irish neutrality. A staunchly Catholic country, Ireland had a firmly anti-communist ideology. As future Taoiseach John A. Costello declared in the Dáil, 'whether or not we were neutral in the last war, there can never be any question again of this country being neutral in any future war.'[9] Ireland was not on the fence between the Eastern and Western blocs; partition, not neutrality, had kept Ireland out of NATO, providing 'the *sole* obstacle to Ireland's participation in the Atlantic Pact.'[10] A notable example of the lack of ideological neutrality was Ireland's intervention in the Italian election of 1948, where the communist-led Popular Democratic Front seemed capable of winning a majority in the Italian Parliament. Irish interference, consisting mainly of soliciting contributions to generate anti-communist campaign materials, can hardly be described as the act of a neutral nation.[11] Conor Cruise O'Brien observed that the

> tendency to associate the national interests with those of Britain, anti-Communism, sympathy with Catholic parties and statesmen in Western Europe, traditional respect for the political views of the Irish Catholic hierarchy . . . all these attractions pulled in the same way; towards involvement on the Western side in the Cold War.[12]

Despite Ireland's official non-participation in the Second World War, there were many similarities between the European countries that had been involved in the war and Ireland in the late 1940s: they all experienced stagnant economies, reshuffling of political parties and groupings, developing Cold War loyalties, and a general 'mood of disenchantment'.[13] Yet immediately following the war, European activists virtually ignored Ireland because, as Miriam Hederman points out, it was a relatively poor country, it was not a particular threat to be mollified or challenged, there was little pre-war political or economic upheaval, the major Irish political parties were not involved in any international political movements, and the Irish politicians of the younger generation were unknown to their European counterparts.[14] Moreover, Irish politics could be rather parochial; Irish TDs 'tended to be primarily local . . . representatives, responsible for advocating and advancing of affairs for [their] constituents and [their] locality.'[15] Foreign policy, if a concern at all, was definitely a secondary one. Keatinge points out that a typical TD was unlikely to be well informed about foreign affairs.[16]

Seán was an exception. As Keogh indicates, 'MacBride was a Christian Democrat and it was quite fashionable to speak of European unity in 1948 within those circles. MacBride saw himself in the fashionable company of Alcide de Gasperi in Italy, Robert Schuman in France, Konrad Adenauer in Germany and Pius XII'.[17] He was well suited to a diplomatic life: French was his first language, he had lived in Paris until he was thirteen, he was enthusiastic about European unity, and as a lawyer and founder of a political party, he was familiar with constitutional and international issues.

Another advantage was timing — Seán arrived in government at a propitious period. Though Ireland remained bound to Britain in some ways, it was looking to distinguish itself in others. It did not want to be seen as an appendage; the psychological importance of separating from the mother country, especially after repeal, must be taken into consideration. The inter-party Government's self-perception situated Ireland as a 'link between the Old World and the New World'.[18] Such assessments may have been grandiose and misguided; as Keogh concludes, Seán 'suffered from having spent too long in Plato's Cave.'[19] Yet, this perception does provide a cogent reason, other than publicising partition, for favouring closer contact with Europe. Senator James Douglas, one of the first delegates to the Council of Europe, summarised the country's changing mood during a Seanad debate on proposals for a united Europe:

> For years our people were insular in their outlook and only a small minority took a real interest in international affairs. During the war we were prevented by the censorship from reading any news which the powers that be thought might interfere with our neutrality, and, generally speaking, the Government during that period discouraged too much interest or curiosity on the part of the man in the street in what was taking place in Europe. A change took place after the end of the war, and I think I am correct in stating that there is now much more interest in European affairs than there has been for a long time.[20]

Involvement in European movements allowed Ireland to escape the confines of Anglo-Irish preoccupations and a relationship that had become stifling.[21] For the Republic, to be European was a way to be acceptably 'not British'. As Frederick Boland observed, the difference between Seán MacBride and Éamon de Valera, the previous Minister for External Affairs, was that

MacBride believed in Western European cooperation while de Valera looked to Commonwealth cooperation.[22] The inter-party Government marked a change of direction. Neutrality had been de Valera and Fianna Fáil's policy; the new Government looked to formulate a unique course of action.

De Valera believed that the External Relations Act, though ambiguous, could provide a bridge that might end partition; he told his biographer, Frank Gallagher, that repeal of the act was the 'height of folly' which 'troubled' him.[23] He also told Nicholas Mansergh in February of 1952 that he had wanted Ireland to remain associated with the Commonwealth.[24] Whereas de Valera would have preferred to remain just inside the Commonwealth, the inter-party Government took Ireland out in 1949, and, as Mansergh states, a distinctive voice within the Commonwealth was lost.[25]

The counterpoint then to secession was membership in the European Recovery Programme and the Council of Europe, a return to the cultural area of which Ireland was a part. As Ireland chose not to join NATO and was not yet a member of the United Nations, participation in European integration provided the country with an opportunity to make itself known. The relationship with Britain, the United States, and the Commonwealth may have been the focus in the immediate post-war period, as emigration made Britain and America the two foreign countries Ireland was most familiar with, yet it also took an interest in fellow Catholic states like Italy, Spain, Portugal, and France, especially because of the perceived threat of atheistic communism.[26] Seán proved willing to support Spain and Portugal's entry into the Council of Europe despite their fascist regimes. In late 1948, the Director of the Political Division of the Spanish Foreign Office Señor Juan Sebastián de Erice suggested that a neutral bloc consisting of Spain, Portugal, Argentina and Ireland be formed to defend Catholicism, especially in regard to access and defence of the Holy Places in Palestine and resistance to communism.[27] Nothing came of the proposal, as Ireland preferred to consult with the Vatican regarding Catholic associations, and Ambassador to the Holy See Joseph Walshe believed that the Vatican 'would prefer to see us maintain our extremely strong position in the English speaking Catholic world, as a defender of Catholic principles . . . rather than as an ally of countries where the use [is] made by politicians of the Catholic religion to uphold essentially undemocratic regimes.'[28] The discussion shows that an alliance had at least been contemplated.

Post-war plans for integration 'offered Ireland an opportunity to develop beyond the confines of Commonwealth and diaspora.'[29] Yet, there were also pragmatic reasons for encouraging relationships with other European countries; Ireland was tied to Britain economically — 90 per cent of Irish food exports went to the UK, and Ireland wanted to improve the stagnant post-war economy with other agricultural markets and trading partners.[30] Seán believed that increased foreign trade was necessary for economic development and the improvement of living standards.[31]

Similar to neutrality, the idea of a closer relationship with Europe provided cohesion within the Republic. Wider involvement in European affairs would help decrease any leftover preoccupation with civil war politics; 'a new generation is rising, which, I trust, will approach the problems of Ireland's reconstruction objectively and with a mind free from past dissensions.'[32] MacBride accurately surmised that no major disagreements existed in the foreign policy of the Irish political parties; 'Fundamentally, there is no difference of policy between the Parties in the House in relation to our external policy. My function, therefore, is to give effect to the best of my ability, to the general policy upon which the Government and all Parties in the House are agreed.'[33] Participation would also provide the opportunity to show sovereignty and independent decision-making power. Britain and Ireland were equal in terms of international law and would later possess the same status in the European Community.

Ireland's first post-war integration undertaking began with the Council of Europe, the result of attempts at international cooperation after the end of the war. The idea to form a 'United States of Europe' was first proposed by Winston Churchill in his address in Zurich on 19 September 1946. Other concepts regarding the tightening of cooperation among European countries emerged almost simultaneously. The goal was to create some form of closer association to recover and reassert influence in the post-war world.[34] Founded in 1949, it was the first European post-war political organisation. Its aim was to create a common democratic and legal area structured around the European Convention on Human Rights and to develop ways of cooperation on a wide range of issues. The basic structure has remained unchanged since its founding.

As Ireland did not join the European Economic Community until 1973, from 1945 to 1973 the Council of Europe provided the most important link to Western Europe and, until Ireland was permitted to join the United Nations in 1955, the only international forum where Ireland could participate as an equal, and learn how international organisations operated.

In addition, with the notable exceptions of Churchill and Ernest Bevin, Britain did not appear enthused: the 'official attitude of Great Britain toward the young Council of Europe was cold and disinterested, and even in some cases almost hostile.'[35] When Churchill asked for Clement Attlee's support before the Hague Conference, Attlee replied that 'it would be undesirable for the Government to take any official action in regard to this Conference.'[36] The Irish sensed this ambivalence; a 1950 External Affairs memo indicated that 'British policy seems to have been directed, in the main, to the task of slowing up or side-tracking any proposals for a greater degree of European cooperation.'[37] British aloofness could provide a chance for the Irish to distinguish themselves as well as providing an opportunity to prove that military neutrality did not mean political isolationism.

An International Committee of Movements for European Unity convened a meeting to demonstrate support for the cause of union and to make recommendations for its execution, believing that 'only a genuine European federation would be able to ensure the permanent peace of the continent.'[38] Ireland sent a delegation to the Hague for the Congress of Europe which began on 7 May 1948. The delegation consisted of Senator James Douglas, President of University College Dublin Michael Tierney, and Labour Senator Eleanor Butler. The *Irish Independent* called the Hague Congress 'one of the most remarkable gatherings of our time'.[39] Professor Tierney reported that he was 'greatly impressed by the representative character of the Congress and by the sincerity and extent of the movement for a united Europe.'[40]

The delegates reported back to MacBride, stressing the atmosphere of Christian Democracy present at the assembly. This attitude encouraged Seán, who 'combined enthusiasm for aspects of European cooperation and convergence — particularly in respect of individual rights, democratic values and the defence of Christianity.'[41] He believed that a united Europe would be safe from communism, which he then felt was 'an ideology that takes little or no cognisance of the elementary principles of democracy and personal liberty.'[42] The Church also supported the idea; Archbishop of Dublin John Charles McQuaid was 'very interested in, and favourable to' European unity and church–state relations were important to Seán.[43]

Aside from MacBride, few other politicians in Ireland were excited about closer ties with the continent. The Irish delegates at the Hague found themselves among prime ministers, elected parliamentary representatives, and distinguished national figures, which may say something about the official level of commitment, as Ireland sent senators rather than the Taoiseach or cabinet ministers.[44] While reporting to the Seanad regarding the Hague conference, Seán was quick to point out that 'I am speaking on my own, without the authority of the Government and without in any way committing the Government to any proposals contained in this resolution or to the proposal for the formation of a united states of Europe put forward at The Hague.'[45] Ireland did not send delegates to the Interlaken meeting beginning on 1 September, believing that 'it was not of sufficient importance.'[46] Only one Irish delegate was sent to the Paris meeting to draw up the Statute and Agenda for the Consultative Assembly in Strasbourg.

Like the British, Irish political parties seemed to prefer traditional, intergovernmental organisations like the OEEC to the Assembly of the Council of Europe, a new concept, which can explain this lack of participation.[47] A recent Anglo-Irish trade agreement had shown the importance of the British market, and during his tenure in office, de Valera had tried to maintain good relations with Britain and was wary of pooling sovereignty in a federal Europe, as he argued in the Dáil regarding free trade agreements, 'Only the powerful States can, in any sense, regard themselves as completely sovereign, and you deprive yourself of the means of doing as you please the moment you sign any international agreement.'[48] There was also a question of funds: sending delegations to the Continent may have been seen as a luxury that the Irish economy of the time could not afford.

Despite any early misgivings, there was little debate anywhere else in the country on integration and MacBride declared that 'Ireland should begin to think about these plans . . . isolationism is no longer possible.'[49] Seán pointed out that taking part would publicise the partition issue, another point that all parties agreed on; while addressing the Seanad, he declared that the Irish 'would achieve the unity of Ireland . . . by playing their part in European affairs and not by sulking in the corner.'[50]

The International Committee of United European Movements, formed to organise the Congress of Europe, became the 'European Movement', involving de Gasperi, Paul-Henri Spaak, Leon Blum, and Churchill, and the programmes outlined led to proposals for a Council of Europe. The Council came into being nine months later and Ireland received an invitation to join in 1949. In an extensive, well-researched speech, providing a detailed outline of the growth of the concept of European unity and reasons for Irish participation, as well as describing how the Council would work, Seán asked the Dáil to approve Irish participation:

> As the memorandum itself put it, the new organisation was to be a 'federation based on the idea of union and not of unity', that is to say, a federation elastic enough to respect the independence and national sovereignty of each State while guaranteeing to all the benefits of collective solidarity . . . At the outset, I should emphasise that there is no desire in this statute to interfere in any way with the independence and sovereignty of the participating nations . . . The one thing that is all-important is the elimination of the causes of war. Destructive as the last two wars have been, it is now abundantly clear that another war must lead to the complete

material destruction of the countries through which the war passes. The material destruction caused by war is only part of the damage which war causes to the structure of our civilisation and society. It destroys and distorts moral values that have taken centuries to build . . . Communism, in the main, was built out of the wreckage of the last two wars. World War I, in effect, created a situation in Central Europe which caused World War II. The last war has created a situation which at present disrupts Europe . . . The Council of Europe is a recognition of the dangers and of the remedy for these dangers to which I have just referred . . . In broad outline the statute seeks to provide for closer co-operation and contact between European States. It provides machinery for this purpose at Governmental level and at Parliamentary or representative levels. Its success will depend on the degree of understanding and co-operation it can bring about, not merely between Governments and representatives of different countries . . . It can . . . help in both spheres by creating a public opinion that will emphasise the ethical and moral basis which must govern human action and relationship . . . it is, in my view, one of the most important and constructive developments that have taken place in Europe.[51]

The Irish Times remarked that this Dáil speech was a 'masterly exposé of the project on which he has set his heart', and that 'every intelligent Irishman will rejoice that his country is taking a useful part in the plan for a federated Europe, and the Minister is to be congratulated on his personal initiative.'[52] Two days later, The Irish Times wrote that 'he is trying to bring Ireland into the main stream of European progress. He is taking a keen interest in international politics; and, although he has made mistakes, he deserves full credit for the work he has been doing abroad.'[53]

Seán felt that there should be a solid Irish presence in the Council of Europe because, 'As a predominantly Christian nation and as a people with a long tradition of idealism devoid of any desire to dominate, politically or economically, any other nation, we can and should take a leading part in steering Europe to a co-operative basis of organisation.'[54] Ireland sent strong delegations to the first sessions of the Assembly: William Norton (Labour Party leader and Tánaiste), James Everett (Minister for Posts and Telegraphs), de Valera, and Seán MacEntee. The substitutes were Frank Aiken, Deputy Gerard Sweetman, Senator James Crosbie, and Senator John Finan. The selection of delegates suggests cross-party cooperation as well as a departure from the initial cautious interest in integration.

Many have argued that Ireland took such an active role in the Council of

Europe only to raise the partition matter, part of the 'sore thumb' strategy to publicise whenever possible the injustice of its situation. As Costello stated at Fine Gael's 1949 ard-fheis, 'we have brought the partition question up to the international plane, as we intended to bring it, and on that plane we will succeed in ending partition.'[55] Some, like Norton, saw the Council of Europe as a way to reach an international audience about the evils of partition while others believed that the anti-partition references were mere posturing for domestic political considerations. As Conor Cruise O'Brien observed, 'our Parliamentary delegates to the Council of Europe seemed to devote their time to making speeches about partition; speeches which were designed to be read at home, but which unfortunately had to be listened to abroad.'[56] He later admitted that MacBride was 'well fitted to play a useful and acceptable role in the major international organs to which Ireland then belonged', but was hamstrung because the Government, who could not appear less than vigilant regarding the topic, obliged him to administer 'pin pricks to Great Britain in the councils of these institutions.'[57]

This may have been an effective strategy for drumming up support at home, but it did not win Ireland friends in the Council. The Council's reaction to the partition speeches tended to be 'boredom mingled with bewilderment' at best, frustration at worst.[58] At the second session of the Council, in response to MacEntee's speech linking partition with human rights abuses, President Spaak replied, 'We must not allow every Debate to become the object of a dispute between the Representatives of Ireland and Great Britain . . . I beg you to keep to the matter at hand.'[59] At a meeting to discuss a potential European Army, Spaak became so exasperated that he beat furiously on his desk with a ruler to stop the partition conversation.[60]

The division of Ireland was a comparatively small dilemma and was not seen as a sufficient reason for offending Britain, whom many European politicians felt grateful to in the aftermath of the Second World War. During the opening address of the Consultative Assembly of the Council of Europe, given by Edouard Herriot, Herriot thanked Churchill 'for in many moments of deep tragedy he bore upon his shoulders the whole weight of the world crying out for help. From his mind sprang the movement which has brought us together here.'[61] *The Leader* pointed out 'while it is well that our statesmen should draw attention to the end of partition, it must be quite obvious that no western European governments or non-communist politicians are prepared to seriously embarrass Great Britain under existing conditions.'[62] It was not only a matter of obliging Britain; *The Irish Times* editorial of 13 August 1949 pointed out that 'most of the delegates at Strasbourg have lived at one time under the rule of real dictatorships' and references to a six-county 'police state' left them cold.[63] Larger issues than an Irish domestic dispute were in question; Churchill himself at a speech at the Hague stated that 'territorial ambitions must be set aside and national rivalries must be resigned to the question of who can render the most distinguished service to the common cause.'[64]

In the Dáil, MacBride defended the anti-partition strategy:

Obviously, if close co-operation is to be achieved between European nations, the first essential is to discuss and, if possible, remove the causes of friction that may exist between the nations that compose the Council of Europe. Partition is certainly one of the outstanding causes of friction in Western Europe to-day. As Irishmen, we make no apology for desiring the territorial unity of our nation . . . As Europeans, we make no apology for seeking to remove one of the causes of disunity in Europe.[65]

Although his claim that the division of Ireland was an outstanding cause of friction was grandiose, he also accurately pointed out that

our representatives, however, did not confine themselves to matters of purely national interest. On the broader plane, of international co-operation, they were to the fore with their contributions to the discussions on the many complex problems that arose; these included such matters as the future political structure of Europe, economic co-operation, human rights, cultural co-operation and co-operation in the field of social security. They made important contributions to the work of the various Assembly Committees, as well as to the debates in the Assembly itself.[66]

Speeches on partition were not just political posturing for the Irish; their delegates did sincerely consider partition to be unjust. Furthermore, Irish initiatives went wider than the rhetorical focus on partition might suggest.[67] Once anti-partition fever died down, Ireland became a model member of the Council, the first country to accept the jurisdiction of the European Court of Human Rights. Delegates of the Council commented that 'Ireland had an individual approach to many questions, that their suggestions were made with cogency and that they were constructive.'[68] The widespread portrayal of Irish delegates bringing up the issue at every possible opportunity is inaccurate — the transcript of the August 1950 sessions shows that they were focused on the issues at hand.[69] MacBride involved himself in improving the structure and function of the group, making efforts to achieve closer unity between the Committee of Ministers and the Consultative Assembly. 'Mr MacBride already has managed to keep on excellent terms with all his European colleagues.'[70] He worked well with others and proved to be dynamic, or at least this is how the world press perceived him — 'a trio of "little ministers" — Belgium's Spaak, Austria's Gruber and Ireland's MacBride — have been giving the hot-foot to the slower-moving Ministers of the larger Western European countries.'[71] The Belgian pictorial, Le Face-à-main, reported that 'avec Churchill et Spaak, dont la popularité est énorme, c'est Sean MacBride, le brillant ministre des Affaires étrangères d'Irlande, qui a le plus de succès.'[72]

Ireland's initial involvement in the Council concerned the spheres of democratic values and human rights. Seán insisted that human rights be at the top of the Council of Europe's priorities, which was the realm where the Council excelled, and he played a significant part in its development.[73] He was partly responsible for the negotiation and ratification of the European Convention on Human Rights, the greatest accomplishment of the Council of Europe, as Bevin wrote to Seán 'a positive achievement of the first importance'.[74] Ratification of the document, which guarantees the right to life, liberty, security, fair trial, freedom of thought, conscience, religion, and speech, became a condition of membership of the Council. Seán hoped that it could help to bring about a federal union of Ireland; at least it would protect the rights of the nationalist minority in the North.[75] In addition, in 1948, he sponsored and signed the Convention for European Economic Cooperation, in 1949 the Statute of the Council of Europe, and in 1949 the Geneva Convention for the Protection of War Victims. He also utilised the Council to emphasise the importance of civil liberties and highlight the plight of political prisoners, which were long-standing concerns of his.

Ireland also benefited from the fact that it possessed an equal say within the Assembly. When asked about the allocation of delegates within the Council, MacBride replied, 'I am glad to say that the number of delegates allocated was not based on population or national income figures. It was intended . . . to give adequate representation to small countries irrespective of their size, population or wealth. To that extent, I think that the small nations of Europe have benefited.'[76] Thus, sovereignty was not compromised and Ireland had just as much of a say as larger, more populous countries. The Council did not rely on military measures, a detail which differentiated it from NATO. As de Valera compared, 'membership of the Council of Europe imposes on us no obligation which is inconsistent with our national rights. Membership of NATO, on the other hand, implies acceptance by each member of the territorial integrity of each of the several states comprising it.'[77]

In the beginning, there was confusion about protocol, procedure, and points of order during the first session because of the newness of the assembly and the different parliamentary traditions of members. Seán MacEntee remarked that 'it has been somewhat difficult for those of us who have not attended a conference of this sort before to know exactly what facilities we have at our disposal.'[78] After the general election on 30 May 1951, de Valera and Fianna Fáil were returned to power and were not as enthusiastic about the Council, becoming the 'most articulate group of Cassandras in the early days of the Council of Europe.'[79] Discussion on European topics diminished until Seán Lemass became Taoiseach in 1959. Yet Ireland's successful participation in the Council of Europe provided the fundamental springboard for moving into European mainstream. Such experience would serve Ireland well after entry into the United Nations and the European Union.

Where the Council of Europe helped to integrate Ireland politically, the Organisation for European Economic Co-operation (OEEC) provided a forum for economic incorporation. The OEEC was formed to administer American aid under the Marshall Plan for the reconstruction of Europe after the Second World War. It developed, in 1961, into the Organisation for Economic Co-operation and Development (OECD). Conference negotiations led to the creation of the OEEC in order to meet Secretary of State George Marshall's request for 'some agreement among the countries of Europe as to the requirements of the situation and the part those countries themselves will take.'[80]

By 1947, Ireland's international reputation had faltered as a result of neutrality, the memory of de Valera's visit to the German legation to offer condolences upon Hitler's death, and the veto of Ireland's application to join the United Nations. Neutrality had also put strain on Ireland's rapport with the United States. However, the country's geographical location made a good relationship important to both British and United States security. The case for Ireland to be offered aid was very strong despite its lack of a threatening communist presence; Ireland's immediate economic difficulties were similar to those of most Western European countries, and there were political, diplomatic, and security arguments for inclusion.[81] There was no real public opposition in Ireland itself and the state of the Irish economy meant that Ireland would seriously consider the American offer.

Ireland received an invitation on 4 July 1947 to attend a meeting in Paris on 12 July to 'take part in the drawing up of a programme covering both the resources and needs of Europe for the following four years.'[82] Here was the 'the first time that Ireland has had an opportunity of cooperating in an international organisation in which the members of the British

Commonwealth of Nations were not also participating'.[83] Representatives of sixteen Western European Countries gathered in Paris to frame a joint response to the American offer. On 16 April 1948, the CEEC met and adopted a convention, establishing a permanent organisation of sixteen participating countries, thus officially forming the OEEC. An *Irish Independent* editorial supported the idea, stating that there was 'good ground for hoping that the agreement signed yesterday in Paris will endure and be of lasting value to the world.'[84]

Organising Irish participation in the ERP and meeting the steps to qualify for aid fell to MacBride, as did how the money should be spent. Participation in the OEEC was useful for receiving Marshall Aid, but it was more beneficial because it forced the Government to consider its position on European cooperation as well as to formulate an economic programme, not something previous governments had done. Seán saw the value in this, 'one of the most essential and urgent steps to give effect to economic planning . . . is to be in a position to plan for and integrate the economy as a whole.'[85] He was enthusiastic, stating that 'the task of the OEEC is not merely to divide the aid which the US have so generously provided, but it is to provide an impetus and a plan for the development of economic co-operation in Europe.'[86] He saw the organisation in broader terms, as he wrote to Spaak, 'the OEEC could fulfil a valuable function if it could formulate a long distance policy for the development and the integration of the participating countries . . . the council of the OEEC could become, in effect, an economic government for Western Europe.'[87] He then wrote that 'I think that it is necessary that the Ministers of all participating countries should meet at frequent intervals and discuss informally current problems as well as long range policy. Such meeting would ensure greater interest and greater co-operation on the part of the Governments and nations concerned.'[88] During their time in the OEEC, MacBride and Spaak corresponded often, Spaak addressing MacBride as 'Mon cher Ministre et Ami,' while MacBride addressed him as 'Mon cher Président et Ami'. The two ministers had much in common: both came from prominent political families; both had lied about their ages to enter the military, Seán joining the IRA in 1918 and Spaak enlisting in the Belgian Army during the First World War; both had spent time in prison, Seán during the Civil War and Spaak in a German prisoner-of-war camp; both had studied law and became foreign ministers of small nations that chose neutrality during the Second World War (although Belgium's situation was very different); and both shared an interest in European unity. MacBride and Spaak may have believed that the OEEC should be strengthened and expanded, but the British and the Scandinavian countries preferred limited economic cooperation.

In February of 1949, a committee of nine ministers of the OEEC met in Paris, on Seán's initiative, to figure out how the OEEC could become more effective to hasten European recovery and encourage economic cooperation. MacBride received from member nations and the Economic Cooperation Administration 'unstinted praise' for his resourcefulness.[89] American diplomat Vinton Chapin wrote of Seán on 4 March 1949:

> Ireland has participated in the Paris meetings of the OEEC wherein MacBride's special abilities and temperament have filled him to perform useful services among the most important nations as a 'leg man', who had no special interest in European power politics. This ability conforms to the Irish contention that it is a nation with a long tradition of resistance to religious and political oppression and therefore in a position to find friends among other nations.[90]

As the OEEC was an international body, it too was subjected to the 'sore thumb' strategy of publicising partition. Fianna Fáil Deputy Dr J.P. Brennan asked Seán if he would give an assurance that on his proposed visit to Paris on the following 14 March, to attend the Committee on European Economic Cooperation, 'he will not discuss thereat any political — other than economic — matter, until the partition of the country will have been solved to the complete satisfaction of the people of Ireland.' MacBride responded by stating that 'the matters to be discussed at the resumed meeting of the C.E.E.C. on March 14th appertain primarily to the economic sphere,' but, when pressed, promised that 'in any question of importance that may arise in the relationship of this country with Great Britain . . . the question of Partition will be considered and discussed.'[91] Despite this, Seán remained sincere about making the organisation work; in a speech to the OEEC Council, he suggested meeting more often and not being afraid of making unpopular decisions:

> the work should not be left merely at an official level, otherwise this organisation runs the risk of many other such international organisations that we have had over the last quarter of a century or more. It will just become an organisation for the compilation of statistics, but it will mean nothing to the people of Europe.[92]

Ireland received Marshall Aid and the OEEC's main task involved removing obstacles to intra-regional commerce after 1951. Ireland remains a member of the OECD, which grew from the OEEC to discuss, develop and refine economic and social policies, advocating a commitment to a market economy and pluralistic democracy. While membership in the OEEC and the Council of Europe did not remove the border, it did raise the country's profile and Ireland enjoyed a renowned reputation in European circles in some part due to Seán, whose 'contributions to the work of the OEEC have done much to enhance [Ireland's] national prestige abroad.'[93]

MacBride gave External Affairs the prominent profile it had previously lacked, as well as providing a sense of direction, and undertaking needed administrative reforms. During his tenure, External Affairs was responsible for the administration of the ERP, the creation of an Irish News Agency, the extension of the American embassy and Washington, DC, office as well as increased contact with European embassies and missions, also a separate trade section, a second assistant secretary in 1948, in 1949 a third assistant secretary and two new sections, political affairs and information, as well as establishing a Cultural Relations Advisory Committee, a Public Relations office at the Consulate General in New York, and increasing international distribution of the Department's *Weekly Bulletin* from 2,000 copies in November 1949 to 4,300 copies in March 1951.[94]

With these expansions and new responsibilities came an increase of staff and requests for more money. As Seán pointed out,

> Some of our most important missions abroad were so understaffed that their members were unable to get away from their desks to maintain essential contacts with the outside world. The headquarters of the Department itself was in the same position. The staff were overwhelmed with the mass of work arising in the ordinary course of Departmental duties, and there was little or no provision for the steady systematic work which must be done if our major objectives in the political field are to be achieved.[95]

He highlighted the contributions of the Department and its staff in its first year of operations in the Dáil:

> From the point of view of the Department of External Affairs, this year has been one of tremendous importance in many fields. Events of paramount importance have occurred in the course of the year, both in our relationship with Britain and in the international field generally; the passage of the Republic of Ireland Act, the Atlantic Pact; the passage of the Ireland Act in the British Parliament; the launching of the Council of Europe; the increasing importance of the Organisation for European Economic Co-operation; the making of trade agreements and the

development of cultural relations. These were all events that cast tremendous work and responsibility on our small Department of External Affairs. Before proceeding further, I should like to pay special tribute to the staff of the Department for the manner in which they responded to the extra calls which are being constantly made upon them by the pressure of events and by the resulting additional burdens . . . I cannot praise their self-sacrificing enthusiasm and devotion to their work too highly; many times I have been reminded of the spirit and enthusiasm that prevailed in the national movement. It is, of course, this type of spirit that should prevail in a small foreign service such as ours at times of crisis.[96]

His request was necessary: because of the frenetic pace of the previous year and Seán's future plans, the Department had an increased workload and certainly needed more personnel and more funding. He continued by predicting that

in present circumstances I see no hope of the work of the Department becoming lighter. On the contrary, if we are to perform our functions effectively in regard to the Council of Europe, the Organisation for European Economic Co-operation and Partition, as well as the many other functions which fall on the Department, the work is bound to increase. In these circumstances, additional staffs are essential.[97]

He then asked the Government

to provide for an expenditure on external affairs higher by £74,025 than that provided last year. I should say quite frankly that I do not feel called upon to make any apology for this increase. We cannot expect to make political headway abroad and attain our national aims unless we are prepared to tackle the task of putting our point of view across much more actively and vigorously than we have done in the past.[98]

The increased volume of correspondence between Dublin and other nations abroad demonstrates the growth of the Department and Seán's efforts to expand its profile. Also, by actively promoting the Department, MacBride encouraged young and talented people like Conor Cruise O'Brien to work at Iveagh House and take an interest in foreign affairs. Such contact and recruitment would benefit the Department when Ireland was admitted into the United Nations; able, experienced people were already on hand to provide support. In the post-war years, External Affairs developed in stature to reduce Finance's dominance in the administration and become one of the primary departments of state. Seán's ability to see the bigger picture, at least in the realm of European unity, made him 'a pioneer in the sense that he articulated long-term national objectives in a Dáil which all too frequently succumbed to the temptations of short-term partisan advantages.'[99]

Despite MacBride's desire to involve Ireland in international organisations, he proved ambivalent about an Irish role in the United Nations. Ireland's official application for membership was submitted in August 1946. There was domestic and international interest in the application; *The Irish Times* commented on the 'considerable array' of foreign representatives gathered in the Dáil Gallery to hear the debate.[100] There was a very full attendance of members as well. Though de Valera saw Irish membership in the United Nations as incompatible with absolute sovereignty, he felt that joining was the better alternative because, 'it is natural that small States should strive to bring about an international organisation which would guarantee their independence and general freedom. The trouble is that no such organisation can come into being without very great sacrifices on the part of all its members.'[101] No note of opposition existed, though very few TDs were overly enthused, feeling that 'we must play our modest part in international affairs.'[102] *The Irish Times* was confident, believing that no 'serious opposition will be raised against Eire's application.'[103]

The prediction proved to be untrue. The Soviet Union vetoed the application's entry, ostensibly on the grounds that Ireland had no diplomatic presence in the Soviet Union and that during the war, Ireland had not helped the Allies, instead offering support to the Axis powers and Franco's Spain. Ireland's anti-communist stance was probably more responsible; the membership of the General Assembly was weighted toward the Western bloc and the Soviet Union did not want its position in the Assembly weakened.[104] This argument is confirmed by the fact that, when Ireland was finally admitted into the United Nations, it still had no diplomatic relations with the Soviet Union. Before official admission, Ireland was involved in specialised United Nations agencies like the World Meteorological Organisation, and the Food and Agricultural Organisation, as membership in the General Assembly was not necessary for participation.

The decision to apply for membership was unanimous and Seán was enthusiastic at first. He recounted in the Dáil:

The decision to apply for membership of the United Nations Organisation was taken by this House on the 25th July, 1946 . . . Ireland possesses the qualifications for membership laid down by Article 4 of the United Nations Charter[105] and should, therefore, be admitted to membership; it further requested the Security Council to reconsider Ireland's application in the light of that determination.[106]

Unlike participation in other international organisations, MacBride did not associate UN membership with the removal of partition; Commonwealth Secretary Philip Noel-Baker remarked on Seán's mature outlook toward the United Nations and the lack of an attempt to link partition to Irish participation.[107] While he conceded that neutrality in theory might be affected, he did not foresee any future problems in practice due to the ideological differences among the permanent members of the Security Council:

> Membership of the organisation involves acceptance of the obligations contained in the charter of the United Nations . . . The most far-reaching of these obligations are those obliging members to carry out the decisions of the Security Council with respect to threats to, or breaches of, the international peace which have not been settled by peaceful methods. It is important to note, however, that such decisions require the concurrence of all the permanent members of the Security Council, namely, the United States, Great Britain, Russia, France and China. In this connection, I should point out that lack of unanimity amongst the permanent members has, so far, prevented the implementation of Article 43 of the charter, that is, the article requiring each member to conclude an agreement with the council specifying the armed forces and other facilities to be made available to the council for the purpose of maintaining international peace and security . . . there is no obligation, by virtue of Ireland's application for membership of the United Nations Organisation, to take any sides . . . The question of what Ireland's attitude would be in the event of a war would be a matter for this House to decide.[108]

However, the veto remained in place and a few months later, Seán seemed to have doubts, both about Ireland's future role in the UN and the efficacy of the organisation itself:

> The fact . . . that we have been excluded from it [the United Nations] demonstrates that its mechanism is open to abuse. In this connection I should mention that, at some time in the near future, it may become

necessary that the Government should consider whether our application for membership of the United Nations Organisation should not be withdrawn . . . [109]

In a letter to Vinton Chapin of the American Legation, MacBride mentioned the 'natural resentment created by the rejection of our application', and 'a growing scepticism with regard to the effectiveness of the United Nations as at present constituted'.[110] The Irish people also may have been wary of joining, feeling disenchanted with the organisation. *The Leader* editorial of 13 March 1948 commented, 'The Palestine problem, at least, is valuable in showing that UNO (United Nations Organisation) as an international force against aggression and war is virtually powerless when prompt action is necessary.'[111] Not only did the Government have doubts about the organisation of the United Nations, but the experience with the League of Nations, a loss of face at being eager to join, then being forced to wait, and the aversion to being seen striking a bargain with the Soviet Union to lift its veto, also led to apprehension about becoming a UN member.

Yet Seán's faith in organisational assemblies themselves remained undiminished:

> I have delayed in bringing this matter formally before the Government and the Dáil as I did not wish, in the present situation, to take any steps that would indicate a lack of faith in any attempt that was being made to discuss world problems at a conference table. No matter how abortive or fruitless such conferences may prove, it is still the only way of avoiding conflict. The more representatives of different nations meet to discuss their problems, the greater the possibility of reaching understanding and peaceful solutions.[112]

Nearly a year afterwards, Seán was asked in the Dáil if the Government would continue to seek admission. He replied that the application was still pending and that 'the Government is not called upon to take any further action in the matter.' Independent Deputy Patrick Cogan then asked, 'is the Minister aware that Ireland's application for membership of the United Nations Organisation has been twice rejected, on the veto of Russia? Would it not be exposing this country to unnecessary humiliation to repeat the application?'[113] Cogan later suggested that Ireland withdraw its application, calling it 'a more dignified course' because any change of attitude by the Soviet Union toward Ireland might be interpreted by freedom-loving nations as a change of our policy towards Russia, which is a thing we would not like to have happen. On the other hand, I do not think we would like to have our admission ticket into the United Nations Organisation peddled about in exchange for the admission of some countries under Communist rule.[114]

MacBride seemed nonchalant about the waiting game, stating that his Department was quite busy without UN membership:

In the midst of all the work that has had to be performed by the Department in the course of the year, I have been very thankful indeed that the Russian veto on our admission to the United Nations Organisation has been maintained. Frankly, the prospect of having to provide representatives at another international body such as the United Nations Organisation and to have to attend yet another series of international conferences, was frightening in existing circumstances.[115]

Ireland's application was vetoed again in September of 1949, along with the applications of Portugal, Italy, Austria, Finland, Jordan, and Greece. Eventually Ireland was admitted to the United Nations in exactly the type of situation Cogan had predicted, as part of a package deal with Soviet-bloc countries.

The United Nations became an arena where Ireland could further some of its political aims, strengthen long-standing contacts throughout Europe and North America, establish relationships with Africa and Asia, and help to preserve the international order.[116] From the mid-1950s until the mid-1960s, the Irish delegation 'led by an extraordinary team of talented, dedicated diplomats, occupied a prominent place in the General Assembly.'[117] Ireland was one of ten non-permanent members elected by the General Assembly of the United Nations to serve on the Security Council in 1962, 1981–1982, and 2001–2002. The United Nations became a vital focal point of Irish foreign policy, both for making diplomatic contact with other nations and as a forum to state opinions on international issues. The Irish delegates never formally raised the issue of partition in the General Assembly but they did argue against it as a way of solving political conflicts.[118] Ireland defended the rights of minorities in Tibet and South Tyrol and supported resolutions on decolonisation. Ironically the United Nations, which Seán once, in a moment of frustration, had said that he was happy not to be in for the time being, would shape his later career to a large extent.

Cruise O'Brien once lampooned MacBride as living in a 'dream world in which he is a brilliantly successful statesman, elegant, eloquent, strolling with the leaders of Europe; what he is doing is not very clear, but with what distinction he does it!'[119] Such a characterisation is unfair, as Seán did much to raise Ireland's profile within Europe. Cruise O'Brien later wrote in 1969 that 'Ireland has acquired an adequate measure of international respect. Her spokesmen find a hearing, when they have something to say. They can exercise a small, but not insignificant influence, on the great movements which help to shape world politics.'[120] Though Cruise O'Brien does not mention it, MacBride can take credit for establishing such respect.

Many of the decisions of the inter-party Government had enduring significance even if they made little impact at the time. This is especially true of foreign policy. Many believe that serious foreign policy pursuits began with admission to the United Nations, as they believe that economic planning began with Whitaker's memo, but both had their roots during the inter-party Government. Choosing not to participate in NATO and the repeal of the External Relations Act may have shown a lack of purpose and foresight in foreign policy, but European integration demonstrated that the inter-party Government was indeed forward thinking in some respects. Seán MacBride gave some of his best, most articulate and well-thought-out speeches in the Dáil on foreign policy issues and travelled more than any previous Minister for External Affairs. Unfortunately domestic problems, like the Mother and Child controversy, would overshadow both the Government's foreign policy gains and Seán's contribution to them.

His focus on foreign affairs meant that he was out of the country much of the time, 'promenading on the world stage . . . [and] must have felt culture shock on returning to the provincial mundanities of Dublin.'[121] His absences led to his influence in the cabinet waning and the Clann, as a relatively recent party, did not receive the attention it needed. Yet MacBride's attempts to break with the past and look toward broader horizons for the future ultimately benefited him personally as well as Ireland. As Mary Robinson, then President of Ireland, explained in 1991,

I myself feel that because we were so uncertain of ourselves when we were first of all ruled by Britain, and then in this century when we achieved the Free State and then the independent republican status from 1937, we still lacked self-confidence as a nation.[122] We still were defensive, ambivalent, self-deprecating. And I believe that it has been an enriching experience to have become part of a wider European continent; that's partly psychological. I think that there has been an awareness that we have of ourselves as strong a culture, that in many areas we can stand on equal terms. That has been good for the national psyche and for the sense of our identity.[123]

What the *Irish Independent* wrote regarding the OEEC could also be applied to this period of Irish international relations: 'the preliminaries have concluded. The edifice has been built and the work is about to begin.'[124]

Chapter 8

CATHOLIC FIRST, IRISHMAN SECOND: SEÁN MacBRIDE, CLANN NA POBLACHTA, AND THE CHURCH

'In this country a man must have upon his side the Church or the Fenians.'

— JOHN O'LEARY

While in office, Seán MacBride attempted to cultivate a close relationship with the hierarchy of the Catholic Church, especially the Archbishop of Dublin, John Charles McQuaid. While earlier attempts to work with the Church did not prove divisive, Seán's role in the Mother and Child controversy split his party and led to the end of his career in Irish politics.

The inter-party Government was overtly Catholic and one of the first actions the Government took was to send to Pope Pius XII a message authored by the Taoiseach, affirming,

> on the occasion of our assumption of office and of the first Cabinet meeting, my colleagues and myself desire to repose at the feet of your Holiness the assurance of our filial loyalty and of our devotion to your August person, as well as our firm resolve to be guided in all our work by the teaching of Christ, and to strive for the attainment of a social order in Ireland based on Christian principles.[1]

Seán himself wrote to McQuaid on 30 October 1947, the day of his election to the Dáil, stating, 'I hasten, as my first act, to pay my humble respects to Your Grace and place myself at Your Grace's disposal', and that he would 'always welcome any advice which Your Grace may be good enough to give me and shall be at Your Grace's disposal should there be any matters upon which Your Grace feels that I could be of any assistance'.[2] McQuaid replied, 'I shall not fail to take advantage of your generous suggestion that you are at my disposal for any matters in which you could assist', but he promised to do so only if 'the good of the faith was in question'.[3]

After the 1948 election, Seán again promised that he would, as 'a Catholic, a public representative and the leader of a party', welcome 'any advice or views' which McQuaid might express 'officially or informally'.[4] The correspondence provides an excellent example of the deference the inter-party Government demonstrated to the Catholic hierarchy. The two letters that Seán wrote to the Archbishop were handwritten on Roebuck House stationery, not Department of External Affairs or Clann na Poblachta letterhead; presumably Seán intended only McQuaid to see the letters, as there are no other copies on file except in McQuaid's papers. John Bowman points this out in his *Irish Times* article of 13 November 1999, questioning the wisdom of giving such 'blank cheques' to the hierarchy.[5] Bowman felt that MacBride's supporters could excuse the initial letter, as he was politically inexperienced, but his repetition in 1948 is inexcusable. As Seán wrote in a tone 'wholly inappropriate for a leader with Clann na Poblachta's roots, policies, and membership', Bowman concludes the article by wondering if he wasn't a bit of a hypocrite.[6] In Seán's 1948 letter to McQuaid, 'Catholic' came before 'public representative'. J.T. Morahan, a Clann candidate in North Tipperary, stated at a public meeting in Ballinrobe that the Clann 'were Christians and Catholics before they were Irishmen . . . The better Catholics they were the better Irishmen they were.'[7]

MacBride continued to affirm his loyalty and ask for advice throughout his political career. In a letter to McQuaid after his re-election in 1954, he wrote, 'It is my aim to serve Catholicism in Ireland to the best of my ability and I shall deem it a favour to receive any guidance and advice which Your Grace may, at any time, time [sic] think fit to give me.'[8] Seán asked for his views about the Clann's National Government idea but asked that McQuaid 'Please do not trouble to acknowledge this letter; I know that Your Grace is already overburdened with work.' Strangely enough, this time he did. In a reply dated 26 May 1954, McQuaid promised that he would 'carefully read' the National Government proposal. Despite the quick reply, Seán's surname is misspelled 'McBride' three times in the letter.

Bowman points out that, in his retirement, MacBride was 'very touchy on the subject of Church–State relations', culminating in a public disagreement between himself and Bowman during a live radio interview in 1980. Bowman mentioned Frederick Boland's having witnessed MacBride being deferential in a phone conversation with McQuaid, then speaking contemptuously of him once he had put the receiver down.

Whatever Seán's personal feelings about McQuaid, the inter-party Government took a similar line to the Church on two political issues early in its tenure: the 1948 elections in Italy and recognition of the state of Israel. Joseph Walshe, the Irish Ambassador to the Holy See, warned the Government of an imminent communist victory in Italy in the elections of April 1948, 'a communist victory in Italy, according to the best minds I can contact, will be followed by Communist penetration of the whole of Western Europe.'[9] Believing this dire prediction, Seán urged McQuaid and John D'Alton, the Archbishop of Armagh, to appeal publicly for funds. Contributions came from religious organisations like the Knights of Saint Columbanus, the Ancient Order of Hibernians, and the Legion of Mary, as well as wealthy Catholic individuals — Seán himself sent a personal contribution. Collections were taken at churches, shops, and factories throughout Ireland. As *The Irish Times* editorialised on 14 April, 'all true democrats must hope for a communist defeat for the sake not alone of Italy, but all of Europe. Ireland, by virtue of her historic attachment to the Holy See, has a particular interest in the outcome, in which the position of the Vatican is immediately involved.'

In the event, 48.5 per cent of the vote went to the Christian Democrats, giving them over half the seats in the Chamber of Deputies. The win was an immediate success for MacBride, but as Dermot Keogh points out, the victory was ultimately dangerous for the Irish Government as it 'brought the Catholic Church into the domain of political decision making' in Ireland.[10] Seán effusively praised McQuaid for his help: 'the real work was done by Your Grace, without whose tireless help and intervention I would have been powerless . . . I feel that Ireland's contribution, for which Your Grace was in the main responsible, was of very material help to the Italian Catholics in their hour of stress and to the cause of world peace.'[11]

The Church also seemed to influence Ireland's position on Israel. The Government had given Israel *de facto* recognition on 15 February 1949, but would not provide *de jure* recognition until 1963.[12] The Department of External Affairs recommended that Ireland give 'the virtual minimum of recognition' to Israel.[13] This hesitation was in direct contrast to the United

States, United Kingdom, and Soviet Union, all of whom gave fairly quick *de jure* recognition.

Surprisingly, Ireland did not draw parallels based on partition, either through a diaspora connection championing a national homeland for the Jews or a decision that the partitioning of Palestine was illegitimate. Instead, the Government seemingly chose religion over politics: the main rationale for Ireland's rebuff was the protection of the Holy Places in and near Jerusalem. McQuaid and Irish public opinion were concerned over their safety and availability to Catholic pilgrims. Seán elucidated the Government's official position in the Dáil, that they supported the demand 'that the Holy Places in Palestine should be suitably protected, that free access should be ensured for all religions and that . . . the whole area of Jerusalem should be placed under international control.'[14] However, Paula Wylie has convincingly argued that the Irish Government may also have been trying to delay Israeli diplomatic representation in Ireland because of a fear of Jewish infiltration into Ireland.[15] As Joseph Walshe, Ireland's Ambassador to the Holy See, reported to Frederick Boland, visiting Irish priests and nuns had told him that 'something ought to be done to prevent the jews [sic] buying property and starting and acquiring businesses in Ireland. There was a general conviction that the jewish [sic] influence is . . . anti-Christian and anti-national, and consequently, detrimental to the revival of an Irish cultural and religious civilisation.' Walshe goes on to write that 'Some of them say that jewish [sic] materialism encourages communism.'[16]

As with the Italian elections, and the Northern Ireland elections in 1949, the Government worked closely with the Irish Catholic hierarchy on the issue. McQuaid wrote to Mgr Gino Paro, at the Nunciature in Dublin, 'I cannot see de jure recognition being accorded to Israel without definite guarantees being given concerning the Holy Places. In this context, I am constantly in touch with the Government.'[17]

Even though the Government's position reflected Irish public opinion, it appeared that the Government was taking guidance from the Irish hierarchy and the Vatican on how to handle a political matter, that church had a direct influence over state.

The hierarchy's power in Irish politics appeared clinched by its role in the implementation of a health service for mothers and children, a matter of vigorous debate more than fifty years later. Many of Seán's contemporaries have written about the Mother and Child conflict and its aftermath.[18] There are also engaging secondary works detailing the origins and outcomes of the crisis.[19] However, these can be difficult to sift through because of the diverse theories and differing interpretations that the various authors propose. Recollections and explanations both at the time of the controversy and later on are conflicting. Noël Browne did publish the correspondence between himself, MacBride, Costello, and the hierarchy, but certain unrecorded face-to-face meetings and discussions are still open to interpretation.[20]

What can be accurately determined is that Browne, as Minister for Health, was given the task of improving and implementing a programme for mother and child health care. Mother and child health care was a concern of his as Ireland had the highest infant mortality rates in Europe. The 1947 Ryan Act, passed by the previous Fianna Fáil Government, made provision for free medical treatment of expectant mothers and children up to age sixteen. The hierarchy expressed objections privately to then-Taoiseach Éamon de Valera after the bill had passed, claiming that the plan was 'entirely and directly contrary to Catholic teachings, the rights of the family, the rights of the Church in education, the rights of the medical profession and of voluntary institutions'.[21] De Valera replied to these concerns on 16 February 1948, two days before his Government fell. He wrote that because the Act had been referred to the Supreme Court to test its constitutionality, 'I think it better to make no personal comment on the matter at this stage.'[22]

A health service for mothers and children was first mentioned by the inter-party Government in the Dáil on 6 July 1948 when Browne requested money for the Department, stating, 'I have not made up my mind as to the exact method of providing the mother and child service and am awaiting the outcome of the deliberations of the council which I have recently established to advise me on matters relating to child health.'[23] Browne had already asked for and received cabinet approval to redraft the previous Act.[24]

At this time, no one objected to the lack of a means test. In the first years of his Ministry, Browne focused on eradicating tuberculosis; several members of his family had died from the disease and he proved committed to that venture, both in increasing the number of sanatoriums and in providing access to medicines. By July 1950, 2,000 new beds had been provided for tuberculosis patients and the death rate dropped from 123 out of 100,000 in 1947 to 73 out of 100,000 in 1951.[25] In 1950, he began in earnest to formulate the mother and child welfare scheme. By June 1950, the draft proposals were completed and details of the plan appeared in the 10 September 1950 issue of the *Sunday Independent*. The scheme would involve free, but voluntary, care for mothers as well as children under sixteen, with no means test. Although the principle of no means test was publicly part of his party's platform, and in the early stages of the plan raised no objections in cabinet, Browne would soon find himself under fire.

It is sometimes assumed that Browne, a politician with a reputation as a radical, was looking for a showdown with the Catholic hierarchy. It is far more likely that he was looking for a showdown with the Irish Medical Association (IMA), and perhaps with his party leader over the management and direction of Clann na Poblachta.

He first encountered problems from the Irish medical profession, who would have to staff and run the scheme. Doctors opposed the plan because they feared a reduction in their incomes and argued that the plan resembled 'socialised medicine'.

Because the struggle with the bishops became more public, the role of the IMA is often underestimated. *The Irish Times* of 9 April 1951 remarked on the front page that 'most of the controversy which has raged around the Mother and Child scheme for the last nine months has been conducted by the Irish Medical Association.'[26] In his article, 'Church–state relations and the development of Irish health policy: the mother-and-child scheme, 1944–53', Eamonn McKee concludes that 'it was Browne's commitment to taking on the doctors in the name of a free-for-all service which set him against the Irish Medical Association and thus against a large section of the cabinet and hierarchy.'[27]

J.H. Whyte believes that Browne, as a radical who wanted social change, deliberately behaved in a contentious manner during the mother and child crisis because he was hoping for a showdown between the Irish state and the IMA.[28] He also indicates that Browne 'appeared to develop a pathological hatred of the doctors' in private practice.[29] His experiences as a house officer in Newcastle Sanatorium in Wicklow may have contributed to an unsympathetic attitude for the medical establishment and he seemed to 'have set out deliberately to provoke the profession, in particular, the Dublin consultants, by criticising in public their manner of practice and preoccupation with money.'[30] MacBride confirmed this view when he stated in the Dáil that 'little or no attempt was made by my late colleague to avoid the clash, and I am not even certain that he [Browne] did not provoke it.'[31]

Whyte further posits that Browne was so preoccupied with his battle with the IMA that he never anticipated problems with the Catholic hierarchy. Furthermore, Browne had been unaware of the previous correspondence between de Valera and the bishops. Dr Ruth Barrington agrees, stating that Browne treated the hierarchy's objections 'in a somewhat cavalier manner and considered that the doctors were the chief opponents to be beaten.'[32] The earlier difficulties with the IMA and cabinet colleagues, especially MacBride, would make his problems with the Church hierarchy much more difficult to solve.

Browne's more public problem would come with the Irish Church's response to the scheme. The bishops also sympathised with the Irish Medical Association's worries about socialised medicine: Archbishop McQuaid's father and uncle were doctors. He also belonged to the Knights of Saint Columbanus, an organisation that included many doctors and provided contact between the IMA, the hierarchy, and the cabinet.[33] In addition, McQuaid was fervently anti-communist, and examples in Eastern Europe of the state taking over from the Church made him vigilant about the Government superseding ecclesiastical authority in realms normally dominated by the Church. McQuaid biographer John Cooney concludes that 'Browne, a democratically elected politician with a social vision, was a pawn in McQuaid's Cold War struggle against communism and its milder but no less insidious from of "socialised medicine", which had spread to Britain and Northern Ireland in the guise of the Welfare State.'[34]

Strong Church opinion on medical issues was not surprising. Although no accord between church and state officially existed, the Catholic Church had an immensely powerful position in Irish public life and in law, particularly in matters involving social welfare and education. The leading hospitals and most secondary schools were run by religious orders, the clergy held a number of university chairs and taught most of the leading people in government.[35] In *Against the Tide*, Browne pointed out that not only did the Church have a huge measure of control in the operation of health services but it 'had for so long not been subjected to any serious criticism or examination in her administration of the health services.'[36] The hierarchy feared that the education of women for motherhood provided under the plan would include instruction on 'sex relations, chastity, and marriage', which, in the view of the Church, was not the state's job.[37] The scheme might also result in Catholic women being treated by non-Catholic doctors, and 'education' could someday lead to contraception and abortion, although both were illegal at the time.

After Browne presented the plan to the cabinet, Costello submitted the scheme to the bishops for their advice. In their reply to Costello, dated 10 October 1950, they declared that

> In their opinion the powers taken by the State in the proposed Mother and Child Health Service are in direct opposition to the rights of the family and of the individual and are liable to very great abuse . . . If adopted in law they would constitute a ready made instrument for future totalitarian aggression.[38]

Browne did agree to make concessions, but remained firm on the no-means-test principle. He submitted a revised memo for the hierarchy's review and gave it to Costello to send on. Costello did not deliver it immediately and there was a delay of several months before the hierarchy received it. Browne heard no more after the meeting with bishops in October 1950 and assumed that all was well until he received a letter, dated 9 March 1951, that showed that the bishops were intent on preventing implementation.[39]

Browne had never secured cabinet approval for details of the proposal — leaving himself in an exposed position when the cabinet later rejected the scheme. As he later said, 'I had no reason to believe that there would be opposition from the Hierarchy. Even if I had known I would still have expected the Cabinet to implement the law.'[40] There had been no criticism from the Irish hierarchy regarding the more comprehensive National Health Service in Northern Ireland, which is odd because the possibility of Catholic women being treated by Protestant doctors was much greater there.

Browne had consulted independently with a theologian who could see no problem with the scheme and assured him that nothing in the plan went against Catholic faith and moral teaching.[41] Browne did not reveal the theologian's identity at the time or later in his memoirs, but John Horgan discovered that it was Monsignor P.F. Cremin, Professor of Theology at Maynooth.[42] Cremin reasoned that if a more radical scheme was tolerable for co-religionists on the other side of the border, then no problem should exist for implementing Browne's scheme in the Republic. The bishops, however, replied that the scheme did go against Catholic *social* teaching. In April 1951, the cabinet decided to drop the scheme after continued protest from the IMA and extensive correspondence from the hierarchy.

At a special seven-hour-long meeting of the Clann na Poblachta National Executive, the party gave MacBride permission to ask for Browne's resignation. On 10 April, he delivered a letter demanding that Browne resign as Minister for Health; in this he was backed by Costello.[43] Browne replied to MacBride and Costello, then arranged for the correspondence to be published in *The Irish Times* of 12 April.

This action was sensational; at the time, such correspondence was kept out of the public domain. Costello was shocked at the disclosure, proclaiming that 'all this matter was intended to be private and to be adjusted behind closed doors and was never intended to be the subject of public controversy.'[44] Browne's action also put both the Government and Clann na Poblachta in the position of having to defend themselves. After his resignation, he received immense public support; letters to the major Irish papers praised Browne and noted that 'he can gain satisfaction from the thought that he has the sympathy of the vast majority of the people of Ireland, and that the way he was coerced to bring his scheme to a conclusion and resign his Ministry has disgusted one and all.'[45] Browne had been the first Minister to use the media to publicise his policies, broadcasting regularly on the radio and managing a publicity section in the Department producing pamphlets in Irish and English. He may not have been politically astute, but he was media savvy, so much so that MacBride later commented that Browne had 'manoeuvred himself in an extremely capable fashion into becoming a martyr.'[46]

Colleagues' assessments of Browne vary, but most agree that he was hard working and 'a person of passionate social concern'.[47] While researching his *Church and State in Modern Ireland*, J.H. Whyte found that for the 'first two years or so in office, Dr Browne's ministerial career was generally applauded' and he had 'won a generally respected opinion for himself among the officials with whom he had to deal.'[48] Even MacBride later admitted that 'Noël Browne was a first-class Minister for Health. He did a first-class job of work on the eradication of TB.'[49]

Some TDS preferred Browne to MacBride; as Independent Oliver Flanagan declared, if given the choice, he would rather have Browne in government than MacBride because 'the Minister for External Affairs has his heart in Paris, his notebook in Strasbourg, his ambitions in Washington and his intentions in the United States, but Deputy Dr Browne's body and soul and ambitions lie in the sick beds of the poor of this country, and that cannot be forgotten.'[50]

However, Browne did have his critics. While James Deeny, the Chief Medical Advisor in the Ministry of Health, admitted that he was compassionate and 'had a lot going for him', he ultimately found Browne 'intolerant, and begrudging of others' efforts and, while a magnificent destructive critic . . . he had few constructive or practical ideas.'[51] Seán MacEntee, known for his acid tongue, called him 'the strangest piece of flotsam the stormy sea of Irish politics has thrown up in three generations',[52] largely because of his liberal outlook and his education in England and at Protestant Trinity College Dublin. He resented that Browne was taking credit for projects begun under the previous Fianna Fáil administration. His fellow cabinet ministers were also critical — Costello declaring that

> I had formed in my own mind, having regard to my experience over the last six months and the history of the affairs I have given in the barest outline, the firm conviction that Deputy Dr Browne was not competent or capable to fulfil the duties of the Department of Health. He was incapable of negotiation; he was obstinate at times and vacillating at other

times. He was quite incapable of knowing what his decision would be to-day or, if he made a decision to-day, it would remain until to-morrow.[53]

Clann member and Deputy Con Lehane stayed true to the Clann's party line and agreed with Costello:

> My experience of the ex-Minister for Health has been that he is constitutionally incapable of listening to criticism. Perhaps that is not anything for which he should be particularly blamed; but I have had the experience of seeing him walk out over a fairly long period, a period of a year or more, from five, if not six, different committee meetings.[54]

Browne later defended himself by disclosing that 'in my opinion it hardly mattered whether I attended meetings or not' as they were ultimately a waste of his time.[55] While this attitude is admirable in the sense that he wanted to get back to what he viewed as important work, it provides proof of a lack of political instinct — further demonstrated when he arrived at the Archbishop's House to meet with McQuaid wearing a Trinity College scarf.[56] In addition, Browne did not bring anyone with him to take notes at the decisive meeting with McQuaid.

Was Browne well respected and dedicated? Or was he inconsistent and unwilling to compromise? His competence is not in doubt; it is questioned only after the scheme fell apart and the cabinet seemed pleased with his performance up to then. As Deeny concluded, the Government gave Browne the post, allowed him free rein, and then withdrew support and reneged on its stated policy when trouble started.[57] As for his inability to compromise, in the Dáil at the start of his Ministry, Browne asserted that

> I am always at the disposal of Deputies on either side of the House if there is any suggestion they have to make which they feel may lead to the improvement or betterment of our health services. I am very glad to have the assistance of the medical members of the House and also the lay members in giving me some idea of the reactions throughout the country to our suggestions and plans for the improvement of the general health of the people.[58]

Browne was determined rather than stubborn; he believed in keeping the plan free of a means test and saw no logical reason for his party, his Government, or the bishops to object. After his resignation, expelled Clann member Peadar Cowan stated,

I say deliberately, that Deputy Dr Browne, if not the most popular Minister, was certainly one of the most popular. The Party to which he belonged, Clann na Poblachta, were claiming credit all over the country for the magnificent work being done by Deputy Dr Browne in the Department of Health.[59]

It is doubtful that Browne would have been so popular if he were so incredibly obstinate. His early accomplishments in eradicating tuberculosis and building and improving hospitals would have been unlikely without some compromise and ability to work constructively with others. Deeny admitted that Browne was 'patently sincere' and possessed 'great energy'.[60] Horgan points out in his biography of Browne that he suffered from partial deafness and, though he was comfortable in one-to-one conversations, Browne was withdrawn in meetings because he was not always aware of everything that was being said.[61]

Few figures in twentieth-century Ireland are as controversial as Noël Browne. To his supporters he was a dynamic liberal who stood up to conservative and reactionary Catholicism. To his opponents he was an unstable, temperamental, and difficult individual who was the author of most of his own misfortune. Browne further alienated the middle ground in 1986 with the release of his memoir, *Against the Tide*. Historians like Dr Barrington, who has written extensively about Irish health policy and had access to the files from the 1940s and 1950s, and biographer John Horgan questioned the book's reliability. Of his cabinet colleagues, only MacBride was alive to protest Browne's version of events, and the relatives of the people involved also disputed the accuracy of the book.

One of the most entrenched myths about the Mother and Child controversy is that it showed the enormous extent of Catholic Church control over the State. Tim Pat Coogan certainly sees it as such, believing that 'the Church, and in particular John Charles McQuaid . . . was the main architect of the Mother and Child Scheme's destruction' and Browne's impertinent independence from the bishops had to be reined in.[62] Coogan also calls attention to the fact that Costello had McQuaid's help in drafting his 15 April Dáil rebuttal of Browne's position. However, the aspect of Church intervention in politics is more complex than it seems. On the whole, bishops intervened very rarely and the Irish Government did not automatically defer to the hierarchy on every point — there were other factors involved in the Mother and Child controversy, such as Browne's growing unpopularity within the cabinet, the cabinet's dislike of the scheme in general, and the cabinet's willingness to choose its battles. Costello had asked the hierarchy to comment on the bill, which the bishops did. Politicians, it could be argued, were the ones to blame for quashing the bill.

There may be other reasons why the cabinet did not back Browne besides the distastefulness of tangling with the Church; 'As far as most of his cabinet colleagues were concerned, the hierarchy's decision suited them well. Some of them disliked the mother and child scheme in itself.'[63] Fine Gael ministers were sympathetic toward IMA arguments, Costello stating several times that 'I would not be a member of a Government or take part in any Government that was in favour of or tried in any way to socialise medicine.'[64] Some had close links with the medical profession: Minister for Defence Dr Tom O'Higgins was a senior officer of the IMA. At best, Fine Gael was not inclined to fight for the scheme; at worst the party encouraged the bishops to intervene because it knew they would find problems with the scheme and anticipated Browne's reaction.

Another theory posits that not only did the Government, especially Fine Gael, dislike the scheme; but it may have been trying to encourage Browne to resign. As Seán Lemass later mused, 'I am not so sure that it was not allowed to develop this way because the coalition leaders were anxious to get an excuse to drop Browne who must have been a very difficult colleague in the Government at the time.'[65] There is no real evidence that Costello cunningly intended for the Church to do his dirty work in an attempt to get rid of a fractious colleague. Cowan believed something very similar, but placed the blame on MacBride:

> Why has Deputy Dr Browne, from being the Minister that was held up by Clann na Poblachta all over the country as such a wonderful man, been brought to the position that he is described as a scoundrel and a liar, as incompetent, incapable and unfit to be Minister in this or any other Government? What has brought about that change? Is it not clear that what has brought about the change is that Deputy Dr Browne, because of his great work for the people, was becoming more popular than his Leader? Because he was more popular than his Leader, he must be downed and he must be damned.[66]

Did MacBride set Browne up because he was overtaking him in popularity? It must be kept in mind that Cowan, having been expelled from Clann na Poblachta by Seán, was probably not the most objective observer. If Cowan is correct, it means that Seán, declining in popularity, was somehow able to encourage Costello, Clann na Poblachta, and the bishops to blacken Browne's name. Unlikely as that is, MacBride should shoulder some of the responsibility, but his behaviour was that of a short-sighted politician rather than a clever conspirator.

Browne may not have been courting confrontation with the hierarchy, but he was almost certainly courting it with Seán. Animosity between the two had been growing for some time. Both men seemed uncomfortable with those who disagreed with them and personality conflicts would feature heavily in both of their careers.

Browne believed that Clann na Poblachta was losing its radicalism and that this development was Seán's fault. They argued over the Baltinglass scandal, where the Minister for Posts and Telegraphs, James Everett, appointed a political friend to the postmastership of Baltinglass, Co. Wicklow, over a well-qualified popular local candidate. The scandal caused rumbles in the Clann, who had promised to stamp out the petty jobbery associated with previous Fianna Fáil governments. Both Browne and Hartnett felt that Clann na Poblachta should protest, but MacBride felt that the scandal was not worth bringing down the Government. Hartnett resigned from Clann na Poblachta, mainly over Seán's nonchalance regarding the Baltinglass affair, commenting that MacBride 'had become obsessed with power and had abandoned any political or social philosophy.'[67] The situation was certainly awkward, as Hartnett was living in the Red Roof Bungalow on Roebuck House grounds. Anna MacBride White recalled seeing Hartnett and Browne in whispered conferences around the grounds, making the Mother and Child controversy seem almost secondary to a violent clash of personalities as the cause of the party's demise.

Hartnett and Browne were close; it was Hartnett who brought Browne into the party. After the relationship between Hartnett and MacBride worsened, so did relations between Browne and MacBride. Browne agreed that MacBride 'had fallen in love with the trappings and aura of politics.'[68]

The conflict culminated in a dinner at the Russell Hotel in November 1950.[69] According to MacBride, Browne told him that he had failed as a party leader, that the Clann was stagnant, and that Browne intended to bring down the Government and break the party up. Seán compiled a memorandum that night to keep the details of the meeting straight. His secretary, Louie O'Brien, confirms this, as, that same night at Iveagh House, she typed the memorandum, a copy of which rests in the Clann archives.[70] According to Seán,

I told him that I had had the distinct impression for over a year that his main purpose whenever he talked to me was to be insulting and to find some issues — any issue — to have a row with me. That he pursued this policy at first only in private conversations with me, but subsequently had pursued it publicly at meetings. I asked him if I were correct in this impression . . . He said that I was perfectly right and that for over a year he had set himself deliberately to pick a row with me. That he had done so on every occasion we met privately and that, having failed in that way, he had decided to do it openly at meetings so as to force an issue with me. If he didn't succeed he could resign and force an issue that way. That he would have done this before now but that he wanted to get his Mother and Child Scheme through first, or resign on that issue. That if this did not provide him with an issue upon which to bring down the Government he could find another . . .

Browne in his memoir remembers the dinner, but does not recall making threats of any kind, merely pointing out that giving in to the bishops might harm the prospects of a united Ireland.[71] He claimed that he did not threaten to resign, calling the charge 'typical of the lies which Seán MacBride spread' and denying that he would ever 'indulge in such histrionics'. He said 'that he never talks to MacBride now because it is a waste of time and because he has become quite inaccessible to the public and refuses to see anyone. This is probably in part due to '"his ivory tower complex"'.[72]

In MacBride's letter to Browne asking for his resignation, written on 10 April 1951, he wrote that

I should like to assure you that, in reaching the decision that has compelled me to write this letter, I have sincerely sought to eliminate from my mind the other events, not connected with the mother and child services, which have rendered our collaboration increasingly difficult in the course of the last year . . . [73]

Browne's understandably vituperative reply to Seán declared that his party leader's letter was

in full conformity with the standards of behaviour which I have learned to expect from you . . . Your letter is a model of the two faced hypocrisy and humbug so characteristic of you . . . I entered politics because I believed in the high-minded principles which you were expounding on political platforms. I do you no injustice when I state that I have never observed you hearken to any of these principles when practical cases came before us . . . [74]

He resigned from Clann na Poblachta as well, writing, 'I have bidden farewell to your unwholesome brand of politics.'

Browne felt betrayed by his colleagues, stating:

> I as a Catholic accept unequivocally and unreservedly the views of the Hierarchy on this matter, I have not been able to accept the manner in which this matter has been dealt with by my former colleagues in the Government . . . I trust that the standards manifested in these dealings are not customary in the public life of this or any other democratic nation and I hope that my experience has been exceptional.[75]

Costello had informed Browne that 'Whatever about fighting the doctors, I am not going to fight the Bishops and whatever about fighting the Bishops, I am not going to fight the doctors and the Bishops.'[76] As *The Irish Times* points out, 'with a united Cabinet on his side, he might have prevailed against the doctors . . . but . . . he was left to fight a single-handed battle once the Church entered the arena.'[77]

Whether or not he was trying to take on the IMA or bring down the Government, Noël Browne did succeed in enlarging the area of political discourse in Ireland between church and state. Two important immediate effects of the fallout were the response of the North and the dissolution of the Clann.

The resulting crisis led to accusations in the North of 'Rome Rule' and strengthened the unionist perception that whenever the Church chose to interfere, it was able to influence decisions. The Ulster Unionist Council pamphlet proclaimed that 'in any matter where the Roman Catholic Church decides to intervene the Eire Government must accept the Church's policy and decision irrespective of all other considerations.'[78] The 14 April *Irish Times* editorial lamented that 'an honest, far-sighted man has been driven out of active politics. The most serious revelation, however, is that the Roman Catholic Church would seem to be the effective Government of this country.'[79] That phrase, however misleading, 'has been reprinted thousands of times in the intervening half-century and . . . helped to define the parameters of analysis for as long'[80] and provided fuel for unionist fire. Harry Midgley, Northern Ireland's Minister of Education, addressed the Unionist Association: 'There is no doubt that the Roman Catholic Hierarchy has entered the political arena and that it is becoming more and more aggressive in extending the pointers of Roman Catholic authority in the fields of medicine and education,' suggesting that there would be no spiritual or temporal freedom in a united Ireland.[81]

The dispute also highlighted the difference in availability of social services. The *Belfast Telegraph* wrote that 'this controversy shows how partition is a wise recognition of fundamental differences . . . a radical difference of outlook between North and South in social reform.'[82] The fact that the skirmishes occurred behind closed doors also caused suspicion. Some hard-line publications enjoyed the fracas; the *Unionist* editorial of May 1951 concluded with: 'the Dr Browne affair is the best propaganda Ulster has had for years, let us see that we use it.'[83]

Costello attempted to defend the Government's position in the face of such unionist propaganda:

> There will be suggestions made as to the intervention of the Church authorities in State affairs. That, I'm afraid, is now inevitable . . . I regret that it may be misrepresented in the North but I wanted to make it clear, as the last thing that I say, that there was no intention of the Hierarchy interfering in any way in politics or with the activities of my Government or the activities of the State. They confine themselves strictly to faith and morals.[84]

Yet many felt that the Government had chosen between blind obedience to the Church and improving chances of reunification and as the *Belfast Telegraph* observed, 'the division between North and South is wider to-day than it has been for a long time.'[85]

McQuaid felt that the outcome was a triumph for the Catholic Church in Ireland, writing to Papal Nuncio Archbishop Ettore Felici that the defeat of the Mother and Child Scheme was the most important event in Irish history since Daniel O'Connell achieved Catholic Emancipation in 1829.[86] Yet, the 'popular memory remains of McQuaid as a clerical villain and Browne as a medical Robin Hood.'[87] The hierarchy's response to the scheme also demonstrated how out of touch the bishops were with the people to whom they claimed to minister. As Browne observed after his first meeting with McQuaid:

> Dr McQuaid asked why it was necessary to go to so much trouble and expense simply to provide a free health service for the 10 per cent necessitous poor. This comment was not only wrong, since the percentage involved was 30 not 10, but surely represented a strange attitude from a powerful prelate of a Christian Church towards the life and death of the necessitous poor and their children.[88]

As British Ambassador Gilbert Laithwaite explained in a letter to London, 'Since the core of the hierarchical objection was the absence of a means test, there are signs . . . of a degree of underground criticism of the attitude of the bishops among the poorer classes in this country, which is far from usual.'[89] The hierarchy's response to the plan showed the bishops' inability to trust their congregations; their position on the Mother and Child scheme hinted that Catholic women had no judgment on matters of faith and morals and would take the advice of their doctor even if it went against Church teaching. The hierarchy appeared to be 'sheltered from the harsher side of Irish life, fearful of hidden dangers to faith and morals and susceptible to the arguments of the medical profession', and 'the bishops' objections to the scheme seem wide of the mark.'[90]

The controversy also affected the Catholic Church in Ireland in the longer term; as Coogan states, the fallout led to 'a reservoir of hostility which is probably only finally overflowing'.[91] The current historical verdict places blame on the Church for dictating to the state on matters of public health. This change of attitude was slow and tentative, but it was fateful and ultimately irrevocable. From then on, the power and prestige of the Catholic hierarchy in Ireland began to wither slowly, 'though few observers recognised this for a long time.'[92]

Costello did not dissolve the Dáil after Browne's resignation. He replaced Browne as Minister for Health and attempted to formulate a plan to satisfy both the IMA and the hierarchy. However, weeks after Browne's departure, rural TDs threatened to withdraw their support unless the Government raised milk prices in order to help farm incomes — it was then that Costello decided to hold a general election. The electorate supported Browne, who was returned to the Dáil as an Independent with more votes than before.

At first glance, Seán's response to the crisis is surprising for two reasons, the obvious one being that his party took a strong stand on social welfare issues. The other is his close relationship with his strong-willed mother, sometimes regarded as the paragon of an independent woman. This too is more complex than it seems. Maud Gonne MacBride never specifically concerned herself with women's rights; she concentrated more on prisoners' rights and the republican cause. She was a political activist, but never claimed to be a feminist. The only feminist position she publicly took regarded marriage; in an interview during her divorce proceedings, she told the *New York Evening World* that 'I believe any woman with independent instincts with the dream of making her individual personality count for something in the world might just as well shun marriage.'[93] This statement was based more on personal experience and the desire to maintain her own independence than on any dedication to expanding the rights of single women. She came from a Protestant upper-class background and had never had the experience of an ordinary Irish woman, despite her 'lifelong concern for the well-being of children and their mothers'.[94]

Mother and son were not always in agreement politically. In 1917, William Butler Yeats wrote that the thirteen-year-old Seán 'is going to be very clever and to my amusement has begun to criticise his mother's politics. He has a confident analytical mind.'[95] He had broken ranks before, joining the IRA at fourteen without his mother's knowledge or permission and opposing the 1921 Treaty while she supported it. Maud never publicly commented on the Mother and Child scheme, but she was ill at the time. Her biographer Margaret Ward posits that her younger self may have argued with the Church, as she did when it refused to cooperate with her school meals for children campaign.[96] She did contribute to the Clann na Poblachta periodical, *Our Nation*, formed to help MacBride in the 1951 general election. When actor Micheál MacLiammóir asked her about her son, she replied, 'Oh, he must go his own way. We all do in the end.'[97] Whatever their political disagreements, she was proud of all he had achieved.

Moreover, Seán was more traditional than his mother. As a convert to Catholicism, she took what she needed from Catholic dogma and discarded anything else.[98] Yet Seán, raised a Catholic and educated in French and Irish Catholic schools, took his faith from Rome. He advised Maud not to include her affair with Millevoye and the details of her divorce from John MacBride when writing her memoir. In the conservative Irish atmosphere, Seán was 'especially anxious that none of the family skeletons should be aired in public'.[99] He did later attempt to ease the stigma of illegitimacy by supporting the introduction of a shortened birth certificate that left out parents' names but he opposed the 1986 referendum on deleting the prohibition of divorce from the Irish Constitution.

Kid MacBride never publicly commented on the controversy. An activist before her marriage, she later devoted herself to her husband's causes. Whether behind closed doors she criticised her husband's behaviour during the Mother and Child controversy remains a mystery.

There is no correspondence from this time between McQuaid and MacBride despite Seán's offer to be available at any time and McQuaid's reply that 'I shall not fail to take advantage of your generous suggestion that you are at my disposal for any matters in which you could assist.'[100] This would have been the time to take Seán up on this offer, but McQuaid chose to communicate through Costello, despite MacBride's position as leader of Browne's party. This may be because McQuaid distrusted Seán because of his

IRA background and his alleged role in the denial of a Red Hat to McQuaid, but there is no extant written evidence to confirm this hypothesis or support any other explanation.

The outcome of the Mother and Child controversy is best seen as another example of the reactive nature of the inter-party Government and its willingness to hang together rather than disagree and risk losing power. It became more obvious that there were five political parties with divergent views, and the doctors and the bishops exploited these differences.[101] The repeal of the External Relations Act is an earlier example of such reactive behaviour, a hasty compromise in order to keep the Government afloat. Repeal worked in the Government's and Clann na Poblachta's favour, but now the danger for MacBride was that he would lose the radical element of his party.

The controversy and the 1951 general election saw the decline of the Clann, once viewed as the party of the future. Both the Government and MacBride wanted to avoid controversy and he showed little of the radicalism of Clann na Poblachta in founding days. What might have happened if MacBride had brought the Government down? He would have been justified in doing so; the no-means test principle was agreed-upon Clann policy. It probably would have been the wisest course of action for the longevity of his party; as Coogan colourfully declares, 'MacBride would have been better advised to support his stormy petrel minister and lead the Clann out of government in defiance of the brandished crosiers.'[102] The coalition had lasted longer than anyone thought possible and withdrawing support would have satisfied the social welfare element in the party, as the republicans had already been placated somewhat by the declaration of the Republic and leaving might have soothed the hurt feelings of those who had questioned the wisdom of joining a Fine Gael coalition. Browne's resignation was a pyrrhic victory for both the Government and MacBride. His behaviour split the party; speaking in the Dáil, Deputy Patrick Smith called him 'Pontius Pilate'[103] and the image of his washing his hands is very evocative.

Why then did he choose to stay in government? His reasoning is unclear. Perhaps he remembered his godfather John O'Leary's advice to William Butler Yeats that in Ireland a man must have the Catholic Church or the Fenians on his side. He had lost much of the Fenian backing with Clann's decision to join the inter-party Government; old IRA and republican supporters were unhappy with the Fine Gael alliance. The republicans in Clann na Poblachta felt betrayed when Clann went into government and the radical section dissipated because of the official Clann response to the Mother and Child scheme. Supporters looking toward the party for radical change revolted against his alleged yielding to the Church. MacBride made a mistake in jettisoning the radical Clann vote and chose to split the party's support base rather than the Government.[104]

The Government chose to fight the election as a government, rather than as individual parties. Seán delivered speeches on their accomplishments, highlighting lower luxury taxes, increased pensions, lower unemployment, the absence of military courts or political prisoners, and the declaration of the Republic: 'From being a part of the British Empire this State was now an independent sovereign Republic recognised as such by the nations of the world.'[105] Other than this reference, the election was silent on partition and international affairs.

De Valera and Fianna Fáil fought the election on the premise that a coalition was an unstable form of government and one party would provide a greater degree of stability. MacBride countered by stating that 'our first inter-party government would indicate that it is more stable than those which were provided by the Fianna Fáil party.'[106] Fianna Fáil candidate Gerald Boland accused both Fine Gael and Clann na Poblachta of letting down their supporters while in power: Fine Gael by leaving the Commonwealth, the Clann by abandoning Browne.[107] Browne, meanwhile, decided to run for re-election as an Independent and was attracting good receptions and enthusiastic crowds at his speeches. Seán did not address the controversy in his speeches, but did write to *The Irish Times* that 'Dr Browne has made many reckless and malicious statements in recent weeks impugning my integrity, honesty of purpose and motives. I have ignored these . . . as they are only intended to confuse the issues in these elections.'[108]

Yet there appeared to be no concrete issues addressed in the election and 'none of the parties has deigned to submit a clear picture of what it proposes to do if returned to power.'[109] 'An Irishman's Diary' in *The Irish Times* commented that 'I have never known a duller election . . . there always was a certain amount of excitement at Irish elections; but this time public interest seems to have flagged completely.'[110] The *Irish Independent* called the campaign 'orderly and unexciting.'[111] Both *The Irish Times* and the *Irish Independent* urged their readers to vote, pointing out that there was the choice between a single-party government and an inter-party government to decide upon, as Fianna Fáil had refused to enter a coalition.[112]

Despite the apparent apathy, more people voted than in the previous general election: 1,334,256 compared to 1,189,558 in 1948.[113] The electorate supported Browne, who was returned to the Dáil as an Independent with more votes than before. In the 1951 election, the Clann lost eight out of ten seats. Former Clann TDS Peadar Cowan and Jack McQuillan were also re-elected as Independents. MacBride was re-elected from his Dublin constituency but his vote fell substantially from 8,648 in 1948 to 2,853, and he was elected on the last count.

The party held only two seats after 1951, including MacBride's. Fine Gael were the winners, getting nine extra seats and it looked like another inter-party government would convene. Both *The Irish Times* and the *Irish Independent* pointed out that people had preferred an inter-party government to a single-party one.[114] Fianna Fáil got only one extra seat, but was able to form a government with Independent support. MacBride had sacrificed long-term gain for short-term reward. He was re-elected as TD in 1951 and 1954, but was never again to hold a position of political importance in the Republic.

Browne remained in Irish politics in the Dáil and Seanad until 1982, though a *Manchester Guardian* editorial predicted in 1951 that 'he can command much sympathy in the country, but no politician of ordinary prudence after reading his reply to MacBride will ever be willing to have him for a colleague.'[115] The prediction was somewhat accurate in that Browne had very few long-term colleagues. Browne joined Fianna Fáil in 1954, then formed his own party, the National Progressive Democrats, in 1958, finally joining the Labour Party in 1969. However, he would end his political career as an Independent.

A derivative of the Mother and Child scheme was implemented subsequently by the new Fianna Fáil Government. The 1952 Social Welfare Act extended national health insurance, unemployment insurance and widows' and orphans' schemes, though Browne's wider vision of universal social insurance would have to wait.

In its simplest form, the crisis was seen as the first major undermining of the Irish state by the Catholic Church, but it is a mistake to judge it as a straightforward conflict between church and state — to paraphrase Oscar Wilde, the truth is not that pure and simple — but the perception was damaging as it provided evidence, particularly in Northern Ireland, that Home Rule was indeed Rome Rule and led public opinion in the Republic to blame the hierarchy rather than the politicians.

Chapter 9 ∽

A STATESMAN OF INTERNATIONAL STATUS: SEÁN MacBRIDE'S LATER CAREER

'The value of an idea has nothing whatever to do with the sincerity of the man who expresses it.'

— OSCAR WILDE

After the fall of the inter-party Government in 1951 and the collapse of Clann na Poblachta in 1965, it seemed that Seán MacBride's career in Irish politics was over. However, his legal skills, his diplomatic experience, and his fluency in French made it possible for him to take up a new international role as a spokesman for human rights issues.

Seán possessed a high profile as Minister for External Affairs and his political career had once shown much future promise. Dermot Keogh referred to him as a 'rival Taoiseach' and after the first cabinet meeting, Richard Mulcahy commented that 'we [he and Thomas O'Higgins] both looked at one another and it was as if the two of us said together, "another de Valera."'[1]

However, by 1951 his reputation was 'effectively in tatters'.[2] As Noël Browne remembers,

He would scan the cabinet agenda, and on those subjects in which he had a special interest, would submit a treatise to the Taoiseach. In the early days, this memorandum was carefully unfolded and conscientiously read out by the Taoiseach to a politely attentive Cabinet. It was treated with some respect . . . As the memoranda proliferated, it became obvious that

all was not well in Clann na Poblachta; they were now treated with a
tolerant amusement, and the epistles filed somewhere.[3]

There are several reasons for this decline in influence. The increase in
Taoiseach John A. Costello's confidence and authority meant that Seán had
less leverage within the cabinet. He was also losing influence within his party;
the decision to enter a coalition government had already alienated some of
the party's republican sector; minor government scandals and the response to
the Mother and Child controversy helped further to divide opinion within
Clann na Poblachta.

In addition, Seán's ability to control his party was weakened because he
travelled more than any previous occupant of his office, and his frequent
absences led to his power diminishing in both the party and the Government.
For example, he spent much of March 1951, the lead-up to the Mother and
Child controversy, in France and the United States. As Sir Gilbert Laithwaite
wrote, MacBride 'is thought by some to pay less attention to holding his little
Clann na Poblachta party together than is wise'.[4]

Personality conflicts, which seemed a common feature of his political
career, were also a factor. By 1951, Seán had fallen out with Clann member
Peadar Cowan, expelling him from the party, and with the Secretary of his
Department, Frederick Boland, as well as Noel Hartnett and Noël Browne.
Todd Andrews, a fellow IRA member in the 1920s, commented that Seán was
'industrious in whatever interested him but sustained effort did not appear to
be one of his characteristics . . . He worked best in an organisation when he
was the leader.'[5] As leader, he expected to be obeyed without debate and did
not deal well with contention. Although he had much in common with de
Valera, the differences were more striking: MacBride did not have De Valera's
character or political acumen. He had de Valera's self-righteousness without
the emotional discipline and could not gather an effective team around him,
essential for longevity as a party leader.[6]

Cruise O'Brien offered a remarkable, if cruel, appraisal of Seán's time in
office. Shortly after MacBride's fall, he wrote a comment on his career which
appeared anonymously in a local periodical, *The Leader*, where he compared
Seán to both Charlie Chaplin and Don Quixote, inspired by lofty and
chivalrous but false or unrealisable ideals:

> There are those who say . . . that he is in fact constantly acting a part . . .
> This gibe, although it often merely voices the envy of the inarticulate and
> drab, is not altogether unjust. The professions of law, politics and
> diplomacy are not conducive to unconditional sincerity . . . Certainly the

new, purged, party follows its leader with uncritical devotion, unsupported by either talent or numbers.[7]

He did credit Seán with building up his Department:

> He managed, with the aid of General Marshall, to induce these gentlemen to put their fingers into the pies of various other Departments . . . and he got Mr Blowick to plant a great deal of Sithca [sic] Spruce. He also — and it was not an inconsiderable achievement — got the money for Dr Browne to build his hospitals . . . In the sphere of justice . . . his interventions were aimed at saving men from the gallows . . . The gaunt knight, wistful yet severe, in the dilapidated La Mancha of Roebuck, has been reading tales of chivalry, from Standish O'Grady to Patrick Pearse. He will rescue the fair lady Cathleen Ní Houlihan from the castle Discrimination, where the British giant Gerrymandering, holds her thrall. The ogre Sterling bars the way with his famous Link, which will have snapped. The good fairies from America will help to accomplish this. (They have all been expelled from the State Department, but Quixote does not know this.) He saddles his spavined mare, Poblaclante, and gallops down the drive. But something is missing. He calls aloud for Sancho Panza. But Sancho will never come again. Sancho has locked himself into the lodge.

Years afterward, Cruise O'Brien felt a bit ashamed of the piece. Seeing himself as the Sancho Panza character, 'hoping that in serving his master in his wild career, he might attain the governorship of an island. But unlike Sancho Panza I not merely obtained from my master the civil service equivalent of the governorship of an island, but retained that prize after my master's fall.'[8]

Seán suffered a further blow in April 1953 when Maud Gonne MacBride died, aged eighty-six. She was buried in the republican plot at Glasnevin cemetery, a fitting tribute for the woman known as 'Ireland's Joan of Arc'. Iseult died of coronary thrombosis less than a year later. No matter how impervious Seán had become to the deaths of relatives and close friends, the loss of both his mother and sister in a short space of time must have been devastating. Roebuck House must have had a very different dynamic. Both Kid and Anna were close to Maud and Iseult, Anna naming a daughter after her.

Seán campaigned during the general election of 1954 on familiar themes such as emigration, partition, protecting natural resources, and allowing representatives from the North to join the Dáil and Seanad. Clann na

Poblachta still advocated making partition an international issue. Though MacBride received enthusiastic receptions wherever he spoke, he did not attract the crowds that de Valera or Costello did and *The Irish Times* called 1954 'the dullest election campaign in recent years'.[9] That newspaper half-heartedly endorsed de Valera and Fianna Fáil, admitting that it was a 'less of two evils' vote, as the alternative was an inter-party government with vague policies and principles.[10]

Despite the apparent lack of enthusiasm, the usual polling level of 70 per cent was exceeded in many places.[11] Fine Gael increased its representation. MacBride also saw an increase of support and the Clann gained one seat from 1951. After the results were in, Seán urged all parties to form a National Government similar to Switzerland's, with the main planks of encouraging reunification and full employment, increasing productivity, reducing emigration, and preserving the Gaeltacht. He conceded that 'by reason of the small representation of my party in the Dáil, I would not seek or expect representation in such a National Government.'[12] The *Irish Independent* liked the idea, writing that 'one-party rule has not solved the nation's problems; it has kept alive old feuds and old personal spleens.'[13]

Instead, a second inter-party Government took power, with a cabinet consisting of Fine Gael, Labour, and Clann na Talmhan. Clann na Poblachta lent 'external support' to the Government, but did not join it. In a letter to Kid MacBride, Costello wrote, 'we are sorry that Seán will not be more closely associated with us than he is.'[14]

The Clann did make two important contributions to the second inter-party Government. The first was by electing Liam Kelly to the Senate. Kelly was the leader of Saor Uladh, a Northern breakaway republican group. Kelly had been elected MP for mid-Tyrone in 1953 and when he was chosen as Senator was serving a jail sentence for making a seditious speech. In November 1955, Saor Uladh raided an RUC barracks in Fermanagh in the first of a series of raids which led to the IRA launching its border campaign a year later. Even though Kelly led the raid, he continued to attend the Seanad for some time afterwards.

The second contribution Clann na Poblachta made to the Government was to bring it down. In early 1957, the party decided to withdraw support from the Government because of the poor economic situation and the Government's offensive against the IRA. Seán opposed the decision, but was outvoted and so proposed a vote of no confidence in the Government, claiming that rising unemployment was the major reason for his vote.[15] Many in Fine Gael were puzzled by Seán's action, especially as Clann na Poblachta had expressed confidence in the Government's fresh declaration of aims and development policies. In a letter to MacBride, regarding the anti-partition movement, Costello informed him that 'I do not intend, for my part, to permit recent events to add to any further bitterness [between personalities and parties].'[16]

By then the Clann had lost much of its freshness and innovation. Only eleven Clann candidates stood at the resulting general election. The Clann received only 22,000 votes and only one seat. Seán was not re-elected; his defeat and his subsequent failure to get re-elected in a by-election in 1959 and a general election in 1961 meant the end for the party.

Talks of a Labour–Clann merger came to nothing, as they could not agree on the focus of a merged party — republican or Labour — the composition of the alliance, and the inclusion of Sinn Féin or Noël Browne's newly formed National Progressive Democrats. John Tully continued as the only Clann TD in the Dáil until 1965. An ard-fheis of 10 July 1965 officially dissolved the party.

Even before the Clann's end, MacBride had become disillusioned with Irish politics. His inability to regain his seat in the Dáil probably contributed. But rather than continue to fight elections, establish a lucrative legal practice, or travel on the speaking circuit, he began to broaden his perspective. His failure in home politics to build up a stable political base, or to maintain for himself for long a significant role in Irish parliamentary affairs, left him free to pursue, with a success denied to him at home, a new and impressive career on an international level, where his considerable diplomatic and legal skills could be used in the cause of a better world order.[17]

Seán's interest in human rights, the treatment of prisoners (no doubt influenced by his and his mother's experiences in prison), and work towards European integration led him to return to the legal profession. Even after his ministry had ended, he continued to be involved in foreign affairs, asking Costello in 1956 if the Government would consider sending food and medical supplies to Hungary, recently battered after a failed revolt against Soviet communism: 'I would willingly place myself at the Government's disposal. I make this offer as I know personally Dr Figl the Austrian Foreign Minister and representatives of the Hungarian nationalist movement in exile, and might be able to get things done more expeditiously than through normal diplomatic channels.'[18]

The Greek Government had asked Seán to advise it at the United Nations regarding the occupation of Cyprus, then a British crown colony. He proposed official recognition of the right of Cyprus to self-determination, a civil government to be vested in the Council of Europe for five years, and naval and military defences vested in NATO for the interim. He believed that the Greeks would agree but the Turks might take more persuasion, as they had been 'reinforced into taking an uncompromising attitude by the British', who were opposed to any compromise proposal. As MacBride wrote to Liam Cosgrave, 'the Cyprus question has done more to weaken faith in the concept of Western democracy than anything else that has happened in the Western world.' He felt kinship with 'a small island being trampled upon'.[19]

MacBride began to practise in Irish and European courts as an advocate. One of his most celebrated cases took place in 1958 when the Greek Government asked him to challenge the deportation of Archbishop Makarios, the Cypriot nationalist leader who the British Government claimed was actively supporting terrorism. The case came before the European Court where Seán was able to prove that conditions in Cyprus did not justify Makarios's deportation. In 1959, Makarios became the President of an independent Cyprus.

The achievement for which Seán MacBride is most recognised is his co-founding and help with the development of Amnesty International (AI). English lawyer Peter Benenson's concern for political prisoners provided the impetus for the formation of the organisation, a worldwide movement campaigning for internationally recognised human rights. Benenson was concerned with law reform and cases of injustice; in the 1950s, he worked at helping those persecuted for political and religious beliefs in various countries, acting as an observer and defence counsel and writing and broadcasting about abuses of autocratic governments. In 1959, he founded Justice, an all-party organisation of British lawyers, to campaign for the maintenance of the rule of law and observation of the United Nations Universal Declaration of Human Rights. While travelling to work one morning on the London Underground, Benenson read an article about two Portuguese students arrested for raising their glasses in a toast to freedom. He recalled that

> it was on the 19th November 1960 as I was reading [the *Daily Telegraph*] in the Tube . . . that I came on a short paragraph that related how two Portuguese students had been sentenced to terms of imprisonment for no other offence than having drunk a toast to liberty in a Lisbon restaurant. Perhaps because I am particularly attached to liberty, perhaps because I am fond of wine, this news-item produced a righteous indignation in me that transcended normal bounds.[20]

Benenson was not only profoundly shocked; he decided that he would try to help the two young men who had been the victims of this injustice. His initial idea involved a one-year campaign to draw public attention to the plight of political and religious prisoners. Benenson's London office would collect and publish information on 'prisoners of conscience' in a year-long 'Appeal for Amnesty'.

He decided to begin by publicising the appeal through a newspaper article published in *The Observer* of 28 May 1961. Entitled 'The Forgotten Prisoners', it began, 'Open your newspaper any day of the week and you will find a report from somewhere in the world of someone being imprisoned, tortured or executed because his opinions are unacceptable to his government.' He maintained that common action was necessary: a world campaign to mobilise public opinion quickly with a 'broadly based, international, non-sectarian and all-party' movement that would not publicise any political views; instead they would focus on humanitarian concerns. The aims of the 'Appeal for Amnesty 1961' were to work impartially for the release of those imprisoned for their opinions, to seek for them a fair and public trial, to enlarge the Right of Asylum and help political refugees to find work, and to urge effective international machinery to guarantee freedom of opinion. Success 'depends . . . upon the campaign being all-embracing in its composition, international in character and politically impartial in direction.'[21] A simultaneous article was published in France's *Le Monde*.

The articles generated an unexpected number of letters, donations, information on other prisoners, and editorial support. The *New York Times*, *Irish Independent*, London *Times*, *New York Tribune*, West Germany's *Die Welt*, Switzerland's *Journal de Genève*, and Sweden's *Politiken* commented favourably and appealed to their readers for help. *The Irish Times* editorial stated that 'no reasonable and humane person could quarrel with these objectives'[22] and The *Guardian* editorial pointed out that 'there are few countries today which can proudly boast that they have no prisoners of conscience in their gaols, and the fact demonstrates eloquently a deep malaise in our world.'[23] The first international meeting was in Luxembourg in July 1961, where it was decided to turn the appeal into a permanent international movement, named Amnesty International the following year.

MacBride and Benenson had much in common. Both were lawyers with an interest in human rights issues and both were Catholic, Benenson having converted in 1958. Seán helped to plan the first Amnesty 'Missions', formulating what tactics to use to aid individual prisoners. His high profile helped both in publicising the movement and in gaining access to world leaders, especially in Amnesty's early years.

The idea was to collect information on prisoners incarcerated for political views and bombard the offending governments with letters, postcards, and telegrams calling for the prisoners' release. Amnesty's regional offices never adopted prisoners in their own countries or accepted the cases of those who had advocated the use of violence. Amnesty did not widely publicise its victories for fear of government reprisals on remaining prisoners or unwillingness to respond to later pressure. Yet Amnesty soon established itself as the leading organisation protecting the rights of political refugees and dissidents and opposing arbitrary imprisonment and torture. MacBride said in 1964, 'Although it cannot be said that the release of two or three thousand people was the actual work of Amnesty International, its influence is obvious.'[24]

Seán was an active ambassador for the movement, travelling to Czechoslovakia, Brazil, and Guinea to negotiate for the release of prisoners and the protection of their rights. Amnesty International soon established itself as the leading body opposing arbitrary arrest, imprisonment and torture.

Though the organisation was meeting with some success, problems developed. In 1966, Benenson began to suspect that British Intelligence was infiltrating Amnesty, and the following year he accused the British Government of tapping Amnesty's phone lines.[25] He expressed a desire to move the organisation to a neutral country, but he was unable to convince anyone else. He then decided to resign, not just because of Amnesty International's decision to remain based in London, but also because of a rift with Seán and his desire to retire.

He reconsidered soon after and decided to stay. He later learned that CIA money had helped to fund the International Commission of Jurists (ICJ), where Seán was Secretary. He grew paranoid about Seán being linked to the CIA, despite the fact that when Seán found out about the ICJ's links to the CIA, he protested and resigned.[26] However, Benenson himself was not without fault; it was later discovered that he had accepted money from the British Government to help British subjects in Rhodesia and Nigeria. This situation was notable, as the idea of Amnesty was to be independently funded and apolitical. Seán acknowledged that Benenson was responsible for 'a number of erratic actions'. Benenson refused to attend Amnesty International's March 1967 meeting, resigning instead. MacBride appointed Peter Calvocoressi, a former Bletchley Park intelligence officer and a member of the Working Group on Minorities, to investigate the charges and to inquire into the internal structures of Amnesty. A special two-day executive meeting convened in March 1967 in Denmark, to discuss Calvocoressi's findings, and Benenson then retired.

His relationship with the organisation was eventually restored, but he continued to believe that Amnesty should be headquartered in a neutral country. The relationship with MacBride was also restored; they corresponded by phone and letter until Seán's death in 1988.[27]

Seán chaired Amnesty International for thirteen years, resigning in November 1974, one month before he received the Nobel Peace Prize. Jonathan Power calls MacBride 'critically important' to the movement by keeping it going, managing to straddle the Cold War East–West ideological divide better than most, and helping establish high-level contacts as well as undertaking regular missions to explore human rights abuses.[28] The founding and development of Amnesty International are credited among the great successes of Seán's career.

MacBride also served as Secretary-General for the previously mentioned International Commission of Jurists, a non-governmental organisation devoted to promoting throughout the world the understanding and observance of the Rule of Law and legal protection of human rights; it operated from 1963 to 1970. Though not allied to any government, the Commission was seen as pro-Western, concerned more with the abuses of human rights in Eastern Europe. Yet Seán would later take stands on issues that were decidedly anti-American. For example, he denounced the United States bombing of Vietnam. In 1969, he travelled to North Vietnam and was appalled by the use of civilian targets and anti-personnel weapons.[29] He also met with the Shah of Iran, whose Prime Minister informed him that the regime used torture, but employed only the most modern scientific techniques under the guidance of their US and British advisors.[30] Later, Seán did not approve of the Ayatollah Khomeini's repressive regime, but he viewed it as a result of the Shah's rule, supported for so many years by the West.

He became United Nations Commissioner for Namibia (South West Africa) from 1973 to 1976, gaining the title of Assistant Secretary-General of the UN. Namibia was a German colony until the 1919 Treaty of Versailles. The League of Nations placed it under the protection of South Africa. In 1966, the United Nations declared that South Africa's mandate to administer Namibia had expired. South Africa refused to adhere to the UN request to vacate the territory and the UN set up a Council for Namibia to implement its policy. As MacBride maintained later, 'South Africa has been systematically flouting the international law and the decisions of the International Court of Justice and the United Nations.'[31]

The appointment of MacBride is not as surprising as it first appears. The International Commission of Jurists (ICJ) had taken cases relating to Namibia, so he was familiar with the country's situation. Seán had visited South Africa in 1958 and condemned its policy of apartheid. He was a good publicist, proven by his work with Amnesty International, and the United

Nations wanted him to organise international opinion against South African rule. In addition, there was the instinctive sympathy he felt for an illegally occupied nation.

He concluded that the foreign policy followed by NATO countries was partly responsible for the situation, and the procrastination of Western nations allowed South Africa to hold out against the UN's request.[32] His public relations work on Namibia allowed him to express a larger opinion that 'be it in Afghanistan, Angola, El Salvador or Cambodia — no superpower has the right to intervene by direct or covert actions. These are matters which should be referred to and dealt with by the United Nations.'[33] Free elections should be organised under UN control to let the people decide the government they desired. He distinguished himself in the post, a road in Namibia's capital Windhoek is named 'Seán MacBride Avenue', and Namibia gained independence in 1990.

From 1968 to 1974, he was also the Chairman of the International Peace Bureau, the parent body for pacifist organisations worldwide, dedicated to resolving international conflicts in a non-violent way; in 1985, he became its President, a post he held until 1985. In the late 1970s, he chaired the UNESCO International Commission for the Study of Communication Problems, culminating in its report 'Many Voices — One World' in 1980. The report sharply criticised the imbalances in world information flows and attacked Western news agencies' reporting of Third World issues, which led to protest from the US Government. Not all of his endeavours met with success; despite his skills as a negotiator, he was unable to break the deadlock between the United States and Iran over the holding of American hostages at the American Embassy in Tehran.

The role of international diplomat suited Seán well. Cruise O'Brien makes the point that in his previous career in Irish parliamentary politics, MacBride had been striving to please 'ghosts', his mother's reputation and his father's martyrdom, rather than possessing a sincere desire to be a politician. When Seán was Secretary-General of the ICJ, they had dinner together:

> Looking back on it now, I can see that MacBride, as Minister in Dublin, had been doomed to appease ghosts . . . at a high cost to himself as a person. But by driving him from office into exile, the Irish people had set MacBride free for a time at least from the ghost-appeasing business. He was now free to be his natural, humorous and pleasant self.[34]

MacBride's post with the ICJ required relocation to Geneva in 1963. He moved to Switzerland without his wife. Biographer Anthony Jordan revealed that

Seán did not ask Kid to accompany him, but it could have been that she did not want to go.[35] Both of their children had remained in Dublin and she did not seem to mind staying at Roebuck House, cooking, gardening, and volunteering as a driver at Cerebral Palsy Ireland's Sandymount School Clinic.

Seán did not cultivate a strong relationship with his family. He and Kid had a 'friendly' rather than passionate marriage and he had devoted little time to bringing up Anna and Tiernan.[36] This is not surprising; not having had a father himself, he probably had little idea how to engage actively with his children. In 1953, Anna underwent a major operation in Peamount Sanatorium. In the six months that she was there, only Iseult visited her: 'the family was too busy to come themselves.'[37] Anna felt that her father 'didn't like children', and even if he related better to them as adults, he did not know them all that well. Work was also a priority throughout Seán's life. When in government, he would sometimes forget to come home for supper and his occupations with various international organisations meant that he travelled often. As Kid told the *New York Times* after Seán's Nobel Peace Prize was announced, 'He works all the time and doesn't even have time to relax. He used to enjoy sailing but doesn't have the time for that now. He comes home when he can, which isn't often.'[38]

Several books featuring Seán MacBride refer obliquely to a 'fondness for women', but none provides specific details.[39] Jordan explains that he preferred to hire women as they were 'less independent and more willing to take and follow instructions'.[40] This was not the case with Ruth Sweetman, MacBride's secretary in Geneva and the daughter of The O'Rahilly. Seán lived in a hotel and rather than keep his belongings there in between trips, he would check out and leave his suitcases in Ruth's flat. When she wanted to get a flatmate, he objected, as he thought it would affect their arrangement. Máire Cruise O'Brien, in her memoir *The Same Age as the State*, refers to the 'fairly worldly fashion' in which the foreign service spent their evenings in Strasbourg when Seán was Minister.[41] One of his colleagues was shocked when Seán went up to receive Communion at Sunday Mass. Cruise O'Brien does not specify why Seán's action was so surprising. It may have merely been a failure to observe proper fasting procedures before receiving or it may have been something deeper. There were vague rumours of an affair with his long-time secretary Louie O'Brien. If so, it would have been a fairly incestuous relationship. She and her husband lived on the top floor of Roebuck House and she worked with Kid for the Irish Sweepstakes as well as being a good friend to Anna.

Seán may have sacrificed a close relationship with his family, but his devotion to his pet causes had benefits, including the Nobel Peace Prize which he was awarded in 1974, the first Irishman to be so honoured. He shared the Prize with Eisaku Sato of Japan. The Nobel Committee commended him for his 'many years of efforts to build up and protect human rights all over the world'.[42] The honour was well received in Ireland; no Irish political figure had achieved such international recognition since de Valera's tenure as President of the League of Nations Assembly in the 1930s. The *Irish Independent* reported that 'most people here see Mr MacBride as a very deserving Prize winner.'[43] An *Irish Times* editorial praised the achievement:

> Ireland can take a proper pride in Mr Seán MacBride's latest distinction . . . With his legal talents, he could have easily made a fortune at the Bar and relapsed into selfish, moneyed complacency . . . Instead he looked outward at the tormented world, and immersed himself in it. He will not feel proud himself, so Ireland has the right to feel proud on his behalf.[44]

In the Dáil, the Fianna Fáil TD and future Minister for Foreign Affairs, Michael O'Kennedy, congratulated MacBride:

> Finally, it is noteworthy that a former Minister for External Affairs in this House has been nominated for the Nobel Peace Prize. This is a great honour for our country, and on behalf of the Fianna Fáil Party I would like to convey to him publicly our appreciation of what he has done and our best wishes for future achievements by him.[45]

MacBride was surprised at the honour: 'It came as a bombshell and I did not even know that I was being considered.'[46] He hoped that the Prize would give him greater prestige in putting forward proposals for Namibia's future. He donated his share of the £45,000 Prize money to Amnesty International and other various humanitarian organisations.

The presentation speech was given by Aase Lionæs, Chairman of the Norwegian Nobel Committee, who noted that Seán was a 'citizen of a country that for many years had been the scene of bitter, grievous conflict'. Strangely, for a 'sore thumb' strategy advocate who had once believed in publicising partition at every opportunity, MacBride did not mention in his acceptance speech partition or the Troubles in the North, despite the fact that the conflict was intensifying. Perhaps he failed to mention it because he was not receiving the Prize for work done in Ireland and he had been unable to alter that situation in his previous interventions: 'MacBride came to Oslo very much as the president of the International Peace Bureau and as the United Nations Commissioner for Namibia.'[47] His acceptance speech, entitled 'The

Imperatives of Survival' and delivered on 12 December 1974, reported knowledgably and at length about disarmament and ways to improve world problems:

> The tremendous scientific and material developments that have taken place in this period have altered radically the whole structure of human society — and even threatened the survival of the human race. This stupendous scientific and material revolution has brought basic changes into every aspect of our lives and of the ecology in which we live. These scientific developments were accompanied by equally radical changes in our social and political structures.[48]

Not surprisingly, Seán mentioned the treatment of prisoners and the resulting cycle of violence:

> Force, or threat of force, are constantly used to dominate other countries . . . Prisoners are not only ill-treated but are tortured systematically in a worse manner than at any barbaric period of history. In many cases this is done with the direct or tacit approval of governments that claim to be civilized or even Christian . . . If those vested with authority and power practise injustice, resort to torture and killing, is it not inevitable that those who are the victims will react with similar methods?[49]

He also made statements that would later be perceived as anti-Western:

> The socialist countries do not have a profit-motivated industrial-military complex. They can therefore adjust more readily to disarmament. The military industrial complex is state owned and controlled. To them disarmament means an automatic switch from increased arms production to increase in production for industrial development and for the consumer and export markets. They cannot lose by disarmament, they can only gain . . . This, no doubt, accounts for the much more sincere and far-reaching approach of the Soviet Union to General and Complete Disarmament than that of the Western powers.[50]

These views represented a vast change from his anti-communist stance while in government. Had his view really altered so completely? He had flirted with socialist principles with Saor Éire early in his political career, and much of MacBride's anti-communist posturing may have been done to please the electorate. Perhaps his new research on disarmament and the knowledge about the dangers of building and storing weapons of mass destruction influenced his opinion. However, it is more likely that Seán's ability to compartmentalise allowed him to hold this viewpoint comfortably. He had demonstrated this ability on previous occasions: he was a constitutional politician who maintained links with extreme republicans, while in government; he disliked the British stance on partition, but was on friendly terms with Clement Attlee and Ernest Bevin and partnered with Britain in the Council of Europe and the OEEC; he founded a political party based on social welfare reform, but did not support Noël Browne during the Mother and Child controversy. Similarly, he disliked the atheistic and repressive parts of communist philosophy, but recognised the benefits of their approach to disarmament.

MacBride also addressed familiar themes from his own work:

> Structures which deprive persons of their human rights and dignity prevent justice from being realized; and systems which condemn people to starvation or to substandard conditions are a denial both of human rights and human dignity.
>
> The Universal Declaration of 1948 is both universal and comprehensive . . . It provides a basis for the relationship between human beings and states inter se. The political and religious leaders of the world should utilize it as part of an effort to rebuild standards of morality that have crumbled in the decadence of this age.[51]

He praised non-governmental organisations both for their achievements and for their lack of political bias and suggested what could be done to make the United Nations more effective:

> In recent years the non-governmental organizations have been playing an increasingly important role. They are virtually the only independent voices that are heard and that can alert public opinion through the press and the media . . . In my view the role of voluntary organizations is becoming more and more essential. They are the only bodies that will have the necessary independence and initiative to restore some faith and idealism in our world. They deserve a great deal more support and encouragement.[52]

Seán's speech demonstrates just how universal and comprehensive his later concerns became. Perhaps his time away from the country educated him and made him aware of problems greater than partition. The lecture was well received at home, *The Irish Times* calling it 'a wide-ranging and profound survey of present discontents and life enhancing expectations . . . rich in humane passion and reasoned argument'.[53]

Three years after Seán's award, Amnesty International won the Nobel Peace Prize. The presentation speech was again given by Lionæs, who commented that Amnesty deserved the prize because the organisation had 'sprung spontaneously from the individual's deep and firmly rooted conviction that the ordinary man and woman is capable of making a meaningful contribution to peace.'[54] The Nobel Lecture was delivered on 11 December by Mümtaz Soysal, a Turkish politician and law professor who was Chairman of Amnesty International from 1974 to 1978.

MacBride also won the 1977 Lenin Peace Prize, which had been established in 1928 as a socialist rival to the Nobel Peace Prize. He was chosen for his 'outstanding merits in the struggle for maintaining and strengthening peace'.[55] He responded that the honour was 'an indication of the interest which the Soviet Union has in putting an end to the arms race and in pursuing the goal of general and complete disarmament'.[56] The award was presented to Seán in Dublin by Nicolai Blokhain, Chairman of the International Lenin Committee, for his work in Namibia and his policy on disarmament. He is among a few Westerners to have been given the award from a Soviet Government-approved committee and was the first to have won both prizes. Though there were no Irish newspaper editorials praising the achievement, there was also no protest at Seán's acceptance of the award. MacBride was popular with the Soviet Government by virtue of his denouncement of the Western military-industrial complex, but he protested just as strongly the Soviet occupation of Afghanistan and martial law in Poland. MacBride was also the first non-American to win the American Medal for Justice, which he was awarded in 1978.

The Seán MacBride Collection at Iona College in New York, consisting of books, pamphlets, and journals, was presented to the American Fund Raising Institute by MacBride's family after his death and provides some clue as to what his concerns were.[57] Most of the material he collected and saved concerns disarmament, poverty and discrimination, showing the range of his later interests, from copies of the Commission of Enquiry into the Irish Penal System to reports on renewable energy resources in developing countries.

Seán's later career reinforces the idea of transition; the shift from concentrating on Ireland to involvement in more universal concerns is similar to his earlier transformation from insurgent to constitutional politician. Conor Cruise O'Brien posits that MacBride needed a niche once his political career was at a standstill. Was his later vocation motivated by altruism or was it a calculated way of ensuring that his fame would continue? This, like many other aspects of his career, is subject to debate. Some, like MacBride's biographer Anthony Jordan thought that the conversion was genuine while others like former colleague Noël Browne believed that it was mere opportunism — use of Seán's skill as a 'versatile performer'.[58] Regardless of the motivation, it is undeniable that he accomplished a substantial amount not only within international politics.

Despite the shift in priorities, his actual views did not substantially alter. Seán had always been concerned with human rights issues, particularly the treatment of prisoners. He had defended republican prisoners, often without compensation, early in his legal career. His commitment to the rule of law had always existed — when he felt that the Government was legitimate. Furthermore, he had always been socially conservative and this did not change, even later in life when he was seen to be more 'liberal'. Senator David Norris recalls that in the early 1970s, he asked Seán to review abuses suffered by a Finnish gay group at the hands of the Russian police. MacBride read the letter, reinserted it in the envelope, parcelled the package up and posted it back without as much as an acknowledgement:

> I had not expected such brutal ignorance from a man such as MacBride but I would have done so had I known of his views on homosexual behaviour which he subsequently expressed in an interview with the *Crane Bag* with Peadar Kirby. When Kirby raised the question of discrimination against gay people MacBride blithely dismissed it bracketing homosexuals with heroin addicts, a not entirely flattering companionship.[59]

Norris was also peeved that Amnesty refused to grant Swedish diplomat and humanitarian Raoul Wallenberg, held in a Soviet gulag, prisoner-of-conscience status. He believes that this exclusion was either an effort by MacBride to ingratiate himself with the Soviet Union who had awarded him the Lenin Peace Prize or was because he knew that Wallenberg was homosexual. Seán also maintained that there was no legal discrimination whatever in the Republic: 'presumably he thought gay people didn't exist at all even though I had attempted on numerous occasions to draw his attention to the state of affairs here regarding this oppression.'

Although he is often viewed as 'the patron saint of Irish radicalism', MacBride remained socially conservative. His memoir carefully avoids what he considered the skeletons in the Gonne-MacBride closet, Iseult's parentage and his parents' separation. When she was young, Iseult's daughter Kay used to come to Roebuck House after school. When visitors enquired about who she was, he would reply, 'She's Anna's cousin.'[60] Seán's opinions on social issues in the Republic, such as the legality of divorce and abortion, could hardly be considered liberal.

However, despite his traditionalism and his reluctance to accept social change, he did much for the causes he espoused. His cousin Paul Durcan recounts visiting the Holocaust Museum in Hiroshima and finding that the only Irish name among the visiting foreign statesmen was Seán MacBride; he says, 'It is fashionable nowadays in self-righteous, politically correct, liberal Dublin to scorn the name of Seán MacBride, but I, not only as a citizen of Ireland but also as his cousin and godson, felt proud to see his name there.'[61]

Chapter 10 ~

NEVER LOST HIS FENIAN FAITH: SEÁN MacBRIDE IN IRELAND

'Politicians, public buildings, and whores all get respectable if they last long enough.'

— NOAH CROSS, *Chinatown*

Assessments of Seán MacBride's life emphasise his international role, which is not surprising as that is where he made his most public and long-lasting contributions. As yet, there is no real examination of his impact on Ireland at this time. Brian Inglis remarks in his memoir *Downstart* that 'I thought it safe to label MacBride as the Grey Subsidence of Irish politics — as politically he was, and remained, though he was to bounce back into international eminence in his old age.'[1] Such labelling was only partially accurate because, despite its international scope, his later career also had an immense impact on Ireland. Seán's participation in non-governmental and peace-keeping bodies and his role in founding and developing Amnesty International served as a counterpoint to growing tensions in the North, and his Nobel Peace Prize improved Ireland's image; *The Irish Times* commented that 'it is no bad time for the world to be reminded that there are Irishmen dedicated to peace and order.'[2] The *Irish Independent* observed that 'in a way too Ireland is being honoured.'[3] The Prize gave credit to the nation as well as to MacBride.

In addition to the reflected glory of Seán's international achievements, he also had more direct involvement in events happening within the country, indirectly through his prominence and directly by returning to the Irish bar in the 1980s, participating in the New Ireland Forum in 1983, and sponsoring the MacBride Principles to encourage American investors to employ fair hiring practices in Northern Ireland.

In 1957, faced with increasing IRA violence, the Fianna Fáil Government reintroduced internment. MacBride took the case of Gerard Lawless, a dissident IRA man who was about to emigrate when he was arrested and interned. It was the first case to be heard by the European Court of Human Rights, in 1959. He lost, but the proceedings established the principle that the Court could investigate whether a state of emergency exists in a country that is sufficient to allow the use of internment or other measures.

During the Irish presidential election of 1966, Tom O'Higgins proposed Seán as a potential candidate whom opposition parties could support against incumbent Éamon de Valera. Liam Cosgrave's response to the suggestion was, 'Are you mad?'[4] Whoever ran against de Valera would most likely lose and there was talk of allowing him to run unopposed, 'but the party [Fine Gael] would never consent to giving Dev a free run.'[5] Eventually Tom O'Higgins was chosen as the Fine Gael candidate and came within 10,000 votes of de Valera.

Seán continued to be active in the anti-partition movement, particularly after conflict in Northern Ireland escalated, suggesting production of pamphlets, a history of partition, and an outline of events since 1968, as the 'need for basic factual information is greater now than ever before.'[6] Despite his anti-partition stance, MacBride strongly opposed the renewed IRA campaign in Northern Ireland in the 1970s, stating, 'I think violence is justified only in certain circumstances. I do not think it is justified in Northern Ireland.'[7] There was still scope for political resistance to injustice in the North. He argued that the only way to end violence in the North was to remove its cause — partition.

In 1976, he and Northern QC Desmond Boal acted on behalf of the IRA and the Ulster Loyalist Central Coordinating Committee respectively in an attempt to find a peaceful solution to the conflict, a negotiated settlement not involving politicians or third parties.[8] Secret talks continued for several months but the initiative was ultimately unsuccessful. In the early 1980s, he resumed practice at the Irish Bar, defending political prisoners in Irish law courts, just as he had at the beginning of his career. Consistently, he supported Ireland's entry into the European Community, but did not want Ireland to participate in any common European defence or security policy.[9] MacBride no longer spoke publicly regarding Irish affairs when he was out of the country, but in later life he proved willing to share his opinions with the media.

Seán suffered upheaval in his personal life with the death of his wife on

11 November 1976. Although she had bequeathed her body to medical research, she was buried at Glasnevin Cemetery with Maud and later Seán.

Kid's death brought changes to Roebuck House. When she was alive, the atmosphere was relaxed; visitors often sat in the kitchen, having tea and a chat with Kid before seeing Seán. With Kid gone, he depended more and more on Caitriona Lawlor who worked for him from 1977 until his death. She was more of a gatekeeper, making visitors wait in the drawing room in a much more formal manner. Lawlor was young and perhaps did not have an established relationship with Seán's callers or as informal a manner as Kid. She did possess a reverence for Seán and a wish that he should not be disturbed. His wife's absence may also have indirectly caused the end of Seán and Louie O'Brien's association. After a minor argument, Seán asked her to leave Roebuck House. O'Brien was shocked and Anna was of the opinion that the incident never would have happened when Kid was alive; she would have provided a 'gentle brake' on her husband.[10] The argument's wounds must have retained their sting: O'Brien is left out of his memoirs, despite having lived and worked with him for over thirty years. Although he enjoyed being around women, Seán did not want to marry again.

He did not publicly involve himself in one of the most controversial events in Northern Ireland in the 1980s, the H-Block hunger strikes, where IRA prisoners in Long Kesh prison, demanding the right to recently denied 'special category' status as political prisoners, protested by fasting.[11] Seán subsequently stated, 'I do not agree with violence. Throughout the hunger strikes, I did not participate in any of the H Block Committee activities lest this might be construed as an approval of violence . . . I did make my views known to the British authorities in no uncertain terms but did not do so publicly.'[12] Despite Seán's silence, the strike affected him deeply. It resulted in the deaths of ten men and it was first time Lawlor saw Seán cry.[13]

He did contribute to the introduction to *Bobby Sands: Writings From Prison*, published in 1988, and he reiterated his position on partition. He wrote that the British public is 'oblivious to the fact that the partition of Ireland has been created, imposed and fostered by the British establishment'.[14] Seán's position on partition remained firm: he never changed his mind about the issue, either about the necessity of its immediate end or about who was to blame. Todd Andrews remarked that, 'on the question of separation, MacBride never lost his Fenian faith.'[15]

Still holding fast to his belief in Britain's culpability, Seán wrote in 1985, 'I had hoped that persuasion and common sense would ultimately persuade the British to withdraw gracefully from Ireland without inflicting more suffering on any section of Ireland or further damaging Britain's reputation.'[16] He still applied the concept of 'self-determination' to the entire island. He had been away from political office for quite a few years, so he no longer needed to 'bang the anti-partition drum' for the electorate — either he had made anti-partition statements so often that they became second nature or he sincerely believed in his position.

In 1983, Irish political parties Fianna Fáil, Fine Gael, Labour, and the SDLP met to review their position on the national question. They were seeking a peaceful solution to renewed IRA violence and were also looking for a way to curb growing support for Sinn Féin as a result of the hunger strikes. The New Ireland Forum was 'established for consultations on the manner in which lasting peace and stability could be achieved in a new Ireland through the democratic process and to report on possible new structures and processes through which this objective might be achieved.'[17] These new structures did not necessarily mean the end of partition. As Taoiseach Garret FitzGerald explained, the goal was to 'seek in discussion with all in Northern Ireland who may see merit in reducing tension within our island their help in identifying those aspects of the Constitution, laws and social arrangements of our state which pose obstacles to understanding amongst the people of this island.'[18] Participation was open to all democratic parties that rejected violence; the four parties together represented over 90 per cent of the nationalist population in the North and almost three-quarters of the entire population of Ireland.[19]

The Forum brought together for the first time elected nationalist representatives from the North and the Republic to deliberate on the form of a new Ireland. The first session took place at Dublin Castle on 30 May 1983. The convenors visited the North on 26–27 September 1983, then from 23 to 24 January 1984 travelled to London for discussions with groups from Conservative, Labour, Liberal, and Social Democratic Parties.

Seán was invited to attend the New Ireland Forum Public Session on 4 October 1983, to communicate his views on the partition issue and the continuing violence in the North. He suggested a Swiss cantonal model for the government of a united Ireland, with a strong emphasis on decentralisation and each county having more autonomy.[20] He also advocated more cooperation between the Republic and the North in areas like afforestation, environmental protection, and the arts. His position on partition remained; he asked the Forum to reiterate 'Ireland's claim to national unity and independence' and still believed that the responsibility for ending partition rested with the British.[21] The *Irish Independent* did not take to Seán's cantonal suggestion, pointing out that 'the Swiss have arrived at their present system through a process of trial and error over a couple of centuries' and such a structure could not be instantly imposed on Ireland, but *The Irish Times* praised the Forum as a whole for its 'impressive variety of ideas' which would help 'stimulate debate and fresh thinking'.[22]

The Forum concluded by suggesting new structures accommodating two sets of legitimate rights, 'the rights of nationalists to effective political, symbolic and administrative expression of their identity' and 'the right of unionists to effective political, symbolic and administrative expression of their ethos and way of life'.[23] Despite all the effort put into the Forum, after the second meeting with FitzGerald, British Prime Minister Margaret Thatcher's summary dismissal of the proposals, 'the unified Ireland was one solution — that is out. A second solution was a confederation of the two States — that is out. A third solution was joint authority — that is out', made it appear that it was wasted time.[24]

Yet, despite Thatcher's seeming unwillingness to include the Republic in the governance of the North, 'it was precisely after the second meeting between Thatcher and FitzGerald that work began in earnest toward the establishment of a treaty of co-operation between Great Britain and the Republic of Ireland regarding the political and security problems afflicting both countries and Northern Ireland', the 1985 Anglo–Irish Agreement.[25] The Agreement was a precedent-setting document in which Britain recognised that the Republic of Ireland did have some say in the affairs of Northern Ireland, and the Republic of Ireland acknowledged the unionist position. Structures proposed by the Forum can be found in the current power-sharing Government instituted by the Good Friday Agreement.

Despite his desire for reconciliation, Seán disagreed with the Anglo–Irish Agreement, believing that it would result in an increase in violence in the North, that it reinforced partition and that all the advantage was with Britain.[26]

He also became an active supporter of the Irish National Caucus, an American lobby formed to fight discrimination against Catholics in the North. He lent his name to a series of conditions for American companies operating in Northern Ireland to follow in order to prevent discrimination. These became known as the MacBride Principles because 'his nationalist and human rights credentials gave him unrivalled credibility among the constituency which the leaders of the campaign sought to mobilize — Irish-American groups and US human rights groups.'[27]

The MacBride Principles are American in origin, consisting of fair employment measures, affirmative action principles, a corporate code of conduct for US companies doing business in Northern Ireland: a direct, meaningful and non-violent means of addressing injustice and discrimination. The idea began with New York City Comptroller Harrison Goldin in 1983, and was embraced by the Irish National Caucus, headed by Fr Sean MacManus. They were modelled on the Sullivan Principles for American companies with subsidiaries in South Africa.

The Principles included increasing the representation of individuals from underrepresented religious groups (namely Catholics) in the work force; adequate security for the protection of minority employees both at the workplace and while travelling to and from work; the banning of provocative religious or political emblems from the workplace; ensuring that lay-off, recall and termination procedures did not in practice favour a particular religion; and abolition of job reservations, apprenticeship restrictions and differential employment criteria which discriminated on the basis of religion.

Most groups responded favourably to the idea. The European Parliament issued a report in March 1994 endorsing the campaign's moral principles, stating that US pressure had been 'responsible for reopening the question of discrimination in Northern Ireland . . . Northern Ireland Catholics see the worldwide "MacBride Principles" campaign as a great source of support in overcoming their problems.' The Principles have been passed in sixteen states, passed and endorsed in forty cities, and are pending in more. They have been adopted by state legislatures; city councils; church groups, including the Archdiocese of New York, the American Baptist Convention, the Episcopal Church in America, the Society of Jesus; and American companies such as AT&T, Federal Express, Ford, General Motors, IBM, McDonald's, Philip Morris, Proctor & Gamble, Texaco, and Xerox among others.

The Irish Government supported the aims of the Principles, but worried that they could discourage investment in Northern Ireland. Foreign Minister Peter Barry commented in the Dáil, 'we believe that, while the philosophy underlying the MacBride Principles presents no difficulties for us, any action which, in the serious economic situation of Northern Ireland, might lead to disinvestment and to the discouragement of US firms investing in Northern Ireland should be avoided.'[28] However, a change of government in Dublin and America's favourable response to the Principles led to a new attitude; Brian Lenihan remarked in the Dáil three years later that 'the Government's view is that there is nothing objectionable in the MacBride principles. We fully understand and share the anxieties of Irish Americans about discrimination in employment in Northern Ireland.'[29]

However, the MacBride Principles were not wholly welcomed in Northern Ireland or Britain. The use of MacBride's name was controversial because of his previous IRA connections and he was still perceived as a symbol of some of the worst aspects of Irish Catholic social conservatism.[30] The Principles themselves appeared too vague about how to achieve a fair proportion of Catholics and Protestants employed, and it was feared that they might discourage new investment or cause already-established companies to pull out. They were opposed by Irish Protestant Churches as well as the SDLP, as John Hume felt that depriving Protestants of jobs would not alleviate the plight of jobless Catholics.[31] Not surprisingly, Sinn Féin endorsed the Principles. The Catholic bishops took no formal position. The MacBride Principles were successful at putting pressure on the British as new anti-discrimination legislation was introduced and the Principles remain a force for change in Northern Ireland should the British Government's own efforts falter in the future.[32]

In late 1983, Seán volunteered to stand for the presidency of Ireland, an offer that was not accepted by the parties. This snub probably resulted more from the popularity of the outgoing President, Dr Patrick Hillery, than from any problem with Seán's candidacy. In fact, the leaders of the major Irish parties, Fine Gael's Garret FitzGerald, Fianna Fáil's Charles Haughey, and Labour's Dick Spring, persuaded Hillery to stand for a second term.[33] Though Seán made it known in the *Sunday Press* newspaper that he was willing to contest the office, only Hillery was nominated and he was declared re-elected for a second seven-year term of office without the need for a popular vote.

In 1986, Noël Browne published his memoir *Against the Tide*, which was described by J.J. Lee as 'etched in vitriol'. Clearly Browne harboured resentment toward MacBride, even in retrospect.[34] Browne makes clear in his preface that he wrote the book to correct certain inaccuracies about his political career. His venom is not reserved exclusively for Seán; he eviscerates most of the cabinet, especially Tánaiste William Norton. He described MacBride as insecure and somewhat manipulative. He delved into Seán's personality, especially his upbringing, and, like many, found his later peace campaign difficult to reconcile with his former violent ways.[35] Browne felt that MacBride was dominated by a formidable mother and needed to find some way to fulfil his destiny as an important political figure; when he lost his cabinet post, his Dáil seat, and Clann na Poblachta, he had to find another role, another way to achieve.[36]

MacBride's rivalry with Browne had continued long after the Mother and Child Scheme fell apart. In a letter to McQuaid, dated 25 May 1954, he enquired about Our Lady's Hospital for Sick Children, Crumlin, which Browne had initiated and built. MacBride questioned Browne's right to take credit: 'my recollection is that the project for this hospital was initiated by His Grace long before Dr Browne was ever heard of. Can you confirm my recollection on this point?'[37] Seán suggested that 'if my recollection is correct in this respect should something not be done to let it be known that it was not Dr Browne who was responsible for the erection of this hospital but that it was His Grace?' Seán also wrote about a proposed speaking engagement at Marian College, Ballsbridge. He did not realise that Browne (whose name was written in red ink) would also be speaking. He fumed that he had 'no desire to appear with Dr Browne at any time' and added that he believed that 'no Catholic College should have invited him.'[38]

MacBride wrote a review of *Against the Tide* for the *Irish Press*, where he admitted that the book was 'well written', but said that it was not short of 'self pity nor in venomous innuendoes against those to whom he took a dislike'.[39] MacBride praised Browne's initial drive: 'Our relations, that first year, were excellent and Dr Browne was working with great enthusiasm.' He had also succeeded in infusing his own enthusiasm to the officials and the local authorities. MacBride did comment on Browne's 'irregular attendance at Cabinet meetings', recalling that when he chided him, 'his reply was that he was bored by Cabinet meetings and had other more important things to do!' Seán took particular offence at Browne's accusation that he was working in collusion with the Special Branch and that he had had Browne followed by them, calling the charges 'utterly false'. He addressed Browne's repeated assertion about the repeal of the External Relations Act and the alleged 'secret Cabinet meeting' held by Costello.

Browne's views on the repeal of the External Relations Act seemed to be a main concern of Seán's, which is not surprising, as the event was viewed as the first inter-party Government's greatest achievement. It is likely that he did not want the canon questioned or disturbed. In a letter to Patrick Lynch in March 1981, he asked for Lynch's recollections of Costello's announcement, as Seán had begun working on his memoir and wanted to ensure that his details were straight.[40]

MacBride's depiction of Browne in his own memoir is unflattering as well as inaccurate. He describes Browne as 'a young man who was or had come from Trinity College and that kind of conservative, Unionist background. I don't think that at that time I knew that he was the son of an RIC man.'[41] David Norris, who knew Browne well, called this portrait a 'classic smear tactic', as Browne, from an impoverished TB-ridden family in the West of Ireland, was most certainly not a member of the Trinity establishment with a conservative unionist background.

Although the enmity between the two men would last for the rest of their respective careers, Browne did attend MacBride's funeral in 1988. While Seán often came into conflict with his political associates, he did remain on friendly terms with many of his former colleagues. He corresponded with Philip

Noel-Baker, Lord Rugby and Paul O'Dwyer after he left politics. In his memoirs, he was fairly restrained and polite about his cabinet colleagues. John A. Costello, James Dillon, William Norton, and Patrick McGilligan receive praise, as do Seán MacEoin and Tom O'Higgins. Seán states that he didn't have much to do with Richard Mulcahy, which is hardly surprising considering their respective roles in the civil war. He did not hold Joseph Blowick in high regard, poking fun at his obsession with the cattle trade, again hardly surprising as Blowick was the Minister for Lands as well as the leader of Clann na Talmhan, a party dedicated to farmers' interests.

Despite Paul Durcan's observation that it is now popular to disparage Seán MacBride in liberal circles, the 'Petition to the United Nations 1998 by 32 County Sovereignty Movement' demonstrates just how influential he remained within Irish politics. The movement, founded in December 1997, was formed by Sinn Féin members who felt that the Northern Ireland Peace Process did not allow for full Irish sovereignty and would ensure that the Six Counties would be forever marginalised. As their manifesto explains,

> Simply put we are a group of individuals who recognise that the root cause of the conflict in Ireland is Britain's refusal to respect the Sovereignty of all-Ireland. We believe that the only way in which Britain can show respect for Irish Sovereignty is to declare publicly its intention to withdraw from Ireland permanently.[42]

The 32 County Sovereignty Movement's petition to the United Nations included Seán's introduction to the Bobby Sands book, posthumously appropriating him as an example of a non-violent Irishman.

The petition neglects to mention that the passage was taken from the Bobby Sands book and not written by Seán specifically for their organisation. This omission makes it seem that Seán was in line with their cause, which he could not have been, as he had died ten years earlier. Moreover, the 32 County Movement supported the re-formation of the IRA, which Seán would not publicly have done. Finally, the authors misspelled 'McBride' and mentioned that he was 'an international jurist; a former U.N. High Commissioner and winner of both the Nobel and the Lenin Peace Prizes'.

Although he continued to advise IRA chiefs-of-staff, he was in agreement with their goals, but not their methods. He often said that he did not agree with violence used by the IRA, but some believe that this was his 'official' line. A source close to the Army Council in the thirty years up to 1994 hinted that he was always available for consultations and advice about political matters in dealing with the British. The exact nature of the consultations and the amount of weight his advice carried will likely remain a mystery.

After Seán MacBride's death from pneumonia on 15 January 1988, a remarkable number of tributes were paid to him from around the world, reflecting the strength of his commitment to a variety of causes. United Nations Secretary-General Javier Pérez de Cuéllar declared that 'Sean MacBride was widely recognised in the international community as a champion of peace, justice and the universal respect for human rights. Indeed, these concerns of his, and the non-violent settlement of disputes, lie at the very heart of the United Nations' Charter of which he was a most eloquent partisan.'[43] The President of the African National Congress, Oliver Tambo, saluted 'the contribution of Sean MacBride to the cause of freedom and human emancipation throughout the world. He was a great beacon, guiding and assisting oppressed people to the path of national liberation and self-determination.'[44] Sergei Losev, director-general of the Soviet News Agency, Tass, said that MacBride was widely known in the Soviet Union and Soviet journalists wholeheartedly respected him.[45] The Green Alliance praised his support of ecological causes 'long before it was fashionable to do so'.[46] Massachusetts Congressman Joseph Kennedy declared that 'he was a man who dedicated his life to the pursuit of peace and justice . . . his voice and compassion will be missed' and Congressman Hamilton Fish Junior of New York said that Seán 'rightly understood that ability and religion should be the basis for employment opportunity in Ireland.'[47]

Most obituaries focused on his career as an international statesman. Yet some did mention his IRA past and the idea of transition in his career. *The Irish Times* wrote that

> the young gunman came to be the most fervent convert to peace. His commitment to the rule of law and to the protection of human rights was absolute . . . His conversion from unconstitutional to constitutional methods in his vision of Ireland's future was matched by a recognition that the evolution of all civilised society had to be similarly grounded.[48]

The *Irish Independent* 'Weekender' section contained articles about MacBride and assessments of his career, including an article by Ronan Fanning entitled 'A man for his times', which maintained that 'he reflected the dreams of a young nation' and 'the long life of Sean MacBride is best seen as a personification of the history of 20th century Irish Republicanism.' He described Seán's role in the IRA during the civil war and stated that his 'finest hour as Minister for External Affairs was when the Republic of Ireland Act of 1948 severed Ireland's last link with the Commonwealth.' Seán's 'international acclaim which he enjoyed in later life as an elder statesman was closely linked with his reputation as one of Ireland's most famous radical republicans.'

Historian John A. Murphy, Professor at University College Cork, commented in the 'Tributes' box that MacBride was one of the outstanding Irish men of the twentieth century, but 'really a Chief of Staff of the IRA at heart, it seems to me, in his attitude toward the National question'. This statement is true in the sense that he always held the British responsible for partition, but incomplete, as it ignores work later in life towards acceptance of non-violence.

Seán was also eulogised in newspapers abroad. A 16 January *Times* article mentions that he was a former IRA chief-of-staff as well as being the 'Irish Republic's most celebrated constitutional and criminal lawyer . . . he was also a principal architect of the European Convention on Human Rights.'[49] Another *Times* article, entitled 'Irreconcilable Irish Republican', mentions his prominence as an 'international advocate of human rights and disarmament', then details his career in the Irish republican movement, as a 'suave and sophisticated' foreign minister and a 'shrewd tactician and a tireless worker', but 'neither an outstanding advocate nor a specially acute lawyer' who 'indulged in the luxury of advocating ideal solutions without having to accept responsibility for the tasks involved in dismantling Western defences'.[50] The article concluded that 'he seemed oblivious to positions other than his own, and in argument he showed little understanding of opposing viewpoints' but 'never hesitated to commit his own money to causes which he supported.'

The Times editorial of 18 January 1988, entitled, 'His Infamous Career' was even less flattering. The 'interpretations of the career of Mr Sean MacBride . . . have tended to suggest that his life was synonymous with the short history of his own Republic of Ireland . . . His biographical trajectory, which took him from IRA chief of staff to recipient of both the Nobel and Lenin peace prizes, has been seen as mirroring the transformation of a state born in violence to fully fledged democracy.' However, the editorial went on to claim that MacBride's international reputation 'was not put to the service of reconciling the state he had helped to found, nor to the service of its future' and stated that his absence would help put away Ireland's violent past and the romantic appeal of violence.[51] This assessment seems unfair, as MacBride had both publicly altered his position on violence and, it can be argued, had done his best as an advocate to improve the state he had helped to found.

There were responses to the editorial. On 23 January 1988, Reverend Dr Vincent Twomey of St Patrick's College, Maynooth, wrote that MacBride had had a beneficial influence on Ireland's development:

the violent revolution which eventually brought the Irish State into being has been transformed over the past five decades into authentic democratic republicanism of the classical and Christian traditions which can only be a source of pride to any self-respecting Irish man or woman ... His championship of human rights throughout the world was his most significant contribution to that development since rights are the basis of democracy.

Another response, from former Secretary-General of Amnesty International Martin Ennals, maintained that the editorial was 'too dismissive of his international role, particularly in the field of human rights', as Seán had worked 'tirelessly' for Amnesty, the Council of Europe, and the United Nations.[52]

Like his contemporaries, his obituaries would assess him differently, but most would agree that 'In all that he touched, MacBride showed extraordinary dedication and tenacity', and 'He worked tirelessly without thought for any tangible reward. Of him it can truly be said that he was faithful to the tradition of passionate political commitment in which he had been nurtured.'[53]

The Irish papers provided extensive coverage of his funeral: 'the variety of accents and indeed languages to be heard at the graveside bore ample testimony to the unrivalled international esteem in which Sean MacBride was held.'[54] Cardinal Tomás Ó Fiach declared in his sermon in Glasnevin Cemetery, 'He would be equally at home among the patriots, the jurists, the politicians, the international statesmen, the defenders of human rights, the protagonists of peace and spokesmen of minorities'

The editorial in *The Irish Times* of 19 January reported the 'huge crowds' at MacBride's 'scarcely standing room' funeral with its long, varied list of attendees: 'no one's funeral could have drawn together so many people so far from each other in mind.' Presidents, Taoisigh, other dignitaries, even Noël Browne attended. If further proof were needed, his significance as a humanitarian could be seen by the fact of U2's Bono attending the funeral. Paul Durcan read a poem at the graveside.

Praise also came in from Irish politicians. Fianna Fáil Taoiseach Charles Haughey led the tributes, stating that Seán was 'a statesman of international status and was listened to with respect around the world'.[55] President Patrick Hillery praised his 'exemplary commitment and generosity' and Tánaiste Brian Lenihan mused that if he was a controversial figure, it may have been because his thinking was too challenging, his perspective too broad for conventional wisdom. He was often ahead of his time in his awareness of the position in international affairs of the newly independent nations, in his determination to bridge the divide between East and West, and in his belief in the force of justice in international relations.[56]

Tributes were heard in the Seanad and the Dáil. Senator Mick Lanigan called MacBride 'a statesman of international standard. His work for the underprivileged, not alone here but abroad, has been acknowledged through the world.'[57] Senator Maurice Manning admitted that 'Perhaps by conventional Irish standards his political career was not a great success ... The party he founded did not make a lasting impact.' However, 'at almost every stage when he entered Irish politics he made a lasting mark; in his work in the courts in the thirties and in his work in the first inter-Party Government. Most of all he will be remembered for his work in the international forum, his work for humanitarian, libertarian causes right around the world.'[58] He relayed a story about Seán merely glancing at his Nobel Peace Prize cheque, signing his name on the back, and sending the prize money to Amnesty International. John A. Murphy, though praising Seán's achievements, disliked 'the absurd attempts at instant canonisation over the weekend', calling them hypocritical because 'In Seán MacBride's cause it has to be recorded, regrettably, that his contribution to the cause of peace at home, to the national debate on the North, was in inverse proportion to his service to peace worldwide. It is a pity that his thinking in the area of this tragic problem remained dangerously simplistic to the end.'[59]

In the Dáil, Haughey summarised Seán's international human rights achievements while also recognising his contributions during the inter-party Government:

> He did much to foster economic and social progress in this country at an important stage in its development, and his contributions to international economic co-operation were numerous and distinguished ... He was an important influence in the creation of the Council of Europe and also served as Vice-President of the Organisation for European Economic Co-Operation. He helped to draft the European Convention on Human Rights.[60]

Fine Gael leader Alan Dukes also paid tribute:

There are very few of us who can look back over a lifetime that contained three separate identifiable careers. I think that it is mostly for his career as a former Member of this House and Minister and for his later career as an international jurist of wide repute that we would remember Seán MacBride. . . . He was a man who was involved in many controversies during his lifetime. On many issues there are many of us who are here today who disagreed very strongly with him but all of us would recognise that, in our personal dealings with him, we always found him — whether he agreed with us or not — to be a man of very considerable personal charm and warmth.[61]

Tomás MacGiolla of the Workers Party said that 'few Irish people have made a greater contribution to world affairs than Seán MacBride. It is for that that he will be remembered most.'[62]

Yet it was Labour leader Dick Spring who gave the most precise assessment:

Seán MacBride was a man of many parts. At one time he appeared to be on the verge of engineering a fundamental change in the development of the Irish political system but ultimately it was on the world stage that he made his greatest contribution . . . Throughout his career he was a man in search of change for the better, as he saw it. In his later years I, together with many others in the House, found myself on the opposite side to Seán MacBride on a number of important social issues. I did not agree with the position he adopted and he was not always an easy man to disagree with but I respect the sincerity with which he held and maintained his views. It is difficult to sum up a career as varied as his in the few moments available to us. Perhaps, in the fullness of time he will be remembered at home for things that are not so obvious now. He may be remembered, for instance, for his commitment to the development of our natural resources or he may be remembered as one who believed passionately that there was room on this island for every one of its young people and that we had an economy that could provide for all.[63]

| CONCLUSION

*'I mean about our papers. Are there any? You must know
now.'*

*'Yes, there are a great many; more than I supposed.' I was
struck by the way her voice trembled as she told me this.*

*'Do you mean that you have got them in there — and
that I may see them?'*

*'I don't think you can see them,' said Miss Tita with an
extraordinary expression of entreaty in her eyes, as if the
dearest hope she had in the world now was that I would not
take them from her.*

HENRY JAMES, *The Aspern Papers*

Seán MacBride's obituaries and testimonials focused on his international reputation and his contributions to world peace and human rights. Few emphasised his career in Irish politics. Perhaps Dick Spring was correct: his political accomplishments in Ireland were not so obvious. Although his most enduring legacy will be his international reputation — the Irish Amnesty International section is now located in Seán MacBride House in Dublin, and an annual peace prize is awarded in his name by the International Peace Bureau — a lasting influence in Irish politics can be seen in the continued enthusiasm for European integration and the willingness of the Irish people to accept a substantial commitment to the United Nations, though, as Kevin Nowlan points out, it was not just MacBride who inspired this development.[1]

Seán's legacy in Irish politics was mixed. He entered the cabinet in 1948 with an enormous reputation. Why did his influence diminish?

Personality conflicts were certainly a key factor. The reactive nature of the inter-party Government, which is especially seen in the management of the repeal of the External Relations Act, the declaration of the Irish Republic and the handling of the Mother and Child controversy, also played a part. Such reactivity is not difficult to understand; an inter-party government was a new phenomenon and its loose structure allowed Seán leeway in establishing his authority and showing interest in topics outside his portfolio, such as finance, environment, and social welfare. However, as the Government settled, it was inevitable that Costello would assert his authority as Taoiseach and 'MacBride's wings would be clipped as other departments tried to assert their command in their traditional areas.'[2]

The Government as a whole made mistakes. It did not respond skilfully to the invitation to join NATO, overestimating the American willingness to become involved in solving the partition issue. The increase of anti-partition rhetoric did not erase the border and it can be argued that government policy further entrenched it. Instead of taking advantage of opportunities for rapprochement with the North, the Government misjudged the strength of Northern unionism and fell prey to bellowing louder instead of engaging in slow but constructive solutions. The 'sore thumb' policy was counterproductive; it alienated other countries and made Ireland appear insular. It also affected the relationship with Belfast, where the real decision-making power to end partition lay. The Government's reliance on rhetoric instead of attempting cross-border cooperation demonstrates a conservatism echoed in its behaviour during the Mother and Child controversy. Members of the Government were not willing to risk offending the Church, the Irish medical lobby, or their constituents.

The repeal of the External Relations Act, though considered one of the Government's major achievements, should be viewed as a bit of a draw. The Irish were fortunate that other Commonwealth countries were willing to lend support and an otherwise preoccupied Britain decided to be generous. While declaring Ireland a republic was an important psychological step, it was not ideal for ending partition; and the manner in which it was handled caused confusion, which still remains.

However, the inter-party Government did more than give Fianna Fáil a short holiday and, because of one spectacular failure, has not been recognised for smaller successes. The inter-party Government showed that coalition government was a workable option and it managed to make it last longer than most contemporary observers thought possible. The Government ended sixteen years of Fianna Fáil domination and restored true parliamentary democracy to Ireland, providing hope for a genuine party system. The emergence of Clann na Poblachta began a decline of Civil War-influenced politics. The coalition achieved success in revitalising land policy, developing agriculture, and introducing the Industrial Development Authority and Córas Trachtála, established to promote Irish exports. MacBride helped to bring about an increased awareness of economic planning and cooperation, energised his department, and his later awards and accomplishments reflected well upon the Irish nation. He also helped to bring Ireland into Europe, and European Union funding would help the Irish economy at a later stage. Many of these activities would bear fruit later, particularly Seán Lemass's enthusiasm for European integration and T.K. Whitaker's venture at economic planning.

Evaluations of the inter-party Government's performance are as divergent as opinions of the man himself. Most agree that he was controversial. Most also agree that he was charming, but differ on whether his charm was sincere. Noël Browne wrote of him:

> Though a forbidding-looking figure he was a man of much personal charm, and impeccable drawing-room manners, reserved for whomever he wished to impress. As I came to know him better, he seemed to me to be an insecure person, a product, no doubt, of his disturbed and turbulent upbringing.[3]

Browne's wife Phyllis recalled meeting him for the first time: 'he wore an air of seriousness, as though he was carrying the troubles of the world on his shoulders. I could see no sense of humour in his face, but he did display a little charm, at times — which I felt was false.'[4] Former government colleague Tom O'Higgins reflected that, 'when he was with you he was forceful and charming, but when the sun went in he was a different man.'[5]

Some contemporaries have questioned the sincerity of his later career as a humanitarian. Phyllis Browne wondered, 'How MacBride was given the Lenin Peace Prize and the Nobel Peace Prize also, is a mystery to me, and many others.'[6] Brian Inglis, who worked with MacBride at the Irish News Agency, wrote of his 'slippery political manoeuvrings — which survived all his climb to international fame and to a Nobel Prize.'[7] As mentioned above, many feel that he lived his life to please ghosts as well as his formidable mother. As Browne, who was interested in psychology, wrote in his memoirs,

> His later campaign for peace following [his mother's] death, is hard to reconcile with his former violent lifestyle . . . To what extent was the powerful and dominating personality of this notorious rebel mother responsible for his earlier career of violence? . . . Was it that, subsequently deprived of all political power — he had lost his Cabinet post, his Dáil seat and his party — he was left with no choice but to play peacemaker?[8]

Cruise O'Brien, who called a chapter in his *Ancestral Voices* 'Son of Maud

Gonne', wrote that MacBride was under the spell of 'the power of the ghosts of a nation . . . Seán MacBride was brought up under that power . . . You could sense the presence of ghosts all right; his face, when in repose, had a perpetually haunted expression.'[9]

MacBride had a strong personality and was determined to get his own way — he was sometimes self-righteous and sometimes self-deceiving, but he was undeniably remarkable.

He had a long and eventful career with stints as a guerrilla fighter, brilliant barrister, politician, diplomat, human rights advocate, and peace campaigner. His roles may have changed but throughout his life certain objectives remained constant: the defence of political prisoners and human rights, self-determination for colonial countries, and an end to partition.

The photo that Maud Gonne showed Phyllis Browne with 'Seán, Man of Destiny' written across it, led her to muse, 'I wonder did he live up to her expectations?'[10] As his contemporary, Todd Andrews, noted, 'whatever one may think of MacBride's role in Irish politics, Nobel and Lenin Prizes are not conferred on people of no merit.'[11] It is doubtful that he was insincere in his beliefs; he devoted so much time and energy to human rights causes. Whether or not MacBride was motivated by the desire for distinction, it cannot be questioned that he and the organisations with which he was involved accomplished a great deal and his interventions benefited a great many people.

Seán MacBride continues to cause controversy even after his death. He willed his library at Roebuck House to Caitriona Lawlor rather than to his children, effectively making her custodian of his archive. He may have done this to reward Lawlor, who worked for him for about ten years, often travelling with him. But it appears likely that he extracted a promise that she would not publish or deposit the documents.[12] Despite the existence (and Lawlor's later publication) of his memoir, he never wanted a biography published; as Lawlor put it, 'Sean MacBride invited neither historian nor biographer to examine his life.'[13] Ever the conservative, he was sensitive about his half-sister's illegitimacy and his parents' divorce, and a biography would dredge those issues up. This explanation is borne out in the memoir, as his early childhood is virtually ignored.

Anna MacBride White believes that her father did not trust her or Tiernan with his papers.[14] Tiernan had once advised him to organise his papers and deposit them somewhere and Anna had inherited her grandmother Maud Gonne's letters and shared her intention to publish them, which she did after MacBride's death. Her husband Declan White agreed, saying, 'He never forgave you for the letters.'[15]

MacBride had also left Lawlor his medals and personal items. Anna asked for a pair of cufflinks for Tiernan. Lawlor complied, but never offered any mementoes to family members. There was further acrimony over what precisely had been left to Lawlor, as she laid claim to personal papers outside the Roebuck House library. Rumours persist that some of the documents have been destroyed. A man whom Kid MacBride had hired to do odd jobs around Roebuck House informed Anna that Lawlor had been burning important papers.[16] Despite Tiernan's acknowledgement of her at Seán's funeral, Lawlor and MacBride's family are not on good terms.

The truth about MacBride's intentions for his archive, what that archive contains, and what fate is in store for the papers remains unclear. Lawlor wrote in the preface to Seán MacBride's memoir, 'There has been no accurate, in-depth chronological account of MacBride's contribution to the development of this nation.'[17] If she releases more of his writings or if the papers ever enter the public domain, more academic studies will become possible. Although this volume provides the most accurate, in-depth account to date, I hope that more analyses of his life are forthcoming as well as analyses of his impact on Irish foreign policy and Irish political and social history.

Whether one admires or reviles him, Seán MacBride constructed a career of extraordinary extent and deep complexity. Perhaps his was not quite the legacy his mother envisioned when she emblazoned his childhood photo with the words 'Man of Destiny', yet it is an impressive and substantial one.

ENDNOTES

Preface (PP. IX–XI)

1. Charles Lysaght, email to the author, 8 February 2002.
2. J.J. Lee, *Ireland 1912–1985: Politics and Society* (Cambridge, 1989), p. 605.
3. F.S.L. Lyons, *Ireland Since the Famine* (London, 1985), p. 563.
4. This is a term Noël Browne also uses to describe MacBride, though in a much less flattering way!
5. Letter, Seán MacBride to Patrick Lynch, 9 March 1981, courtesy of Caitriona Lawlor.
6. Dermot Keogh, 'Ireland, the Vatican and Cold War: The Case of Italy 1948', *Irish Studies in International Affairs* 3 (1991), p. 70.

Chapter One (PP. 1–29)

1. Phyllis Browne, *Thanks for the Tea, Mrs. Browne: My Life with Noël* (Dublin, 1988), p. 101.
2. Conrad A. Balliett, 'The Lives — And Lies — of Maud Gonne', *Éire-Ireland*, vol. XIV, no. 3, Fall 1979, pp. 17–44.
3. Introduction, Maud Gonne MacBride, *A Servant of the Queen*, A. Norman Jeffares and Anna MacBride White, eds. (Gerrards Cross, 1994), p. xii.
4. Balliett, 'Lives', p. 17.
5. Introduction, *A Servant of the Queen*, p. xi.
6. 24 October 1897.
7. Quoted in Balliett, 'Lives', p. 23.
8. *Irish Literary Supplement*, Fall 1991, p. 23.
9. Margaret Ward, *Maud Gonne: A Life* (London, 1990), p. 176.
10. Gonne MacBride, *A Servant of the Queen*, pp. 41–42.
11. Dublin Castle State Papers, CBS, 1833/S 22/8, 1890, National Archives, Ireland.
12. *Irish Times*, 28 April 1953.
13. W.B. Yeats, *Memoirs*, Denis Donoghue, ed. (London, 1988), p. 40.
14. Yeats, *Memoirs*, pp. 47–48.
15. 4 August 1894 is the date given by her niece, Seán's daughter Anna MacBride White, in *Letters to W.B. Yeats and Ezra Pound from Iseult Gonne: A Girl that Knew All Dante Once* (London, 2004). However, 6 August 1894 is the date mentioned in Janis and Richard Londraville, eds., *Too Long a Sacrifice: The Letters of Maud*

Gonne and John Quinn (London, 1999). 6 August is the more likely date; Iseult's husband Francis Stuart and her daughter Kay remember celebrating her birthday on the 6th and her death certificate lists her birthday as 6 August (See Balliett, 'Lives', p. 28).

16. *Too Long a Sacrifice*, footnote 6, p. 257.
17. Yeats, *Memoirs*, p. 133.
18. Gonne to Quinn, 22 June 1909, *Too Long a Sacrifice*, p. 44. She felt that the Abbey Theatre kept Yeats from his poetry. Gonne and Yeats would often disagree strongly about literature being subordinate to nationalism.
19. Yeats, *Memoirs*, p. 134.
20. Gonne MacBride, *A Servant of the Queen*, pp. 318–319.
21. Anna MacBride White and A. Norman Jeffares, eds., *Always Your Friend: The Gonne–Yeats Letters 1893–1938* (London, 1992), p. 130.
22. R.F. Foster, *W.B. Yeats: A Life, The Apprentice Mage, 1865–1914* (Oxford, 1997), p. 284.
23. John MacBride, 'The Irish Brigade in South Africa', *Freeman's Journal*, 13 October 1906.
24. See Denis Judd and Keith Surridge, *The Boer War* (London, 2002).
25. John MacBride, 'Irish Brigade'.
26. See Keith Jeffery, 'The Irish Soldier in the Boer War' in John Gooch, ed., *The Boer War: Direction, Experience, and Image* (London, 2000).
27. D.P. McCracken, 'Irish Settlement and Identity in South Africa before 1910', *Irish Historical Studies*, vol. 28 (1992–3), p. 146.
28. See *Sunday Press*, 15 January 1989.
29. Something of the revolutionary tradition was also passed on; MacBride's alleged grandson Derek was arrested in 1986 for helping African National Congress rebel Gordon Webster to escape from prison, and his son Robert MacBride was known as the 'Magoo's Bomber' in South Africa because of a car bomb planted outside Magoo's Bar in Durban that killed three and injured eighty-nine in 1984.
30. *United Irishman*, 17 February 1900.
31. Brian Walker, ed., *Parliamentary Election Results in Ireland 1801–1922* (The Royal Irish Academy, 1978).
32. Gonne MacBride, *A Servant of the Queen*, p. 308.
33. Quoted in introduction to *Gonne–Yeats Letters*, by Jeffares, p. 29.
34. Donal P. McCracken, *MacBride's Brigade: Irish Commandos in the Anglo-Boer War* (Dublin, 1999), p. 150.
35. *Gonne–Yeats Letters*, p. 139.
36. Quoted in Balliett, 'Lives', p. 31.
37. Ibid.
38. 10 February 1903, *Gonne–Yeats Letters*, p. 167.
39. Letter, Gonne to Mme Avril, undated, MS 10,714, National Library of Ireland (NLI).

40. Letter, Gonne to John O'Leary, 29 September 1905, John O'Leary Papers, MS 29,593, NLI.
41. John MacBride's notebook, written between March and November 1905, Frederick Allan Papers, MS 29,817, NLI.
42. Ibid.
43. Yeats to Lady Gregory, 5 May 1903, in *The Collected Letters of W.B. Yeats, vol. 3, 1901–1904*, John Kelly and Ronald Schuchard, eds. (Oxford, 1994), p. 357.
44. 10 February 1903, *Gonne–Yeats Letters*, p. 166.
45. Letter, Gonne to Yeats, 7 May 1903, *Gonne–Yeats Letters*, p. 170.
46. Gonne MacBride, *A Servant of the Queen*, p. 344.
47. Balliett, 'Lives', p. 32.
48. Gonne MacBride, *A Servant of the Queen*, p. 348.
49. Ibid.
50. Anthony Jordan, *Major John MacBride 1865–1916* (Westport, Ireland, 1991), p. 61.
51. *United Irishman*, 28 February 1903.
52. Ward, *Maud Gonne*, p. 78.
53. Joseph Hone, *W.B. Yeats 1865–1939* (London, 1942), pp. 188–189.
54. Richard Ellmann, *Yeats: the Man and the Masks* (London, 1948), pp. 162–163.
55. Yeats to Lady Gregory, 5 May 1903, *The Collected Letters of W.B. Yeats, vol. 3, 1901–1904*, Kelly and Schuchard, eds., p. 356.
56. John MacBride to John Daly, 5 December 1903, quoted in Jordan, *John MacBride*, p. 66.
57. 15 July 1905, *Gonne–Yeats Letters*, p. 207.
58. John MacBride's notebook, written between March and November 1905, NLI.
59. Friday January 1905, *Gonne–Yeats Letters*, p. 186.
60. 'Statement of facts on behalf of Major John MacBride', 3 March 1905, Frederick Allan Papers, MS 29,819, NLI.
61. John MacBride's notebook, written between March and November 1905, NLI.
62. Ibid.
63. Ibid.
64. 12 February 1904, *Gonne–Yeats Letters*, p. 180.
65. Ward, *Maud Gonne*, p. 85.
66. Ibid.
67. Mistakenly reported as the Church of the Three Patrons, Rathgar. MacBride said in *Survivors* that the police report got the church wrong, and he was actually baptised at St Joesph's Church, Terenure. Uinseann MacEoin, *Survivors* (Dublin, 1980), p. 130 (fn).
68. Email from Caitriona Lawlor to the author, 3 May 2005.
69. 10 August 1905, *The Mail*, Paris edition.
70. *Gonne–Yeats Letters*, p. 203.
71. *Irish Literary Supplement*, Fall, 1991, p. 24.
72. *Too Long a Sacrifice*, p. 259, fn, interview Anna MacBride White.

73. See Foster, *Apprentice Mage*, p. 331, *Too Long a Sacrifice*, p. 259, fn 3, and Brenda Maddox, *George's Ghosts: A New Life of W.B. Yeats* (London, 1999), p. 43. All treat the allegation as true, Maddox asserting that John MacBride assaulted both Eileen and Iseult.

74. Francis Stuart, *Black List Section H* (London, 1971), p. 34.

75. 'Statement of facts on behalf of Major John MacBride', 3 March 1905, Frederick Allan Papers, MS 29,819, NLI.

76. 'Major MacBride's observation on the evidence of petitioner's witnesses', Frederick Allan Papers, MS 29,820, NLI.

77. Ibid.

78. John MacBride's notebook, written between March and November 1905, NLI.

79. Ibid.

80. Ibid.

81. 'Major MacBride's observation on the evidence of petitioner's witnesses', NLI.

82. John MacBride's notebook, written between March and November 1905, NLI.

83. Ibid.

84. 'Statement of facts on behalf of Major John MacBride', 3 March 1905, NLI.

85. Letter, John MacBride to Barry O'Brien, 29 December 1904, Frederick Allan Papers, MS 29,812, NLI.

86. Tuesday January 1905, *Gonne–Yeats Letters*, pp. 184–185.

87. Letter, Barry O'Brien to Maud Gonne, 1 January 1905, Frederick Allan Papers, MS 29,814, NLI.

88. Quinn to Yeats, 6 May 1905, Berg Collection, New York Public Library.

89. Annie Horniman to Lady Gregory, 11 April 1905, The Berg Collection, NYPL.

90. *Gonne–Yeats Letters*, p. 226.

91. 'Statement of facts on behalf of Major John MacBride', 3 March 1905, NLI.

92. Gonne to John Quinn, 25 March 1908, *Too Long a Sacrifice*, p. 37.

93. Mary Colum, *Life and the Dream* (Dublin, 1966), p. 124.

94. 25 February 1905, *Gonne–Yeats Letters*, p. 192.

95. Ward, *Maud Gonne*, p. 91.

96. Yeats to John Butler Yeats, dated 17 July 1908, quoted in Foster, *Apprentice Mage*, p. 387.

97. James P. O'Donnell, 'Ireland's New Man of Destiny', *Saturday Evening Post*, 23 April 1949 (copy in MS 26,423, NLI).

98. *Letters from Iseult Gonne*, Prologue, p. 19.

99. Conor Cruise O'Brien, *Ancestral Voices: Religion and Nationalism in Ireland* (Dublin, 1994), p. 132.

100. 'Major MacBride's observation on the evidence of petitioner's witnesses', NLI.

101. Gonne to Quinn, 11 July 1908, *Too Long a Sacrifice*, p. 37.

102. Gonne to Quinn, 22 April 1915, *Too Long a Sacrifice*, p. 149.

103. *Letters from Iseult Gonne*, Prologue, p. 33.

104. *Gonne–Yeats Letters*, p. 337.

105. 4 February 1916, *Too Long a Sacrifice*, p. 165.

106. Quinn to Gonne, 14 November 1910, *Too Long a Sacrifice*, p. 59.

107. MacEoin, *Survivors*, p. 108.

108. 28 September 1907, *Gonne–Yeats Letters*, p. 246.

109. Anna MacBride White, in *Gonne–Yeats Letters*, p. 5.

110. 31 December 1910, *Too Long a Sacrifice*, p. 62.

111. MacEoin, *Survivors*, p. 107.

112. Seán MacBride, *That Day's Struggle* (Dublin, 2005), p. 16.

113. *Gonne–Yeats Letters*, p. 286. See *Sunday Chronicle*, 31 October 1948.

114. Gonne to Quinn, 13 February 1911, *Too Long a Sacrifice*, p. 70.

115. Ellmann, *Man and the Masks*, p. xxiv. See also Balliett, 'Lives', pp. 41–42; Jeffares, introduction, *Gonne–Yeats Letters*, p. 34; Maddox, *George's Ghosts*, pp. 44–45; Foster, *Apprentice Mage*, pp. 393–395.

116. Crime Department, Special Branch, 'Report on Secret Societies' 19 December 1910, CO 904 (microfilm), National Archives Ireland.

117. Michael Foy and Brian Barton, *The Easter Rising* (Phoenix Mill, 1999), p. 139.

118. Jordan, *John MacBride*, p. 90.

119. 4 May 1911, *Gonne–Yeats Letters*, p. 300.

120. January 1912, *Gonne–Yeats Letters*, p. 307.

121. O'Donnell, 'Man of Destiny'.

122. *Too Long a Sacrifice*, p. 166.

123. See R.F. Foster, *Modern Ireland 1600–1972* (London, 1988), pp. 471–493; Lee, *Ireland 1912–1985*, pp. 24–38; Lyons, *Ireland Since the Famine*, pp. 329–399; Alvin Jackson, *Ireland 1798–1998* (Oxford, 1998), pp. 201–208; and Tim Pat Coogan, *1916: The Easter Rising* (London, 2001).

124. See Paul Bew, *Ideology and the Irish Question: Ulster Unionism and Irish Nationalism 1912–16* (Oxford, 1994), p. 120.

125. Foster, *Ireland*, p. 477.

126. Lee, *Ireland 1912–1985*, p. 25.

127. Coogan, *1916*, p. 137.

128. 'Proceedings of court martial of John MacBride', 5 May 1916, War Office WO 71/350, National Archives, Kew.

129. Ibid.

130. Coogan, *1916*, pp. 151–157.

131. 'Proceedings of court martial of John MacBride'.

132. J.B. Lyons, *The Enigma of Tom Kettle* (Dublin, 1983), p. 294.

133. Quinn to Gonne, 29 July 1916, *Too Long a Sacrifice*, p. 172.

134. Lee, *Ireland 1912–1985*, p. 29

135. Gonne to Yeats, April 1916, *Gonne–Yeats Letters*, p. 372.

136. Yeats to Florence Farr, 19 August 1916, see *Irish Times*, 16 July 1988.

137. MacBride, *That Day's Struggle*, p. 1

138. 11 May 1916, *Too Long a Sacrifice*, p. 169.

139. Gonne to Yeats, 11 May 1916, *Gonne–Yeats Letters*, p. 375.

140. Gonne to Quinn, 8 October 1916, *Too Long a Sacrifice*, p. 178.

141. 11 May 1916, *Too Long a Sacrifice*, p. 169.

142. *Letters from Iseult Gonne*, Prologue, p. 51.

143. Cruise O'Brien, *Ancestral Voices*, p. 133.

144. Conor Cruise O'Brien, *Memoir: My Life and Themes* (Dublin, 1998), p. 138.

145. May 1916, *Gonne–Yeats Letters*, p. 379.

146. W.B. Yeats to Lady Gregory, Yeats MS 30995, NLI.

Chapter Two (PP. 30–56)

1. Dillon to Lloyd George, 11 June 1916, David Lloyd George Papers (LG/D/14/2/25), Parliamentary Archive, Record Office, House of Lords.

2. Home Office, HO 144/1465, 321,387, National Archives, Kew.

3. Gonne to Quinn, 24 November 1916, *Too Long a Sacrifice*, p. 181.

4. MacBride, *That Day's Struggle*, pp. 13–14.

5. *Letters from Iseult*, p. 85.

6. Ibid., p. 107.

7. *Irish Times*, 16 January 1988.

8. The Home Office had actually predicted her disguise: 'She is likely to be dressed as a very old woman, probably dressed in black.' (Memo to Aliens Officer, 21 December 1917 HO 144/1465/321387, National Archives, Kew.)

9. MacBride, *That Day's Struggle*, p. 15

10. HO 144/1465, 20 December 1917.

11. Ibid.

12. MacBride, *That Day's Struggle*, p. 16.

13. W.B. Yeats to George Russell (Æ), 28 June 1918, quoted in Foster, *Apprentice Mage*, p. 127.

14. Constance Markiewicz to Eva Gore-Booth, 22 June 1918, in Constance Markiewicz, *Prison Letters of Countess Markievicz* (London, 1986).

15. Letter to Governor, 8 July 1918, HO 144/1465.

16. 18 June 1918, HO 144/1465.

17. Last week in October 1918, *Letters from Iseult*, p. 111.

18. HO 144/1465, 11 September 1918.

19. Ibid.

20. 16 November 1918, HO 144/1465.

21. R.F. Foster, *W.B. Yeats: A Life, The Arch-Poet 1915–1939* (Oxford, 2003), p. 135.

22. Iseult to Ezra Pound, late November 1918, *Letters from Iseult*, p. 141.

23. 18 October 1918, *Letters from Iseult*, p. 110.

24. 18 August 1918, *Gonne–Yeats Letters*, p. 396.

25. Yeats to Quinn, 4 September 1918, Berg Collection, NYPL.

26. Yeats to Lady Gregory, 14 December 1918, Yeats MS 30,994, NLI.

27. *Letters from Iseult*, p. 107.

28. Ibid., p. 212, fn 5.

29. MacBride, *That Day's Struggle*, p. 18.

30. Ibid., p. 21.
31. *Irish Freedom*, May 1912.
32. Karl Beckson, 'Arthur Symon's Iseult Gonne': A Previously Unpublished Memoir, *Yeats Annual #7* 1990, p. 204.
33. C.S. Andrews, *Man of No Property: An Autobiography*, vol. 2, (Dublin, 1982), p. 192.
34. Breandán Ó hEithir, *Over the Bar: A Personal Relationship with the GAA* (Dublin, 1984), p. 212.
35. Iseult to Pound, early December 1918, *Letters from Iseult*, p. 142.
36. MacBride, *That Day's Struggle*, p. 34.
37. Seán MacBride interview with Tim Pat Coogan, quoted in his *Michael Collins* (London, 1990), p. 143.
38. MacBride, *That Day's Struggle*, pp. 28–29.
39. 10 October 1920, *Prison Letters of Countess Markievicz*, p. 251.
40. October 1920, *Gonne–Yeats Letters*, p. 415.
41. Ward, *Maud Gonne*, p.127.
42. MacBride interview with Coogan, *Michael Collins*, p. 143.
43. MacBride, *That Day's Struggle*, p. 28.
44. Geoffrey Elborn, *Francis Stuart: A Life* (Dublin, 1990), p. 7.
45. MacBride, *That Day's Struggle*, p. 31. It was most likely Thomas Whelan. He protested his innocence and was hanged on 14 March 1921, the date mentioned by MacBride in his memoir. MacBride claimed that he had 'inside information' that Whelan was not involved in the ambush.
46. MacBride, *That Day's Struggle*, p. 33.
47. Ibid., p. 39.
48. Ibid.
49. Ibid., p. 42.
50. Ibid., p. 44.
51. Ibid., p. 46.
52. *Irish Press*, 18 October 1982.
53. Quoted in Meda Ryan, *Liam Lynch: The Real Chief* (Cork, 1986). See also MacEoin, *Survivors*.
54. MacBride, *That Day's Struggle*, p. 54.
55. MacEoin, *Survivors*, pp. 115–116.
56. Lyons, *Ireland Since the Famine*, p. 445.
57. Lee, *Ireland 1912–1985*, p. 53.
58. MacBride, *That Day's Struggle*, p. 72–73.
59. Ibid., p. 55.
60. Foster, *Ireland*, p. 503.
61. MacBride, *That Day's Struggle*, p. 57.
62. MacEoin, *Survivors*, p. 117.
63. MacBride, *That Day's Struggle*, p. 56.
64. Ibid.
65. Ibid., pp. 62–63.

66. 'Copy of statement issued by Executive on the attack on the Four Courts', 28 June 1922, Éamon de Valera Papers, University College Dublin, P150/1627.
67. John P. McCarthy, *Kevin O'Higgins: Builder of the Irish State* (Dublin, 2006), pp. 94–95.
68. *Sunday Independent*, 17 February 2002.
69. MacBride, *That Day's Struggle*, p. 71.
70. Ibid., p. 83.
71. Ibid., p. 67.
72. Ibid., p. 72.
73. *Too Long a Sacrifice*, Foreword, p. 9.
74. *Belfast Telegraph*, 15 December 1924.
75. MacBride, *That Day's Struggle*, p. 97.
76. Michael MacEvilly, 'Sean MacBride and the Republican Motor Launch St George', *Irish Sword*, 16 (1984).
77. Ibid., p. 56.
78. Ibid.
79. MacBride, *That Day's Struggle*, p. 91.
80. Dermot Keogh, *The Vatican, the Bishops, and Irish Politics 1919–1939* (Cambridge, 1986), p. 131.
81. MacBride, *That Day's Struggle*, 94.
82. 'Synopsis of political history of Sean MacBride s.c.' copy found in Seán MacEntee Papers, University College Dublin, P67/139 (1).
83. Gonne to Ethel Mannin, 20 November 1945, NLI.
84. Andrews, *Man of No Property*, p. 35.
85. *Irish Times*, 1 May 1953.
86. N. Browne, *Against the Tide*, p. 111.
87. Andrews, *Man of No Property*, p. 38.
88. MacBride, *That Day's Struggle*, p. 100.
89. A similar incident had happened before when Seán was a boy. French officials told Gonne that her documents were being photographed by British agents. It turned out that the family cook and her son were the spies.
90. Interview, Anna MacBride White.
91. Ward, *Maud Gonne*, p. 144.
92. MacBride, *That Day's Struggle*, p. 106.
93. Moss Twomey to Kid MacBride, 9 October 1927, Moss Twomey Papers, University College Dublin, P69/60 (7).
94. See Harry White, *Harry: The Story of Harry White as Related to Uinseann MacEoin* (Dublin, 1985), p. 106 and McCarthy, *Kevin O'Higgins*, pp. 288–289.
95. *Irish Times*, 7 October 1985.
96. Ibid., see also Tim Pat Coogan, *The IRA* (London, 2000 ed.), p. 55.
97. MacBride, *That Day's Struggle*, p. 106–107.
98. *Irish Times*, 7 October 1985.

99. Ibid.
100. *New York Times*, 15 September 1931.
101. Seán Cronin, *The McGarrity Papers: Revelations of the Irish Revolutionary Movement in Ireland and America 1900–1940* (Tralee, 1972), p. 158.
102. MacBride, *That Day's Struggle*, 112.
103. 'Minutes of General Army Convention', 17 March 1934, copy in MacEntee Papers, P67/525.
104. 'Office of the Minister for Justice, Departmental Notes on Events from 1 January 1931 to 31 December 1940' copy in MacEntee Papers, P67/534.
105. MacBride, *That Day's Struggle*, p. 116
106. 18 October 1931, MacEntee Papers, P67/545(9).
107. Interview with Declan White and Anna MacBride White.
108. De Valera to McGarrity, text in Seán Cronin, *The McGarrity Papers*, p. 157.
109. See Fearghal McGarry, *Irish Politics and the Spanish Civil War* (Cork, 1999).
110. MacEoin, *Survivors*, p. 123.
111. J. Bowyer Bell, *The Secret Army: The IRA* (third edition) (London, 1997), p. 130.

Chapter Three (PP. 57–70)

1. Bell, *Secret Army*, p. 100.
2. Ibid., p. 130.
3. Andrews, *Man of No Property*, p. 35.
4. David Norris, 'Speaking Ill of the Dead' Conference, 31 March 2006, Norris email to author.
5. Bob Bradshaw in Uinseann MacEoin's *The IRA in the Twilight Years 1923–1948*, Dublin, 1997, p. 428.
6. Andrews, *Man of No Property*, p. 192.
7. C.S. Andrews, *Dublin Made Me: An Autobiography*, vol. 2 (Dublin, 1979), p. 220.
8. MacBride, *That Day's Struggle*, p. 121.
9. Clare O'Halloran, *Partition and the Limits of Irish Nationalism* (Dublin, 1987), p. 175.
10. Joseph Lee, 'The Irish Constitution of 1937', Seán Hutton and Paul Stewart, eds., *Ireland's Histories: Aspects of State, Society and Ideology* (London, 1991), p. 83.
11. Ibid.
12. *Irish Times*, 16 January 1988.
13. MacBride, *That Day's Struggle*, p. 123.
14. Interview with Anna MacBride White.
15. MacEoin, *IRA*, p. 430.
16. MacEntee Papers, P67/542 (31).
17. Donal Lowry, 'New Ireland, Old Empire and the Outside World 1922–49: The Strange Evolution of a "Dictionary Republic"'. In *Ireland: The Politics of Independence, 1922–49*, Mike Cronin and John M. Regan, eds. (London, 2000), p. 164.

18. In 1945, the War Office estimated that 42,665 Irish soldiers served in the British Armed Forces during the war, quite high for a neutral country. See Robert Fisk, *In Time of War* (London, 1985) pp. 523–524.

19. There was secret military cooperation between the British and Irish armies to repel a German invasion of Ireland; it was known as the 'W' Plan. The operational papers for the plan were destroyed in the Luftwaffe bombing of Belfast in 1941. See Fisk, *In Time of War*, pp. 233–244.

20. As of September 1939, the Department of Defence, Dublin, estimated the Irish Army to number 19,783–7,494 Regulars, 5,066 A and B Reservists, and 7,223 Volunteers with 21 armoured vehicles, two tanks, a tiny air force, and no navy.

21. Nicholas Mansergh, *Survey of British Commonwealth Affairs: Problems of Wartime Cooperation and Postwar Change, 1939–1952* (Oxford, 1958), p. 75.

22. See Martin S. Quigley, *A U.S. Spy in Ireland* (Dublin, 1999).

23. Quigley, *U.S. Spy*, p. 101.

24. Dáil Eireann Debates, vol. 123, col. 1045, 22 November 1950.

25. Lee, *Ireland 1912–1985*, p. 248.

26. Coogan, *IRA*, p. 217.

27. Found in 'Invasion! If the British Come Back? If the Germans Land? If Both Come — What Then? A Republican Answer' written by Peadar O'Donnell and George Gilmore — undated, but around 6 July 1940, Dominions Office, DO 130/8 National Archives, Kew.

28. Letter to Maffey from J.E. Stephenson, Dominions Office, 18 April 1940, DO 130/8.

29. Eunan O'Halpin, *Defending Ireland: The Irish State and its Enemies since 1922* (Oxford, 1999), p. 126.

30. Stuart, *Black List*, p. 291.

31. John P. Duggan, *Neutral Ireland and the Third Reich* (Dublin, 1985), p. 64.

32. *Irish Times*, 25 August 1947.

33. Ibid., 29 August 1947.

34. *Letters from Iseult*, pp. 151–152.

35. Typescript of letter to *Irish Press*, dated 20 Deire Fomhair (October) 1947, MacEntee Papers, P67/372 (24).

36. 'Minister for Local Government on some "national" records', MacEntee Papers, P67/373 (1).

37. MacEntee Papers, P67/373 (3).

38. *Irish Times*, 14 October 1947.

39. 21 October 1947, MacEntee Papers, P67/374.

40. *Irish Press*, 1 June 1946.

41. MacBride to de Valera, 23 March 1944, de Valera Papers, P150/2571.

42. Coogan, *IRA*, pp. 138–139.

43. Ibid., p. 139.

44. O'Donnell, 'Man of Destiny'.

45. Bell, *Secret Army*, p. 163.

46. Ibid., p. 171.
47. *Irish Times*, 8 April 1940.
48. A transcript of the inquest can be found in *The Irish Times*, 23 April 1940.
49. See Coogan, IRA, pp. 178–183 and 'Eire and the war' pamphlet, undated, de Valera Papers, P150/1997.
50. *Irish Times*, 13 May 1946.
51. Ibid.
52. MacBride, *That Day's Struggle*, p. 132.
53. Interview with Anna MacBride White.
54. MacBride, *That Day's Struggle*, p. 130. Italics mine.

Chapter Four (PP. 71–92)

1. MacDermott, *Clann na Poblachta*, p. 2.
2. Reported in *Irish Times*, 18 March 1943.
3. N. Browne, *Against the Tide*, p. 97.
4. Lyons, *Ireland Since the Famine*, p. 558.
5. *The Times*, 17 July 1948.
6. John A. Murphy, *Ireland in the Twentieth Century* (Dublin, 1975), p. 107.
7. MacBride, *That Day's Struggle*, p. 108.
8. Ibid., p. 109.
9. Brian Inglis, *West Briton* (London, 1962), p. 100.
10. Cruise O'Brien, *Memoir*, p. 134. Cruise O'Brien was Head of Information in the External Affairs Department during Seán's ministry.
11. This assertion is difficult to believe given Seán's high public profile. See P. Browne, *Thanks for the Tea*.
12. Inglis, *West Briton*, p. 105.
13. MacDermott, *Clann na Poblachta*, p. 40.
14. All major political parties in the Irish Free State chose Irish names, with the exception of the Irish Labour Party, perhaps because its party ethos was more international, although as I have pointed out, Labour in Ireland never wanted to appear too far to the left. According to Lyons, the Irish political community was deeply opposed to communism (*Ireland Since the Famine*, p. 591) and John Coakley and Michael Gallagher remark on the 'absence of a significant classical revolutionary left' in Ireland [*Politics in the Republic of Ireland*, second edition (Limerick, 1996), p. 18]. As Seán Lemass once commented, Labour in Ireland was always 'a harmless shade of pink' (Quoted in MacDermott, *Clann*, p. 5).
15. MacDermott, *Clann na Poblachta*, p. 14.
16. Alvin Jackson, *Ireland 1798–1998*, p. 305.
17. MacBride, *That Day's Struggle*, p. 131.
18. Kees van Kersbergen, 'The Distinctiveness of Christian Democracy' in David Hanley, ed., *Christian Democracy in Europe: A Comparative Perspective* (London, 1994), p. 35. For other treatments of the phenomenon and influence of Christian

Democracy in Europe, see R.E.M. Irving, *Christian Democracy in France* (London, 1973), R.A. Webster, *Christian Democracy in Italy 1860–1960* (London, 1961), Emiel Lamberts, *Christian Democracy in the European Union 1945–1995: Proceedings of the Leuven Colloquium* (Leuven, 1997), M.P. Fogarty, *Christian Democracy in Western Europe 1820–1953* (London, 1957), and Geoffrey Pridham, *Christian Democracy in Western Germany: The CDU/CSU in Government and Opposition 1945–1976* (London, 1977).

19. J.H. Whyte, *Church and State in Modern Ireland 1923–1979*, second edition (Dublin, 1980), p. 158.

20. See John Cooney, *John Charles McQuaid: Ruler of Catholic Ireland* (Dublin, 2000), pp. 94–106. Popular perception of McQuaid's role may differ from the reality; as Cooney states, 'McQuaid's efforts to enshrine the absolute claims of the Catholic Church as the Church of Christ were frustrated by de Valera' (p. 94).

21. Whyte, *Church and State*, p. 159.

22. *Irish Times*, 8 July 1946.

23. Newspaper clipping, undated, found in MacEntee Papers, P67/542 (28).

24. Newspaper clipping, undated, found in MacEntee Papers, P67/542 (29).

25. *Irish Times*, 10 May 1947, 6 February 1947.

26. Ibid., 6 April 1968.

27. P. Browne, *Thanks for the Tea*, p. 103.

28. *Irish Independent*, 27 October 1947. Seán's comment on the family unit was an odd statement to make, considering that Seán and his half-sister had been raised by a single parent. As he lived in France until his father's death, perhaps he did not consider France as 'Christian' a state as Ireland.

29. Seán to McQuaid, 1 November 1948, Dublin Diocesan Archives. McQuaid referred the matter to the Youth Unemployment Council, but did not offer any advice directly to Seán.

30. *Irish Independent*, 25 November 1947.

31. In 1944, this amount stood at £130.9 million.

32. *Irish Independent*, 13 December 1947.

33. Ibid., 16 January 1948.

34. N. Browne, *Against the Tide*, p. 97.

35. Lee, *Ireland 1912–1985*, p. 241.

36. *Irish Independent*, 5 January 1948.

37. Ibid., 2 January 1948.

38. *The Economist*, 8 November 1947.

39. 29 December 1980, quoted in MacDermott, *Clann na Poblachta*, p. 63.

40. F.S.L. Lyons, 'The Years of Readjustment 1945–51' in K.B. Nowlan and T.D. Williams, eds., *Ireland in the War Years and After, 1939–1951* (Dublin, 1969), p. 69.

41. MacDermott, *Clann na Poblachta*, p. 23.

42. Cruise O'Brien, *Memoir*, p. 138.

43. N. Browne, *Against the Tide*, pp. 22–23 and 198–201.

44. Lee, *Ireland 1912–1985*, p. 318.

45. MacBride, *That Day's Struggle*, p. 146.
46. *Irish Times*, 27 January 1948.
47. *Irish Independent*, 9 October 1947.
48. Ibid., 25 October 1947.
49. Interview with Eithne MacDermott in *Clann na Poblachta*, p. 79.
50. *Irish Times*, 27 October 1947.
51. Ibid., 8 November 1947.
52. MacDermott, *Clann na Poblachta*, p. 48.
53. During the general election campaign, Seán suggested that, as a result of the inclement weather which prevented the electorate from attending open meetings, radio time be given to political parties. The Secretary to the Taoiseach, Maurice Moynihan, replied that 'it is not considered desirable to depart from the long standing rule that the national broadcasting service should not be used for the purpose of political party controversy' (15 January 1948, Department of the Taoiseach, S14204, National Archives, Dublin).
54. MacDermott, *Clann na Poblachta*, p. 39.
55. *Irish Times*, 16 October 1947.
56. Ibid., 18 October 1947. At various times, MacEntee labelled Seán a communist, fascist, socialist, and Nazi sympathiser, which makes for an interesting political philosophy!
57. *Irish Times*, 29 October 1947.
58. *Irish Independent*, 29 October 1947.
59. Ibid., 1 November 1947.
60. *Irish Times*, 1 November 1947.
61. Ibid., 31 October 1947.
62. *Irish Independent*, 1 November 1947.
63. Dáil Éireann Debates, vol. 108, col. 1379, 5 November 1947.
64. Ibid., cols. 1443–1444, 5 November 1947, also reported in *Irish Times*, 6 November 1947.
65. MacBride, *That Day's Struggle*, p. 137.
66. Ran in the *Irish Independent*, 30 January 1948.
67. Quoted in David McCullagh, *A Makeshift Majority: The First Interparty Government 1948–1951* (Dublin, 1999), p. 20.
68. MacDermott, *Clann na Poblachta*, p. 57.
69. N. Browne, *Against the Tide*, p. 99.
70. Liam Ó Laoghaire to booking managers, dated 7 January 1948, MacEntee Papers, P67/379 (1).
71. Inglis, *West Briton*, p. 114.
72. Editorial, *Irish Times*, 17 January 1948.
73. Colm and Liam Ó Laoghaire in conversation with MacDermott, in *Clann na Poblachta*, p. 62.
74. *Irish Times*, 4 February 1948.
75. *Irish Independent*, 13 December 1947.

76. N. Browne, *Against the Tide*, p. 103.

77. Kevin Rafter, *The Clann: The Story of Clann na Poblachta* (Cork, 1996), p. 35.

78. *Irish Independent*, 6 January 1948.

79. Lord Rugby to the Commonwealth Relations Office, 1 November 1947, Dominions Office, 35.3955, p. 3, National Archives, Kew.

80. *Observer*, 18 January 1948.

81. Inglis, *West Briton*, p. 114.

82. *Limerick Leader*, 31 January 1948.

83. Ballina is in Co. Mayo, the native county of John MacBride who was born in Westport.

84. *Irish Independent*, 4 February 1948.

85. Ibid., 29 January 1948.

86. John A. Murphy, 'The Irish Party System' in Nowlan and Williams, eds., *Ireland in the War Years*, pp. 158–159.

87. Ronan Fanning, *Independent Ireland*, p. 165. Italics his.

88. MacBride, *That Day's Struggle*, pp. 138–139.

89. Murphy, *Ireland in the Twentieth Century*, p. 119.

90. *Irish Times*, 1 January 1979.

91. Fanning, *Independent Ireland*, p. 165.

92. MacBride, *That Day's Struggle*, p. 151.

93. 1 October 1927, *Gonne–Yeats Letters*, p. 436.

94. Andrews, *Man of No Property*, p. 191.

95. Keogh, 'Ireland, the Vatican, and the Cold War', p. 68.

96. Dáil Éireann Debates, vol. 108, col. 1604, 7 November 1947.

Chapter Five (PP. 93–134)

1. Lecture to Royal Institute of International Affairs, Chatham House, 24 February 1949 — given by MacBride (Patrick McGilligan Papers, University College Dublin, P35b/148).

2. O'Halloran, *Partition*, p. xv.

3. Dáil Éireann Debates, vol. 117, col. 853, 13 July 1949.

4. Cruise O'Brien, *Memoir*, p. 145.

5. John Bowman, *De Valera and the Ulster Question 1917–1973* (Oxford, 1982), p. 128.

6. Dáil Éireann Debates, vol. 112, col. 95, 20 July 1948.

7. Quoted in Cronin, *Washington's Irish Policy 1916–1986* (Dublin, 1987), p. 201.

8. John Dulanty to External Affairs, 8 November 1948, Frank Aiken Papers, University College Dublin, P104/4463.

9. Memoranda of conversations, 11 April 1949, Dean Acheson Papers, Box 73, Harry S. Truman Library, Independence, MO.

10. O'Halloran, *Partition*, p. 7.

11. Patrick McGilligan Papers, University College Dublin, P35b/148.

12. *Irish Press*, 6 May 1949.

13. H. Duncan Hall, *A History of the British Commonwealth of Nations* (London, 1971), p. 819, fn.

14. *Irish Times*, 19 March 1947.

15. Dáil Éireann Debates, vol. 111, col. 2447, 8 July 1948.

16. The special position of the Catholic Church was removed in 1972, causing then Senator Mary Robinson to comment, 'I regret so little being done so late' (Seanad Éireann Debates, vol. 73, col. 795, 3 November 1972). Articles 2 and 3 were amended in 1998 as part of the Good Friday Agreement. A referendum to lift a ban on divorce was approved by a slim margin in November 1995. After a contentious court battle contesting the referendum, legalised divorce was finally enacted on 27 February 1997. Ireland's divorce law is a very conservative piece of legislation, one of the most conservative in any Western country, requiring at least four years' separation, and the courts must be satisfied that there is no prospect of reconciliation.

17. John Hickerson to George Garrett, 24 May 1948, State Department Decimal File, 841D 00/3.2448, National Archives, Washington, DC.

18. Troy Davis, 'Anti-partitionism, Irish America and Anglo-Irish Relations, 1945–51' in *Irish Foreign Policy: From Independence to Internationalism* (Dublin, 2000), p. 195. Inglis, *West Briton*, pp. 135–136.

19. Quoted in Cronin, *Washington's Irish Policy*, p. 183.

20. Letter to Minister of External Affairs from E. McAteer, 5 March 1949. Copy found in McGilligan Papers, P35b/146 (4).

21. Dáil Éireann Debates, vol. 117, col. 2, 5 July 1949.

22. Lord Rugby report of General Election in Eire, Report from Lord Rugby to Commonwealth Relations Office, 1 November 1947, Foreign Office 371.707175, National Archives, Kew.

23. Bowman, *De Valera*, pp. 274–275.

24. *Westmeath Examiner*, 21 August 1948.

25. Anthony Jordan, *Seán MacBride: A Biography* (Dublin, 1993), p. 105.

26. H. Duncan Hall, *A History of the British Commonwealth of Nations* (London, 1971), p. 811.

27. Jackson, *Ireland 1798–1998*, p. 309.

28. Dáil Éireann Debates, vol. 97, col. 2570, 17 July 1945.

29. *Irish Times*, 27 January 1948.

30. Dáil Éireann Debates, vol. 113, col. 25, 18 February 1948.

31. *Irish Times*, 19 February 1948.

32. Dáil Éireann Debates, vol. 112, col. 910, 20 July 1948.

33. Copy found in Frank Aiken Papers, P104/4442 (2).

34. Dáil Éireann Debates, vol. 110, cols. 27–28, 18 February 1948.

35. Nicholas Mansergh, *Nationalism and Independence* (Cork, 1997), pp. 188–189.

36. Lyons, *Ireland Since the Famine*, p. 564.

37. MacBride, *That Day's Struggle*, pp. 157–158.

38. Dáil Debates, vol. 112, col. 992, 21 July 1948.

39. Ibid., col. 2441, 6 August 1948.

40. Cabinet minutes, 10 August 1948, CAB 2/10, pp. 99–102, National Archives, Dublin.

41. Michael McInerney profile of John A. Costello, *Irish Times*, 4 September 1967. Copy of Costello's initial answers to McInerney's questions found in Patrick McGilligan Papers, p35c/205 (3).

42. MacDermott, *Clann na Poblachta*, pp. 115–116.

43. *Ireland in International Affairs*, text found in John A. Costello Papers, University College, Dublin, p190/532.

44. Costello to F.S.L. Lyons, 6 January 1967, in Lyons, *Ireland Since the Famine*, p. 565.

45. 'Dinner on 4 September, Diary of Taoiseach's visit to the USA and Canada', John A. Costello Papers, p190/526 (3).

46. Patrick Lynch, 'Pages from a Memoir' in P. Lynch and J. Meenan, eds., *Essays in Honour of Alexis Fitzgerald* (Dublin, 1987), pp. 50–52.

47. 'Memorandum for the Secretary of State for External Affairs', 28 February 1949, Department of External Affairs, File 50021–40 (Record Group 25, vols. 4480–4481), National Archives of Canada, Ottawa.

48. Lynch, 'Pages', pp. 52–53.

49. Memorandum, 15 June 1972, written by Costello, John A. Costello Papers, p190/546 (14). In an *Irish Times* interview on 25 March 1961, the Governor-General denied ever having intended an 'insult to this country'. Costello later acknowledged the statement and accepted the apology.

50. Memorandum, 15 June 1972, by Costello, John A. Costello Papers, p190/546 (14).

51. John J. Hearne to Costello, 23 January 1949, John A. Costello Papers, p190/414 (11).

52. N. Browne, *Against the Tide*, pp. 130–132 and Mansergh, 'Conversation with Frederick Boland – 1952,' *Nationalism and Independence*, pp. 188–189.

53. Nicholas Mansergh, *The Unresolved Question: The Anglo-Irish Settlement and Its Undoing 1912–72* (New Haven, CT, 1991), p. 331.

54. Clement Attlee, *As It Happened* (London, 1954), p. 190.

55. Lyons, *Ireland Since the Famine*, p. 562.

56. 29 July 1948, quoted in Ian McCabe, *A Diplomatic History of Ireland 1948–9: The Republic, the Commonwealth and NATO* (Dublin, 1991), p. 36.

57. 'Memorandum for file', 28 February 1949, Department of External Affairs, File 50021–40 (Record Group 25, vols. 4480–4481), National Archives of Canada, Ottawa.

58. Jordan, *Seán MacBride*, pp. 106–107.

59. Mansergh, *Nationalism and Independence*, p. 187.

60. Maffey report to the Commonwealth Relations Office, 12 June 1948, CAB 134/118, National Archives, Kew.

61. Patrick Lynch to Seán MacBride, 12 March 1981, courtesy of Caitriona Lawlor.

62. Second draft of memo, July 1972, John A. Costello Papers, p190/546 (16).

63. *Irish Times*, 8 September 1948.

64. Ibid., 5 April 1999.

65. Murphy, *Ireland in the Twentieth Century*, p. 126.

66. Lyons, *Ireland Since the Famine*, p. 567.

67. *Irish Times*, 4 July 1962.

68. Ibid., 19 January 1979.

69. Ibid., 10 July 1962.

70. N. Browne, *Against the Tide*, p. 131.

71. *Sunday Independent*, 1 February 1984.

72. Patrick Lynch to Seán MacBride, 17 January 1984, courtesy of Caitriona Lawlor.

73. MacDermott, *Clann na Poblachta*, p. 130.

74. Lynch, 'Pages', p. 39.

75. Coogan, *Ireland*, p. 349.

76. Cabinet minutes, 11 October 1948, CAB 2/10, pp. 159–160, National Archives, Dublin.

77. Attlee, *As It Happened*, p. 190.

78. Garret FitzGerald, *All In A Life: An Autobiography* (Dublin, 1991), p. 45.

79. Seanad Éireann Debates, vol. 36, col. 84, 9 December 1948.

80. *Irish Times*, 1 January 1979.

81. Ibid., 25 November 1948.

82. Nicholas Mansergh 'The Implications of Eire's Relationship with the British Commonwealth of Nations', *International Affairs*, January 1948, p. 4.

83. Nicholas Mansergh, *The Unresolved Question*, p. 328.

84. Quoted in *Irish Times*, 27 October 1948.

85. Fitzgerald to Costello, Wednesday, October 1949, John A. Costello Papers, P190/390.

86. Michael Gallagher, *Political Parties in the Republic of Ireland* (Manchester, 1985), p. 49.

87. MacDermott, *Clann na Poblachta*, p. 96.

88. Report to the Department of External Affairs by John Dulanty, 7 October 1948. Frank Aiken Papers, P104/4449 (2).

89. *The Citizen*, May 1967.

90. Copy found in Sighle Humphreys Papers, University College Dublin, P106/2148 (1).

91. Patrick Keatinge, *Formulation of Irish Foreign Policy* (Dublin, 1973), pp. 80–81.

92. Cruise O'Brien, *Memoir*, p.159.

93. *Irish Times*, 26 October 1948.

94. Keatinge, *Formulation of Irish Foreign Policy*, p. 63.

95. MacDermott, *Clann na Poblachta*, p. 131.

96. Alexis Fitzgerald to Costello, Wednesday, October 1949, John A. Costello Papers, P190/390. Italics his.

97. N. Browne, *Against the Tide*, p. 133.

98. *Irish Times*, 22 December 1948.

99. The conference took place from 2 April to 3 May. Easter Monday fell on 18 April in 1949.

100. Samuel Levenson, *Maud Gonne* (London, 1976), p. 405; *Life*, 2 May 1949.

101. *Life*, 2 May 1949.

102. *Times*, 19 April 1949.

103. *Irish Times*, 19 April 1949.

104. Records of the Cabinet Office, 129/29 CP(48) 205, National Archives, Kew.

105. Report by High Commissioner for Ireland John J. Hearne to External Affairs, 5 October 1949. Department of Foreign Affairs 313/3A, National Archives, Dublin.

106. Maffey to Sir Eric Machtig, 27 January 1948, CAB 134/118/annex 11, National Archives, Kew.

107. Ronan Fanning, 'The Response of the London and Belfast Governments to the Declaration of the Republic of Ireland 1948–1949', *International Affairs*, 58 (Winter 1981–1982), p. 113.

108. 'Notes of a conversation between the Prime Minister of Canada and the Prime Minister of Ireland', 9 September 1948, Department of External Affairs, File 50021-40 (Record Group 25, vols. 4480–4481), National Archives of Canada, Ottawa.

109. Copy found in Frank Aiken Papers, P104/4443 (1).

110. Quoted in Mansergh, *Nationalism and Independence*, p. 208.

111. House of Commons Debates, vol. CLIX, col. 1090, 15 December 1948.

112. CAB 128/13/143–4, National Archives, Kew.

113. *Times*, 18 October 1948, *Irish Times*, 18 October 1948.

114. Ronan Fanning, 'Anglo-Irish Relations — Partition and the British Dimension in Historical Perspective', *Irish Studies in International Affairs*, vol. 2, no. 1, 1985, p. 15.

115. Dáil Éireann Debates, vol. 113, col. 715, 26 November 1948.

116. Clement Attlee Papers, Bodleian Library, Oxford, MS Attlee, dep. 82, 172.

117. D.G. Boyce, *The Irish Question and British Politics 1868–1996*, second edition (London, 1996), pp. 97–98.

118. Attlee, *As It Happened*, p. 190.

119. House of Commons Debates, vol. 464, col. 1858, 11 May 1949. Fanning arrives at a similar conclusion, 'Response of London and Belfast Governments', p. 114.

120. *Irish Times*, 29 October 1948.

121. Ibid., 27 January 1948.

122. Lyons, *Famine*, p. 567.

123. Dáil Éireann Debates, vol. 113, col. 385, 24 November 1948.

124. Lee, *Ireland 1912–1985*, p. 301.

125. Dáil Éireann Debates, vol. 113, col. 385, 24 November 1948.

126. Copy found in Patrick McGilligan Papers, P35b/148.

127. Lyons, *Famine*, p. 570.

128. Mansergh, *Unresolved Question*, p. 341.

129. Telegram from Noel-Baker to Maffey, 9 May 1949, CAB, 21/184, National Archives, Kew.

130. MacBride to Dulanty, 15 May 1949, Department of Foreign Affairs 305/14/36, National Archives, Dublin.

131. Report to External Affairs by Dulanty, 10 May 1949. Department of Foreign Affairs 305/14/36, National Archives, Dublin.
132. R.F. Foster, *Modern Ireland 1600–1972*, p. 567.
133. Dáil Éireann Debates, vol. 115, cols. 785–786, 10 May 1949.
134. *Irish Times*, 8 September 1967.
135. David Harkness, *Ireland in the Twentieth Century: Divided Island* (London, 1966), p. 80.
136. Attlee, *As It Happened*, p. 190.
137. Attlee Papers, MS Attlee, dep. 83, 15.
138. Attlee, *As It Happened*, pp. 186–187.
139. Mansergh, 'Ireland: the Republic Outside the Commonwealth', in *Nationalism and Independence*, p. 176.
140. Lee, *Ireland 1912–1985*, p. 300.
141. *Irish Times*, 7 September 1967.
142. 14 April 1949 radio interview reprinted in *Irish Times*, 16 April 1949. Seán MacEoin Papers, University College Dublin, P151/619 (1).
143. Lee, *Ireland 1912–1985*, p. 301.
144. Coogan, *Ireland*, p. 350.
145. McCabe, *Diplomatic History*, p. 149.
146. MacDermott, *Clann na Poblachta*, p. 113.
147. *Irish Times*, 20 November 1999.
148. Ibid., 19 April 1949.
149. Speech in Mullingar, Co. Westmeath, undated, Seán MacEoin Papers, P151/615 (2).
150. *Manchester Guardian*, 21 September 1948.
151. *Irish Times*, 2 October 1948.
152. Cruise O'Brien, *Memoir*, p. 141.
153. *Irish Times*, 6 May 1949.
154. Attlee, *As It Happened*, p. 190.
155. Seán MacEoin Papers, P151/618.
156. Costello's speech at the 1950 Fine Gael party convention. Copy found in Mulcahy Papers, P7/c/123.
157. Dáil Éireann Debates, vol. 113, col. 392, 24 November 1948.
158. Cronin, *Washington's Irish Policy*, p. 194.
159. Inadequate representation was not entirely the fault of the Stormont Government. Most nationalist parties followed an absentionist policy until 1925, which allowed the Government to tighten control.
160. *Irish Independent*, 28 January 1949.
161. *Irish Press*, 28 January 1949.
162. *Irish Times*, 3 February 1949.
163. *Irish Independent*, editorial, 26 January 1949.
164. *Irish Times*, editorial, 28 January 1949.
165. CAB, 9F/123/11, Public Record Office, Northern Ireland.
166. Dáil Éireann Debates, vol. 117, col. 757, 13 July 1949.

167. Ibid., col. 761, 13 July 1949.

168. Cruise O'Brien, *Memoir*, p. 145.

169. Ibid., pp. 144–148; N. Browne, *Against the Tide*, pp. 106–107, 137–138.

170. As Cruise O'Brien explains in his memoirs, 'to have been favoured by MacBride and then be dropped by him was not a promising career option.' Cruise O'Brien, *Memoir*, p. 147.

171. Cruise O'Brien, *Memoir*, p. 148.

172. Akenson, *Conor*, p. 137.

173. Ibid.

174. Inglis, *West Briton*, p. 142.

175. Ibid.

176. Cruise O'Brien, *Memoir*, p. 150.

177. Miriam Hederman, *The Road to Europe: Irish Attitudes 1948–61* (Dublin, 1983), p. 78.

178. Douglas Gageby, 'The Media 1945–70' in J.J. Lee, ed., *Ireland 1945–70* (Dublin, 1979), p. 130.

179. *Irish Times*, 8 March 1948.

180. Dáil Éireann Debates, vol. 112, col. 2113, 5 August 1948.

181. Ibid.

182. CAB 9F/140/28, PRONI.

183. McWilliam to Brooke, 23 August 1950, CAB 9F/140/28, PRONI.

184. Cabinet meeting, 8 March 1951, CAB 9F/140/29, PRONI.

185. *Irish Independent*, 9 May 1950.

186. *Irish Times*, 10 May 1950.

187. Curran to Lavery, 4 April 1949, Department of the Taoiseach, s 14414 A, National Archives, Dublin.

188. Quoted in McCabe, *Diplomatic History*, p. 129.

189. Unfortunately, Cosgrave goes on to say, 'These three instances demonstrate the absurdity of Partition and the necessity for ending it as quickly as possible.' Dáil Éireann Debates, vol. 126, col. 2227, 19 July 1951.

190. McCullagh, *A Makeshift Majority*, p. 128.

191. John Whyte, 'Dynamics of Social and Political Change in Northern Ireland' in Dermot Keogh and Michael H. Haltzel, eds., *Northern Ireland and the Politics of Reconciliation* (Cambridge, 1993), p. 116.

192. *Irish Times*, 8 May 1950.

193. Basil Chubb, *The Politics of the Irish Constitution* (Dublin, 1991), p. 81.

194. *Irish Independent*, 8 May 1950.

195. *That Day's Struggle*, p. 180.

Chapter Six (PP. 135–62)

1. Quoted in Dermot Keogh, 'Ireland', in Zara Steiner's *Times Survey of Foreign Ministries of the World* (London, 1982), p. 279.

2. Dáil Éireann Debates, vol. 4, col. 11, 18 August 1921.
3. Donald Harmon Akenson, *The United States and Ireland* (Cambridge, MA, 1973), p. 34.
4. Akenson, *United States and Ireland*, p. 37.
5. Troy D. Davis, *Dublin's American Policy: Irish-American Diplomatic Relations 1945–1952* (Washington, DC, 1998), p. 92.
6. T.N. Brown, *Irish-American Nationalism 1870–1890* (New York, 1966), pp. 63–64.
7. Patrick J. Blessing, 'Irish Emigration to the United States, 1800–1920: An overview' in P.J. Drudy, ed., *The Irish in America: Emigration, Assimilation, Impact* (Cambridge, 1985), p. 31.
8. Akenson, *United States and Ireland*, p. 44.
9. Though no reliable published work on the Irish ancestry of American Presidents exists, nineteen American Presidents have claimed Irish ancestry. However, their backgrounds were 'Scotch-Irish' and only one American President was an Irish-American Catholic.
10. Daniel Patrick Moynihan, 'The Irish', in Daniel Patrick Moynihan and Nathan Glazer, eds., *Beyond the Melting Pot: The Negros, Puerto Ricans, Jews, Italians, and Irish of New York City* (Cambridge, MA, 1963), p. 241.
11. Thomas N. Brown, 'Social Discrimination Against the Irish in the United States,' quoted in Moynihan, p. 241.
12. Lawrence J. McCaffrey, 'Irish-American Politics: Power with or without Purpose?' in Drudy, *The Irish in America*, p. 169.
13. Moynihan, 'The Irish', p. 229.
14. Lowry, 'New Ireland', p. 195.
15. Memorandum from Matthew Connelly to Secretary of State George Marshall, 18 June 1947, Harry S. Truman Papers (HSTP), White House Central Files, Official File 218, Box 823, Harry S. Truman Library (HSTL), Independence, Missouri.
16. Hickerson to Gray, 1 January 1945, Record Group 59, Box 20, File UK D-5 (B), National Archives and Records Administration, Washington, DC.
17. British Embassy to Foreign Office, 10 March 1949, Foreign Office (FO) 371 1967, 74190, National Archives, Kew.
18. T. Ryle Dwyer, *Strained Relations: Ireland at Peace and the USA at War, 1941–45* (Dublin, 1988), p. 172; Davis, *Dublin's American Policy*, pp. 29–57.
19. Davis, *Dublin's American Policy*, pp. 58–59.
20. Oral History, Nathan M. Becker, State Department, 19 January 1973, Box 27, OH-159, p. 7a, HSTL.
21. Hickerson to Garrett, 4 May 1948.
22. Memorandum for the President, 11 April 1949, Myron C. Taylor File, HSTP, White House Confidential Files, Box 47, HSTL.
23. Memorandum on the state of Ireland, 10 October 1942, President Secretary's Files, Vatican Diplomatic Files, Box 51, Franklin Delano Roosevelt Library, Hyde Park, New York.

24. Raymond J. Raymond, 'The Marshall Plan and Ireland 1947–1952,' in Drudy, *Irish in America*, p. 297.
25. Moynihan, 'The Irish,' p. 244.
26. *New York Times*, 1 May 1945.
27. Memorandum, 21 May 1945, Dominions Office (DO) 130/56, National Archives, Kew.
28. Dáil Éireann Debates, vol. 96, col. 2037, 13 April 1945.
29. Dwyer, *Strained Relations*, p. 161.
30. Quoted in Earl of Longford and Thomas P. O'Neill, *Eamon de Valera* (London, 1970), p. 411.
31. Lewis W. Douglas to Ernest Bevin, 6 April 1948, BEVN II 6/5, Misc. Correspondence, 1948 Foreign Office #7, Ernest Bevin Papers, Churchill College, Cambridge.
32. Ronan Fanning, *Independent Ireland* (Dublin, 1983), p. 177.
33. Memorandum for the President, Subject Policy Manual, p. 46, 16 April 1945, HSTP, President Secretary Files, Subject File Cabinet, Box 138, HSTL.
34. MacBride to Nunan, 26 October 1948, Department of Foreign Affairs 305/74, National Archives, Dublin.
35. Cronin, *Washington's Irish Policy*, p. 191.
36. Quoted in Cronin, *Washington's Irish Policy*, p. 248.
37. *Congressional Record* — House of Representatives, vol. 96, 81st Congress, second session, 29 March 1950, p. 4344.
38. The Amendment was passed by a teller vote. According to Congressional Quarterly's *American Congressional Dictionary*, this procedure required Members to pass through the centre aisle to be counted, but not recorded by name. The teller vote is no longer practised in the House of Representatives.
39. Truman cleverly ran his 1948 presidential campaign not against Republican opponent Thomas E. Dewey, but against a 'do-nothing' Republican Congress. See David McCullough, *Truman* (New York, 1993).
40. *New York Times*, 30 March 1950.
41. *Washington Post*, 30 March 1950
42. *Irish Times*, 30 March 1950.
43. Ibid., 31 March 1950.
44. See Department of Foreign Affairs, File D24, National Archives, Dublin.
45. *New York Times*, 2 April 1950.
46. Ibid., 31 March 1950.
47. *Washington Post*, 30 March 1950.
48. *Irish Times*, 31 March 1950.
49. See *Congressional Record* — House of Representatives, vol. 96, 81st Congress, second session, 31 March 1950, p. 4552.
50. Jack K. McFall, Assistant Secretary of State, to Tom Connally, 13 April 1951, United States State Department Decimal File, 740A.00, National Archives, Washington, DC.

51. Michael Farrell, 'The Extraordinary Life and Times of Sean MacBride, Part 2' *Magill*, January 1983, p. 31.

52. American League to Marshall, 12 May 1948, HSTP, HSTL.

53. HSTP, White House Central Files, Official File 218, Box 823, HSTL.

54. 'Ireland' written by Colonel H.D. Kehm, Dublin Army Attaché to Psychological Strategy Board, dated 20 September 1951, HSTP, Psychological Strategy Board Files, Box 7, 091.

55. Lee, *Ireland 1912–1985*, p. 301.

56. CIA Situation Report Ireland April 1949, p. 15, HSTP, PSF, Intelligence File 1946–1953, Box 219.

57. Rugby to Sir Eric Machtig, Under-Secretary of State at Dominions Office, 30 March 1948, DO 35/3928, National Archives, Kew.

58. Memorandum for Truman, dated 22 March 1951, re: MacBride appointment for meeting of 23 March, Signed by Dean Acheson. HSTP, President Secretary's File, Subject File, Foreign Affairs 1945–1953 'Ireland' Box 157.

59. HSTP, White House Confidential Files, State Department Correspondence, Box 42, HSTL.

60. Truman to Sir Basil Brooke, 23 September 1949, HSTP, White House Central Files, Official File 218, Box 823, HSTL.

61. HSTP, White House Central Files, Official File 218, Box 823, HSTL.

62. Cronin, *Washington's Irish Policy*, p. 220.

63. Davis, *Dublin's American Policy*, p. 134.

64. Conor Cruise O'Brien, 'Ireland in International Affairs', in Owen Dudley Edwards, ed., *Conor Cruise O'Brien Introduces Ireland* (New York, 1969), p. 127.

65. Dáil Éireann Debates, vol. 126, col. 2024, 19 July 1951.

66. 'Against hunger, poverty, desperation and chaos', George C. Marshall's speech at the Harvard University Commencement, 5 June 1947, reprinted in *Foreign Affairs*, May–June 1997, vol. 76, p. 160.

67. Bernadette Whelan, 'Integration or Isolation? Ireland and the Invitation to Join the Marshall Plan' in Kennedy and Skelly, eds., *Irish Foreign Policy*, p. 204.

68. Marshall never explicitly stated this in his speech; aid was not directed 'against any country or doctrine'. However, Sallie Pisani convincingly argues that the Marshall Plan was 'coordinated intervention' used to combat communism. Sallie Pisani, *The CIA and the Marshall Plan* (Lawrence, Kansas, 1991).

69. Till Geiger and Michael Kennedy, eds., *Ireland, Europe and the Marshall Plan* (Dublin, 2004), p. 29.

70. Whelan, 'Integration' in *Irish Foreign Policy*, p. 221 and *Ireland and the Marshall Plan 1947–57* (Dublin, 2000), p. 17.

71. HSTP, President's Secretary File, Box 256, SR 48, CIA Ireland, 1 April 1949, HSTL.

72. Raymond, 'Marshall Plan', pp. 299–300.

73. This was possibly because Spain, as a fascist dictatorship under Franco, was not invited to participate in the OEEC and, by association, the Marshall Plan.

74. HSTP, PSF: Intelligence File 1946–1953, Box 219, CIA: Situation Report, Ireland April 1949, p. 13, HSTL.
75. Dáil Éireann Debates, vol. 114, col. 324, 23 February 1949.
76. Whelan, 'Integration', p. 213.
77. 4 July 1947, Department of External Affairs to the Government, Department of the Taoiseach, s 14106/A, National Archives, Dublin.
78. Irish Independent, 17 April 1948.
79. MacBride's role in the OEEC is more fully explored in Chapter Seven.
80. Memorandum, Hickerson to Marshall, 18 May 1948, State Department Decimal Files 841D.021, National Archives, Washington, DC.
81. Oral History, W. John Kenney, Chief of Mission, ECA 1949–1950, OH 322, Box 56, 29 November 1971, HSTL.
82. Raymond, 'Marshall Plan', p. 306.
83. MacBride — submitted to ECA, May 1948, p. 1, HSTP, White House Central Files, Official File 218, Box 823, HSTL.
84. Ibid., p. 3.
85. Northern Ireland was receiving three-quarters of its aid in grant form in 1949–1950.
86. Memorandum, Department of Finance to Government, 18 April 1952, Taoiseach s 141061, National Archives, Dublin.
87. Lee, Ireland 1912–1985, p. 304.
88. Alan S. Milward, The Reconstruction of Western Europe, 1945–51 (London, 1987), p. 83.
89. Memorandum for Government from Finance, 8 June 1948, Department of Finance, 121/21/48 F Series, National Archives, Dublin.
90. Hickerson, Memorandum of Conversation, 20 May 1948, quoted in Cronin, Washington's Irish Policy, pp. 196–197.
91. Geiger and Kennedy, Marshall Plan, p. 21.
92. Daniel Davies, '"It is More Important to us that Eire Should Receive Adequate Aid than it is for Eire Herself": Britain, Ireland and the Marshall Plan', in Geiger and Kennedy, Marshall Plan, p. 69.
93. HSTP, PSF: Intelligence File 1946–1953, Box 219, CIA: Situation Report, Ireland April 1949, p. 38, HSTL.
94. Ibid., p. 11.
95. Memoranda of conversations, 13 February 1951, with John J. Hearne, Dean Acheson Papers, Box 77, HSTL.
96. Quoted in Ronan Fanning, The Irish Department of Finance 1922–58 (Dublin, 1978), p. 411.
97. Quoted in Fanning, Finance, p. 406.
98. 3 February 1948, Department of Finance 121/10/48, National Archives, Dublin.
99. Fanning, Finance, pp. 434–442.
100. Quoted in Fanning, Finance, p. 405.

101. Text found in HSTP, Foreign Affairs File, Ireland — General News Clippings, Box 151.

102. Raymond, 'Marshall Plan', p. 321.

103. Fanning, *Finance*, p. 406.

104. Michael Kennedy, 'The Challenge of Multilateralism: The Marshall Plan and the Expansion of the Irish Diplomatic Service', in Geiger and Kennedy, *Marshall Plan*, p. 103.

105. HSTP, President Secretary's File, Intelligence File, Box 219, CIA Situation Report, Ireland, April 1949, p. 1, HSTL.

106. 8 February 1949, Department of Foreign Affairs 305/74, National Archives, Dublin.

107. Dáil Éireann Debates, vol. 114, col. 324, 23 February 1949.

108. Quoted in Cronin, *Washington's Irish Policy*, p. 225.

109. Hickerson to Nunan, 31 March 1949, Department of Foreign Affairs 305/72/5 part 1, National Archives, Dublin.

110. McCabe, *Diplomatic History*, p. 97.

111. HSTP, PSF: Intelligence File 1946–1953, Box 219, CIA: Situation Report, Ireland April 1949, p. 38, HSTL.

112. N. Browne, *Against the Tide*, p. 134. Browne was unhappy about MacBride overlooking 'the hardworking and experienced' Noel Hartnett for a Seanad nomination. He goes so far as to suggest that Denis Ireland may have been 'a secret member of British Intelligence whose job it was to bring the Republic into NATO' (p. 135).

113. Garrett to Truman, 10 July 1950, HSTP, White House Central Files, Official File 218, Box 823, HSTL.

114. Cronin interview with MacBride, 12 February 1986 in *Washington's Irish Policy*, p. 248.

115. Memoranda of conversations, 11 April 1949, Dean Acheson Papers, Box 73, HSTL.

116. Department of Foreign Affairs, 305/74, National Archives, Dublin.

117. HSTP, PSF, Subject File, NSC Meetings, 2 November 1950, NSC Staff Study, Box 181, HSTL.

118. Ibid.

119. NSC note, reported in *Irish Times*, 5 November 1980.

120. HSTP, PSF, Subject File, NSC Meetings, 2 November 1950, NSC Staff Study, Box 181, HSTL.

121. Dáil Éireann Debates, vol. 112, col. 903, 20 July 1948.

122. Cronin, *Washington's Irish Policy*, p. 233.

123. Lyons, *Ireland Since the Famine*, pp. 557–558.

124. NSC note, *Irish Times*, 5 November 1980.

125. Report 'Eire and the Paris Conference', 12 March 1948, FO, 371.70175, National Archives, Kew.

126. Dáil Éireann Debates, vol. 106, col. 2333, 20 June 1947.

127. Francis H. Heller and John R. Gillingham, eds., NATO: *The Founding of the Atlantic Alliance and the Integration of Europe* (New York, 1992), p. 2.

128. 14 March 1951. Text can be found in HSTP, Foreign Affairs File, Ireland — General News Clippings, Box 151, HSTL.

129. Quoted in McCabe, *Diplomatic History*, p. 108.

130. Cronin interview with MacBride, 12 February 1986, *Washington's Irish Policy*, pp. 247–248.

131. *Irish Times*, 29 January 1949.

132. Ibid., 19 March 1949.

133. Referenda take place only in matters of constitutional alteration.

134. Ronan Fanning, 'Irish Neutrality: An Historical Perspective', in *Irish Studies in International Affairs*, vol. 1, no. 3 (1982), p. 34.

135. Quoted in Ronan Fanning, 'The United States and Irish Participation in NATO: The Debate of 1950', *Irish Studies in International Affairs* 1 (1979), p. 39.

136. 28 January 1949, 'Outline of conversation between MacBride and Garrett', FO 371.79224, National Archives, Kew.

137. Garrett to Truman, 10 July 1950, HSTP, White House Central Files, Official File 218, Box 823, HSTL.

138. HSTP, PSF, Subject File, NSC Meetings, 2 November 1950, NSC Staff Study, Box 181, HSTL.

139. Memoranda of conversations, 13 March 1951, Dean Acheson Papers, Box 77, HSTL.

140. This was approved by Truman on 3 November 1950. HSTP, PSF, Subject File, NSC Meetings, 2 November 1950, Box 181, HSTL.

141. Cronin, *Washington's Irish Policy*, pp. 248–249.

142. Boland to Walshe, 9 February 1949, Department of Foreign Affairs, 305/72/5, part 1, National Archives, Dublin. Canadian intervention also proved elusive; the Canadian High Commissioner in London told MacBride that repeal of the External Relations Act coupled with the refusal to join NATO meant that 'not only are the United Kingdom and Northern Ireland less disposed to discuss partition, but other North Atlantic countries, including Canada, have, for the first time, a strategic interest in maintaining partition' (Quoted in McCabe, *Diplomatic History*, p. 112).

143. Cronin, *Washington's Irish Policy*, p. 249.

144. Dwyer, *Strained Relations*, p. 1.

145. Dermot Keogh, *Twentieth Century Ireland* (Dublin, 1994), p. 194.

146. Desmond Dinan, 'After the Emergency: Ireland in the Post-War World, 1945–50', *Éire-Ireland*, vol. 24 (Fall 1989), p. 98.

147. 'Eire and the Paris Conference', 12 March 1948, FO, 371.70175, National Archives, Kew.

148. McCabe, *Diplomatic History*, p. 107.

149. Quoted in Cronin, *Washington's Irish Policy*, p. 254.

150. *Irish Times*, 19 March 1949.

151. Conor Cruise O'Brien, 'Ireland in International Affairs', pp. 124–125.

152. Memorandum to Department of External Affairs from John Dulanty, 10 May 1949, Department of Foreign Affairs 305/14/36, National Archives, Dublin.

153. Cronin, *Washington's Irish Policy*, p. 239.

154. Farrell, 'Life and Times', p. 33

155. Richard Bourke, *Peace in Ireland: The War of Ideas* (London, 2003), p. 17. See also George Mitchell, *Making Peace* (London, 1999).

156. Record Group 84 File (2) 1948, Box 703. National Archives, Washington, DC.

157. Keogh, 'Ireland' in *Foreign Ministries*, p. 279.

Chapter Seven (PP. 163–85)

1. As J.J. Lee wrote in 1989, Ireland 'has chosen to ignore the study of international relations, including the study of neutrality, to an extent unparalleled in any other small Western European neutral.' J.J. Lee, *Ireland 1912–1985*, p. 605.

2. Keatinge, *Formulation*, p. 81.

3. Basil Chubb, *The Government and Politics of Ireland* (Oxford, 1974), p. 46. Trevor Salmon and Patrick Keatinge also make this point. Salmon, *Unneutral Ireland: An Ambivalent and Unique Security Policy* (Oxford, 1989), p. 1.

4. Michael Kennedy and Eunan O'Halpin, *Ireland and the Council of Europe: From Isolation Toward Integration* (Strasbourg, 2000), p. 12.

5. Michael Kennedy, *Ireland and the League of Nations 1919–1946: International Relations, Diplomacy, and Politics* (Dublin, 1996), p. 27.

6. Norman MacQueen, 'Ireland's Entry to the United Nations' in Tom Gallagher and James O'Connell, eds., *Contemporary Irish Studies* (Manchester, 1983), p. 77. See also Fisk, *In Time of War*, Fanning, 'Irish Neutrality: An Historical Perspective', Trevor Salmon, *Unneutral Ireland*, and Dennis Driscoll, 'Is Ireland Really Neutral?' in *Irish Studies in International Affairs*, vol. 1, no. 3, 1982.

7. Dinan, 'After the Emergency', p. 85.

8. Interview with United Press, 12 February 1949, Department of the Taoiseach, s 14291 A/1, National Archives, Dublin.

9. Dáil Éireann Debates, vol. 102, col. 1374, 24 July 1946.

10. Irish *aide-mémoire*, 25 May 1949 in *Texts Concerning Ireland's Position in Relation to the North Atlantic Treaty* (Dublin, 1950). Italics mine.

11. See Keogh, 'Ireland, the Vatican and the Cold War', pp. 931–952.

12. Conor Cruise O'Brien, 'Ireland in International Affairs', p. 124.

13. Miriam Hederman, 'The Beginning of the Discussion on European Union in Ireland', Walter Lipgens and Wilfred Loth, eds., *Documents on the History of European Integration, Vol. 3, The Struggle for European Union by Political Parties and Pressure Groups in Western European Countries, 1945–1950* (Berlin, 1988), p. 766.

14. The Labour Party is an exception, though Irish Labour had little in common with other European Labour movements. Clann na Poblachta's connection with European Christian Democrats is another exception.

15. Basil Chubb, *A Source Book of Irish Government* (Dublin, 1983), pp. 157–158.

16. Keatinge, *Formulation*, p. 224.

17. Dermot Keogh, *Ireland and Europe 1919–1989: A Diplomatic and Political History* (Cork, 1990), p. 219.

18. MacBride speech in Sligo, 17 November 1950, Department of Foreign Affairs, GIS/1/255, National Archives, Dublin.

19. Keogh, *Ireland 1919–1989*, p. 218.

20. Seanad Éireann Debates, vol. 35, col. 748, 5 August 1948.

21. Miriam Hederman, *The Road to Europe: Irish Attitudes 1948–61* (Dublin, 1983), p. 16.

22. In conversation with Mansergh in 1952, *Nationalism and Independence* (Cork, 1997), p. 189.

23. John Bowman, *De Valera*, p. 273.

24. Mansergh, *Nationalism and Independence*, p. 209.

25. Ibid.

26. Though Spain and Portugal were at the time under authoritarian regimes, both Franco and Salazar allied themselves with Catholicism, and Fascist Catholic countries appeared to be lesser evils than Communist Russia. Ireland had diplomatic relations with both Spain and Portugal during MacBride's tenure (the Taoiseach expressed regret in the Dáil at the death of President Carmona [Dáil Éireann, vol. 125, col. 978, 18 April 1951])and Ireland worked with both in the OEEC.

27. 29 December 1948, Department of Foreign Affairs 305/62/1, National Archives, Dublin.

28. Joseph Walshe to Secretary of the Department of External Affairs, 20 January 1949, Department of Foreign Affairs, 305/62/1, National Archives, Dublin.

29. Dermot Keogh, *Ireland and Europe 1919–48*, p. 212.

30. Mansergh, *Nationalism and Independence*, p. 184.

31. MacBride speech in Sligo, 17 November 1950. Department of Foreign Affairs, GIS/1/255, National Archives, Dublin.

32. Ibid.

33. Dáil Éireann Debates, vol. 117, col. 850, 13 July 1949.

34. See Hederman, *Road*, pp. 21–23.

35. Paul-Henri Spaak, 'Strasbourg: The Second Year', Stevenson Memorial Lecture, delivered 30 October 1950, Chatham House (Oxford, 1952), p. 13.

36. Attlee to Churchill, 4 February 1948, Winston Churchill Collection, Churchill College, Cambridge, CHUR 2/21.

37. Memorandum from External Affairs, 13 June 1950, Department of Foreign Affairs, 4/17, National Archives, Dublin.

38. European Parliamentary Union Memorandum on the Structure of Europe, 16 December 1949, Department of Foreign Affairs, 417/24 Part I, National Archives, Dublin.

39. *Irish Independent*, 8 May 1948.

40. *Irish Times*, 15 May 1948.
41. Kennedy and O'Halpin, *Council of Europe*, p. 23.
42. Dáil Éireann Debates, vol. 112, col. 903, 20 July 1948.
43. 16 June 1949, Department of Foreign Affairs, 417/39, National Archives, Dublin.
44. Whelan, *Marshall Plan*, p. 172.
45. Seanad Éireann Debates, vol. 35, col. 805, 5 August 1948.
46. Frederick Boland to John Costello, 11 August 1948, Department of Foreign Affairs, 417/24 Part I, National Archives, Dublin.
47. Hederman, *Road*, p. 29.
48. Dáil Éireann Debates, vol. 112, col. 2435, 6 August 1948.
49. Ibid., col. 903, 20 July 1948.
50. Seanad Éireann Debates, vol. 35, col. 813, 5 August 1948.
51. Dáil Éireann Debates, vol. 117, cols. 696–706, 12 July 1949.
52. *Irish Times*, editorial, 14 July 1949.
53. Ibid., editorial, 16 July 1949.
54. Dáil Éireann Debates, vol. 122, col. 1601, 12 July 1950.
55. *Irish Times*, 16 February 1949.
56. Conor Cruise O'Brien, *To Katanga and Back: A UN Case History* (London, 1962), p. 14.
57. Cruise O'Brien, 'Ireland in International Affairs', p. 126.
58. Lyons, *Ireland Since the Famine*, p. 591.
59. *Official Reports of Council of Europe Consultative Assembly*, 10 August–8 September 1949, p. 238.
60. *Irish Independent*, 12 August 1950.
61. Quoted in Hederman, *Road*, p. 31.
62. *The Leader*, editorial, 27 August 1949.
63. *Irish Times*, editorial, 13 August 1949.
64. *Irish Times*, 10 May 1948.
65. Dáil Éireann Debates, vol. 122, col. 1592, 12 July 1950.
66. Ibid.
67. Kennedy and O'Halpin, *Council of Europe*, p. 80.
68. *Irish Independent*, 10 September 1949.
69. *Summary of the Debates in the Consultative Assembly of the Council of Europe*, August 1950, Winston Churchill Collection, Churchill College, Cambridge, CHUR 2/76.
70. *Irish Times*, 3 August 1949.
71. O'Donnell, 'Man of Destiny'.
72. 'With Churchill and Spaak, whose popularity is enormous, it is Sean MacBride, the brilliant Foreign Minister of Ireland, who has the most success' (vol. 34, 20 August 1949).
73. Kennedy and O'Halpin, *Council of Europe*, p. 59.
74. Bevin to MacBride, 30 October 1950, Department of Foreign Affairs, 417/39/64, National Archives, Dublin.

75. *Irish Independent*, 8 November 1950.
76. Dáil Éireann Debates, vol. 117, col. 746, 13 July 1949.
77. Quoted in *Éire/Ireland*, Bulletin of Department of External Affairs, no. 136, 19 May 1952.
78. Quoted in Hederman, *Road*, p. 33.
79. Hederman, *Road*, p. 147.
80. 'Against Hunger, Poverty, Desperation and Chaos', George C. Marshall speech at Harvard University Commencement, 5 June 1947, reprinted in *Foreign Affairs*, May–June 1997, vol. 76, no. 3, p. 160.
81. Bernadette Whelan, 'Integration or Isolation?' p. 213.
82. External Affairs to the Government, 4 July 1947, Department of the Taoiseach, s 14106/A, National Archives, Dublin.
83. External Affairs to the Government, June 1947, Department of the Taoiseach, s 14106/A, National Archives, Dublin.
84. *Irish Independent*, 17 April 1948.
85. Report of final session of the Conference on European Economic Cooperation, reported in the *Irish Independent*, 17 March 1948.
86. Address to Institute of International Affairs, 24 February 1949, Department of the Taoiseach, s 14406, National Archives, Dublin.
87. MacBride to Spaak, 6 September 1948, Department of the Taoiseach, s 14106, National Archives, Dublin.
88. Ibid.
89. Department of External Affairs Report, 28 February 1949, Department of Foreign Affairs, 305/57/140, National Archives, Dublin.
90. Quoted in Cronin, *Washington's Irish Policy*, p. 241.
91. Dáil Éireann Debates, vol. 110, cols. 331–335, 10 March 1948.
92. Speech before the OEEC Council on 25 July 1948, File: OEEC 1010; 106, C(48)106, European University Institute Archives, Florence.
93. *Irish Times*, editorial, 22 February 1950.
94. Department of External Affairs Report, 31 March 1951, Department of the Taoiseach, s 15067/B, National Archives, Dublin.
95. Dáil Éireann Debates, vol. 117, cols. 857–858, 13 July 1949.
96. Ibid., cols. 850–851, 13 July 1949.
97. Ibid.
98. Dáil Éireann Debates, vol. 117, col. 857, 13 July 1949.
99. Keatinge, *Formulation*, pp. 80–82.
100. *Irish Times*, 25 July 1946.
101. Dáil Éireann Debates, vol. 102, col. 1312, 24 July 1946.
102. *Irish Independent*, 25 July 1946.
103. *Irish Times*, 25 July 1946.
104. MacQueen, 'Ireland's Entry', p. 69.
105. Article 4 of the Charter states, 'Membership in the United Nations is open to all other peace-loving states which accept the obligations contained in the present

Charter and, in the judgment of the Organization, are able and willing to carry out these obligations.'

106. Dáil Éireann Debates, vol. 110, col. 622, 14 April 1948.
107. 'Record of a conversation between the Secretary of State and Sean MacBride', 16 June 1948, DO 35/3958, National Archives, Kew.
108. Dáil Éireann Debates, vol. 110, col. 623, 14 April 1948.
109. Ibid., vol. 112, cols. 903–904, 20 July 1948.
110. Department of Foreign Affairs 417/33/Part 3, National Archives, Dublin.
111. *The Leader*, editorial, 13 March 1948.
112. Dáil Éireann Debates, vol. 112, col. 904, 20 July 1948.
113. Ibid., vol. 116, cols. 865–866, 21 June 1949.
114. Ibid., vol. 117, col. 999, 14 July 1949.
115. Ibid., col. 851, 13 July 1949.
116. Joseph Morrison Skelly, 'National Interests and International Mediation: Ireland's South Tyrol Initiative at the United Nations 1960–1' in *Irish Foreign Policy*, p. 288.
117. Joseph Morrison Skelly, *Irish Diplomacy at the United Nations 1945–65* (Dublin, 1997), p. 15.
118. In several cases, for example Cyprus, Korea, Vietnam, Germany, West New Guinea, and Algeria, Irish delegates 'in a mature diplomatic fashion' argued against partition as a way of resolving political conflicts. See Skelly, 'National Interests and International Mediation' in *Irish Foreign Policy*.
119. Cruise O'Brien, *Memoir*, pp. 156–160, quotes from his anonymous piece in *The Leader*, also in Jordan, *Seán MacBride*, pp. 138–139.
120. Cruise O'Brien, 'Ireland in International Affairs', p. 134.
121. Lee, *Ireland: 1912–1985*, p. 308.
122. Robinson is perhaps dating Irish independence from the 1937 Constitution rather than the official declaration on Easter Monday, 1949.
123. Quoted in Rosemary Mahoney, *Whoredom in Kimmage: Irish Women Coming of Age* (New York, 1993), p. 290.
124. *Irish Independent*, 17 April 1948.

Chapter Eight (PP. 186–206)
1. Quoted in Whyte, *Church and State*, p. 158.
2. MacBride to McQuaid, 30 October 1947, Seán MacBride file, John Charles McQuaid Papers, Dublin Diocesan Archives.
3. McQuaid to MacBride, 1 November 1947, Dublin Diocesan Archives.
4. MacBride to McQuaid, 7 February 1948, Dublin Diocesan Archives.
5. *Irish Times*, 13 November 1999.
6. Catriona Lawlor responded with an article of her own, writing that Bowman's comments were 'unfair', that MacBride 'deliberately avoided getting too closely involved with the hierarchy concerning matters regarding political developments', and that Bowman had taken MacBride's letters out of context of

the period (*Irish Times*, 20 November 1999). Bowman replied that Lawlor merely summarised MacBride's own self-assessment of his career so 'that he emerges from this scrutiny without blemish is hardly surprising' (*Irish Times*, 29 November 1999).

7. *Irish Independent*, 24 November 1947.

8. MacBride to McQuaid, 25 May 1954 —, DDA, MacBride file.

9. Quoted in Keogh, 'Ireland, the Vatican, and the Cold War', pp. 77–78.

10. Keogh, 'Ireland, the Vatican, and the Cold War', p. 110.

11. 25 August 1948, DDA.

12. Official recognition (*de jure*) would involve the exchange of diplomatic representatives and formal relations.

13. Memorandum Michael Rynne to Frederick Boland, 10 February 1949, DFA, 305/81/1, NAI.

14. Dail Éireann Debates, vol. 117, 13 July 1949, col. 865.

15. See Paula Wylie, '"The Virtual Minimum": Ireland's Decision for *De Facto* Recognition of Israel 1947–9', in *Irish Foreign Policy*.

16. Walshe to Boland, 17 October 1946, DFA 313/6, National Archives, Dublin.

17. 13 June 1949, McQuaid Papers, Dept. of Foreign Affairs file, Box 1, DDA.

18. See N. Browne, *Against the Tide*; P. Browne, *Thanks for the Tea*; Inglis, *West Briton*; James Deeny, *To Cure and to Care: Memoirs of a Chief Medical Officer* (Dublin, 1989); Cruise O'Brien, *Ancestral Voices* and *Memoir*.

19. J.H. Whyte's *Church and State* provides excellent insight into Irish Catholicism and the Church's role in the mother and child controversy as well as intriguing theories about Noël Browne and the inter-party Government's motivations, which may not be obvious at first glance. Ruth Barrington's *Health, Medicine and Politics in Ireland 1900–1970* (Dublin, 1987) focuses on the scheme itself and Browne's problems with the Irish Medical Association. John Horgan's *Noël Browne: Passionate Outsider* (Dublin, 2000) is a useful counterpoint to Browne's memoirs.

20. See John Cooney, *John Charles McQuaid*, pp. 258–260, and N. Browne, *Against the Tide*, pp. 143–147, for vastly differing recollections of the 11 October 1950 meeting between Browne and Archbishop McQuaid.

21. Statement of the Hierarchy on the Health Act 1947, 13 October 1947, de Valera Papers, P150/2904(2).

22. Reply to Dr Staunton, 16 February 1948, de Valera Papers, P150/2904(2).

23. Dáil Éireann Debates, vol. 111, col. 2264, 6 July 1948.

24. Cabinet minutes, 25 June 1948, CAB 2/10, National Archives, Dublin.

25. N. Browne, *Against the Tide*, p. 124.

26. *Irish Times*, 9 April 1951.

27. Eamonn McKee, 'Church-state relations and the development of Irish health policy: the mother-and-child scheme, 1944–53', *Irish Historical Studies*, vol. 25 (November 1986), p. 194.

28. Whyte, *Church and State*, p. 230.

29. Ibid., p. 207.

30. Barrington, *Health, Medicine and Politics*, p. 205.

31. Dáil Éireann Debates, vol. 125, col. 789, 12 April 1951.

32. Barrington, *Health, Medicine and Politics*, p. 220.

33. McKee, 'Church-state relations', p. 177. Cabinet members Richard Mulcahy, Seán MacEoin, William Norton, and Joseph Blowick were also members.

34. Cooney, *John Charles McQuaid*, p. 252.

35. Deeny, *To Cure*, p. 175.

36. N. Browne, *Against the Tide*, p. 143.

37. Letter from Dr James Staunton, Bishop of Ferns, to Taoiseach, 10 October 1950, Éamon de Valera Papers P150/2904 (2), Appendix E.

38. Ibid.

39. N. Browne, *Against the Tide*, p. 167.

40. Ibid., p. 153.

41. Ibid., pp. 163–164.

42. Horgan, *Noël Browne*, p. 142.

43. At the time, Costello declared in the Dáil, 'I want to say here that if Deputy MacBride had not taken that course, I myself would, under the Constitution, have requested Deputy Dr Browne to give me his resignation. It is only right and it is only just to my loyal colleagues that I should make that quite clear' (Dáil Éireann Debates, vol. 125, col. 777, 12 April 1951). Yet, years later, his take on the situation was very different. In a 1974 interview with *The Irish Times*, he said, 'And don't forget it wasn't me that sacked Noël Browne, it was his own party and Mr Sean MacBride' (*Irish Times*, 2 November 1974).

44. Dáil Éireann Debates, vol. 125, col. 739, 12 April 1951.

45. Letter to *Irish Times*, 14 April 1951, signed 'A Catholic'.

46. MacBride, *That Day's Struggle*, p. 225.

47. Cruise O'Brien, *Ancestral Voices*, p. 140.

48. Whyte, *Church and State*, pp. 197–198.

49. Quoted in MacDermott, *Clann na Poblachta*, p. 146.

50. Dáil Éireann Debates, vol. 125, col. 910, 17 April 1951.

51. Deeny, *To Cure*, p. 162.

52. Dáil Éireann Debates, vol. 111, col. 2541, 8 July 1948.

53. Ibid., vol. 125, cols. 777–778, 12 April 1951.

54. Ibid., col. 933, 17 April 1951.

55. N. Browne, *Against the Tide*, p. 127.

56. David Sheehy, archivist, Dublin Diocesan Archives, in conversation with the author, 28 July 2004.

57. Deeny, *To Cure*, p. 178.

58. Dáil Éireann Debates, vol. 117, col. 321, 6 July 1949.

59. Ibid., vol. 125, col. 797, 12 April 1951.

60. Deeny, *To Cure*, p. 166.

61. Horgan, *Noël Browne*, p. 8.

62. Coogan, *Ireland*, p. 368.

63. Whyte, *Church and State*, p. 235.

64. Dáil Éireann Debates, vol. 125, col. 749, 12 April 1951.

65. *Irish Press*, 17 January 1969.

66. Dáil Éireann Debates, vol. 125, cols. 797–798, 12 April 1951.

67. Quoted in N. Browne, *Against the Tide*, p. 139.

68. N. Browne, *Against the Tide*, p. 107.

69. Accounts and recollections of the dinner vary. MacDermott, *Clann na Poblachta*, p. 146; Whyte, *Church and State*, p. 210; Jordan, *Seán MacBride*, p. 127; MacBride, *That Day's Struggle*, p. 220.

70. Jordan, *Seán MacBride*, p. 127.

71. N. Browne, *Against the Tide*, p. 181.

72. Minutes of a discussion between Donal O'Donoghue, Browne, and MacBride, 4 January 1951, Clann na Poblachta Papers, University College Dublin, P125 (8).

73. *Irish Times*, 12 April 1951.

74. Ibid.

75. Dáil Éireann Debates, vol. 125, col. 669, 12 April 1951.

76. Ibid., col. 758, 12 April 1951.

77. Editorial, *Irish Times*, 12 April 1951.

78. 'Southern Ireland — Church or State?' p. 2, cited in Whyte, p. 232.

79. *Irish Times*, 12 April 1951.

80. Horgan, *Noël Browne*, p. 152.

81. *Irish Times*, 13 April 1951.

82. *Belfast Telegraph*, editorial, 12 April 1951.

83. *Unionist*, editorial, May 1951.

84. Dáil Éireann Debates, vol. 125, cols. 783–784, 12 April 1951.

85. *Belfast Telegraph*, editorial, 19 April 1951.

86. Letter to Papal Nuncio Archbishop Ettore Felici, written 16 April 1951, Cooney, *John Charles McQuaid*, p. 252.

87. Cooney, *John Charles McQuaid*, p. 253.

88. N. Browne, *Against the Tide*, p. 161.

89. Quoted in *Irish Times*, 1–2 January 1982.

90. Barrington, *Health, Medicine and Politics*, p. 211.

91. Coogan, *Ireland*, p. 373.

92. Brian Fallon, 'Reflecting on Ireland in the 1950s', in Dermot Keogh, Finbarr O'Shea, and Carmel Quinlan, eds., *The Lost Decade: Ireland in the 1950s* (Cork, 2004), p. 35.

93. Quoted in Samuel Levenson, *Maud Gonne* (London, 1976), p. 231.

94. Ward, *Maud Gonne*, p. 190.

95. Yeats to Lady Gregory, 21 August 1917, in Allan Wade, ed., *The Letters of W.B. Yeats* (London, 1954), p. 630.

96. Ward, *Maud Gonne*, p. 191.

97. Conrad A. Balliett, 'Micheal MacLiammoir Recalls Maude Gonne MacBride', in *Journal of Irish Literature*, May, 1977.
98. Ward, *Maud Gonne*, p. 190.
99. Jeffares and MacBride White, *Servant of the Queen*, Introduction, p. xii.
100. McQuaid to MacBride, 1 November 1947, Seán MacBride file, John Charles McQuaid Papers, Dublin Diocesan Archives.
101. Barrington, *Health, Medicine and Politics*, p. 219.
102. Coogan, *Ireland*, p. 378.
103. Dáil Éireann Debates, vol. 125, col. 677, 12 April 1951.
104. Lee, *Ireland 1912–1985*, pp. 317–318.
105. *Irish Times*, 14 May 1951.
106. Ibid., 7 May 1951.
107. Ibid.
108. *Irish Times*, 29 May 1951.
109. Ibid., editorial, 28 May 1951.
110. *Irish Times*, 19 May 1951.
111. *Irish Independent*, 26 May 1951.
112. *Irish Times*, 28 May 1951; *Irish Independent*, 18 May 1951.
113. *Irish Times*, 2 June 1951.
114. Ibid.; *Irish Independent*, 2 June 1951.
115. *Manchester Guardian*, 25 April 1951.

Chapter Nine (PP. 207–23)

1. Quoted in Fanning, *Independent Ireland*, pp. 168–169.
2. MacDermott, *Clann na Poblachta*, p. 133.
3. N. Browne, *Against the Tide*, p. 128.
4. Sir Gilbert Laithwaite, 8 March 1950, cited in *Irish Press*, 1 and 2 January 1981.
5. Andrews, *Man of No Property*, p. 192.
6. Lee, *Ireland 1912–1985*, p. 307.
7. Cruise O'Brien, *Memoir*, p. 160.
8. Ibid. Anthony Jordan also includes part of this piece in his book, but attributes authorship to Jack B. Yeats, artist, dramatist, son of the artist, John Butler Yeats, and brother of the poet, William Butler Yeats. Jordan does not clarify why Yeats would have written such a piece (Jordan, *Seán MacBride*, p. 138).
9. *Irish Times*, 17 May 1954.
10. Ibid., editorial, 18 May 1954.
11. *Irish Independent*, 19 May 1954.
12. *Irish Times*, 25 May 1954.
13. *Irish Independent*, 17 May 1954.
14. Letter, Costello to Kid MacBride, 23 Meitheamh (June) 1954, Department of the Taoiseach, s15719B, National Archives, Dublin.
15. *Irish Times*, 31 January 1957.

16. Letter, Costello to MacBride, Costello Papers, P190/838.

17. Kevin B. Nowlan, 'The Irish Nobel Peace Prize Winners', in Karl Holl and Anne C. Kjelling, eds., *The Nobel Peace Prize and the Laureates: the Meaning and Acceptance of the Nobel Peace Prize in the Peace Winners' Countries* (Frankfurt, 1994), p. 227.

18. Letter, MacBride to Costello, 28 October 1956, Costello Papers, P190/694 (33).

19. Letter, MacBride to Liam Cosgrave, 19 November 1956, Costello Papers, P190/694 (36).

20. Amnesty International Archives, Oral History Pilot Project, Peter Benenson Memoir, November 1983. However, while researching an article on the beginnings of Amnesty, Tom Buchanan was unable to locate any news items about Portuguese students in the *Daily Telegraph* for November and December 1960. Moreover, their names were never mentioned in the case studies publicised by Amnesty and they were not chosen when the 1961 appeal was launched. *The Times* mentions a few incidents of oppression in Portugal, but not Benenson's particular case. See Tom Buchanan, 'The Truth Will Set You Free: The Making of Amnesty International', *Journal of Contemporary History*, October 2002, vol. 37, no. 4, p. 576 (fn).

21. *Observer*, 28 May 1961.

22. *Irish Times*, 30 May 1961.

23. *Guardian*, 29 May 1961.

24. MacBride quoted in Egon Larsen, *A Flame in Barbed Wire: The Story of Amnesty International* (London, 1978), p. 26.

25. Larsen, *Flame in Barbed Wire*, p. 34.

26. Jordan, *Seán MacBride*, p. 165. MacBride had no love for the CIA, saying in 1987, 'the CIA has extended its tentacles all over the world' ('Reflections on Intelligence', p. 96).

27. Letter, Caitriona Lawlor to *Irish Times*, 14 March 2005.

28. Jonathan Power, *Like Water on Stone: The Story of Amnesty International* (Boston, 2001), p. 123.

29. Farrell, 'Life and Times', p. 36.

30. Ibid.

31. Sean MacBride, 'Namibia', in *Bulletin of Atomic Scientists*, vol. 37, no. 6, June/July 1981, p. 22.

32. See also S.C. Saxena, *Namibia and the World: The Story of the Birth of a Nation* (New Delhi, 1991).

33. MacBride, 'Namibia', p. 24.

34. Cruise O'Brien, *Memoir*, p. 168.

35. Jordan, *Seán MacBride*, p. 162.

36. Ibid.

37. *Letters from Iseult Gonne*, p. 158.

38. *New York Times*, 9 October 1974.

39. 'He loved the company of women and was rarely disappointed by those he sought out for his special attention' (Jordan, *Seán MacBride*, p. 162). 'MacBride, although he was a married man, was also known to be fond of women, especially when in Paris' (Cooney, *John Charles McQuaid*, p. 222).

40. Jordan, *Seán MacBride*, p. 162.

41. Máire Cruise O'Brien, *The Same Age as the State* (Dublin, 2003), p. 213.

42. *Irish Times*, 9 October 1974.

43. *Irish Independent*, 11 December 1974.

44. *Irish Times*, 9 October 1974.

45. Dáil Éireann Debates, vol. 275, col. 994, 5 November 1974.

46. *Irish Independent*, 10 December 1974.

47. Nowlan, 'Irish Nobel Peace Prize Winners', p. 277.

48. Seán MacBride, 'The Imperatives of Survival,' reprinted in *Les Prix Nobel en 1974* (Stockholm, 1975), p. 208.

49. Ibid., p. 209.

50. Ibid., p. 216.

51. Ibid., p. 219.

52. Ibid., pp. 221–222.

53. Editorial, *Irish Times*, 13 December 1974.

54. Reprinted from *Nobel Lectures, Peace 1971–1980* (Singapore, 1981).

55. *Irish Times*, 2 May 1977.

56. Ibid.

57. Sean MacBride Collection, Petronio Room, Iona College Library, New Rochelle, New York.

58. Jordan, *Seán MacBride*; N. Browne, *Against the Tide*, p. 96.

59. David Norris, 'Speaking Ill of the Dead' Conference, 31 March 2006, Norris email to author.

60. Interview with Anna MacBride White.

61. *Paul Durcan's Diary* (Dublin, 2003), p. 100.

Chapter Ten (PP. 224–37)

1. Brian Inglis, *Downstart: The Autobiography of Brian Inglis* (London, 1990), p. 181.

2. *Irish Times*, 9 October 1974.

3. *Irish Independent*, 10 December 1974.

4. *Irish Times*, 7 October 1991.

5. Ibid.

6. MacBride to D. O'Sullivan, Assistant Secretary, Department of the Taoiseach, 24 July 1972, Costello Papers, P190/799 (90).

7. New Ireland Forum Report of Public Session, Dublin Castle, 4 October 1983, p. 16.

8. Jordan, *Seán MacBride*, p. 174; Bell, *Secret Army*, pp. 432–433.

9. Farrell, 'Life and Times', p. 37.

10. Interview with Anna MacBride White.

11. See Padraig O'Malley, *Biting at the Grave: The Irish Hunger Strikes and the Politics of Despair* (Belfast, 1990); David Beresford, *Ten Men Dead: The Story of the 1981 Irish Hunger Strike* (London, 1987); Tim Pat Coogan, *IRA*; and Bobby Sands, *Writings From Prison* (Cork, 1988).

12. Sands, *Writings From Prison*, p. 21.

13. MacBride, *That Day's Struggle*, p. 12.

14. Sands, *Writings From Prison*, p. 14.

15. Andrews, *Man of No Property*, p. 192.

16. Seán MacBride, *A Message to the Irish People* (Cork, 1985), p. 56.

17. New Ireland Forum Report, Stationery Office, Dublin, 1984, Chapter 1, Preface, 1.1.

18. FitzGerald, *All in a Life*, p. 463.

19. Forum Report, Chapter 1, Preface, 1.2.

20. *Irish Times*, 5 October 1983.

21. Ibid.

22. *Irish Independent*, editorial, 5 October 1983; *Irish Times*, 6 October 1983.

23. Forum Report, p. 23.

24. *Belfast Telegraph*, 20 November 1984.

25. Bourke, *Peace in Ireland*, p. 280.

26. *Irish Times*, 16 January 1988.

27. Christopher McCrudden, 'Human Rights Codes for Transnational Corporations: What Can the Sullivan and MacBride Principles Tell Us?' in *Oxford Journal of Legal Studies*, vol. 19, no. 2 (Summer 1999), p. 182.

28. Dáil Éireann Debates, vol. 367, cols. 937–938, 4 June 1986.

29. Ibid., vol. 388, col. 1843, 18 April 1989.

30. McCrudden, 'Human Rights Codes', p. 184.

31. Paul Routledge, *John Hume: A Biography* (London, 1997), p. 14.

32. McCrudden, 'Human Rights Codes', p. 197.

33. FitzGerald, *All in a Life*, p. 604.

34. Lee, *Ireland 1912–1985*, p. 318.

35. N. Browne, *Against the Tide*, p. 96.

36. Ibid.

37. 25 May 1954, MacBride to McQuaid, Seán MacBride file, DDA.

38. c. 6 March 1956, MacBride to McQuaid, Seán MacBride file, DDA.

39. Caitriona Lawlor, email to author, 16 May 2005.

40. Letter, MacBride to Patrick Lynch, 9 March 1981, courtesy of Caitriona Lawlor.

41. MacBride, *That Day's Struggle*, p. 146.

42. The Background and History, 32 County Sovereignty Movement (http://32csm.netfirms.com).

43. *Irish Times*, 16 January 1988.

44. Ibid., 18 January 1988.

45. Ibid.

46. Ibid.
47. *Irish Times*, 16 January 1988.
48. Ibid.
49. The *Times*, 16 January 1988.
50. Ibid.
51. The *Times*, 18 January 1998.
52. Ibid., 23 January 1988.
53. Ibid., 16 January 1988.
54. *Irish Times*, 19 January 1988.
55. Haughey later told Tim Pat Coogan that MacBride was 'as crooked as a ram's horn' (Coogan, *Ireland*, p. 359). One wonders if Haughey then informed Coogan that the kettle was black.
56. *Irish Times*, 16 January 1988.
57. Seanad Éireann Debates, vol. 118, col. 544, 20 January 1988.
58. Ibid.
59. Seanad Éireann Debates, vol. 118, col. 545, 20 January 1988.
60. Dáil Éireann Debates, vol. 377, cols. 439–440, 28 January 1988.
61. Ibid., cols. 440–441, 28 January 1988.
62. Ibid., col. 443, 28 January 1988.
63. Ibid., col. 442, 28 January 1988.

Conclusion (PP. 238–42)

1. Kevin B. Nowlan, 'The Irish Nobel Peace Prize Winners', p. 234.
2. Lee, *Ireland 1912–1985*, p. 307.
3. N. Browne, *Against the Tide*, p. 95.
4. P. Browne, *Thanks for the Tea*, p. 102.
5. *Irish Times*, 7 October 1991.
6. P. Browne, *Thanks for the Tea*, p. 106.
7. Inglis, *Downstart*, p. 175.
8. N. Browne, *Against the Tide*, p. 96.
9. Cruise O'Brien, *Ancestral Voices*, pp. 133–136
10. P. Browne, *Thanks for the Tea*, p. 101.
11. Andrews, *Man of No Property*, p. 192.
12. Interview with Anna MacBride White.
13. *Irish Times*, 7 December 2004.
14. Interview with Anna MacBride White.
15. Ibid.
16. Ibid.
17. MacBride, *That Day's Struggle*, p. 9.

BIBLIOGRAPHY

PRIMARY SOURCES

Private and unpublished papers

Dean Acheson Papers, Harry S. Truman Library, Independence, MO
Frank Aiken Papers, University College, Dublin
Frederick Allan Papers, National Library, Ireland
Clement Attlee Papers, Bodleian Library, Oxford
Clement Attlee Papers, Churchill College, Cambridge
Ernest Bevin Papers, Churchill College, Cambridge
Winston Churchill Papers, Churchill College, Cambridge
John A. Costello Papers, University College, Dublin
Éamon de Valera Papers, University College, Dublin
Paul G. Hoffman Papers, Harry S. Truman Library, Independence, MO
Sighle Humphreys Papers, University College, Dublin
David Lloyd George Papers, Parliamentary Archive, Record Office, House of Lords
Seán MacEoin Papers, University College, Dublin
Seán MacEntee Papers, University College, Dublin
Patrick McGilligan Papers, University College, Dublin
Archbishop John Charles McQuaid Papers, Dublin Diocesan Archives
Francis Matthews Papers, Harry S. Truman Library, Independence, MO
Philip Noel-Baker Papers, Churchill College, Cambridge
Richard Mulcahy Papers, University College, Dublin
John O'Leary Papers, National Library, Ireland
John Quinn Letters, Berg Collection, New York Public Library
Hanna Sheehy Skeffington Papers, National Library, Ireland
Harry Truman Papers, Harry S. Truman Library, Independence, MO
Maurice Twomey Papers, University College Dublin
William Butler Yeats Papers, National Library, Ireland

Government papers
Bunreacht na hÉireann (Constitution of Ireland)
Houses of the Oireachtas
Dáil Éireann Debates
Seanad Éireann Debates
European University Institute Archives, Florence, Italy

OEEC Speeches
MacBride Principles
National Archives, Canada
    Department of External Affairs File
National Archives, Ireland
    Cabinet Minutes
    Department of Finance,
    Department of Foreign Affairs
    Department of the Taoiseach
    Dublin Castle State Papers
National Archives, Kew
    Cabinet Minutes
    Commonwealth Office Records
    Dominions Office Records
    Foreign Office Records
    Home Office Papers
    House of Commons Debates
    Office of Prime Minister Records
    War Office Records
National Archives and Records Administration, Washington, DC
    US State Department
New Ireland Forum Report
Public Record Office, Northern Ireland
    Cabinet Minutes
    Northern Ireland House of Commons Debates
Franklin Delano Roosevelt Library, Hyde Park, New York
    Vatican Diplomatic Files

Newspapers and periodicals
Amnesty International (reports, briefs, newsletters, 1962–84)
Belfast Telegraph
Freeman's Journal
Irish Echo
Irish Freedom
Irish Independent
Irish Literary Supplement
Irish Press
Life Magazine
Limerick Leader
Manchester Guardian
New York Times
Our Nation — Clann na Poblachta periodical
Our Policy — Clann na Poblachta periodical, 1948

Saturday Evening Post
The Citizen
The Economist
The Irish Times
The Leader
The Mail
The Observer
The Times
The Unionist
United Irishman
Washington Post

Oral Histories
Theodore Achilles, Harry S. Truman Library
Nathan M. Becker, Harry S. Truman Library
W. John Kenney, Harry S. Truman Library

Published autobiographies and memoirs
Acheson, Dean, *Present at the Creation: My Years in the State Department* (New York, 1987).
Andrews, C.S., *Dublin Made Me: An Autobiography* (Dublin, 1979).
——, *Man of No Property: An Autobiography, Vol. Two* (Dublin, 1982).
Attlee, Clement, *As It Happened* (London, 1954).
Browne, Noël, *Against the Tide* (Dublin, 1986).
Browne, Phyllis, *Thanks for the Tea, Mrs. Browne: My Life with Noël* (Dublin, 1998).
Colum, Mary, *Life and the Dream* (Dublin, 1966).
Cruise O'Brien, Conor, *Ancestral Voices: Religion and Nationalism in Ireland* (Dublin, 1994).
——, *Memoir: My Life and Themes* (Dublin, 1998).
——, *To Katanga and Back: A UN Case History* (London, 1962).
Cruise O'Brien, Máire, *The Same Age as the State* (Dublin, 2003).
Deeny, James, *To Cure and to Care: Memoirs of a Chief Medical Officer* (Dublin, 1989).
FitzGerald, Garret, *All In A Life: An Autobiography* (Dublin, 1991).
Gonne MacBride, Maud, *A Servant of the Queen* (Gerrard's Cross, Buckinghamshire, 1994).
Inglis, Brian, *Downstart: The Autobiography of Brian Inglis* (London, 1990).
——, *West Briton* (London, 1962).
MacBride, John, 'The Irish Brigade in South Africa', *Freeman's Journal*, 13 October 1906.
MacBride, Seán, *That Day's Struggle* (Dublin, 2005).
MacEoin, Uinseann, *Survivors* (Dublin, 1980).
Markiewicz, Constance, *Prison Letters of Countess Markievicz* (London, 1986).
Mitchell, George J., *Making Peace* (London, 1999).

Ó hEithir, Breandán, *Over the Bar: A Personal Relationship with the* GAA (Dublin, 1984).

O'Higgins, Thomas F., *A Double Life* (Dublin, 1996).

O'Neill, Tip, and Novak, William, *Man of the House: The Life and Political Memoirs of Speaker Tip O'Neill* (London, 1987).

Quigley, Martin S., *A U.S. Spy in Ireland* (Dublin, 1999).

Riddell, Lord, *Intimate Diary of the Peace Conference and After 1918–1923* (London, 1933).

Sands, Bobby, *Writings From Prison* (Cork, 1988).

Stuart, Francis, *Black List Section H* (London, 1971).

Thatcher, Margaret, *The Downing Street Years* (London, 1995).

Truman, Harry S., *Memoirs: Years of Trial and Hope, Vol. Two* (New York, 1955).

White, Harry, *Harry: The Story of Harry White as Related to Uinseann MacEoin* (Dublin, 1985).

Yeats, W.B., *Memoirs*, Denis Donoghue, ed. (London, 1988).

Other published contemporary sources

The Background and History, 32 County Sovereignty Movement (http://32csm.netfirms.com).

Beckson, Karl, '"Arthur Symon's Iseult Gonne": A Previously Unpublished Memoir', *Yeats Annual* #7, 1990.

Costello, John A., *Ireland in International Affairs* (Dublin, 1948).

Durcan, Paul, *Paul Durcan's Diary* (Dublin, 2003).

Ireland's Position in Relation to the North Atlantic Treaty (Dublin, 1950).

Jeffares, A. Norman, MacBride White, Anna, and Bridgwater, Christina, eds., *Letters to W.B. Yeats and Ezra Pound from Iseult Gonne: A Girl that Knew All Dante Once* (London, 2004).

Kelly, John, and Schuchard, Ronald, eds., *The Collected Letters of W.B. Yeats, Vol. 3, 1901–1904* (Oxford, 1994).

Londraville, Janis and Richard, eds., *Too Long a Sacrifice: The Letters of Maud Gonne and John Quinn* (London, 1999).

MacBride, Seán, 'The Imperatives of Survival', reprinted in *Les Prix Nobel en 1974* (Stockholm, 1975).

—, *A Message to the Irish People* (Cork, 1985).

—, 'Namibia', *Bulletin of Atomic Scientists*, vol. 37, no. 6 (1981).

— , 'Reflections on Intelligence', *Intelligence and National Security* 2 (1987).

—, *Nobel Lectures, Peace 1971–1980* (Singapore, 1981).

Spaak, Paul-Henri, 'Strasbourg: The Second Year', Stevenson Memorial Lecture, delivered 30 October 1950, Chatham House (Oxford, 1952).

Wade, Allan, ed., *Letters of W.B. Yeats* (London, 1954).

White, Anna MacBride, and Jeffares, A. Norman, eds., *Always Your Friend: The Gonne–Yeats Letters 1893–1938* (London, 1992).

SECONDARY SOURCES

Books and journal articles

Akenson, Donald Harmon, *Conor: A Biography of Conor Cruise O'Brien* (London, 1994).

—, *The United States and Ireland* (Cambridge, MA, 1973).

Anderson, Benedict, *Imagined Communities: Reflections on the Origin and Spread of Nationalism* (London, 1983).

Balliett, Conrad A., 'The Lives — and Lies — of Maud Gonne', *Éire-Ireland* XIV (1979).

—, 'Michael MacLiammoir Recalls Maude Gonne MacBride', *Journal of Irish Literature* (May, 1977).

Barrington, Ruth, *Health, Medicine and Politics in Ireland 1900–1970* (Dublin, 1987).

Bell, J. Bowyer, *The Secret Army: The IRA* (Dublin, 1998).

Beresford, David, *Ten Men Dead: The Story of the 1981 Irish Hunger Strike* (London, 1987).

Bew, Paul, *Ideology and the Irish Question: Ulster Unionism and Irish Nationalism 1912–16* (Oxford, 1994).

—, Hazelkorn, Ellen, and Patterson, Henry, *The Dynamics of Irish Politics* (London, 1989).

— and Patterson, Henry, *Sean Lemass and the Making of Modern Ireland* (Dublin, 1982).

Bloom, William, *Personal Identity, National Identity, and International Relations* (New York, 1990).

Bourke, Richard, *Peace in Ireland: The War of Ideas* (London, 2003).

Bowman, John, *De Valera and the Ulster Question 1917–1973* (Oxford, 1982).

Boyce, D. George, *The Irish Question and British Politics 1868–1996*, second edition, (London, 1996).

—, and O'Day, Alan, eds., *The Making of Modern Irish History: Revisionism and the Revisionist Controversy* (London, 1996).

Bradshaw, Brendan, 'Irish Nationalism: An Historical Perspective', *Bullán* vol. V, no. 1 (Summer/Fall 2000).

Brown, Terence N., *Ireland: A Social and Cultural History 1922–1979* (London, 1981).

—, *Irish-American Nationalism 1870–1890* (New York, 1966).

Buchanan, Tom, 'The Truth Will Set You Free: The Making of Amnesty International' in *Journal of Contemporary History*, vol. 37, no. 4 (October 2002).

Bullock, Alan, *Ernest Bevin: Foreign Secretary 1945–1951* (Oxford, 1985).

Cardozo, Nancy, *Lucky Eyes and a High Heart: The Life of Maud Gonne* (New York, 1978).

Carroll, Joseph, 'US-Irish Relations 1939–45', *Irish Sword* 19 (1993–94).

Carter, Carrolle J., 'Ireland: America's Neutral Ally', *Éire-Ireland* XII (1977).

Chubb, Basil, *The Government and Politics of Ireland*, third edition (Stanford, 1992).

—, *The Politics of the Irish Constitution* (Dublin, 1991).

—, *A Source Book of Irish Government* (Dublin, 1983).

Coakley, John, and Gallagher, Michael, *Politics in the Republic of Ireland*, second edition (Limerick, 1996).

Coogan, Tim Pat, *1916: The Easter Rising* (London, 2001).

—, *De Valera: Long Fellow, Long Shadow* (London, 1995).

—, *The IRA* (London, 2000).

—, *Ireland in the Twentieth Century* (London, 2003).

—, *Michael Collins* (London, 1990).

Cooney, John, *John Charles McQuaid: Ruler of Catholic Ireland* (Dublin, 2003).

Cox, W.H., 'The Politics of Irish Unification in the Irish Republic', *Parliamentary Affairs*, 38 (1985).

Cronin, Mike, and Regan, John M., eds., *Ireland: The Politics of Independence, 1922–49* (London, 2000).

Cronin, Seán, *Irish Nationalism* (Dublin, 1980).

—, *The McGarrity Papers: Revelations of the Irish Revolutionary Movement in Ireland and America 1900–1940* (Tralee, 1972).

—, 'The Making of NATO and the Partition of Ireland', *Éire-Ireland*, 20 (1985).

—, *Washington's Irish Policy 1916–1986* (Dublin, 1987).

Cruise O'Brien, Conor, 'Ireland in International Affairs', in Owen Dudley Edwards, ed., *Conor Cruise O'Brien Introduces Ireland* (New York, 1969).

—, ed., *The Shaping of Modern Ireland* (London, 1960).

Curtin, Nancy J., *The United Irishmen: Popular Politics in Ulster and Dublin, 1791–1798* (Oxford, 1994).

Davis, Troy D., *Dublin's American Policy: Irish-American Diplomatic Relations 1945–1952* (Washington, DC, 1998).

Dickson, David, Keogh, Dáire, and Whelan, Kevin, eds., *The United Irishmen: Republicanism, Radicalism and Rebellion* (Dublin, 1993).

Dinan, Desmond, 'After the Emergency: Ireland in the Post-War World, 1945–50', *Éire-Ireland*, vol. 24 (Fall 1989).

Driscoll, Dennis, 'Is Ireland Really Neutral?', *Irish Studies in International Affairs*, vol. 1, no. 3 (1982).

Drudy, P.J., ed., *The Irish in America: Emigration, Assimilation, Impact* (Cambridge, 1985).

—, and McAleese, D., eds., *Ireland and the European Community* (Cambridge, 1983).

Dudley Edwards, R., and Moody, T.W., *Irish Historical Studies*, vol. 1, no. 1, March 1938.

Duggan, John P., *Neutral Ireland and the Third Reich* (Dublin, 1985).

Dwyer, T. Ryle, *De Valera's Darkest Hour 1919–1932: In Search of National Independence* (Dublin, 1982).

—, *De Valera's Finest Hour 1932–1959: In Search of National Independence* (Dublin, 1982).

—, *Strained Relations: Ireland at Peace and the USA at War, 1941–45* (Dublin, 1988).

Edwards, Owen Dudley, ed., *Conor Cruise O'Brien Introduces Ireland* (New York, 1969).

Edwards, Owen Dudley and Doyle, David N., eds., *America and Ireland 1776–1976* (Westport, CT, 1980).

Elborn, Geoffrey, *Francis Stuart: A Life* (Dublin, 1990).

Ellmann, Richard, *Yeats: The Man and the Masks* (London, 1948).

Fanning, Ronan, 'The Anglo-American Alliance and the Irish Application for Membership in the United Nations', *Irish Studies in International Affairs*, 2 (1986).

—, 'Anglo-Irish Relations — Partition and the British Dimension in Historical Perspective', *Irish Studies in International Affairs*, vol. 2, no. 1 (1985).

—, *Independent Ireland* (Dublin, 1983).

—, *The Irish Department of Finance 1922–58* (Dublin, 1978).

—, 'Irish Neutrality: An Historical Perspective', *Irish Studies in International Affairs*, vol. 1, no. 3 (1982).

—, 'The Response of the London and Belfast Governments to the Declaration of the Republic of Ireland 1948–1949', *International Affairs*, 58 (Winter 1981–82).

—, 'The United States and Irish Participation in NATO: The Debate of 1950', *Irish Studies in International Affairs*, 1 (1979).

Farrell, Brian, *Chairman or Chief: The Role of the Taoiseach in Irish Government* (Dublin, 1971).

Farrell, Michael, 'The Extraordinary Life and Times of Sean MacBride', *Magill* (January, 1983).

Fisk, Robert, *In Time of War* (London, 1985).

Fitzpatrick, David, *The Two Irelands 1912–1939* (Oxford, 1998).

Fogarty, M.P., *Christian Democracy in Western Europe 1820–1953* (London, 1957).

Foster, R.F., *The Irish Story: Telling Tales and Making It Up in Ireland* (London, 2001).

—, *Modern Ireland 1600–1972* (London, 1988).

—, *Paddy and Mr Punch* (London, 1993).

—, *W.B. Yeats: A Life, The Apprentice Mage, 1865–1914* (Oxford, 1997).

—, *W.B. Yeats: A Life, The Arch-Poet 1915–1939* (Oxford, 2003).

Foy, Michael, and Barton, Brian, *The Easter Rising* (Phoenix Mill, 1999).

Fraser, T.G., *Partition in Ireland, India, Palestine: Theory and Practice* (London, 1984).

Gallagher, Michael, *Political Parties in the Republic of Ireland* (Manchester, 1985).

Gallagher, Tom, 'Fianna Fail and Partition 1926–1984', *Éire-Ireland*, 20 (1985).

—, and O'Connell, James, eds., *Contemporary Irish Studies* (Manchester, 1983).

Garvin, Tom, *1922: The Birth of Irish Democracy* (Dublin, 1996).

—, 'Continuity and Change in Irish Electoral Politics 1923–1969', *Economic and Social Review*, vol. III (March 1972).

—, *The Evolution of Irish Nationalist Politics* (New York, 1981).

—, *The Nationalist Revolution in Ireland* (Oxford, 1997).

Geiger, Till, and Kennedy, Michael, eds., *Ireland, Europe and the Marshall Plan* (Dublin, 2004).

Ginsborg, Paul, *A History of Contemporary Italy: Society and Politics 1943–1988* (London, 1990).

Girvin, Brian, *Between Two Worlds: Politics and Economics in Independent Ireland*

(Dublin, 1989).

Girvin, Brian, and Sturm, Roland, 'Politics and Society in Contemporary Ireland', *Economic and Social Review*, vol. 21, no. 3 (1990).

Gooch, John, ed., *The Boer War: Direction, Experience, and Image* (London, 2000).

Hall, H. Duncan, *A History of the British Commonwealth of Nations* (London, 1971).

Hanley, David, ed., *Christian Democracy in Europe: A Comparative Perspective* (London, 1994).

Harkness, David, *Ireland in the Twentieth Century: Divided Island* (London, 1966).

Harris, Kenneth, *Attlee* (London, 1982).

Hederman, Miriam, *The Road to Europe: Irish Attitudes 1948–61* (Dublin, 1983).

Heller, Francis H., and Gillingham, John R., eds., NATO: *The Founding of the Atlantic Alliance and the Integration of Europe* (New York, 1992).

Hennessey, Thomas, *The Northern Ireland Peace Process: Ending the Troubles* (Dublin, 2000).

Hennessy, Peter, *Never Again* (London, 1993).

Hobsbawm, E.J., *Nations and Nationalism since 1780: Programme, Myth, Reality* (Cambridge, 1990).

Hogan, Michael J., *The Marshall Plan: America, Britain, and the Reconstruction of Western Europe 1947–1952* (Cambridge, 1987).

Hone, Joseph, *W.B. Yeats 1865–1939* (London, 1942).

Horgan, John, *Noël Browne: Passionate Outsider* (Dublin, 2000).

Howe, Stephen, *Anticolonialism in British Politics* (London, 1993).

Hutton, Seán, and Stewart, Paul, eds., *Ireland's Histories: Aspects of State, Society and Ideology* (London, 1991).

'Ireland and the Commonwealth — Mr. Costello's Government and Partition', *Round Table*, vol. xxxix (1948–1949).

Irving, R.E.M., *Christian Democracy in France* (London, 1973).

Jackson, Alvin, *Ireland 1798–1998* (Oxford, 1998).

Jordan, Anthony, *Major John MacBride 1865–1916* (Westport, Ireland, 1991).

—, *Seán MacBride: A Biography* (Dublin, 1993).

Judd, Denis, and Surridge, Keith, *The Boer War* (London, 2002).

Keatinge, Patrick, *The Formulation of Irish Foreign Policy* (Dublin, 1973).

—, *A Place Among the Nations: Issues of Irish Foreign Policy* (Dublin, 1978).

Kennan, George F., *American Diplomacy 1900–1950* (Chicago, IL, 1953).

Kennedy, Michael, *Ireland and the League of Nations 1919–1946: International Relations, Diplomacy, and Politics* (Dublin, 1996).

—, and O'Halpin, Eunan, *Ireland and the Council of Europe: From Isolation Toward Integration* (Strasbourg, 2000).

—, and Skelly, Joseph Morrison, eds., *Irish Foreign Policy 1919–1969: From Independence to Internationalism* (Dublin, 2000).

Kenny, Kevin, *The American Irish: A History* (Harlow, 2000).

Keogh, Dermot, *Ireland and Europe, 1919–1989: A Diplomatic and Political History* (Cork, 1990).

Keogh, Dermot, 'Ireland, the Vatican and Cold War: The Case of Italy 1948', *Irish Studies in International Affairs*, 3 (1991).

—, *Twentieth-Century Ireland* (Dublin, 1994).

—, *The Vatican, the Bishops, and Irish Politics 1919–1939* (Cambridge, 1986).

—, and Haltzel, Michael H., eds., *Northern Ireland and the Politics of Reconciliation* (Cambridge, 1993).

—, O'Shea, Finbarr, and Quinlan, Carmel, eds., *The Lost Decade: Ireland in the 1950s* (Cork, 2004).

Lamberts, Emiel, *Christian Democracy in the European Union 1945–1995: Proceedings of the Leuven Colloquium* (Leuven, 1997).

Larsen, Egon, *A Flame in Barbed Wire: The Story of Amnesty International* (London, 1978).

Lee, J.J., *Ireland 1912–1985: Politics and Society* (Cambridge, 1989).

—, *The Modernisation of Irish Society* (Dublin, 1973).

—, and Ó Tuathaigh, Gearóid, *The Age of de Valera* (Dublin, 1982).

—, ed., *Ireland 1945–70* (Dublin, 1979).

Levenson, Samuel, *Maud Gonne* (London, 1976).

Lipgens, Walter, and Loth, Wilfred, eds., *Documents on the History of European Integration, vol. 3, The Struggle for European Union by Political Parties and Pressure Groups in Western European Countries, 1945–1950* (Berlin, 1988).

Longford, Earl of, *Peace by Ordeal* (London, 1972).

— , and O'Neill, Thomas P., *Eamon de Valera* (London, 1970).

Lynch, P., and Meenan, J., eds., *Essays in Honour of Alexis Fitzgerald* (Dublin, 1987).

Lyons, F.S.L., *Ireland Since the Famine* (London, 1985).

Lyons, J.B., *The Enigma of Tom Kettle* (Dublin, 1983).

McBride, Ian, ed., *History and Memory in Modern Ireland* (Cambridge, 2001).

MacBride, Seán, 'Reflections on Intelligence', *Intelligence and National Security*, vol. 2, no. 1 (January 1987).

McCabe, Ian, *A Diplomatic History of Ireland 1948–1949: The Republic, the Commonwealth and NATO* (Dublin, 1991).

McCarthy, John P., *Kevin O'Higgins: Builder of the Irish State* (Dublin, 2006).

McCracken, Donal P., 'Irish Settlement and Identity in South Africa before 1910', *Irish Historical Studies*, vol. 28 (1992–3).

—, *MacBride's Brigade: Irish Commandos in the Anglo-Boer War* (Dublin, 1999).

McCrudden, Christopher, 'Human Rights Codes for Transnational Corporations: What Can the Sullivan and MacBride Principles Tell Us?', *Oxford Journal of Legal Studies*, vol. 19, no. 2 (Summer 1999).

McCullagh, David, *A Makeshift Majority: The First Interparty Government 1948–51* (Dublin, 1999).

McCullough, David, *Truman* (New York, 1993).

MacDermott, Eithne, *Clann na Poblachta* (Cork, 1998).

MacEoin, Uinseann, *The IRA in the Twilight Years 1923–1948* (Dublin, 1997).

MacEvilly, Michael, 'Sean MacBride and the Republican Motor Launch St George', *Irish Sword*, 16 (1984).

McEvoy, F.J., 'Canada, Ireland and the Commonwealth: The Declaration of the Irish Republic 1948–9', *Irish Historical Studies*, 24 (1985).

McGarry, Fearghal, *Irish Politics and the Spanish Civil War* (Cork, 1999).

McKee, Eamonn, 'Church–state relations and the development of Irish health policy: the mother-and-child scheme, 1944–53', *Irish Historical Studies*, vol. 25 (November 1986).

MacManus, Francis, ed., *Years of the Great Test 1926–1939* (Cork, 1962).

Maddox, Brenda, *George's Ghosts: A New Life of W.B. Yeats* (London, 1999).

Maher, D.J., *The Tortuous Path: The Course of Ireland's Entry into the EEC 1948–73* (Dublin, 1986).

Mahoney, Rosemary, *Whoredom in Kimmage: Irish Women Coming of Age* (New York, 1993).

Mansergh, Nicholas, *The Commonwealth Experience*, second edition (London, 1982).

—, 'The Implications of Éire's Relationship with the British Commonwealth of Nations', *International Affairs*, vol. 24, no. 1 (January 1948).

—, 'Ireland: The Republic Outside the Commonwealth', *International Affairs*, vol. 28, no. 3 (July 1952).

—, *Nationalism and Independence* (Cork, 1997).

—, *Survey of British Commonwealth Affairs: Problems of War-time Cooperation and Postwar Change, 1939–1952* (Oxford, 1958).

—, *The Unresolved Question: The Anglo-Irish Settlement and Its Undoing 1912–72* (New Haven, CT, 1991).

Milward, Alan S., *The Reconstruction of Western Europe, 1945–51* (London, 1987).

Mitrany, David, *Functional Theory of Politics* (London, 1975).

Moody, T.W., and Martin, F.X., eds., *The Course of Irish History* (Boulder, CO, 1994).

Moraes, Frank, *Jawaharal Nehru: A Biography* (New York, 1956).

Morgan, Kenneth O., *Labour in Power 1945–1951* (London, 1985).

Moynihan, Daniel Patrick, and Glazer, Nathan, eds., *Beyond the Melting Pot: The Negros, Puerto Ricans, Jews, Italians, and Irish of New York City*, (Cambridge, MA, 1963).

Moynihan, Maurice, ed., *Speeches and Statements by Eamon de Valera 1917–73* (Dublin, 1980).

Murphy, John A., *Ireland in the Twentieth Century* (Dublin, 1975).

—, 'Put Them Out: Parties and Elections 1948–69', in J.J. Lee, *Ireland 1945–1970* (Dublin, 1979).

Nairn, Tom, *The Break-up of Britain: Crisis and Neo-Nationalism*, second edition, (London, 1981).

Nowlan, Kevin B., 'The Irish Nobel Peace Prize Winners' in Karl Holl and Anne C. Kjelling, eds., *The Nobel Peace Prize and the Laureates: the Meaning and Acceptance of the Nobel Peace Prize in the Peace Winners' Countries* (Frankfurt, 1994).

Nowlan, Kevin B. and Williams, T.D., eds., *Ireland in the War Years and After 1939–1951* (Dublin, 1969).

O'Donnell, James P., 'Ireland's New Man of Destiny', *Saturday Evening Post*, 23 April 1949.

O'Driscoll, Robert, ed., *The Celtic Consciousness* (New York, 1981).

O'Grady, Joseph P., 'Ireland and the Defence of the North Atlantic, 1948–1951: The American View', *Éire-Ireland*, vol. xxv, no. 3 (Fall 1990).

O'Halloran, Clare, *Partition and the Limits of Irish Nationalism* (Dublin, 1987).

O'Halpin, Eunan, *Defending Ireland: the Irish State and its Enemies since 1922* (Oxford, 1999).

O'Higgins, Brian, *Wolfe Tone Annual: Salute to the Soldiers of 1916*, 28 (1960).

O'Malley, Padraig, *Biting at the Grave: The Irish Hunger Strikes and the Politics of Despair* (Belfast, 1990).

Ovendale, Ritchie, *The Foreign Policy of the British Labour Government 1945–51* (Leicester, 1984).

Pelling, Henry, *The Labour Governments, 1945–1951* (London, 1984).

Pisani, Sallie, *The CIA and the Marshall Plan* (Lawrence, KS, 1991).

Power, Jonathan, *Like Water on Stone: The Story of Amnesty International* (Boston, 2001).

Pridham, Geoffrey, *Christian Democracy in Western Germany: The CDU/CSU in Government and Opposition 1945–1976* (London, 1977).

Rafter, Kevin, *The Clann: The Story of Clann na Poblachta* (Cork, 1996).

Raymond, Raymond J., 'Ireland's 1949 NATO Decision: A Reassessment', *Éire-Ireland*, vol. 20, no. 3 (Fall 1985).

Robertson, A.H., *The Council of Europe: Its Structure, Functions and Achievements* (London, 1961).

Routledge, Paul, *John Hume: A Biography* (London, 1997).

Ruane, Joseph, and Todd, Jennifer, eds., *After the Good Friday Agreement: Analysing Political Change in Northern Ireland* (Dublin, 1999).

Ryan, Meda, *Liam Lynch: The Real Chief* (Cork, 1986).

—, *The Tom Barry Story* (Cork, 1982).

Salmon, Trevor, 'Neutrality and the Irish Republic: Myth or Reality?', *Round Table*, 290 (1984).

—, *Unneutral Ireland: An Ambivalent and Unique Security Policy* (Oxford, 1989).

Saxena, S.C., *Namibia and the World: The Story of the Birth of a Nation* (New Delhi, 1991).

Seton-Watson, Hugh, *Nations and States: An Enquiry into the Origins of Nations and the Politics of Nationalism* (London, 1977).

Singh, Kusum, and Gross, Bertram, 'MacBride: The Report and the Response', *Journal of Communication*, 31 (1981).

Skelly, Joseph Morrison, 'Ireland, the Department of External Affairs and the United Nations 1946–55: A New Look', *Irish Studies in International Affairs*, vol. 7 (1996).

—, *Irish Diplomacy at the United Nations 1945–65* (Dublin, 1997).

Smith, Anthony D., *Nationalism and Modernism: A Critical Survey of Recent Theories of Nations and Nationalism* (London, 1998).

Steiner, Zara, ed., *Times Survey of Foreign Ministries of the World* (London, 1982).

Stewart, A.T.Q., *A Deeper Silence: The Hidden Origins of the United Irishmen* (Belfast, 1998).

Thompson, John A., *Woodrow Wilson* (London, 2002).

Tiratsoo, Nick, ed., *The Attlee Years* (London, 1991).

Walsh, James P., *The Irish: America's Political Class,* (New York, 1976).

Ward, Margaret, *Maud Gonne: A Life* (London, 1990).

—, *Maud Gonne: Ireland's Joan of Arc* (London, 1990).

Webster, R.A., *Christian Democracy in Italy 1860–1960* (London, 1961).

Weight, Richard, *Patriots: National Identity in Britain 1940–2000* (London, 2002).

Whelan, Bernadette, *Ireland and the Marshall Plan 1947–57* (Dublin, 2000).

INDEX